Oracle E-Business Suite R12 Core Development and Extension Cookbook

Over 60 recipes to develop core extensions in Oracle E-Business Suite R12

Andy Penver

[PACKT] enterprise

PUBLISHING

professional expertise distilled

BIRMINGHAM - MUMBAI

Oracle E-Business Suite R12 Core Development and Extension Cookbook

First published: May 2012

Production Reference: 1030512

Published by Packt Publishing Ltd.
Livery Place
35 Livery Street
Birmingham B3 2PB, UK.

ISBN 978-1-84968-484-2

www.packtpub.com

Cover Image by David Gimenez (bilbaorocker@yahoo.co.uk)

Credits

Author

Andy Penver

Reviewers

Mariana Angelova

Reuben Filius

Acquisition Editor

Dilip Venkatesh

Lead Technical Editor

Dayan Hyames

Technical Editors

Manali Mehta

Ankita Shashi

Manmeet Singh Vasir

Copy Editors

Leonard D'Silva

Laxmi Subramanian

Project Coordinators

Kushal Bhardwaj

Theresa Chettiar

Proofreader

Aaron Nash

Indexer

Tejal Daruwale

Graphics

Valentina D'silva

Production Coordinator

Aparna Bhagat

Cover Work

Aparna Bhagat

About the Author

Andy Penver currently lives and works in the UK and has studied at Christ Church (University of Kent). He works as an Oracle E-Business Suite consultant and has over 16 years of experience. He has worked in both the private and public sectors and has a strong technical background. He has led various teams using a hands-on approach through full project lifecycles on some very large projects throughout the UK and Europe. Andy has been involved in two large scale, award-winning implementations. Andy has worked largely as an independent consultant and is Managing Director of his own business, NU-TEKK limited. For the past six years Andy has been heavily involved in a large scale government project rolled out UK-wide. Andy is also currently authoring a second book relating to Oracle E-Business Suite. The second book will relate to other areas of E-Business Suite not covered in this book. It will have chapters focusing on OA Framework personalization and extension, integration of EBS with Oracle 11g middleware (SOA and BEPL), and BI Publisher.

I would like to thank my parents, my wife Buaphan and three children, Sangrung, James, and Jack for their support. I would also like to thank my colleagues for their help in reviewing and commenting on the material in the book. I would also like to thank my fellow colleagues, and in particular, Brian Badenhorst, Phill Davey, Andy Collins, and Dermot Moloney who have all helped me in some way to produce this book.

About the Reviewers

Mariana Angelova is an Oracle certified professional with more than 15 years' experience as an Oracle Applications DBA and Oracle DBA, beginning on Oracle RDBMS rel. 5. She has gained thorough knowledge and rich experience supporting Oracle RDBMS (rel. 11g/10g/9i/8i/8/7/5) on a wide range of platforms: AIX, HP UX, Sun Solaris, Linux, Digital VMS, Windows, and also Oracle Applications environments (R11.5.10/11.5.9/11.5.8/11.5.3) including installation, implementations, upgrades, and system assessments.

Reuben Filius has worked in the IT industry since 1995. He has worked as a technical manager, technical team lead, analyst, auditor, and technical consultant/developer on a large number of (international) E-Business Suite projects. Reuben has experience in various market segments and can use business knowledge together with technical knowledge to enable him to build a much needed bridge between technology and business users and be a liaison for customer senior management levels.

Reuben has worked for Oracle Netherlands for nine years and six years in other consulting organizations specialized in Oracle E-Business Suite. In early 2011 Reuben started Distinct Consulting, a company that focuses on bringing more added value and more focus on business processes for customers using E-Business Suite, having the technology be a vehicle to support the business rather than it becoming the main focus.

Reuben has developed training materials for Oracle in the past and has been a trainer for these at Oracle University.

www.PacktPub.com

Support files, eBooks, discount offers, and more

You might want to visit www.PacktPub.com for support files and downloads related to your book.

Did you know that Packt offers eBook versions of every book published, with PDF and ePub files available? You can upgrade to the eBook version at www.PacktPub.com and as a print book customer, you are entitled to a discount on the eBook copy. Get in touch with us at service@packtpub.com for more details.

At www.PacktPub.com, you can also read a collection of free technical articles, sign up for a range of free newsletters and receive exclusive discounts and offers on Packt books and eBooks.

http://PacktLib.PacktPub.com

Do you need instant solutions to your IT questions? PacktLib is Packt's online digital book library. Here, you can access, read and search across Packt's entire library of books.

Why Subscribe?

- ▶ Fully searchable across every book published by Packt
- ▶ Copy and paste, print and bookmark content
- ▶ On demand and accessible via web browser

Free Access for Packt account holders

If you have an account with Packt at www.PacktPub.com, you can use this to access PacktLib today and view nine entirely free books. Simply use your login credentials for immediate access.

Instant Updates on New Packt Books

Get notified! Find out when new books are published by following @PacktEnterprise on Twitter, or the *Packt Enterprise* Facebook page.

Table of Contents

Preface

Extending Oracle E-Business Suite

This book is about extending Oracle E-Business Suite (EBS). Throughout the book there are detailed examples to work through with tips and explanations about how various components are configured and how we can extend standard functionality. The book is aimed at developers who are new to E-Business Suite or those who are strong in one particular area and need to expand their knowledge in other areas. Experienced developers may also use the book to brush up on their skills or to pick up tips that may help them.

The book focuses on core development and extension and each chapter will go through a topic from start to finish. There are plenty of detailed screenshots throughout each chapter giving clear instructions. This helps to provide a clear and full understanding of what we are doing and why. Each topic will develop a solution to a scenario that will focus on starting an extension right from the beginning to deploying it within E-Business Suite. By the end of each chapter, the reader will have a good understanding of what they need to do for each topic to be able to take away the knowledge gained and start using it in practice. Each chapter will explain in detail how to build an extension in a supported manner. The book also comes with complete, fully tested code and scripts that can be downloaded. The examples have been developed using a Vision instance of Oracle E-Business Suite Release 12 (12.1.1). It would be helpful to know some SQL and PL/SQL but it is not essential as the code is already written and fully documented. We will be going through each chapter example step by step so you will not be expected to write any code that is not detailed in the book.

If you are new to Oracle EBS or a consultant who has worked with Oracle E-Business Suite before, you will be aware that there are many technical components to consider; there are many features using a wide range of tools and the footprint seems to be expanding all the time. One of the key features of EBS is its flexibility. Not all organizations are the same and there are many ways you can configure EBS to make it specific to an organization's needs. Whenever possible, an organization should always attempt to use standard functionality to meet their EBS requirements.

However, there are occasions where business requirements cannot be met using the standard Oracle-provided functionality and this can be anything from renaming a label on a screen to automating a process that would take many hours for someone to process manually.

There are various ways in which you can change behavior in Oracle EBS. The simplest way to change the behavior is through configuration. For example, extending Oracle through profile options, values sets, and Descriptive Flexfields are ways to extend apps through configuration. In addition, Oracle also provides a screen that allows us to extend Oracle core forms. This screen is known as the personalization screen and is a powerful feature that allows us to change the behavior without needing to change any standard objects. These are mechanisms provided by Oracle to change how the application looks or how the application behaves. On the other hand, there are extensions that require writing code, creating new objects, or even extending or replacing existing objects. These type of extensions are in addition to the code or objects that Oracle delivers.

A powerful feature of Oracle is the ability to extend EBS but when doing this, there is a strict set of development standards that must be adhered to. There are two primary ways that Oracle EBS can be modified; the first is customization by extension, as we have just described, and the second is customization by modification. Customization by modification is where standard objects are changed, meaning that the change needs to be re-applied when a newer version of the object is released by Oracle.

Customizations by modification are *not* supported by Oracle and should be avoided at all costs. There are very few occasions where there is a real business justification for an intrusive customization. There are often alternatives such as exploring other solutions or looking at ways to change the requirements or processes. It is important to understand the difference between customization by extension and customization by modification as the two terms are often used incorrectly. When we extend Oracle EBS by supported methods, the standard functionality is still supported by Oracle as it has not been amended by the extension whereas customization by modifying a standard object means the standard object also becomes unsupported by them.

A worthwhile feature of Oracle EBS is that it uses a common toolset and also has a vast amount of documentation written about the supported ways in which you can extend the product. The first place to start would be the Oracle Release 12 documentation library. This provides many documents, all relating to Oracle EBS. This is available from Oracle's website and you should pay particular attention to the concepts, user, developer and user interface guides. Another great resource is Oracle Support, which is a portal provided by Oracle for support, documentation, white papers, and patches among many other things related to EBS. To access the portal, you need to register and also provide a support identifier which is only provided when there is a support contract with Oracle Support. So, if you are new to EBS or if have been around a while, you can nearly always find examples or documentation relating to your specific requirements.

There are nearly always numerous business processes and solutions available to satisfy them. The best way to provide a solution is to have an understanding of what methods are available. Having knowledge of the various ways in which we can extend EBS will give us a much better chance of coming up with better solutions. This book will provide recipes which will cover some simple and some more complex solutions. It will utilize a majority of the Oracle toolset and will hopefully broaden your knowledge. Expanding our knowledge of the toolset will allow us to provide a more varied set of solutions, resulting in having a better chance of providing a better, more robust solution for a given problem.

Understanding the EBS architecture

Before we really get into the book, it is important to understand the E-Business Suite architecture in Release 12. We need to understand where files are kept and how it is installed. If you are a beginner, you will need this information to understand some key concepts and pick up some terminology that is often used when we discuss Oracle EBS.

In release 12, there has been a significant change in the filesystem when it is installed. The change quite simply is used to segregate code, data, and configuration. This makes maintenance much easier. There will be a number of terms that you will encounter regularly when we discuss EBS. A server is a term for a number of processes that provide specific functionality on a single machine. A tier is a term used to describe a logical group of services which can be on one or more physical machine. A machine is used to describe a computer or a group of computers. A node is a group of computers that work closely together as a cluster.

Essentially, there are three tiers per instance of EBS. The database tier (DB Tier), the application tier (APPS Tier), and the desktop tier. The *desktop tier* is the client interface where users will connect to Oracle EBS through a web browser. When Oracle is first used, the browser will install a J2SE plugin, which will use Oracle's own Java Virtual Machine (JVM) rather than the browsers own JVM. The *application tier* (also known as the middle tier) processes all of the business logic. It comprises three servers or service groups. These are *web services* which process requests from the desktop client. Then there are the *forms services*, which manage all of the listening and secure requests for Oracle forms. Then there is the *concurrent processing* server, which processes concurrent requests that are submitted.

When Oracle EBS is installed on all variants of Unix, the install is performed by the root user. However, as part of the installation process, there will be two OS users. One will own the application node filesystem (the applmgr user) and the other will own the database node filesystem (the Oracle user). When installed on Windows, there is one OS user that owns the filesystem. The following diagram shows the basic architecture:

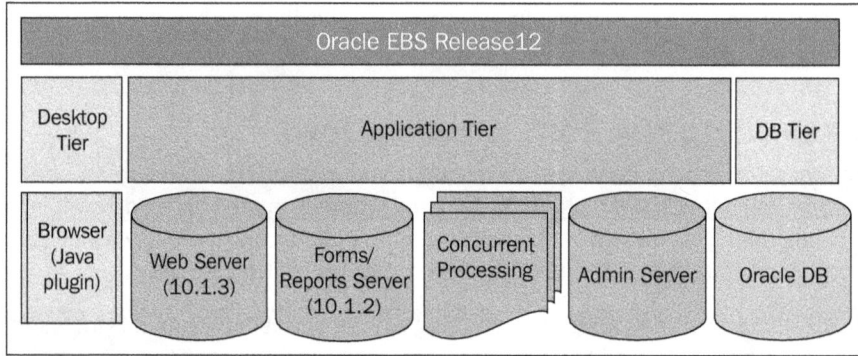

Oracle EBS Release12		
Desktop Tier	Application Tier	DB Tier
Browser (Java plugin)	Web Server (10.1.3) / Forms/Reports Server (10.1.2) / Concurrent Processing / Admin Server	Oracle DB

The directory structure of the Applications Tier and Database Tier will help to understand where files are stored. The following directory structure should help you understand where various files are stored within EBS:

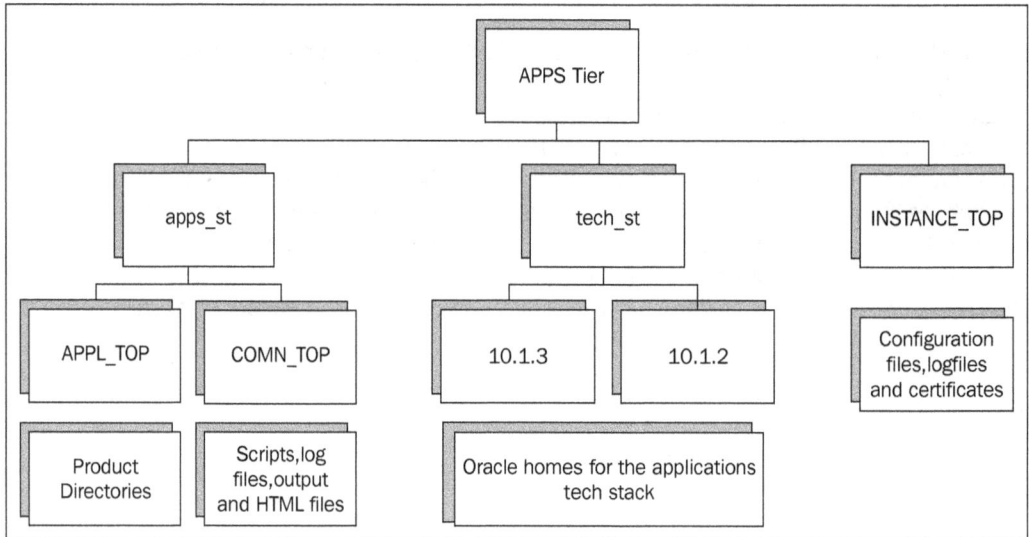

APPS Tier
- apps_st
  - APPL_TOP → Product Directories
  - COMN_TOP → Scripts, log files, output and HTML files
- tech_st
  - 10.1.3 / 10.1.2 → Oracle homes for the applications tech stack
- INSTANCE_TOP → Configuration files, logfiles and certificates

The following table shows the directory structures of some core directories on the applications tier and the database tier:

Apps Tier

Profile	Directory	Description
APPL_TOP	`/apps_st/appl`	This directory is the base directory where all of the product tops are stored.
AU_TOP/forms/US	`/apps_st/appls/au/12.0.0/forms/US`	This directory is where all forms binaries are stored.
AU_TOP/resource	`/apps_st/appls/au/12.0.0/resource`	This directory is where all libraries are stored.
COMMON_TOP	`/apps/apps_st/comn`	This is the base directory for scripts, log files, output files, and HTML files.
ORACLE_HOME	`/apps_st/10.1.2`	This is the directory structure for the forms server files.
iAS_ORACLE_HOME	`/apps_st/10.1.3`	This is the directory structure for the web server files.
INSTANCE_TOP	`/inst/apps/<CONTEXT_NAME>`	This is the top directory for the configuration files.
ADMIN_SCRIPTS_HOME	`/inst/apps/<CONTEXT>/admin/scripts`	This is where admin scripts are stored to start and stop services.

DB Tier

Profile	Directory	Description
ORACLE_HOME	`/db/tech_st/10.2.0`	This directory is the base directory where all of the database files are stored.
Data Files	`/db/apps_st/data`	This directory is the base directory where all of the data files are stored.

Within EBS, each product has its own database user within Oracle. The user will own the objects that store data, such as tables and so on. This is in the form of an abbreviation of the product (AP for Account Payables and HR for Human Resources, for example) and is referred to as a schema. The passwords are by default the same as the schema name but this is nearly always changed after install. On the filesystem on the APPS tier, each product has its own filesystem. The filesystem has the same root directory as the product username in Oracle. For example, there will be a directory structure for Payables (AP) that has a root directory of AP. There is one very important schema called the APPS schema. The APPS schema owns all of the code such as packages, triggers, views, and Java classes. Each product user has grants providing access to the APPS schema for all of its objects. Therefore, the APPS schema has access to all of the objects. That is, the code and the objects owned by the product schemas. It is important that, as a developer, you can access the APPS database schema. All objects that you will require access to are accessible from this schema. When we create custom objects, we need to create a custom schema and all of the data storing objects will reside in this schema. The custom schema will need to be prefixed with XX so that other developers know it's a custom schema. Usually, an onsite DBA will perform this task but we will go through this in one of the recipes we have in the final chapter.

If you would like to understand more relating to the core concepts of EBS, then you can get detailed information from the Oracle Applications Concepts Release 12 from the Release 12 Documentation Library. You can get the documentation from Oracle by following this link: `http://docs.oracle.com/cd/B53825_08/current/html/docset.html`.

Before we start

One final word before we get into the recipes. Hopefully, you will find the book extremely useful. There are thousands of pages written about how to extend and customize Oracle E-Business Suite. This book is not going to cover a solution to every problem. In fact, it will not even come close. The recipes are designed to take us through the different features of the tools and extensions that you may need to utilize in your own solutions. Use the book to get a feel for how each tool and product can be used. It will provide a core understanding of how things can be done and the standards that we need to adhere to. You will need to expand on what you learn here and apply the knowledge you gain to design a solution or solutions to your own scenarios. I personally am a great believer of learning through practice. Expanding your knowledge through understanding the fundamentals is essential to providing the best solutions. Oracle uses many tools and technologies in its suite of applications, of which there are too many to cover in this book alone. However, I am working on a second book which will focus on Integration, OA Framework, and BI Publisher.

What this book covers

Chapter 1, Creating Concurrent Programs, looks at some recipes relating to concurrent programs. Essentially, a concurrent program is used to launch a program. The program could be a PL/SQL package, a report, a host script, or a Java program, for example. The chapter will detail the full list of programs that can be launched. The recipes will focus on creating concurrent programs and defining parameters. They will also show how we can run, schedule, and output data throughout a concurrent program lifecycle. At the end of this chapter, we will have built a concurrent program that runs a PL/SQL program and a host script that sends an e-mail. We will have passed parameters to our executable and written to both output files and log files. We will also schedule the concurrent program and create a request set that allows us to run multiple programs together.

Chapter 2, Oracle Forms, will include developing an Oracle form. Forms have been used in Oracle Applications right from the original release. It started out with forms 2.0, which was character based. Then came forms 4.5 and with it a richer user interface that included widgets such as buttons and toolbars. It is now up to version 10 in Release 12. At the end of the chapter, readers will have developed a form and deployed it within EBS. The form will be built using Oracle Developer 10g and will use the template form that Oracle provides for developers to use. We will go through the changes we need to make to the template form, and develop a form that we can implement for our scenario. The form will have a master-detail relationship. The objects we create will use Oracle's property classes to look and feel like all other professional forms. We will look at the built-in functions that Oracle provides and why we use them instead of the standard forms developer built-in functions. We will also add a number of triggers to the form which will perform actions such as setting the standard WHO fields, inserting update, and deleting records. We will deploy the form in Oracle EBS showing how we transfer and compile the form and how we configure the form and function definitions in EBS.

Chapter 3, Advanced Oracle Forms, looks at implementing more advanced Oracle EBS features such as a query entry screen, messages, tabs, and Descriptive Flexfields. The form will also have a number of widgets such as the standard date lookup and we will also create our own lookup using a query from a record group. We will also show how we can set up a zoom to the form from a standard form. We will also show how we can pass parameters to our form that will allow us to automatically query data upon opening it. As we develop the form we will deploy and test each of the features we add and at the end of the chapters on forms we will have a completed form deployed within the application. The form will have implemented many of the features we would normally require in our custom forms.

Chapter 4, Forms Personalization, discusses configuring forms personalization. Traditionally, changes made to Oracle EBS professional forms were made using the custom library, which requires technical knowledge. However, since version 11.5.10, Oracle has introduced forms personalization as a way of immediately changing the behavior of Oracle standard forms through configuration. Personalization are protected and are generally supported when patches are applied. As they change the behavior of a standard form it is important to re-test any personalization after any patches are applied. This is a must if the patch has introduced new versions of any forms you have personalized. We will demonstrate that to implement personalization you do not have to be technical but a basic understanding of Oracle Forms will help. You can perform some complex functionality through personalization as well but you would need to have a more technical background for this.

At the end of the personalization chapter we will have been through several examples. We will change properties that rename item labels, move items around, disable fields, and rename tab labels. We will also perform some more advanced tasks than just changing properties. We will add a new menu item to launch a form and we will perform validation by calling a database package. We will display user messages to make the user interface functionality more specific to business terminology and processes. We will use personalization to perform activities we used to do in the custom library.

Chapter 5, Workflow, looks at developing and deploying and Oracle workflow within EBS. Oracle Workflow is heavily integrated with Oracle EBS to automate and integrate business processes. Oracle supports workflow extensions as long as they are done in a supported manner. The tool that is used is Oracle Workflow Builder, which is a GUI interface that allows us to drag and drop objects to build or modify processes. At the end of this chapter, users will have a good understanding of how to create a new workflow and deploy it in EBS. We will create functions that call database packages and look at some of the PL/SQL functions used when developing workflows. We will examine the statuses returned back to the workflow from our code and perform activities based upon the responses. We will also create our own lookups and show how they are used within the code and how they are mapped in a process diagram. We will learn a little about advanced queues and how we can create our own queues and trigger events that we can subscribe to. We will build sub processes and add activities such as sending notifications that require responses. We will have created several attributes and store information in the attributes. We will also show how we can monitor and test workflow processes in EBS. Once we have completed the workflow we will examine the role of the workflow background engine and how we deploy our workflow.

Chapter 6, Utilities, looks at a number of utilities that you will find extremely useful when moving extensions from one environment to another. We will show how to create a custom schema and how to configure it on EBS. We will also look at ways to use common utilities, which will reduce risk and save enormous amounts of time. Usually the biggest reason for problems when migrating extensions or configuration is when there are human tasks. We will also look at how to start and stop an environment. There are a number of utilities Oracle provides to make life easier for us. These are used to upload, extract, and bulk load data among other things. It is important to remember that Oracle has spent years developing its applications and there are a great many reusable objects and it is important to use them wherever possible.

What you need for this book

Oracle uses a great many tools to develop extensions. The tools we will mostly focus on in this book are as follows:

- Access to an EBS R12 environment
- Oracle Forms Developer
- SQL Developer
- Oracle Workflow Builder

Other utility programs we will be using are:

- WinSCP
- Putty
- Text Editor

There are a number of languages used for programming and writing scripts that Oracle supports. We are going to primarily focus on the following in this book:

- PL/SQL
- SQL
- Unix shell scripting

Other languages such as Java, Pro*C, and Pro*COBOL are also used within EBS but fall outside the scope of this book.

Who this book is for

This book is written for individuals who want to learn how to develop extensions in Oracle E-Business Suite. If you are involved in development or supporting an E-Business Suite implementation, you should find this book very useful. The book gives detail explanations, so minimal technical expertise is required. It is suitable for beginners who have little experience or developers who may want to use the book to brush up on their skills.

Conventions

In this book, you will find a number of styles of text that distinguish between different kinds of information. Here are some examples of these styles, and an explanation of their meaning.

Code words in text are shown as follows: "The message will get sent to the e-mail address of the employee linked to a role in the WF_ROLES table."

A block of code is set as follows:

```
IF :per_societies.subs_hold = 'Y' THEN
    FND_MESSAGE.SET_NAME('XXHR', 'XXHR_ON_HOLD_WARNING');
    FND_MESSAGE.SET_TOKEN('NAME', :PER_SOCIETIES.NAME);
    FND_MESSAGE.SHOW;
END IF;
```

Any command-line input or output is written as follows:

```
WFLOAD apps/<password> 0 Y FORCE $XXHR_TOP/install/ch5/XXHRIABS.wft
```

New terms and **important words** are shown in bold. Words that you see on the screen, in menus or dialog boxes for example, appear in the text like this: "clicking the **Next** button moves you to the next screen".

[Warnings or important notes appear in a box like this.]

[Tips and tricks appear like this.]

Reader feedback

Feedback from our readers is always welcome. Let us know what you think about this book—what you liked or may have disliked. Reader feedback is important for us to develop titles that you really get the most out of.

To send us general feedback, simply send an e-mail to feedback@packtpub.com, and mention the book title through the subject of your message.

If there is a topic that you have expertise in and you are interested in either writing or contributing to a book, see our author guide on www.packtpub.com/authors.

Customer support

Now that you are the proud owner of a Packt book, we have a number of things to help you to get the most from your purchase.

Downloading the example code

You can download the example code files for all Packt books you have purchased from your account at http://www.packtpub.com. If you purchased this book elsewhere, you can visit http://www.packtpub.com/support and register to have the files e-mailed directly to you.

Errata

Although we have taken every care to ensure the accuracy of our content, mistakes do happen. If you find a mistake in one of our books—maybe a mistake in the text or the code— we would be grateful if you would report this to us. By doing so, you can save other readers from frustration and help us improve subsequent versions of this book. If you find any errata, please report them by visiting http://www.packtpub.com/support, selecting your book, clicking on the **errata submission form** link, and entering the details of your errata. Once your errata are verified, your submission will be accepted and the errata will be uploaded to our website, or added to any list of existing errata, under the Errata section of that title.

Piracy

Piracy of copyright material on the Internet is an ongoing problem across all media. At Packt, we take the protection of our copyright and licenses very seriously. If you come across any illegal copies of our works, in any form, on the Internet, please provide us with the location address or website name immediately so that we can pursue a remedy.

Please contact us at copyright@packtpub.com with a link to the suspected pirated material.

We appreciate your help in protecting our authors, and our ability to bring you valuable content.

Questions

You can contact us at questions@packtpub.com if you are having a problem with any aspect of the book, and we will do our best to address it.

1
Creating Concurrent Programs

In this chapter, we will cover the following:

- ▶ Defining a concurrent program
- ▶ Making a concurrent program available to a user
- ▶ Adding a concurrent program parameter
- ▶ Creating a value set
- ▶ Creating dependent parameters
- ▶ Adding messages to the concurrent program log file
- ▶ Reporting to the concurrent program output file
- ▶ Scheduling the concurrent program
- ▶ Creating multiple concurrent programs
- ▶ Creating request sets
- ▶ Installing the database objects
- ▶ Creating a HOST concurrent program

Introduction

Concurrent programs are commonly used within **Oracle E-Business Suite** as a mechanism to run an executable. Concurrent programs allow users to pass parameters to the executable, which enables it to behave in different ways. We are going to go through some recipes configuring and running concurrent programs. We are also going to show how you can view and write to log files and output files to record what is happening whilst the program is running. Before we get into that, there is a bit of important background knowledge that needs to be highlighted.

Firstly, in release 12, there are additional options when defining a concurrent program to integrate with business events. You can now raise an event at various points throughout the concurrent program lifecycle. This is an extremely useful feature for extending e-Business Suite. For example, developers can subscribe to events and from the event we can launch workflows, send messages to an advanced queue, or launch PL/SQL procedures.

There are some basic concepts that need to be explained before we get into creating concurrent programs and such like. In Oracle EBS, there are users defined on the system and that's how we gain access to the application. There are some pre-configured users such as *sysadmin* and we can also create our own users each time we want to provide access to someone else on the system. Users are assigned one or more responsibilities and these determine the access we have to the system in terms of the forms we can go into, the programs we can run, and the data we can see. A responsibility will have a menu associated with it which will define the forms that can be accessed. It will also have a request group associated with it which will determine which concurrent programs the responsibility can execute. This is a very basic overview and you are probably already familiar with these concepts. However, if you want to understand more then I suggest you do some more reading of the *System Administration* guides from the *Oracle Release 12 Documentation Library portal* available on the Internet.

A few other important points to note are as follows:

- ▶ The responsibility that you will need to configure nearly everything relating to a concurrent program is **Application Developer**. The only thing you cannot do with this responsibility is give access to users. For this you will need to use the **System Administrator** responsibility. (Assign these responsibilities to your user if you do not have them already.)

- ▶ You can launch concurrent programs through an online request, for it to be scheduled automatically or to be triggered programmatically by using Oracle's built-in APIs.

- ▶ Concurrent programs can also be configured so that they can be made incompatible with other concurrent programs meaning that they cannot run simultaneously.

- ▶ You can also group concurrent programs together and form a request set. This feature is useful if you need to create concurrent programs that are linked in some way but need to be run in a certain manner.

- ▶ Concurrent programs can also be scheduled to run on a certain date or to be run on an ongoing basis indefinitely.

We are now ready to get started and in this chapter we will create a concurrent program that launches a PL/SQL procedure. We will look at the parameters that are used internally and we will also add our own parameters using value sets and a dependent value set. In addition, we will write to the log and output files to show runtime information used for logging and reporting. We will schedule the concurrent programs to run automatically at specified time intervals and will look at creating multiple concurrent programs and run them together as a request set. At the end of the chapter we will look at creating a different type of concurrent program.

Defining a concurrent program

In our first recipe, we are going to create an executable and then define a concurrent program that launches the executable. The executable in this example is a PL/SQL package that we want to run. We will start off with a little introduction and look at the types of concurrent programs we can create, the location of executable files on the server, and how to find the output and log files. We will then register a custom application which we need to register our executable and concurrent programs with. Therefore, this recipe will comprise of the following:

- ► Introducing concurrent programs
- ► Register a custom application
- ► Configure an executable
- ► Configure a concurrent program

We do not need any additional development tools to configure a concurrent program. However, the executable that we will be launching will have been developed using the appropriate development tool—Reports Developer, SQL Developer, Java, and so on.

Introducing concurrent programs

There are a number of different types of executables that can be triggered using concurrent programs. We are going to briefly discuss each one as a bit of background before we get started.

Types of concurrent programs

The different types of concurrent programs that we can create are as follows:

- ► **Oracle Reports**: This option is, like the name suggests, used for launching Oracle reports developed using reports builder. It is quite common to have requirements to extend an Oracle standard report. There are a number of options when configuring a concurrent program that specifically relate to Oracle Reports, such as the output format, saving and printing options, columns/rows, and style.

- ► **PL/SQL stored procedures**: These types of concurrent programs call a database stored procedure. There are two mandatory parameters when calling procedures from a concurrent program, which are `errbuf` and `retcode`. The *errbuf* parameter is used to return error messages. The `retcode` is used to return the status of the concurrent program. PL/SQL procedures are stored on the database in the apps schema so this is where Oracle will look for the stored procedure at runtime. The recipes in this chapter have examples of PL/SQL concurrent programs so we will explain this in detail throughout the chapter.

- **Host script:** This is a program that is used to launch a shell script and is commonly used to perform operating system actions such as copying or moving files. Some important points to note are that the program needs to be put in the appropriate BIN (`$PROD_TOP/bin`) directory. Oracle, by default, uses the first four parameters so any parameters used in the shell script will need to start with the fifth parameter (`$5, $6 ...`, and so on). We will go through this in more detail later in the chapter as we will be creating a concurrent program calling a host file in one of the examples.

- **Immediate**: This is for backward compatibility only and was used to launch a subroutine. It is now recommended to use a PL/SQL Procedure or spawned process.

- **Java stored procedures**: As the name suggests, these are executables written using Java. A concurrent program is then defined to execute the code. When interacting with the database, PL/SQL Procedures are still the best way to do any processing as it is a language specifically designed to do so. You can perform many tasks using PL/SQL or Java but there are certain tasks where Java would be the better choice, especially when it comes to interacting with the operating system or third party databases.

- **Multi Language Function**: The execution file is an MLS function used for running programs in multiple languages. This means that a concurrent program can be submitted multiple times, each time in a different language.

- **SQL*Loader**: This is a utility to be able to load bulk data into Oracle E-Business Suite. It uses a data file and a control file. The **data file** is the data and the **control file** is the definition of the fields in the data file. There is a third file which is the **parameter file**, which is also used to pass any additional parameters when processing begins. There are three files produced when processing completes, a log file, a discard file, and a bad file. The **log file** provides information about the execution of the load. The **bad file** is written to if there are any records that are rejected throughout the execution of the load. The **discard file** is written to when there are any discarded records during the load execution, for example, when selectively loading rows.

- **SQL*Plus**: This is used to run an SQL*Plus script or anonymous block. It will get executed as if you were running the script on the command line through SQL*Plus.

- **Spawned**: This is a program that is usually run on the operating system, such as C or Pro*C.

- **Perl Concurrent Program**: This is used for executing programs written in **CGI Perl**. **CGI** stands for **Common Gateway Interface** and Perl is the most common language for writing CGI scripts. It is used for scripting, programming web interfaces/development, and is great for parsing.

Executable file location

It is worth noting that at runtime the executable will need to be placed at a specific location. Files are stored in the $PRODUCT_TOP of the application they are registered with. Under this directory, they will be in the directory related to the type of program it is. The following are a few examples of where executables will need to be stored:

- A spawned program registered in the Payables application would be stored in the $AP_TOP/bin directory.
- A host program registered in the Receivables application would be stored in the $AR_TOP/bin directory.
- An SQL*Plus script registered in a custom application would be stored in the custom application top directory, for example, the $XXHR_TOP/sql directory. If you are unfamiliar with the custom top discussed here then do not worry as we will discuss this throughout the book.
- A report that was registered in the Inventory application would be stored in the $INV_TOP/Reports/Lang directory.

Output and log files

Throughout the chapter we will be looking at the output and log files generated by Oracle EBS when we run a concurrent program. These files are produced during execution and we can write log messages or output messages throughout processing. The output file is used to produce output for the user to see what has been processed and the log file is used to write more technical or debugging messages, which may not necessarily be understood by the end user. An additional way to debug is to use APIs to write to the FND_LOG_MESSAGES table.

The location of log files can be found by querying the FND_CONCURRENT_REQUESTS table. The two columns you are looking for are logfile_name and outfile_name:

```
SELECT logfile_name, outfile_name
FROM FND_CONCURRENT_REQUESTS
WHERE request_id = <request_id>
```

The results of this query will give you the location of the output files for a given request_id. Alternatively, you can search for the files manually in the directory listed in the UTL_FILE_DIR parameter in the init.ora file. The log file will start with an *l* and the output file with an *o*. Both will be followed by the request_id and both will have a .req file extension.

Register a custom application

We must register a new application in Oracle E-Business Suite to register our custom configuration with. A new application allows us to isolate custom code and/or configuration from the standard Oracle Applications code and configuration. When we define a custom application, we register the custom application name, application short name, application basepath, and application description with the **Oracle Application Object Library**. This is used to configure custom application objects such as responsibilities and forms as belonging to our custom application. This identification with the custom application allows any extensions to be preserved during upgrades. The application basepath is an operating system profile variable that points to the directories where the application object library will look to find the files associated with the custom application. At this point we are just going to configure our custom application. We will create the file structure and create a custom schema later in the book.

How to do it...

To register an application, perform the following steps:

1. Log in to Oracle with the **System Administrator** responsibility.
2. Navigate to **Application | Register** and the **Applications** window will open as shown in the following screenshot:

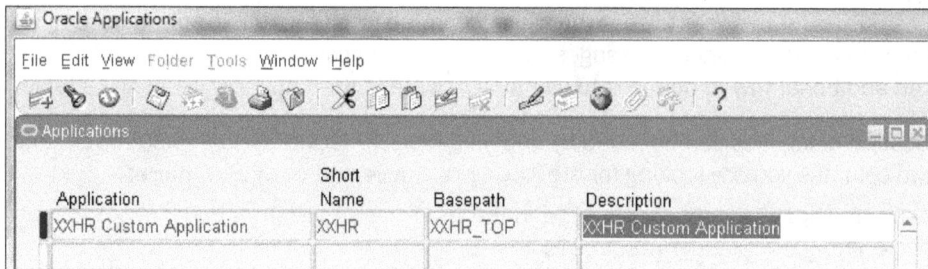

3. Enter a new record with the following data:

Application:	XXHR Custom Application
Short Name :	XXHR
Basepath :	XXHR_TOP
Description :	XXHR Custom Application

4. Save the record.

How it works

We have now registered a custom application called **XXHR Custom Application**. We can see that the application short name and the base path are defined here.

Configure an executable

We will now configure the executable that our concurrent program will execute at runtime.

Getting ready

The responsibility we need to configure the concurrent program is **Application Developer**. The code for the following recipe is available in the following files: XXHREEBS_1_1.pks (specification) and XXHREEBS_1_1.pkb (body). Follow the readme_1_1.txt to install this package.

How to do it...

1. Log in to Oracle with the **Application Developer** responsibility.

2. Navigate to **Concurrent | Executable** and the **Concurrent Program Executable** window will open, as shown in the following screenshot:

3. Enter data as shown in the following table:

Item name	Item value
Executable	XXHR1001
Short Name	XXHR1001
Application	XXHR Custom Application
Description	Executable created for concurrent program recipe
Execution Method	PL/SQL Stored Procedure
Execution File Name	xxhreebs.first_concurrent_program

> Please note that any fields that are not specified in this table should be left as their default value.

4. Click the **Save** button in the toolbar (or *Ctrl* + *S*) to save the record.

5. Exit the form.

How it works...

We have defined an executable that will be launched by the concurrent program we are about to configure next. The executable has to be created before we can configure the concurrent program. This executable is calling a database package which at present has very little in it. When calling a PL/SQL package from a concurrent program there are two mandatory parameters. These are `errbuf` and `retcode`. We must return a value that represents a completion status and this is done by assigning a value to the `retcode` parameter. If we look at the package specification we can see that there are three constant variables defined, called SUCCESS, WARNING, and FAILED. These are set to 0, 1, and 2 respectively and we will assign a constant variable to the `retcode` out parameter to return a value to the concurrent manager upon completion. Valid return values for the `retcode` parameter are as follows:

```
0 - Success
1 - Success & warning
2 - Error
```

We have assigned constant variables to make the code easier to read. The other parameter that is returned is the `errbuf` parameter. We can assign text to this parameter so that we can return error messages if any occur at runtime back to the concurrent program, so it will be displayed in the log file.

Configure a concurrent program

In this recipe, we will configure our first concurrent program. The concurrent program will run the executable that we have just defined.

How to do it...

1. Log in to Oracle and select the **Application Developer** responsibility.

2. Navigate to **Concurrent | Program** and the **Concurrent Programs** window will open, as shown in the following screenshot:

3. Enter data as shown in the following table:

Item name	Item value
Program	**XXHR First Concurrent Program**
Short Name	XXHR_FIRST_CONC_PROG
Application	**XXHR Custom Application**
Description	**XXHR First Concurrent Program**
Executable Name	**XXHR1001**

Please note that any fields that are not defined in this table should be left as their default value.

4. Click the **Save** button in the toolbar (or *Ctrl* + *S*) to save the record.

5. Exit the form.

How it works...

So now we have configured the executable and also defined the concurrent program that launches the executable. These are the basic steps required to configure a concurrent program. As you will see there are a number of other regions on the screen and some buttons, and we will be looking at some of these later in the chapter. The next step is to run the concurrent program.

Making a concurrent program available to a user

We have created our first concurrent program but now we want to run it. That is exactly what we are going to do in this recipe. However, before we can run it we need to do some configuration. The concurrent program needs to be assigned to a request group and the request group needs to be assigned to a responsibility. The responsibility will have a menu that calls the concurrent request functions. So we are going to perform the following tasks so that we can access and run our concurrent program:

- ▶ Configure a menu
- ▶ Register a custom application
- ▶ Create a new request group
- ▶ Create a new responsibility
- ▶ Assign the responsibility to a user
- ▶ Run the concurrent program
- ▶ View the request

> Please note that it may well be the case that there is an existing responsibility, menu, and request group already defined.

Configure a menu

This recipe will configure a menu which will be attached to the new responsibility we are going to create. This will determine the concurrent programs and forms we will be able to access.

How to do it...

To create a menu, perform the following steps:

1. Log in to Oracle with the **Application Developer** responsibility.

2. Navigate to **Application | Menu** and the **Menus** window will open, as shown in the following screenshot:

3. Enter data as shown in the following table for the master record:

Item name	Item value
Menu	XXHR_TEST_MENU
User Menu Name	**Test Menu**
Menu Type	**Standard**
Description	**Test Menu**

4. Enter data as shown in the following table for the detail records:

Seq	Prompt	Submenu	Function	Description	Grant
10	View Requests		View All Concurrent Requests	View Requests	
20	Submit Requests		Requests: Submit	Submit Requests	

5. Click the **Save** button in the toolbar (or *Ctrl + S*) to save the record.

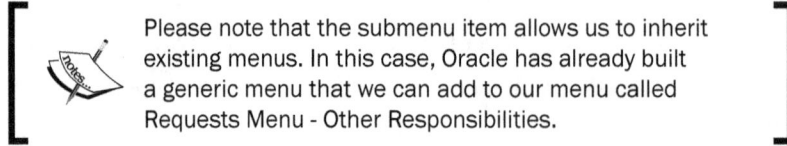

> Please note that the submenu item allows us to inherit existing menus. In this case, Oracle has already built a generic menu that we can add to our menu called Requests Menu - Other Responsibilities.

6. Exit the form.

How it works...

The menu is what a user will see in the navigator when they are assigned a responsibility that has our menu assigned to it. More specifically the user will see the **Prompt** value which when selected will launch the function assigned to it. The menu can also be assigned a submenu. If you add a submenu the whole menu will be inherited and any functions it contains. We have created a simple menu that has the standard concurrent request functions added to it, so that we can run and view our concurrent program.

There's more...

We can see the menu structure that we have created and how it may look to the user.

Viewing a menu structure

If after we have saved the menu we wish to see how it will look, we can click on the **View Tree** button from the **Menus** screen. It will open a new window which will show us the menu we have just created. The following screenshot shows what we have just created (the menu has been fully expanded):

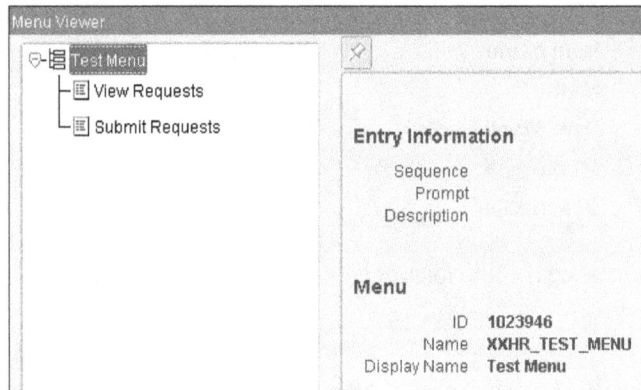

Create a new request group

When we define a responsibility we can also assign a request group to it. A request group is a list of concurrent programs or request sets that a responsibility will see when they run a concurrent request. We are going to add a request group that will have our concurrent program in it.

How to do it...

To create a request group perform the following:

1. Log in to Oracle with the **System Administrator** responsibility.

2. Navigate to **Security | Responsibility | Request** and the **Request Groups** window will open as shown in the following screenshot:

3. Enter data as shown in the following table for the master record:

Item name	Item value
Group	**XXHR Request Group**
Application	**XXHR Custom Application**
Code	XXHR_REQUEST_GROUP
Description	**XXHR Request Group**

4. Now we are going to add the concurrent program we created in the *Defining a concurrent program* recipe. Navigate to the **Requests** region and enter data as shown in the following table for the detail record:

Type	Name	Application
Program	**XXHR First Concurrent Program**	**XXHR Custom Application**

5. Click the **Save** button in the toolbar (or *Ctrl* + *S*) to save the record.
6. Exit the form.

How it works...

We have now created a request group that contains our concurrent program. When we assign the request group to our responsibility the concurrent program will appear as a list of concurrent programs when we want to run a request. The responsibility only has access to programs in the request set assigned to it.

Create a new responsibility

Now to create our new responsibility that will run the concurrent program.

How to do it...

Perform the following steps to create a new responsibility called **XXEBS Extending e-Business Suite**:

1. Log in to Oracle with the **System Administrator** responsibility.
2. Navigate to **Security | Responsibility | Define** and the **Responsibilities** window will open as shown in the following screenshot:

3. Enter data as shown in the following table for the master record:

Item name	Item value
Responsibility Name	**XXEBS Extending e-Business Suite**
Application	**XXHR Custom Application**
Responsibility Key	**XXEBSEEBS**
Description	**XXEBS Extending e-Business Suite**
Data Group: Name	**Standard**
Application	**XXHR Custom Application**
Menu	**Test Menu**
Request Group: Name	**XXHR Request Group**

4. Click the **Save** button in the toolbar (or _Ctrl_ + S) to save the record.
5. Exit the form.

How it works...

We have now created a responsibility that has the menu we created earlier and our request group assigned to it.

Assign the responsibility to a user

Now we are going to create a user and assign the responsibility we created to the user.

How to do it...

To create a new user, perform the following steps:

1. Log in to Oracle with the **System Administrator** responsibility.

2. Navigate to **Security | User | Define** and the **Users** window will open, as shown in the following screenshot:

3. Enter data as shown in the following table:

Item name	Item value
User Name	TEST01
Password	*<enter your password>*
Description	TEST01 User
Password Expiration	*<None>*

> Please note that when you enter a password and press the *Tab* key the cursor will remain in the password field as you have to enter the password again.

4. In the **Direct Responsibilities** tab, add **XXEBS Extending e-Business Suite** to the responsibility field.

> You can also just type the first few characters and then the *Tab* button. If there is more than one record then a list of values will appear. In this case, you could have typed XXEBS and then the *Tab* key.

5. Click the **Save** button in the toolbar (or *Ctrl* + *S*) to save the record.
6. Exit the form.

How it works...

We have now created a user so that we have access to the responsibility we created. If you already have a user that you have created, you can add the responsibility to that user if you prefer.

Run the concurrent program

Now we can run the concurrent program we have created.

How to do it...

To run the concurrent program, perform the following steps:

1. Log in to Oracle with the user that has the **XXEBS Extending e-Business Suite** responsibility assigned to it.

2. Navigate to **Submit Requests | Submit** and a **Submit a New Request** window will open, as shown in the following screenshot:

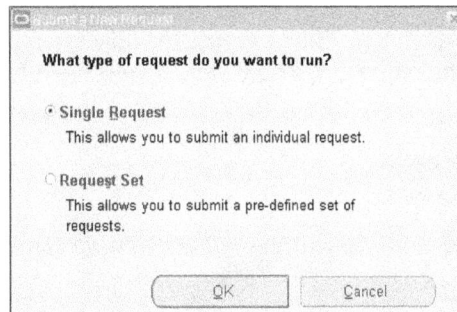

3. Select **Single Request** and click the **OK** button.

4. The **Submit Request** screen will open, as shown in the following screenshot:

5. Click on the **Name** field and select **XXHR First Concurrent Program** from the list of values.

6. Click on the **Submit** button.

7. A decision box will appear informing us that the request has been submitted.

8. Click on the **No** button as we do not wish to submit another request at this time.

9. Exit the form.

How it works...

The request has now been submitted. The next time the concurrent manager runs in the background it will execute the request. We now want to view the request to see if it has completed successfully.

View the request

We want to see the outcome of the concurrent request and we can do this from the menu.

How to do it...

To view the request, perform the following:

1. Navigate to **View | Requests**, as shown in the following screenshot:

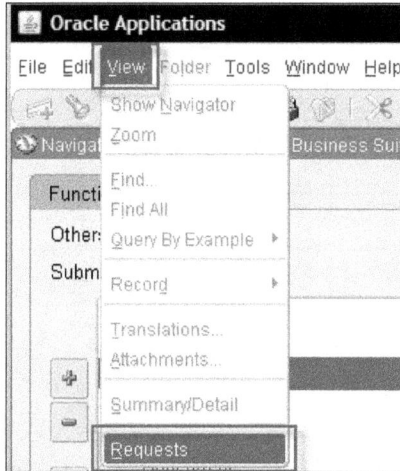

2. The **Find Requests** window will appear, as shown in the following screenshot:

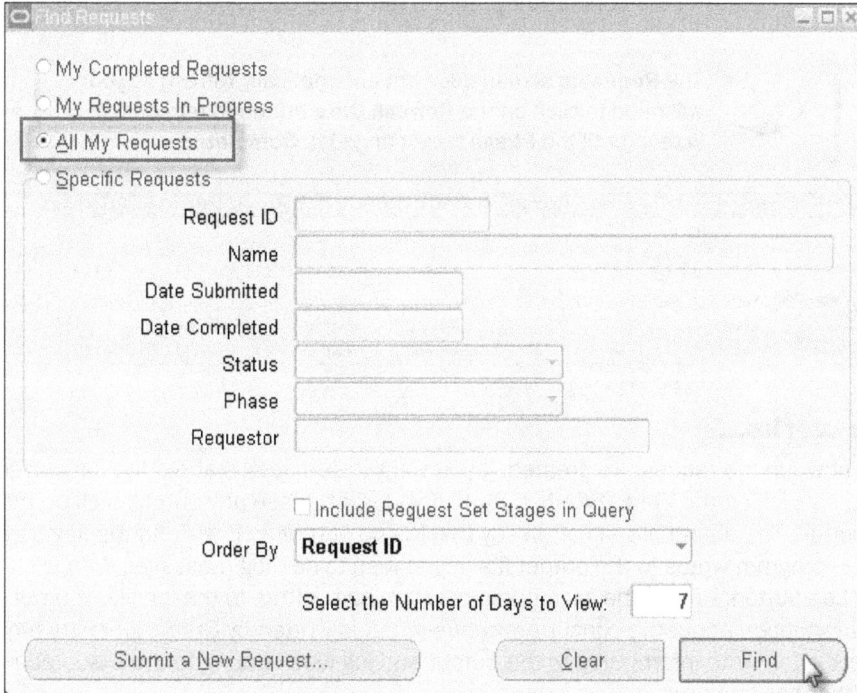

3. Click on the **Find** button in the bottom-right hand side corner.

4. The **Requests** window will appear and you will see the concurrent program that was executed, as shown in the following screenshot:

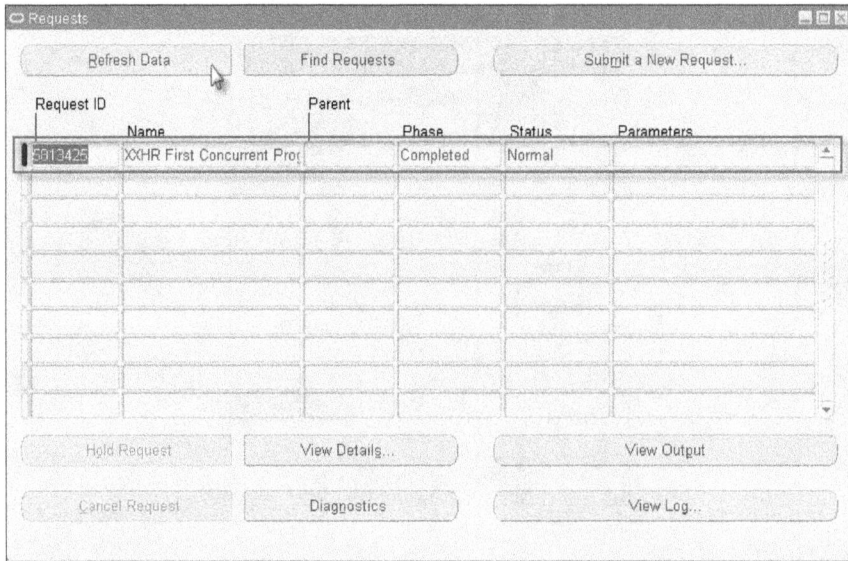

5. You can see that the concurrent program has been completed successfully.

> The **Requests** screen does not automatically refresh so you will need to click on the **Refresh Data** button to refresh the screen until the **Phase** has changed to **Completed**.

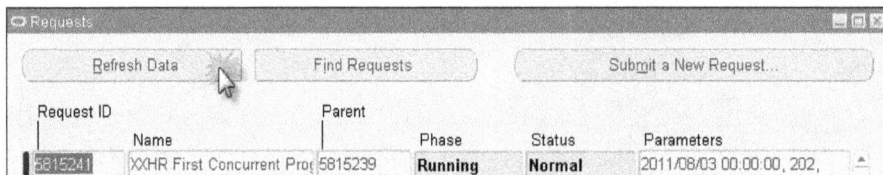

How it works...

We have now run the request we created. If you want to see details about the concurrent request then click on the **View Details** button. If you want to see any output click on the **View Output** button. The output file will often say there is no output as it will only display data if the executable program writes to the output file. If you wish to see log messages then click on the **View Log** button. Unless the executable program has written to the log file, you will see generic information about the concurrent request that is written by Oracle for every request. Developers often write information to the output and log files relating to the executable program that has been run.

See also...

Adding messages to the concurrent program log file.

Reporting to the concurrent program output file.

Adding a concurrent program parameter

In this recipe, we are going to add a parameter to the concurrent program **XXHR First Concurrent Program**. Parameters allow the users to pass values into the concurrent program. This can be used by the executable to impact the way it performs the intended task. We are going to add the parameter to the PL/SQL package and then change the return code based upon the value we pass in.

We will be adding a parameter to the concurrent program we have already created. We will also need to add the parameter to the code in the XXHREEBS package and we will use SQL Developer to make these changes. The following tasks will be performed in this recipe:

- ▸ Adding a parameter to the concurrent program
- ▸ Amend the XXHREEBS package to add the new parameter
- ▸ Amend the XXHREEBS to change the completion status of the concurrent program
- ▸ Testing the concurrent program

Adding a parameter to the concurrent program

We are now going to add a parameter to the concurrent program to pass the date on which the request was run.

How to do it...

To add a parameter, perform the following steps:

1. Log in to Oracle with the **Application Developer** responsibility.
2. Navigate to **Concurrent | Program** and the **Concurrent Programs** window will open.
3. Press the *F11* key to enter a query.
4. Type **XXHR First%** into the **Program** field and press the *Ctrl + F11* keys together to execute the query.

5. The concurrent program we created in an earlier recipe will be returned, as shown in the following screenshot:

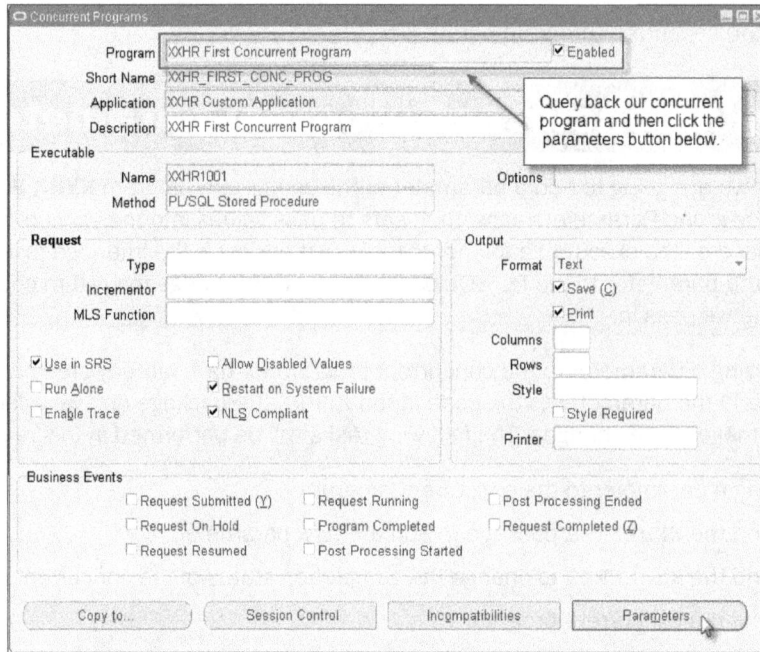

6. Click on the **Parameters** button to open the **Concurrent Program Parameters** window, as shown in the following screenshot:

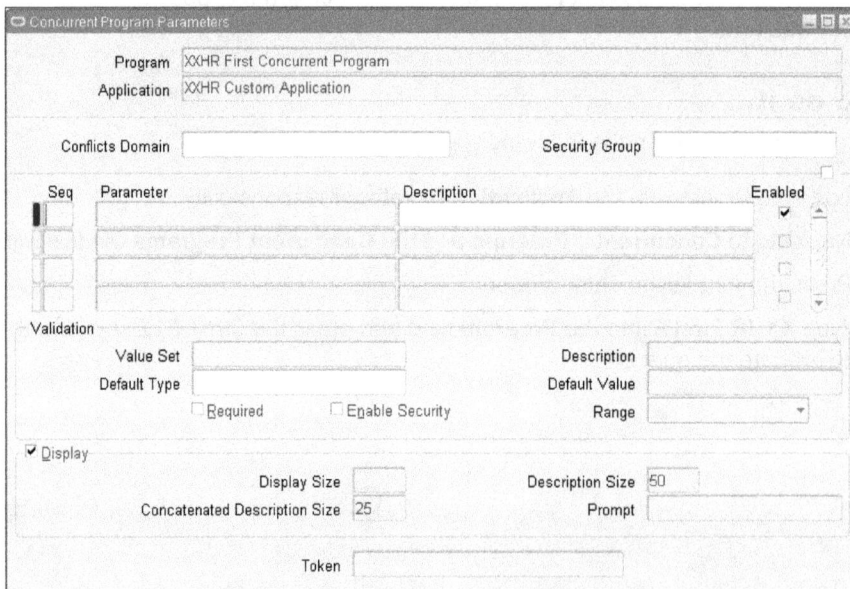

7. Enter the following details as per the following table:

Item name	Value
Seq	10
Parameter	P_RUN_DATE
Description	Concurrent program run date
Enabled	☑
Value Set	FND_STANDARD_DATE
Default Type	Current Date
Required	☒
Display	☑
Display Size	11
Description Size	50
Concatenated Description Size	25
Prompt	Run Date

> The value entered in the **Parameter** field is the name of the parameter we will define in the PL/SQL package in the next task.
>
> The value entered in the **Value Set** field is a pre-defined value set. It is for selecting a date and we are going to re-use this rather than create our own.

8. Click the **Save** button in the toolbar (or *Ctrl + S*) to save the record.
9. Exit the form.

How it works...

We have now added a date parameter to the concurrent request. When we run the concurrent request, Oracle uses the records entered here to dynamically create a parameter screen. We can add parameters that are mandatory and based on a list of values if we wish. Also, we can hide a parameter to the user by checking the **Display** checkbox if required. We are going to add some more parameters to the concurrent program in the next few tasks but first we must add the parameter we just created to the procedure we call in the executable.

Amend the XXHREEBS package to add the new parameter

Now we are going to amend the XXHREEBS package to accept the new parameter we have configured. The parameter we configured is P_RUN_DATE.

Getting ready

We will need to use SQL Developer to amend the package so if you have not already done so, install SQL Developer. You can download SQL Developer from http://www.oracle.com/technetwork/developer-tools/sql-developer/downloads/index-098778.html.

How to do it...

We are now going to amend the database package to add the parameter we have just configured, as follows:

1. Open SQL Developer and connect to the **apps** user.

2. In the navigator, expand the **Packages** node and select the XXHREEBS package.

> You can add a filter on the **Packages** node in SQL Developer which will refresh the list much quicker. To do this highlight the **Packages** node and click on the filter icon. In the **Filter** window, select **Name | Like | XXHR%** in the filter criteria region and click ok.

3. The package specification will be opened in the editor as shown in the following screenshot:

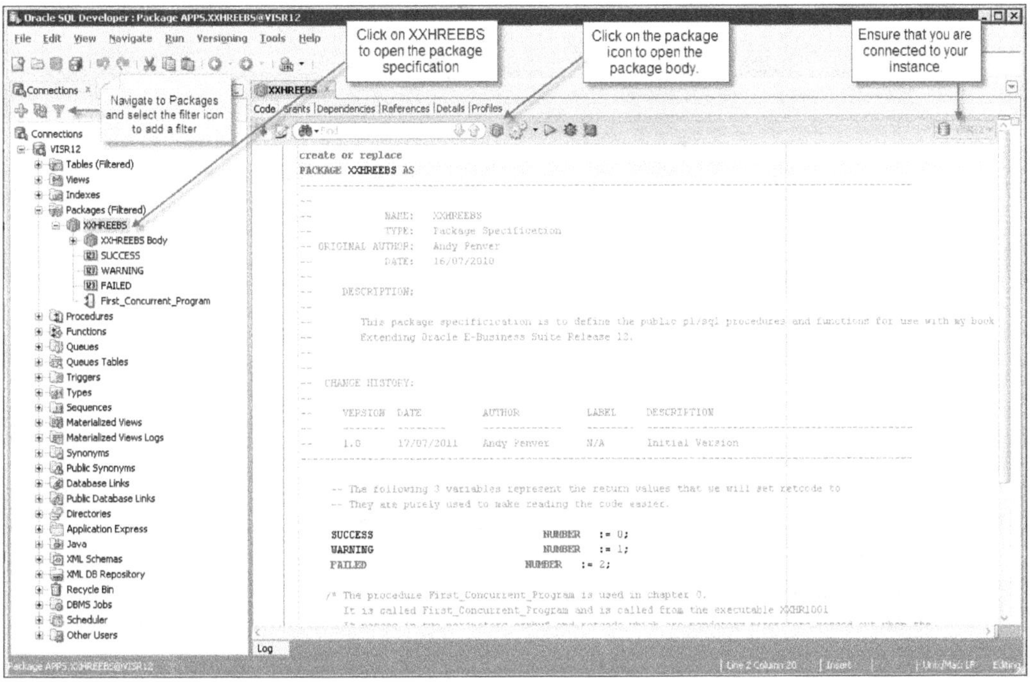

4. Now edit the package specification by clicking on the package specification in the **Packages** node as shown in the following screenshot.

5. Scroll down the package specification code until you reach the First_Concurrent_Program procedure definition, shown as follows:

```
PROCEDURE  First_Concurrent_Program (errbuf        OUT VARCHAR2,
                                     retcode   OUT NUMBER);
```

6. Now add the parameter to the code after the first two mandatory parameters, errbuf and retcode. The program definition will look like the following:

```
PROCEDURE  First_Concurrent_Program (errbuf        OUT VARCHAR2,
                                     retcode   OUT NUMBER,
                                     p_run_date IN VARCHAR2);
```

7. Compile the package specification by clicking the compile icon ( ) in the editor toolbar.

8. The package specification will now look like the following:

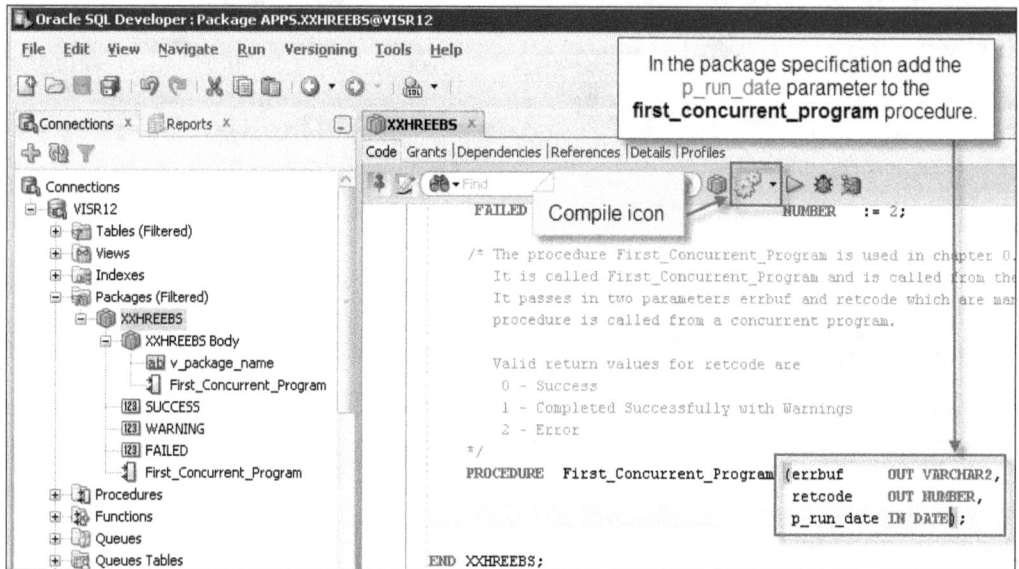

9. Now we need to add the parameter to the package body, so click the open body icon as shown in the following screenshot and a new tab will open displaying the package body in the editor:

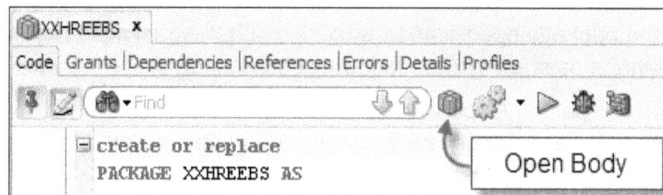

10. Scroll down to the `First_Concurrent_Program` procedure definition and add the `p_run_date` parameter to the list of parameters, shown as follows:

```
PROCEDURE   First_Concurrent_Program (errbuf      OUT VARCHAR2,
                                      retcode     OUT NUMBER,
                                      p_run_date  IN VARCHAR2) IS
```

11. Compile the `First_Concurrent_Program` package body.

How it works...

Now we have created a new parameter and added it to our PL/SQL package executed by our concurrent program.

Amend the XXHREEBS package to change the completion status of the concurrent program

We are now going to add some code to the package to change the return status of the concurrent program. We will return a status of success if the date parameter we enter when we run the concurrent program is equal to the current date. When the date parameter is before the current date we will return a status of warning and if the date parameter is after today's date then we will return an error status.

Getting ready

We are going to amend the XXHREEBS package body to determine the return status of the concurrent program based upon the date parameter P_RUN_DATE that is passed in. The code for the following recipe is available in the following files: XXHREEBS_1_2.pks (specification) and XXHREEBS_1_2.pkb (body). The following are the steps taken to add the code to the existing XXHREEBS package.

How to do it...

To amend the package, perform the following steps:

1. Open SQL Developer and connect to the **apps** user.

2. Navigate to **Packages** and select the XXHREEBS package.

3. Add the following variable to capture the run date passed in and convert it to a date:

   ```
   v_run_date  DATE := TO_DATE(p_run_date,'YYYY/MM/DD
   HH24:MI:SS');
   ```

4. Edit the First_Concurrent_Program procedure by replacing the line of code retcode := SUCCESS; with the following code after the BEGIN statement:

   ```
   IF TRUNC(v_run_date) = TRUNC(SYSDATE) THEN
      retcode := SUCCESS;
   ELSIF TRUNC(v_run_date) < TRUNC(SYSDATE) THEN
      retcode := WARNING;
   ELSIF TRUNC(v_run_date) > TRUNC(SYSDATE) THEN
      retcode := FAILED;
   END IF;
   ```

5. The package body should now look similar to the following screenshot, which shows the three changes to the code we have made:

```
38  ⊟     PROCEDURE  First_Concurrent_Program (errbuf     OUT VARCHAR2,
39                                             retcode    OUT NUMBER,
40                                   (1)       p_run_date IN VARCHAR2) IS -- 1.1 Added p_run_date parameter
41
42           v_procedure_name   VARCHAR2(30) := 'First_Concurrent_Program'; -- local variable containing the n
●   (2)      v_run_date         DATE := TO_DATE(p_run_date,'YYYY/MM/DD HH24:MI:SS'); -- 1.2 added local variab
44        BEGIN
45
●   (3)         -- 1.2 Added the conditions to set the completion status
●                -- If the run date is the same as the date it is run on then complete with success
●                -- If the run date is less than the date it is run on the complete with warning
●                -- If the run date is greater than the date it is run oncomplete the concurrent program as failed
●   ⊟         IF TRUNC(v_run_date) = TRUNC(SYSDATE) THEN
●                 retcode := SUCCESS;
●              ELSIF TRUNC(v_run_date) < TRUNC(SYSDATE) THEN
●                 retcode := WARNING;
●              ELSIF TRUNC(v_run_date) > TRUNC(SYSDATE) THEN
●                 retcode := FAILED;
●              END IF;
57
58           EXCEPTION WHEN OTHERS THEN
59                -- A procedure will always have an EXCEPTIONS section to catch errors
60                -- At a minimum there will be a catch all other errors statement
61              errbuf  := SQLERRM;
62              retcode := FAILED;
63        END;
```

6. Compile the `First_Concurrent_Program` package body.

How it works...

We have edited the package to add some rules, so that the concurrent program will complete either with success, a warning, or an error depending upon the value of the date parameter we run the concurrent program with.

Testing the concurrent program

Now we want to run the concurrent program testing the logic we have added in the PL/SQL code. If the run date parameter is entered as the current date then the concurrent program will complete successfully. If the concurrent program runs with a run date prior to today then the concurrent program will complete with a warning. If the concurrent program runs with a future date then it will complete with an error.

How to do it...

To test the logic we have added, perform the following steps:

1. Log in to Oracle with the **XXEBS Extending e-Business Suite** responsibility.
2. Navigate to **Submit Requests** and submit a single request.

3. Select the **XXHR First Concurrent Program** concurrent program and leave the `Run Date` parameter to the default date (which is the current date) and click **OK**.

4. Click on the **Submit** button and when prompted to submit a new request, select **No** and the form will close down.

5. Navigate to the **View Requests** window and click on the **Find** button (to find all requests).

6. You should see that the concurrent program we just submitted has completed successfully. (If it is still **Pending** then click the refresh button until the status is **Completed**.)

How it works...

We have tested that we have been able to add the parameter to the concurrent program. We have also tested that it still completes successfully.

There's more...

Now we want to test the other conditions so try submitting the concurrent program again but enter a date less than the current date. The program should complete with a warning. Finally, run the program again with a future date and the concurrent program should complete with an error.

Creating a value set

In this recipe, we are going to add a parameter that uses a value set. A value set is a list of values and they are commonly used to extend e-Business Suite and in this recipe we are going to create a value set that is a list of organizations.

We are going to perform the following tasks:

  ▸ Create a value set

  ▸ Create a new parameter for the concurrent program

  ▸ Modify the executable to accept the new parameter

  ▸ Run the concurrent program

Create a value set

We are now going to create the value set that we will use as a list of values for our next parameter. The value set will contain a list of organizations.

How to do it...

To create a value set complete the following tasks:

1. Log in to Oracle with the **Application Developer** responsibility.

2. Navigate to **Application | Validation | Set**, and the **Values Sets** window will open as shown in the following screenshot:

3. Enter the following details as per the following table:

Item name	Value
Value Set Name	XXHR_ORG_LIST_VS
Description	**List of HR Organisations**
List Type	**List of Values**
Security Type	**No Security**
Format Type	**Char**
Maximum Size	**20**
Validation Type	**Table**

4. Click on the **Edit Information** button and the **Validation Table Information** form will appear, as shown in the following screenshot:

5. Enter the following details as per the following table:

Item name	Value	Type	Size
Table Application	**Human Resources**		
Table Name	HR_ALL_ORGANIZATION_UNITS		
Value	ORGANIZATION_ID	Varchar2	**22**
Meaning	NAME	Varchar2	**240**
ID	ORGANIZATION_ID	Number	**22**
Where/Order By	SYSDATE BETWEEN NVL(date_from, SYSDATE) AND NVL (date_to, SYSDATE) ORDER BY name		

6. Click on the **Save** button in the toolbar (or *Ctrl* + *S*) to save the record.
7. Click on the **Test** button to test the code entered.

How it works...

We have created a lookup that we can use in our concurrent program when we define the next parameter. The list will contain a list of organizations from the HR_ALL_ORGANIZATION_UNITS table.

There's more...

We are just going to explore what happens to the information we store in this screen and how it performs at runtime.

What happens to the data entered?

Essentially this screen dynamically creates an SQL statement which is used to generate the list of values. The table columns region defines the values that are visible to the user and the value that is passed to the concurrent program. The Name value is what is displayed to the user. If there is no value entered for ID then it is passed as the parameter value, otherwise the value in ID is passed. The ID field is hidden from the user. In addition, if the value set is already used, that is, already mapped to a concurrent program, it cannot be modified.

Create a new parameter for the concurrent program

We are now going to add a new parameter and use the value set we have just created in the previous recipe.

How to do it...

To create a new parameter, perform the following steps:

1. Log in to Oracle with the **Application Developer** responsibility.
2. Navigate to **Concurrent | Program** and the **Concurrent Programs** window will open.
3. Press the *F11* key to enter a query.
4. Query back the **XXHR First Concurrent Program** concurrent program and click the parameters button.
5. Add a new parameter with the following details:

Item name	Value
Seq	20
Parameter	P_ORG_ID
Description	Organization ID
Enabled	☑
Value Set	XXHR_ORG_LIST_VS
Default Type	
Required	☑
Display	☑
Display Size	20
Description Size	50
Concatenated Description Size	25
Prompt	Organization

6. Click the **Save** button in the toolbar (or *Ctrl + S*) to save the record.

7. The completed screen will look like the following screenshot:

How it works...

We have added a new parameter that will be passed to our concurrent program. The parameter will use the list of organizations we created in the previous task. We must now add the parameter to the PL/SQL package, which we will do next.

Modify the executable to accept the new parameter

We are now going to add the parameter to the executable, which is the package called XXHREEBS.First_Concurrent_Program. If you wish to view the code then it can be found in the files XXHREEBS_1_3.pks and XXHREEBS_1_3.pkb. You can compile the package provided or add the parameter to the code manually below.

How to do it...

To add the parameter, take the following steps:

1. Open SQL Developer and connect to the **apps** user.

2. Navigate to **Packages** and select the XXHREEBS package.

3. In the code editor, scroll down the package specification until you reach the First_Concurrent_Program procedure definition.

4. Now add the parameter to the code AFTER the `p_run_date` parameter. The program definition will look like the following:

```
PROCEDURE  First_Concurrent_Program (errbuf      OUT VARCHAR2,
                                     retcode     OUT NUMBER,
                                     p_run_date IN VARCHAR2,
                                     p_org_id    IN VARCHAR2);
```

5. Compile the package specification and ensure it compiles without error.

6. Now we need to make the same addition to the package body. Open the package body.

7. Scroll down to the `First_Concurrent_Program` procedure definition and add `p_org_id` to the list of parameters, as shown in the following code:

```
PROCEDURE  First_Concurrent_Program (errbuf       OUT VARCHAR2,
                                     retcode      OUT NUMBER,
                                     p_run_date   IN VARCHAR2,
                                     p_org_id     IN VARCHAR2) IS
```

8. Compile the `First_Concurrent_Program` package body.

9. The program specification will look like the following:

```
PROCEDURE  First_Concurrent_Program (errbuf      OUT VARCHAR2,
                                     retcode     OUT NUMBER,
                                     p_run_date IN VARCHAR2, -- 1.1 Added p_run_date parameter
                                     p_org_id    IN VARCHAR2); -- 1.2 Added p_org_id parameter
```

10. The program body will look like the following:

```
PROCEDURE  First_Concurrent_Program (errbuf      OUT VARCHAR2,
                                     retcode     OUT NUMBER,
                                     p_run_date IN  VARCHAR2, -- 1.1 Added p_run_date parameter
                                     p_org_id    IN  VARCHAR2) IS -- 1.3 Added p_org_id parameter
```

How it works...

We have now added the parameter `p_org_id` to the concurrent program definition and also amended the code to add the parameter to the package specification and body.

Run the concurrent program

Now we want to run the concurrent program testing that the concurrent program still runs successfully if the organization parameter is passed in.

How to do it...

To test the changes perform the following:

1. Log in to Oracle with the **XXEBS Extending e-Business Suite** responsibility.

2. Navigate to **Submit Requests** and submit a single request.

3. Select the **XXHR First Concurrent Program** concurrent program and leave the Run Date parameter to the default date (which is the current date).

4. Select an organization from the list of values for the Organization parameter and then click **OK**.

5. Click on the **Submit** button and when prompted to submit a new request, select **No** and the form will close down.

6. Navigate to **View Requests** and click on the **find** button (to find all requests).

7. You should see that the concurrent program we have just submitted has completed successfully. (If it is still **Pending** then click the refresh button until the status is **Completed**.)

If you now look at the following screenshot at the request once it has completed, the parameters field has an extra value which is the ID (your ID may well be different to the one in the screenshot dependent upon the organization you selected) of the parameter we have added:

You can see that the ID of the organization selected has been passed as a parameter.

How it works...

We have tested that the parameter we have added has been passed to the procedure. We don't at present do anything with it but we just want to ensure that the organization identifier is being passed.

Creating dependent parameters

In this next recipe, we are going to create a new parameter but this time we are going to make it dependent upon the parameter we created in the previous recipe.

We will be adding a parameter to the concurrent program we have already created. We will also be looking to change the package XXHREEBS so we will need to use SQL Developer to make these changes. The following tasks will be performed in this recipe:

  ▶ Create a dependent value set
  ▶ Create a new parameter for the concurrent program
  ▶ Modify the executable to accept the new parameter
  ▶ Run the concurrent program

Create a dependent value set

We are now going to create a dependent value set. It will select a list of employees who belong to the organization chosen in the Organization parameter.

How to do it...

Perform the following steps to create the value set:

1. Log in to Oracle with the **Application Developer** responsibility.
2. Navigate to **Application | Validation | Set** and the **Values Sets** window will open.
3. Enter the details as shown in the following table:

Item name	Value
Value Set Name	XXHR_PERSON_DEP_VS
Description	**List of HR person records dependent upon organization**
List Type	**List of Values**
Security Type	**No Security**
Format Type	Char
Maximum Size	**20**
Validation Type	**Table**

4. Click on the **Edit Information** button and the **Validation Table Information** window will open.

5. Enter the details as shown in the following table:

Item name	Value	Type	Size
Table Application	**Human Resources**		
Table Name	`per_people_f ppf, per_` `assignments_f paf`		
Value	`ppf.national_identifier`	`Char`	**20**
Meaning	`ppf.full_name||'- Employee Number` `: '||ppf.employee_number`	`Varchar2`	**240**
ID	`ppf.person_id`	`Number`	**10**

Where/Order By	`TRUNC(SYSDATE) BETWEEN ppf.` `effective_start_date and ppf.` `effective_end_date`
	
	 `AND TRUNC(SYSDATE) BETWEEN paf.` `effective_start_date AND paf.` `effective_end_date AND ppf.` `person_id = paf.person_id AND paf.` `primary_flag = 'Y'`
	
	 `and paf.assignment_type = 'E' AND` `paf.organization_id = :$FLEX$.` `XXHR_ORG_LIST_VS`		

We should just examine the syntax in the **Where/Order By** field. The clause joins the two tables we have defined in the table name field. The syntax I want to focus on is the following line:

```
AND paf.organization_id = :$FLEX$.XXHR_ORG_LIST_VS
```

The `$FLEX$` indicates that we want to base this upon another value set. It is followed by the name of the value set we want this to be dependent upon. A parameter that uses the value set must exist in another parameter defined in the concurrent program.

6. Click the **Save** button in the toolbar (or *Ctrl + S*) to save the record.
7. Click on the **Test** button to test the code entered.

How it works...

We have created a value set that is dependent upon another value set. We have already defined the `p_org_id` parameter that uses the `XXHR_ORG_LIST_VS` value set. When we run the concurrent program the parameter that uses this value set will appear disabled until a value has been entered in the dependent parameter.

Create a new parameter for the concurrent program

We are now going to add a new parameter called `person_id` and use the value set we have just created for the parameter.

How to do it...

Perform the following steps to add the new parameter:

1. Log in to Oracle with the **Application Developer** responsibility.
2. Navigate to **Concurrent | Program** and the **Concurrent Programs** window will open.
3. Press the *F11* key to enter a query.
4. Query back the **XXHR First Concurrent Program** concurrent program and click the **parameters** button.
5. Add a new parameter with the following details:

Item name	Value
Seq	30
Parameter	P_PERSON_ID
Description	Person ID
Enabled	☑
Value Set	XXHR_PERSON_DEP_VS
Default Type	
Required	☒
Display	☑
Display Size	20
Description Size	50
Concatenated Description Size	25
Prompt	Person

The parameter should now look like the following screenshot:

How it works...

We have configured the P_PERSON_ID parameter that is dependent upon the organization parameter. This can be achieved by referencing the Organization value set with the :$FLEX$.XXHR_ORG_LIST_VS syntax.

Modify the executable to accept the new parameter

We are now going to add the parameter to the executable, which is the package called XXHREEBS.First_Concurrent_Program. If you wish to view the code then it can be found in the files XXHREEBS_1_4.pks and XXHREEBS_1_4.pkb. You can compile the package provided or use the following instructions to add the parameter manually.

How to do it...

To add the new parameter to the code, perform the following steps:

1. Open SQL Developer and connect to the **apps** user.

2. Navigate to **Packages** and select the XXHREEBS package.

3. Now edit the package specification.

4. Scroll down the package specification until you reach the `First_Concurrent_Program` procedure definition.

5. Now add the parameter to the code AFTER the `p_org_id` parameter. The program definition will look like the following:

```
PROCEDURE   First_Concurrent_Program (errbuf      OUT VARCHAR2,
                                      retcode     OUT NUMBER,
                                      p_run_date  IN VARCHAR2,
                                      p_org_id    IN VARCHAR2,
                                      p_person_id IN NUMBER);
```

6. Compile the package specification.

7. Open the package body to add the `p_person_id` parameter to the body.

8. Scroll down to the `First_Concurrent_Program` procedure definition and add `p_person_id` to the list of parameters, as shown in the following code:

```
PROCEDURE   First_Concurrent_Program (errbuf      OUT VARCHAR2,
                                      retcode     OUT NUMBER,
                                      p_run_date  IN VARCHAR2,
                                      p_org_id    IN VARCHAR2,
                                      p_person_id IN NUMBER) IS
```

9. Compile the `First_Concurrent_Program` package body.

How it works...

We have added the new parameter to the package specification and body. When we run the concurrent program the `Person` parameter will be dependent upon the organization that is selected.

Run the concurrent program

Now we want to run the concurrent program testing that the concurrent program still runs successfully if the `person_id` parameter is passed in.

How to do it...

To run the concurrent program, perform the following:

1. Log in to Oracle with the **XXEBS Extending e-Business Suite** responsibility.

2. Navigate to **Submit Requests** and submit a single request.

3. Select the **XXHR First Concurrent Program** concurrent program and leave the `Run Date` parameter set to the default date (which is the current date).

> You will notice that the Person parameter is disabled. This is because it is dependent upon the Organization field and will remain disabled until an organization has been entered.

4. Select an organization from the list of values for the Organization parameter and then click **OK**. (If using a Vision instance select 'Vision Corporation', for example.)

5. Select an employee record from the list of values for the Person parameter and then click **OK**.

6. Click on the **Submit** button and when prompted to submit a new request select **No** and the form will close down.

7. Navigate to **View Requests** and click on the **find** button (to find all requests).

8. You should see that the concurrent program we just submitted has completed successfully. (If it is still **Pending** then click the refresh button until the status is **Completed**).

How it works...

We have now added the dependent parameter to the concurrent program. This allows us to control values that are entered by the users.

Adding messages to the concurrent program log file

In this recipe, we are going to write to the log file to show the values of parameters that are passed into the executable. This is useful as we need a way of debugging and logging activity when a program is being executed. We can also write other messages to the log file of the concurrent program to report activity when the executable runs.

The tasks we are going to perform in this recipe are as follows:

▸ Create a profile option to turn logging on or off

▸ Set the profile option value

▸ Add a procedure to write to the log file

▸ Writing to the log file

▸ Running the concurrent program

▸ Viewing the log file

Create a profile option to turn logging on or off

Firstly we are going to create a profile option. This profile option is a simple profile that can be set to 'Y' or 'N'. If it is set to 'Y' then we can use it to write to the log file and if it is set to 'N' then we can choose not to write to the log file.

How to do it...

To create a new profile, perform the following:

1. Log in to Oracle with the **Application Developer** responsibility.

2. Navigate to **Profile** and the **Profiles** window will open, as shown in the following screenshot:

3. Enter data as shown in the following table:

Item name	Item value
Name	`XXHR_WRITE_LOGFILE`
Application	**XXHR Custom Application**
User Profile Name	**XXHR Write to Concurrent Program Logfile**
Description	**XXHR Write to Concurrent Program Logfile**

SQL Validation	`SQL="SELECT MEANING \"Yes or No\",`
	`LOOKUP_CODE`
	`INTO :visible_option_value,`
	`          :profile_option_value`
	`FROM fnd_common_lookups`
	`WHERE lookup_type = 'YES_NO'"`
	`COLUMN="\"Yes or No\"(*)"`

4. Click the **Save** button in the toolbar (or *Ctrl* + S) to save the record.

How it works...

We have created a profile which will allow users to turn logging information on or off. Profile options can be a really useful way of setting values in our code without having to hard code.

There's more...

There are often a number of ways to implement extensions or ways of doing things. As an example we could have created an additional parameter that uses a Yes/No value set that allows the user to write to the log file at runtime by setting a parameter value. It really depends upon how you want the program to run.

Set the profile option value

We will now set the profile to 'Yes' so that we can add code to our program that writes information to a log file.

How to do it...

To set the profile option value, perform the following:

1. Log in to Oracle with the **System Administrator** responsibility.

2. Navigate to **Profile | System** and the **Find System Profile Values** window will open as shown in the following screenshot:

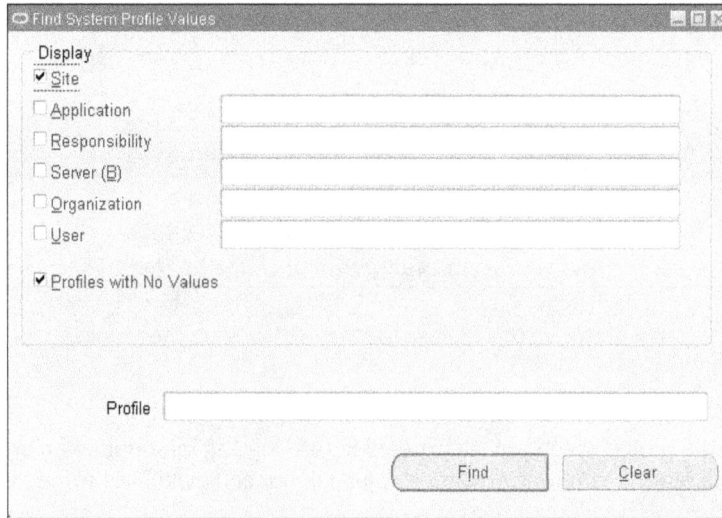

3. In the **Profile** field type **XXHR Write to Concurrent Program Logfile** and click the **Find** button.

> You could have also just typed **XXHR%** and clicked the **Find** button. Then you would retrieve all of the profile options beginning with XXHR. You can use the wildcard (%) to search for specific text such as **%HR%Write%Log%**, which will also be just as acceptable and will help if you cannot remember the full name of the profile you are looking for. Just remember it is also case sensitive.

4. Set the **Profile Option Name** at **Site** level to **Yes**, as shown in the following screenshot:

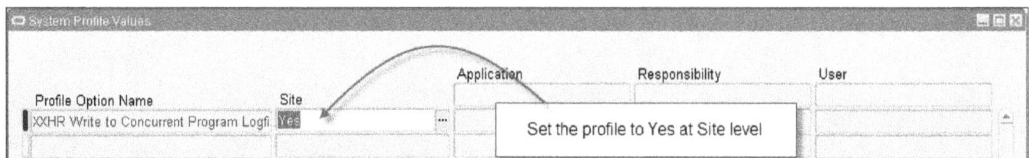

5. Click the **Save** button in the toolbar (or *Ctrl + S*) to save the record.

How it works...

We have now created a profile option that we can use to turn logging on or off after we have added code to our program to use the profile option value.

Add a procedure to write to the log file

We are now going to add the code to the executable, which is our package called XXHREEBS. If you wish to view the code then it can be found in the files XXHREEBS_1_5.pks and XXHREEBS_1_5.pkb. You can compile the package provided or use the following instructions to add the code manually.

How to do it...

To add a new procedure, perform the following steps:

1. Open SQL Developer and connect to the apps user.

2. Navigate to **Packages** and select the XXHREEBS package.

3. Now edit the package specification.

4. Declare a constant variable called cv_write_to_log and assign to it the value of the profile option XXHR_WRITE_LOGFILE, shown as follows:

```
30    SUCCESS                     NUMBER    := 0;
31    WARNING                     NUMBER    := 1;
32    FAILED                      NUMBER    := 2;
33
34    -- 1.4 - add constant to store the value of the XXHR Write to Concurrent Program Logfile profile option
      cv_write_to_log        CONSTANT  VARCHAR2(10) := fnd_profile.value('XXHR_WRITE_LOGFILE');
36
```

> Note that it is the **Profile Option Name** that we use and not the **User Profile Option Name** which is what we see when we set the profile option value.

5. Compile the package specification.

6. Edit the package body.

7. Add a procedure called `write_log`, shown as follows:

```
30    -- This variable is to be used in reporting the name of the package that executued code
31    v_package_name    CONSTANT VARCHAR2(30) := 'XXHREEBS';
32
33    /* 1.5 - the procedure below is a local procedure to write to the concurrent program log file.
34         If the profile option XXHR Write to Concurrent Program Logfile is set to 'Y' then
35         the message passed in is written to the log file. */
36
      PROCEDURE write_log (p_msg IN VARCHAR2) IS
      BEGIN
          -- Check the Debug profile option
          IF cv_write_to_log = 'Y' THEN
              fnd_file.put_line (fnd_file.log, p_msg);
          END IF;
      END;
```

8. Compile the package body.

How it works...

We have added a procedure to our program that will allow us to write messages to the concurrent program log file. This can be switched on or off by changing a profile option value.

Writing to the log file

Now we can add some messages to the `First_Concurrent_Program` procedure to write to the log file. We have already set the profile option to 'Yes' so every time we call the `write_log` procedure, the executable will write a message to the log file. So now we will add some messages to the log file. A good place to start would be to display the values that are being passed in as parameters.

How to do it...

To add messages to the log file perform the following steps:

1. Open SQL Developer and connect to the apps user.
2. Navigate to **Packages** and select the XXHREEBS package.
3. Now edit the package body.

4. Write to the log file with calls to `write_log` in our First_Concurrent Program procedure as follows:

```
55 ☐      PROCEDURE  First_Concurrent_Program (errbuf     OUT VARCHAR2,
56                                             retcode    OUT NUMBER,
57                                             p_run_date IN  VARCHAR2, -- 1.1 Added
58                                             p_org_id   IN  VARCHAR2, -- 1.3 Added
59                                             p_person_id IN NUMBER) IS -- 1.4 Added
60
61           v_procedure_name    VARCHAR2(30) := 'First_Concurrent_Program'; -- local
62           v_run_date          DATE := TO_DATE(p_run_date,'YYYY/MM/DD HH24:MI:SS');
63      BEGIN
64
 ○          -- 1.6 Add messages to the log file showing the parameters passed in
 ○          write_log(v_procedure_name||' Parameters are:');
 ○          write_log(' p_run_date -> '||p_run_date);
 ○          write_log(' p_org_id -> '||p_org_id);
 ○          write_log(' p_person_id -> '||p_person_id);
```

5. Compile the package body.

How it works...

We have added code to write messages to the log file. We have also written the values of the parameters that are passed in to the program to the log file, so that a developer will find it easy to debug the program if there are errors.

Run the concurrent program

Now we want to run the concurrent program testing that the code we have just added writes messages to the log file.

How to do it...

To run the concurrent program, do the following:

1. Log in to Oracle with the **XXEBS Extending e-Business Suite** responsibility.

2. Navigate to **Submit Requests** and submit a single request.

3. Select the **XXHR First Concurrent Program** concurrent program and leave the Run Date parameter to the default date (which is the current date).

4. Select **Vision Corporation** from the list of values for the Organization parameter and then click **OK**.

5. Select an employee record from the list of values for the Person parameter and then click **OK**.

6. Click on the **Submit** button and when prompted to submit a new request select **No** and the form will close down.

7. Navigate to **View Requests** and click on the **Find** button (to find all requests).

8. You should see that the concurrent program we just submitted has completed successfully. (If it is still **Pending** then click the refresh button until the status is **Completed**.)

How it works...

We have run the concurrent program again to test that the log messages are written to the log file.

Viewing the log file

Once the concurrent program has completed successfully we can view the log file. Let's now have a look at the log file and see the messages that have been written to it.

How to do it...

To view the messages written to the log file perform the following:

1. Click on the **View Log** button in the View Requests screen and a browser window will open.

2. You will see that the messages we put into the `First_Concurrent_Program` package have been written to the log file as highlighted in the following image:

```
+---------------------------------------------------------------------------+
Human Resources: Version : 12.0.0

Copyright (c) 1979, 1999, Oracle Corporation. All rights reserved.

XXHR_FIRST_CONC_PROG module: XXHR First Concurrent Program
+---------------------------------------------------------------------------+

Current system time is 28-JUL-2011 15:19:36


+---------------------------------------------------------------------------+

**Starts**28-JUL-2011 15:19:42
**Ends**28-JUL-2011 15:19:42
+---------------------------------------------------------------------------+
Start of log messages from FND_FILE
+---------------------------------------------------------------------------+
First_Concurrent_Program Parameters are:
 p_run_date -> 2011/07/28 00:00:00
 p_org_id -> 202
 p_person_id -> 2446
+---------------------------------------------------------------------------+
End of log messages from FND_FILE
+---------------------------------------------------------------------------+
```

How it works...

The messages have been written to the log file, providing valuable information about events that have occurred at runtime.

Reporting to the concurrent program output file

Now that we have written to the log file to view log information, we want to write more user-friendly information to the user. We will make this more formatted so that it provides useful information to the user about the processing that has taken place.

The tasks we are going to perform in this recipe are as follows:

- Add a procedure to write to the output file
- Add a cursor to get some data
- Add code to fetch data and write to the output file
- Run the concurrent program
- View the concurrent program output file

Add a procedure to write to the output file

We are now going to add the code to the executable, which is our package called XXHREEBS. If you wish to view or copy the code then it can be found in the file XXHREEBS_1_6.pkb. You can compile the package body provided or use the following instructions to add the code manually.

How to do it...

To add a procedure to write to the output file perform the following steps:

1. Open SQL Developer and connect to the apps user.
2. Navigate to **Packages** and select the XXHREEBS package.
3. Now edit the package body.
4. Add a new procedure called `write_output`, shown as follows:

```
41  PROCEDURE write_log (p_msg IN VARCHAR2) IS
42  BEGIN
43     -- Check the Debug profile option
44     IF cv_write_to_log = 'Y' THEN
45        fnd_file.put_line (fnd_file.log, p_msg);
46     END IF;
47  END;
48
    -- 1.6 - the procedure below is a local procedure to write to the concurrent
    PROCEDURE write_output (p_msg IN VARCHAR2) IS
    BEGIN
       fnd_file.put_line (fnd_file.output, p_msg);
    END;
54
```

5. Compile the package body.

How it works...

We have now added a procedure to write messages to the concurrent program output file.

Add a cursor to get some data

We are now going to add a cursor to our procedure to get some data back so that it can be displayed in the output file.

How to do it...

To write a cursor to retrieve some data perform the following steps:

1. Edit the procedure `First_Concurrent_Program` and add the cursor as shown in the following image:

```
65   PROCEDURE  First_Concurrent_Program (errbuf      OUT VARCHAR2,
66                                         retcode     OUT NUMBER,
67                                         p_run_date IN  VARCHAR2, -- 1.1 Added p_run_date parameter
68                                         p_org_id   IN  VARCHAR2, -- 1.3 Added p_org_id parameter
69                                         p_person_id IN NUMBER) IS -- 1.4 Added p_person_id parameter
70
71      v_procedure_name    CONSTANT VARCHAR2(30) := 'First_Concurrent_Program'; -- local variable conta
72      v_run_date          DATE := TO_DATE(p_run_date,'YYYY/MM/DD HH24:MI:SS');
73
        /* 1.8 - cursor to fetch some employee details
             - Note the person_id can be null so that if a person_id parameter is not passed all empl
             - organisation will be returned */
        CURSOR c_emp_dtls (c_org_id IN hr_all_organization_units.organization_id%TYPE,
                           c_person_id IN per_all_people_f.person_id%TYPE) IS
        SELECT ho.name, ppf.full_name
             , ppf.employee_number
             , PPF.NATIONAL_IDENTIFIER
             , PPF.email_address
             , NVL2(payroll_id, 'Yes', 'No') payroll -- is the employee on a payroll
             , NVL2(supervisor_id, 'Yes', 'No') supervisor -- does the employee have a supervisor
          FROM per_people_f ppf
             , per_assignments_f paf
             , hr_all_organization_units ho
         WHERE ppf.person_id = paf.person_id
           AND paf.primary_flag = 'Y'
           AND paf.assignment_type = 'E'
           AND paf.organization_id = ho.organization_id
           AND TRUNC(SYSDATE) BETWEEN ppf.effective_start_date AND ppf.effective_end_date
           AND TRUNC(SYSDATE) BETWEEN paf.effective_start_date AND paf.effective_end_date
           AND SYSDATE BETWEEN NVL(ho.date_from, SYSDATE) AND NVL(ho.date_to, SYSDATE)
           AND paf.organization_id = c_org_id
           AND ppf.person_id = NVL(c_person_id,ppf.person_id)
         ORDER BY ppf.full_name;
98
99   BEGIN
```

> Remember that the cursor is available in the download bundle in the `XXHREEBS_1_6.pkb` package.

How it works...

We have added a cursor that will return data at runtime. We want to format the data and display it in the output file.

Add code to fetch data and write to the output file

We are now going to add a cursor `for` loop to our procedure to get some data back, so that it can be written to the output file.

How to do it...

To add code to fetch data and write to the output file do the following:

1. Edit the `First_Concurrent_Program` procedure and add a cursor `for` loop to get the data. Make some calls to the `write_output` procedure to add the information to the output file as shown in the following image:

```
102    BEGIN
103
104        -- 1.6 Add messages to the log file showing the parameters passed in
105        write_log(v_procedure_name||' Parameters are:');
106        write_log(' p_run_date -> '||p_run_date);
107        write_log(' p_org_id -> '||p_org_id);
108        write_log(' p_person_id -> '||p_person_id);
109
           -- 1.9 Add a report header
           write_output('                              Report Output for Employee Details');
           write_output('                              ------------------------------------'||CHR(10));
           write_output(' Report Date: '||TO_CHAR(v_run_date, 'DD-MON-YYYY')||CHR(10));
114
           -- 1.10 Call the cursor and write details to the output file
           FOR r_emp_dtls IN c_emp_dtls (p_org_id, p_person_id) LOOP

               write_output(CHR(10));
               write_output('       Organisation : '||r_emp_dtls.name);
               write_output('          Full Name : '||r_emp_dtls.full_name);
               write_output('    Employee Number : '||r_emp_dtls.employee_number);
               write_output('National Identifier : '||r_emp_dtls.national_identifier);
               write_output('      Email Address : '||r_emp_dtls.email_address);
               write_output('         On Payroll : '||r_emp_dtls.payroll);
               write_output('         Supervisor : '||r_emp_dtls.supervisor);
               write_output(CHR(10));

           END LOOP;
```

2. Compile the package body.

How it works...

For the employee record that we have entered in the person parameter we will fetch the record from the database and write the details to the output file.

Running the concurrent program

Now we want to run the concurrent program testing that the code we have just added writes messages to the log file.

How to do it...

To run the concurrent program to view the output file, perform the following:

1. Log in to Oracle with the **XXEBS Extending e-Business Suite** responsibility.

2. Navigate to **Submit Requests** and submit a single request.

3. Select the **XXHR First Concurrent Program** concurrent program and leave the `Run Date` parameter set to the default date (which is the current date).

4. Select **Vision Corporation** from the list of values for the `Organization` parameter and then click **OK**.

5. Select an employee record from the list of values for the `Person` parameter and then click **OK**.

6. Click on the **Submit** button and when prompted to submit a new request select **No** and the form will close down.

7. Navigate to **View Requests** and click on the **Find** button (to find all requests).

8. You should see that the concurrent program we just submitted has completed successfully. (If it is still **Pending** then click the refresh button until the status is **Completed**.)

How it works...

We have run the concurrent program to test the code that we added to write to the output file. We can now view the output to ensure that the layout is as expected.

View the concurrent program output file

Now we want to view the output file to see the messages we have written to it.

How to do it...

To open the output file to test our changes do the following:

1. Click on the **View Output** button and a browser window will open.

2. You will see that the messages we put into the `First_Concurrent_Program` package have been written to the output file as shown in the following image:

```
                              Report Output for Employee Details
                              ----------------------------------

    Report Date: 29-JUL-2011



            Organsization : Vision Corporation
                Full Name : Wollard, Ms. Sally
          Employee Number : 248
      National Identifier : 121-09-2039
            Email Address : nobody@localhost
               On Payroll : Yes
               Supervisor : Yes
```

How it works...

As you can see we have generated formatted data that we have written to the output file.

Scheduling a concurrent program

There are two ways in which a concurrent program can be executed; it can be launched manually by a user or it can be scheduled to run automatically either on a one off basis or on a regular basis. In the next recipe, we are going to schedule the concurrent program we have created. It is important to note that when we schedule a concurrent program there is no user there to select the values for the parameters that are defined. Therefore, any required parameters we have added must have a default value. This can be done when entering the concurrent program but we are going to default a value for the organization.

We are going to complete the following tasks in this recipe:

▸ Add default values for any required parameters

▸ Schedule the concurrent program

Add default values for any required parameters

We are now going to add default values for the parameters in our concurrent program that are required.

Getting ready

In our concurrent program **XXHR First Concurrent Program** we have three parameters:

- ▸ P_RUN_DATE
- ▸ P_ORG_ID
- ▸ P_PERSON_ID

The first parameter P_RUN_DATE is not required and is already defaulted to the current date. The second parameter P_ORG_ID is required and so we are going to default this to **Vision Corporation**.

How to do it...

To add default values to our concurrent program parameters complete the following steps:

1. Log in to Oracle with the **Application Developer** responsibility.
2. Navigate to **Concurrent | Program** and the **Concurrent Programs** window will open.
3. Press the *F11* key to enter a query.
4. Query back the **XXHR First Concurrent Program concurrent program** and click the **parameters** button.
5. Click on the P_ORG_ID parameter and enter the following details to set the default parameter:

Item name	Item value
Default Type	SQL Statement
Default Value	SELECT organization_id FROM hr_all_organization_units WHERE name = 'Vision Corporation'

6. Click the **Save** button in the toolbar (or *Ctrl + S*) to save the record.

How it works...

We have set a default value for the Organization parameter in the concurrent program so that it can be scheduled.

Schedule the concurrent program

Now we are going to schedule the concurrent program to run on a daily basis for two days.

How to do it...

To schedule the concurrent program do the following:

1. Log in to Oracle with the **XXEBS Extending e-Business Suite** responsibility.

2. Navigate to **Submit Requests** and submit a single request.

3. Select the **XXHR First Concurrent Program** concurrent program and leave the Run Date and Organization parameters set to their default values and click on **OK**:

4. Now click on the **Schedule** button. The screen dynamically changes when you click on each item of the **Run the Job** radio group.

5. Click **Periodically**.

6. Set **Re-Run** to every **1 Day(s)**.

7. Enter an **End At** value 2 days from the current date.

8. Check the **Increment date parameters each run**.

The steps are shown in the following screenshot:

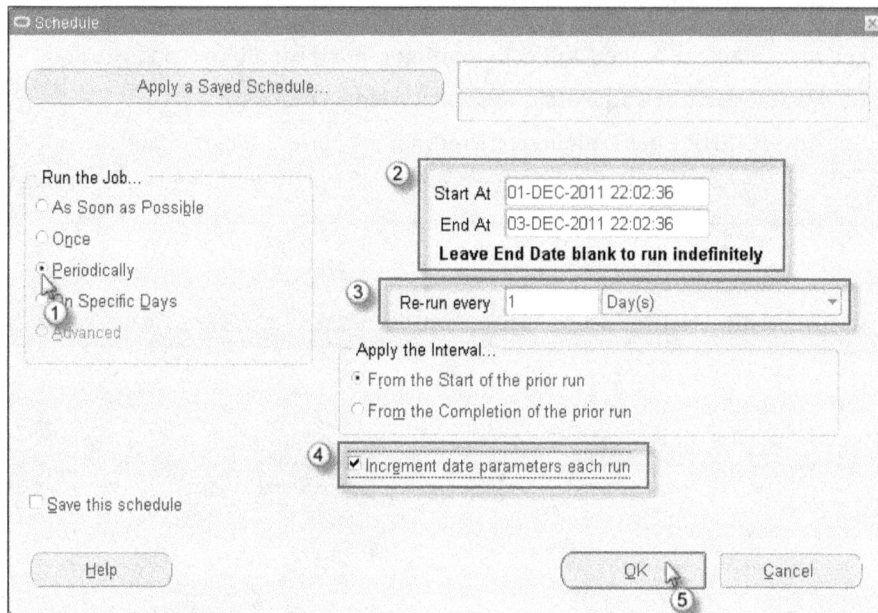

1. Click on **OK** and the window will close.

2. Click on the **Submit** button and when prompted to submit a new request select **No** and the form will close down.

3. Navigate to **View Requests** and click on the **Find** button (to find all requests).

4. You should see that the concurrent program we just submitted has submitted two requests. The first will be set to run immediately and the second concurrent program is **Pending** with a status of **Scheduled**, as shown in the following screenshot:

> You will notice that the date in the **Parameters** field has automatically been incremented because we checked the **Increment date parameters each run** checkbox.

How it works...

We have now scheduled our concurrent program for two days and the program will run automatically unless it is cancelled before the last run has completed.

Creating multiple concurrent programs

It is quite common to have a requirement where we need to configure a concurrent program that is similar to an existing concurrent program. To prevent us having to configure the concurrent program from the beginning, Oracle has created a button that allows us to copy an existing concurrent program. In the next recipe, we are going to create a new concurrent program that is based upon the program we have already created.

The tasks we need to perform to achieve this are the following:

- ▸ Copy an existing concurrent program
- ▸ Add a concurrent program to a request set

Copy an existing concurrent program

We are going to copy the existing concurrent program and use the same parameters. We are also going to change the default parameter for the `Organization` parameter so that it defaults to 'Vision Operations'.

How to do it...

To copy an existing concurrent program definition, do the following:

1. Log in to Oracle with the **Application Developer** responsibility.
2. Navigate to **Concurrent | Program** and the **Concurrent Programs** window will open.
3. Press the *F11* key to enter a query.
4. Type in **XXHR First**% into the **Program** field and press the *Ctrl + F11* keys to execute the query.
5. The concurrent program we created in an earlier recipe will be returned.

6. Now click on the **Copy to** button and the **Copy to** window will open, as shown in the following screenshot:

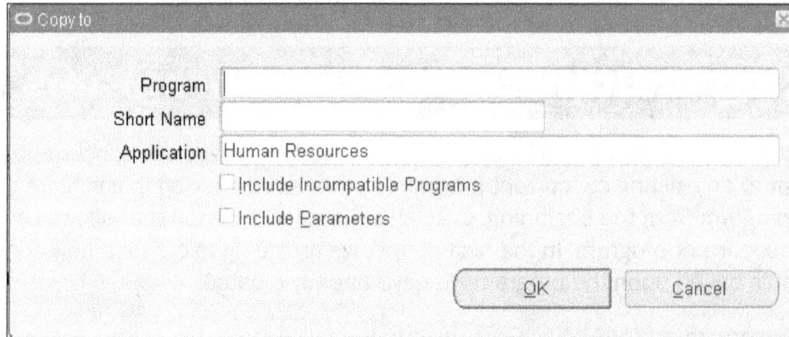

7. Enter the data as shown in the following table:

Item Name	Item Value
Program	**XXHR Second Concurrent Program**
Short Name	XXHR_SECOND_CONC_PROG
Application	**XXHR Custom Application**
Include Incompatible Programs	☒
Include Parameters	☑

8. Click the **OK** button and the window will close and you will be returned to the **Concurrent Programs** window. You will notice that the concurrent program is now the new one we have just copied to, **XXHR Second Concurrent Program**.

9. Now click on the **Parameters** button and the **Concurrent Program Parameters** window will open.

10. Navigate to the parameter P_ORG_ID.

11. Change the select statement in the 'Default Value' field to the following:

```
SELECT organization_id
FROM hr_all_organization_units
WHERE UPPER(NAME) = 'VISION OPERATIONS'
```

> This query assumes that you are using a Vision instance. Modify the organization name in the query if you are using a different development environment.

12. Click the **Save** button to commit the changes.

How it works...

We have now made a copy of an existing concurrent program. We can then amend the details as required to suite our requirements.

Add a concurrent program to a request set

We are now going to add our concurrent program to our request set, so that it will be available from our responsibility when we run a new request.

How to do it...

To add the second concurrent program to our request group, perform the following:

1. Log in to Oracle with the **System Administrator** responsibility.
2. Navigate to **Security | Responsibility | Request** and the **Request Groups** window will open.
3. Query back the **XXHR Request Group** request group.
4. Now we are going to add the second concurrent program we created in the **Requests** region. Enter data as in the following table for the detail records:

Type	Name	Application
Program	XXHR Second Concurrent Program	XXHR Custom Application

5. Click the **Save** button in the toolbar (or *Ctrl + S*) to save the record.
6. Exit the form.

How it works...

We have now added our second concurrent program to our request set assigned to the **XXEBS Extending e-Business Suite** responsibility.

Creating request sets

In this next recipe we are going to link the concurrent programs and run them together as a request set.

We are going to complete the following tasks in this recipe:

▸ Run request set wizard
▸ Add a request set to a request group
▸ Run the request set

Run request set wizard

To create a request set we are going to run a wizard. The request set allows us to link concurrent programs together. Concurrent programs can be run sequentially or in parallel as a group. They can also be dependent upon the outcome of another program within the request set.

How to do it...

To create a request set using the wizard complete the following tasks:

1. Log in to Oracle with the **System Administrator** responsibility.

2. Navigate to **Requests | Set** and the **Request Set** window will open, as shown in the following screenshot:

3. Click the **Request Set Wizard** button.

4. Select the radio button called **Sequentially (One After Another)** and then click **Next**, as shown in the following screenshot:

5. Click on radio button called **Continue Processing**. This is what we want the request set to do if any of the programs end with a status of **Error**:

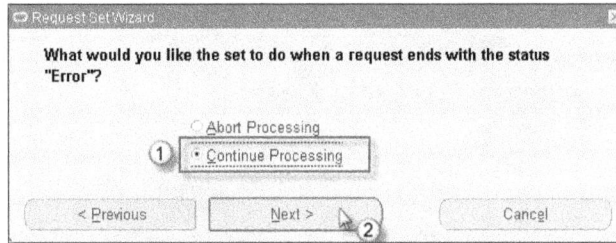

6. We now need to enter the details of our request set in the wizard as shown in the following table and click **Next**:

Item Name	Item Value
Set	XXHR20001
Application	XXHR Custom Application
Description	XXHR Employee By Organization

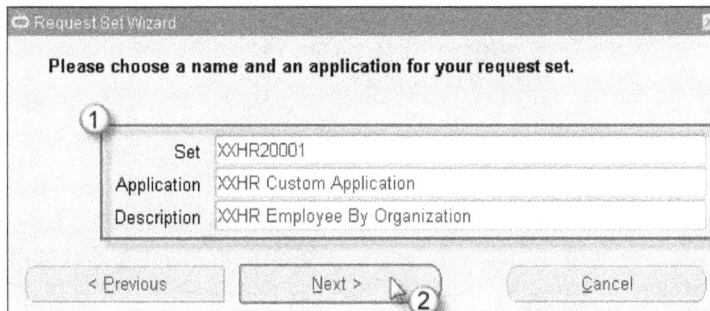

7. We now want to print the output files as each request finishes, so select **As Each Request in the Set Completes** and click **Next** as follows:

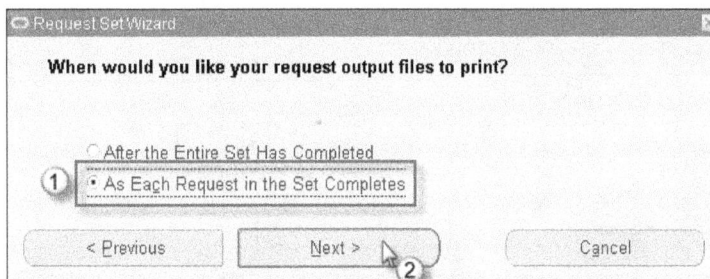

8. Now add the concurrent programs that we want to run in the request set so add the two programs we have created, **XXHR First Concurrent Program** and **XXHR Second Concurrent Program**, and click **Finish** as shown in the following screenshot:

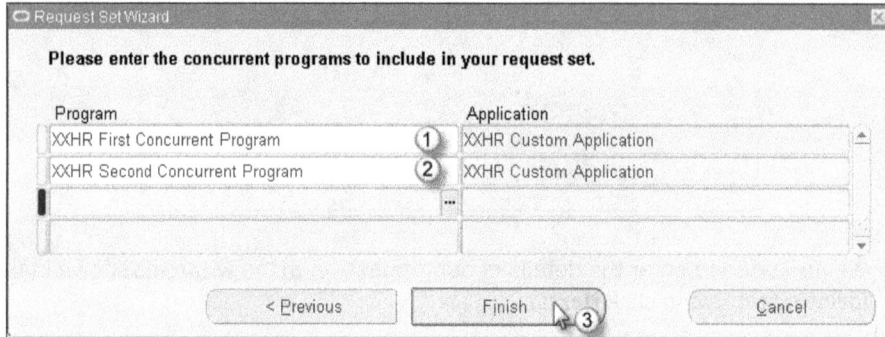

9. The following message will appear; click **OK**:

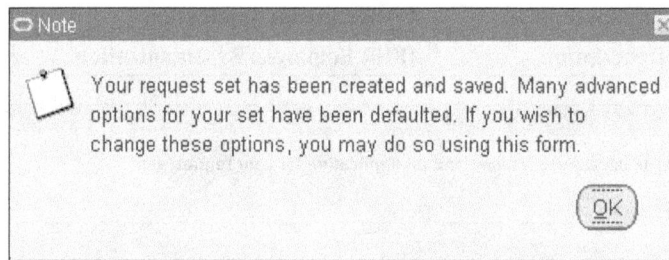

10. The request set is then automatically created and the completed set will appear something similar to the following screenshot. We are going to first look at the **Define Stages** screen and the **Link Stages** screen to check the configuration:

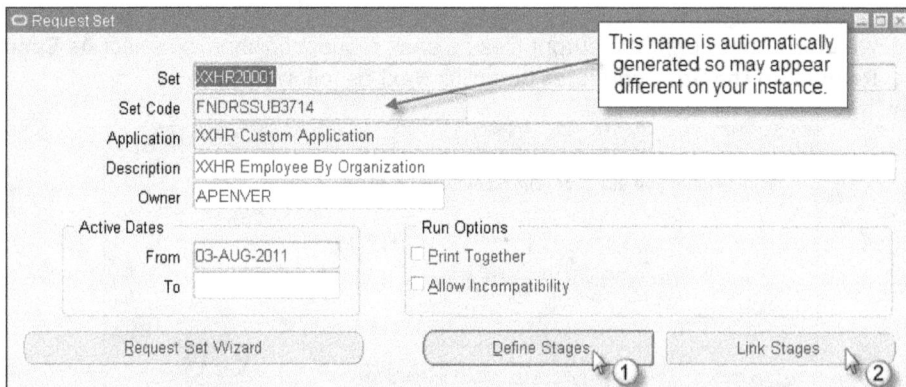

11. Click on the **Define Stages** button to check that the concurrent programs are configured as required:

12. Check that the screen is configured as we expected and then close the **Stages** window to navigate back to the **Request Set** window.

13. Click on the **Link Stages** button and the **Link Stages** window will open as shown in the following screenshot:

How it works...

We have now created a request set using the request set wizard. We can now run the request set, and the concurrent programs will run as we have defined them in the request set.

Add a request set to a request group

We will now add our request set to the request group we have associated with the **XXEBS Extending e-Business Suite** responsibility.

How to do it...

To add the request set perform the following steps:

1. Log in to Oracle with the **System Administrator** responsibility.
2. Navigate to **Security | Responsibility | Request** and the **Request Groups** window will open.
3. Query back the **XXHR Request Group** request group.
4. Now we are going to add the request set we created in the **Requests** region. Enter data as in the following table in the **Requests** block:

Type	Name	Application
Set	XXHR20001	XXHR Custom Application

5. Click the **Save** button in the toolbar (or *Ctrl* + S) to save the record.
6. Exit the form.

How it works...

Okay so now we have added the request set to our request group. Next we are going to run the request set.

Run the request set

Now we want to run the concurrent request set.

How to do it...

To run the request set take the following steps:

1. Log in to Oracle with the **XXEBS Extending e-Business Suite** responsibility.

2. Navigate to **Submit Requests** and click the **OK** button as shown in the following screenshot:

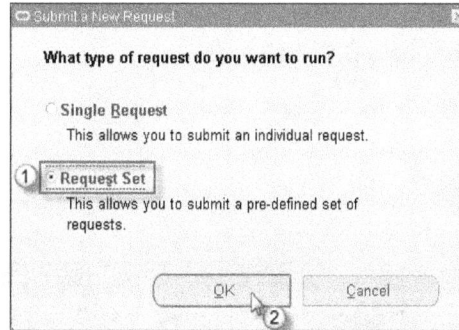

3. Navigate to the **Request Set** field and select the **XXHR20001** request set from the list of values and click **OK**.

4. Click on the **Submit** button and when prompted to submit a new request select **No** and the form will close down.

5. Navigate to **View Requests** and click on the **Find** button (to find all requests) and you will see the request set as shown in the following screenshot:

6. You should see that the request set we just submitted is running.

If you click the refresh button you will see the stages of the request set complete as they are executed. Once the request set has completed you will see three records in the **Requests** block. One for the set and one each for the concurrent programs in the request set as shown in the following screenshot:

[
Note: Remember to click the refresh button as the page does
not refresh automatically, so if you see a program still has a
phase of **Running** you will need to click the refresh button
until the phase is **Completed**.
]

How it works...

We have now run the request set and can see that we can group concurrent programs to be run together.

Installing the database objects

We are going to create the database objects for the next examples, by using a script provided called `4842_01_01.sh` In the next examples we will be configuring a concurrent program that calls a host program. The script we are going to run will create a sequence, synonym, and package for our host program call. We will also create a package that will handle all of the database transactions such as insert, update, and delete. Finally, we will create a sequence that will be used to generate a unique number for new filenames. The following provides details of how to run the script.

How to do it...

To create the database objects required for this chapter perform the following tasks:

1. Create a local directory `c:\packt\scripts\ch1` where the scripts are downloaded and extracted to.

2. Open **Putty** and connect to the application tier user.

3. Create a new directory on the application tier under `$XXHR_TOP/install` as follows:

   cd $XXHR_TOP/install

   mkdir ch1

4. Navigate to the new directory `ch1` as follows:

   cd ch1

5. Open WinSCP and transfer the files from `c:\packt\scripts\ch1` on your local machine to the `$XXHR_TOP/install/ch1` directory on the application server, as shown in the following screenshot:

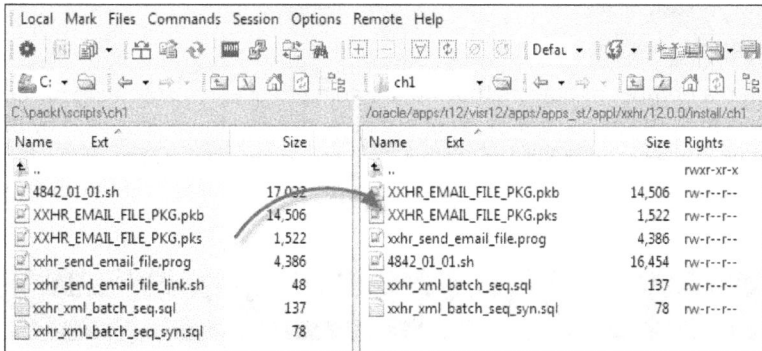

6. In **Putty**, change the permissions of the script with the following command:

   ```
   chmod 775 4842_01_01.sh
   ```

7. Run the following script to create all of the objects by issuing the following command:

   ```
   ./4842_01_01.sh apps/apps
   ```

8. The script checks that all of the files are present in your $XXHR_TOP/install/ch1 directory and will prompt you to continue if they are all there, so type Y and press return.

9. After the script has completed, check the XXHR_4842_01_01.log file for errors. (It will be created in the same directory $XXHR_TOP/install/ch1.)

10. Run the following query to check that all of the objects have been created successfully:

    ```
    SELECT OWNER, OBJECT_NAME, OBJECT_TYPE, STATUS
      FROM ALL_OBJECTS
     WHERE OBJECT_NAME LIKE 'XXHR_EMAIL%'
        OR OBJECT_NAME LIKE 'XXHR%BATCH%'
    ORDER BY 1, 2
    ```

11. This is shown in the following screenshot:

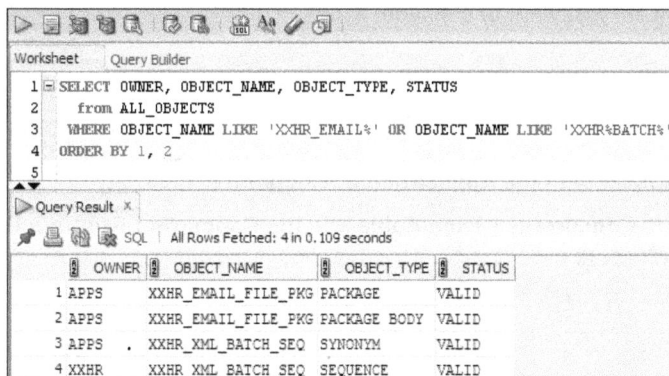

How it works...

We have created a number of objects that we are going to use in the coming recipes. We have created a synonym to the apps user as all of our objects need to be accessed by this user. The sequence we have created will generate a unique number each time a new file is created. Finally, the package we have created contains all of the procedures and functions relating to database activity for calling our host program.

Creating a HOST concurrent program

In this recipe, we are going to create two concurrent programs. The first concurrent program will call the second concurrent program through PL/SQL. The first concurrent program will also generate a file and place it in a directory on the database server. The second concurrent program will call a host program that will get the file we just created and will e-mail it to an e-mail account. To complete the recipe we will perform the following tasks:

- ▸ Creating a PL/SQL executable
- ▸ Configuring a concurrent program to call the PL/SQL executable
- ▸ Creating a HOST executable
- ▸ Configuring a concurrent program to call the HOST executable
- ▸ Adding concurrent programs to a menu
- ▸ Creating an OUT directory
- ▸ Creating a symbolic link
- ▸ Testing a host concurrent program

Creating a PL/SQL executable

The first thing we will do is create an executable that calls a PL/SQL package called `xxhr_email_file_pkg.process_main`. We will look into what the package does later on, so for now we just want to configure it.

How to do it...

To create the executable to call a database package perform the following steps:

1. Log in to Oracle with the **Application Developer** responsibility.
2. Navigate to **Concurrent | Executable** and the **Concurrent Program Executable** window will open.

3. Enter data as shown in the following table:

Item Name	Item Value
Executable	**XXHR Generate File**
Short Name	XXHR_GENERATE_FILE
Application	**XXHR Custom Application**
Description	**Generates a file that is emailed**
Execution Method	**PL/SQL Stored Procedure**
Execution File Name	XXHR_EMAIL_FILE_PKG.process_main

> Note: Any fields that are not specified in this table should be left as their default value.

4. The form should now look like the following screenshot:

5. Click the **Save** button in the toolbar (or *Ctrl* + *S*) to save the record.
6. Exit the form.

How it works...

We have now created a concurrent program executable that will launch a PL/SQL package called xxhr_email_file_pkg.process_main.

Configuring a concurrent program to call the PL/SQL executable

In the following recipe, we will configure our concurrent program that calls the executable we have just defined.

How to do it...

To configure the concurrent program, perform the following:

1. Log in to Oracle and select the **Application Developer** responsibility.

2. Navigate to **Concurrent | Program** and the **Concurrent Programs** window will open, as shown in the following screenshot.

3. Enter data as shown in the following table:

Item name	Item value
Program	**XXHR Generate File and Email**
Short Name	XXHR_GEN_AND_EMAIL
Application	**XXHR Custom Application**
Description	**Generate XML file and email it**
Executable Name	XXHR_GENERATE_FILE

[Note: Any fields that are not defined in this table should be left as their default value.]

4. The form should now look like the following:

5. Click the **Save** button in the toolbar (or *Ctrl + S*) to save the record.

6. Click on the **Parameters** button to open the **Parameters** window.

7. Enter a first parameter with the following details:

Item name	Value
Seq	10
Parameter	P_SUBJECT
Description	Subject
Enabled	☑
Value Set	240 Characters
Required	☑
Display	☑
Display Size	30
Description Size	50
Concatenated Description Size	25
Prompt	Subject

8. The **Parameter** screen should now look like the following screenshot:

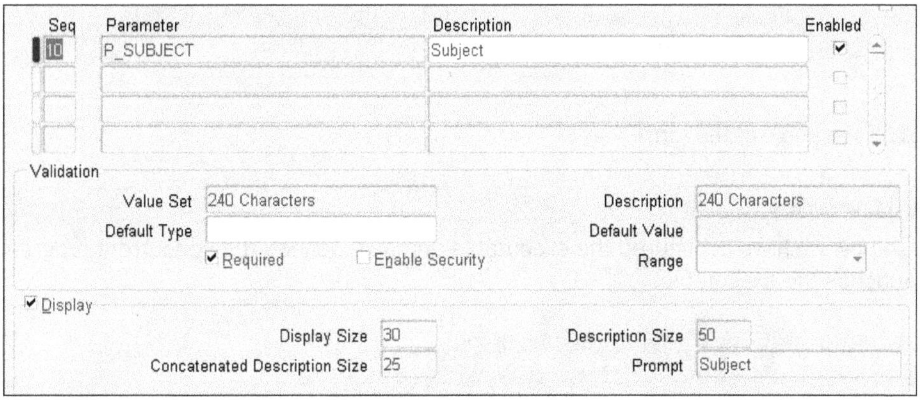

9. Enter a second parameter with the following details:

Item name	Value
Seq	20
Parameter	P_EMAIL_TO
Description	Email Address
Enabled	☑
Value Set	100 Characters

Item name	Value
Required	☑
Display	☑
Display Size	30
Description Size	50
Concatenated Description Size	25
Prompt	Email Address To

10. The screen should now look like the following screenshot:

11. Save and exit the form.

How it works...

Okay, so now we have configured the executable and also defined the concurrent program that launches the executable.

Creating a HOST executable

Now we will create an executable that calls a HOST file called `xxhr_send_email_file`. The name is case sensitive so ensure it is in lower case. Also the host file does not have any extension.

How to do it...

To create the executable to call a HOST file, perform the following:

1. Log in to Oracle with the **Application Developer** responsibility.

2. Navigate to **Concurrent | Executable** and the **Concurrent Program Executable** window will open.

3. Enter data as shown in the following table:

Item name	Item value
Executable	**XXHR Email File From Unix**
Short Name	XXHR_EMAIL_FILE_FROM_UNIX
Application	**XXHR Custom Application**
Description	**XXHR Email File From Unix**
Execution Method	**Host**
Execution File Name	xxhr_send_email_file

Note: Any fields that are not specified in this table should be left as their default value.

4. The form should now look like the following screenshot:

5. Click the **Save** button in the toolbar (or *Ctrl* + *S*) to save the record.
6. Exit the form.

How it works...

We have now created a concurrent program executable that will launch a HOST file called xxhr_send_email_file.

Configuring a concurrent program to call the HOST executable

In the following recipe, we will configure our concurrent program that calls the executable we have just defined.

How to do it...

To configure the concurrent program, perform the following:

1. Log in to Oracle and select the **Application Developer** responsibility.
2. Navigate to **Concurrent | Program** and the **Concurrent Programs** window will open as shown in the following screenshot.
3. Enter data as shown in the following table:

Item name	Item value
Program	**XXHR Email File**
Short Name	XXHR_GEN_EMAIL_FILE
Application	**XXHR Custom Application**
Description	**XXHR Email File**
Executable Name	XXHR_EMAIL_FILE_FROM_UNIX

> Note: Any fields that are not defined in this table should be left as their default value.

4. The form should now look like the following screenshot:

5. Click the **Save** button in the toolbar (or *Ctrl + S*) to save the record.
6. Click on the **Parameters** button to open the **Parameters** window.

7. Enter a first parameter with the following details:

Item name	Value
Seq	10
Parameter	Subject
Description	Subject
Enabled	☑
Value Set	240 Characters
Default Type	Constant
Default Value	Email Generated from EBS
Required	☑
Display	☑
Display Size	30
Description Size	50
Concatenated Description Size	25
Prompt	Subject

8. Enter a second parameter with the following details:

Item name	Value
Seq	20
Parameter	Email Address
Description	Email Address
Enabled	☑
Value Set	100 Characters
Required	☑
Display	☑
Display Size	30
Description Size	50
Concatenated Description Size	25
Prompt	Email Address

9. Enter a third parameter with the following details:

Item name	Value
Seq	30
Parameter	Filename
Description	Filename
Enabled	☑
Value Set	240 Characters
Required	☑
Display	☑
Display Size	30
Description Size	50
Concatenated Description Size	25
Prompt	Filename

10. Enter a fourth parameter with the following details:

Item name	Value
Seq	40
Parameter	Directory
Description	Directory
Enabled	☑
Value Set	240 Characters
Required	☑
Display	☑
Display Size	30
Description Size	50
Concatenated Description Size	25
Prompt	Directory

11. Enter a fifth parameter with the following details:

Item name	Value
Seq	50
Parameter	Sent From
Description	Sent From
Enabled	☑

Item name	Value
Value Set	240 Characters
Required	☑
Display	☑
Display Size	30
Description Size	50
Concatenated Description Size	25
Prompt	Sent From

12. The parameter screen should now look like the following. Note: you need to scroll down to see the fifth parameter.

Seq	Parameter	Description	Enabled
10	Subject	Subject	✔
20	Email Address	Email Address	✔
30	Filename	Filename	✔
40	Directory	Directory	✔

Validation

Value Set 240 Characters	Description 240 Characters
Default Type Constant	Default Value Email Generated from EBS
✔ Required ☐ Enable Security	Range

✔ Display

Display Size 30	Description Size 50
Concatenated Description Size 25	Prompt Subject

13. Save and exit the form.

How it works...

Okay, so now we have configured the executable and also defined the concurrent program that launches the executable. The concurrent program has five parameters which will be passed into the host file.

Adding concurrent programs to a request group

When we defined our responsibility called **XXEBS Extending e-Business Suite** we assigned a request group to it called **XXHR Request Group**. We are going to add our concurrent programs, so that they will be available from the responsibility.

How to do it...

To update our request group perform the following steps:

1. Log in to Oracle with the **System Administrator** responsibility.
2. Navigate to **Security | Responsibility | Request** and the **Request Groups** window will open.
3. Query back the **XXHR Request Group** we created earlier in the chapter.
4. Now we are going to add the concurrent programs we created. Add the two concurrent programs as per the following table:

Type	Name	Application
Program	XXHR Generate File and Email	XXHR Custom Application
Program	XXHR Email File	XXHR Custom Application

5. Click the **Save** button in the toolbar (or *Ctrl + S*) to save the record.
6. Exit the form.

How it works...

We have now added the concurrent programs to the request group used by the **XXEBS Extending e-Business Suite** responsibility. Our concurrent programs will appear in a list of concurrent programs when we want to run a request. The responsibility only has access to the programs in the request set assigned to it.

Creating an OUT directory

Our PL/SQL package uses a PL/SQL utility called UTL_FILE. We are going to write a file to the database server using this utility but we first need to see which directories we have access to. We will then create a name for a directory that we can use as a name for that directory.

How to do it...

To create a named directory, perform the following:

1. Open SQL Developer and connect as the apps user.
2. Run the following query to see what directories the file utility has access to:

   ```
   SELECT * FROM dba_directories order by directory_name
   ```

3. We can see that there is a directory called `/usr/tmp`, which is the one we will use to write our file to.

4. We want to create our own name for it, however; to do this run the following command:

```
CREATE OR REPLACE DIRECTORY XXHR_XML_OUT AS '/usr/tmp'
/
```

5. If you run the query again you should see that our entry now exists in the table `dba_directories`, as shown in the following screenshot:

How it works...

We have created a name for a directory path that we will use to write a file to in our PL/SQL package later on. The name XXHR_XML_OUT is used instead of having to code the file path in our code, and if we need to change the directory we will not have to change our PL/SQL package.

Creating a symbolic link

We are now going to transfer our file over to the application tier in the $APPLBIN directory under the PRODUCT TOP directory. We will then make a symbolic link using the execution filename (without an extension) to fndcpesr, which is located in the $FND_TOP/$APPLBIN directory.

How to do it...

To install our host file, perform the following:

1. Open WinSCP and transfer the xxhr_send_email_file.prog to the $XXHR_TOP/$APPLBIN directory on the application tier as shown in the following screenshot:

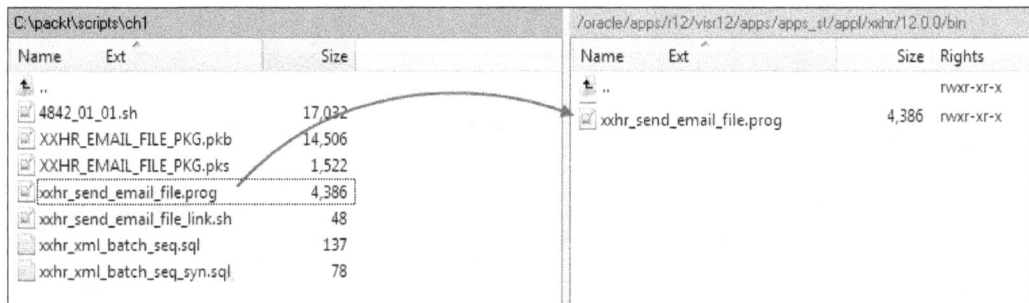

2. Open **Putty** and connect to the application tier with the OS user that owns the application tier. (Ensure that the environment is set—refer to *Chapter 6* about setting the environment.)

3. Navigate to the $XXHR_TOP/$APPLBIN directory by typing the following command:

   ```
   APPS Tier> cd $XXHR_TOP/$APPLBIN
   ```

4. Change the permissions of the xxhr_send_email_prog file with the following command:

   ```
   APPS Tier> chmod 775 xxhr_send_email_prog
   ```

5. Create a symbolic link for the file with the following command:

   ```
   APPS Tier> ln -s $FND_TOP/bin/fndcpesr xxhr_send_email_file
   ```

6. Check that the symbolic link has been created with the following command:

    ```
    APPS Tier> ls -al
    ```

7. You can see that the symbolic link has been created as shown in the following screenshot:

How it works...

We have copied our host program over to the bin directory of the application we registered the executable with. We have given correct permissions to the `.prog` file and then created a symbolic link for the file.

Testing a host concurrent program

We are now going to test the concurrent program but before we do we will take a look at some of the code in the package and the host program we have configured, to see what is happening.

Getting started...

The concurrent program **XXHR Generate File and Email** will execute the PL/SQL package called `XXHR_EMAIL_FILE_PKG.process_main`. This package calls three procedures in the following order:

*   `generate_xml`: This procedure is called first and creates an XML message and stores the message in a `CLOB` variable.

*   `create_xml_file`: This procedure is called next and takes the data in the `CLOB` and creates a file on the server for the named directory we created earlier called `XXHR_XML_OUT`.

*   `email_xml_file`: This procedure is called last and submits a concurrent program through a PL/SQL command. The concurrent program that it runs is the **XXHR Email File** we created to call our host program. The host program gets the file from the server and e-mails it using the UNIX `uuencode` command.

The host concurrent program called **XXHR Email File** launches the host file we created on the application tier. The first four parameters in the host file are reserved for oracle. Therefore, the first parameter that we pass from our concurrent program is actually the fifth parameter in the host file. The host file validates the parameters that we pass in and then sends an e-mail using the UNIX uuencode utility. Now we want to run the concurrent program testing that the file is generated on the server and then e-mailed by calling the second concurrent program.

> Note: The concurrent program that uses the UTL_FILE utility will write to a directory on the database server. However, the host program accesses the application tier. Therefore, we must write the file to a directory that is shared by the application tier and the database tier.

How to do it...

To run the concurrent program, do the following:

1. Log in to Oracle with the **XXEBS Extending e-Business Suite** responsibility.
2. Navigate to **Submit Requests** and submit a single request.
3. Select the **XXHR Generate File and Email** concurrent program.
4. Fill in the parameters as shown in the following table:

Subject	Email sent from EBS
Email Address To	<enter your email address here>

> Note: you will need to enter your own e-mail address in the Email Address To parameter.

5. Click **OK** to submit the request as shown in the following screenshot:

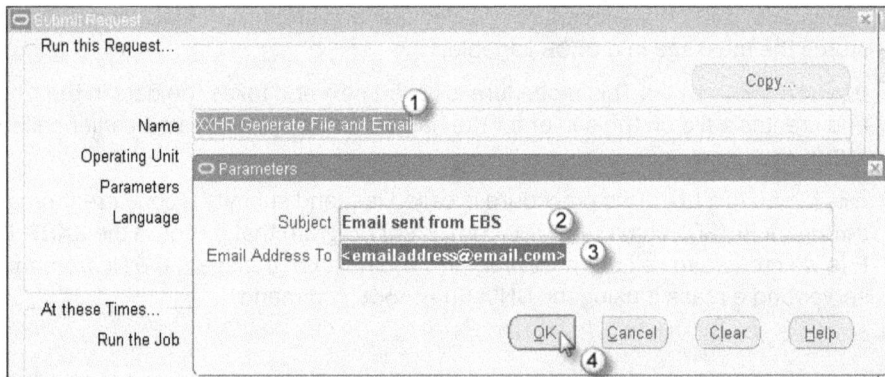

6. Click on the **Submit** button and when prompted to submit a new request select **No** and the form will close down.

7. Navigate to **View Requests** and click on the **Find** button (to find all requests).

8. We can see in the following screenshot that there are two concurrent requests. The first is the one that we launched. The second is the program that is launched from our database package through PL/SQL:

9. You should see that the concurrent program we just submitted has completed successfully. (If it is still **Pending** then click the refresh button until the status is **Completed**.)

We can see from the following screenshot that the e-mail has been received at the e-mail address passed as a parameter when we launched the concurrent program:

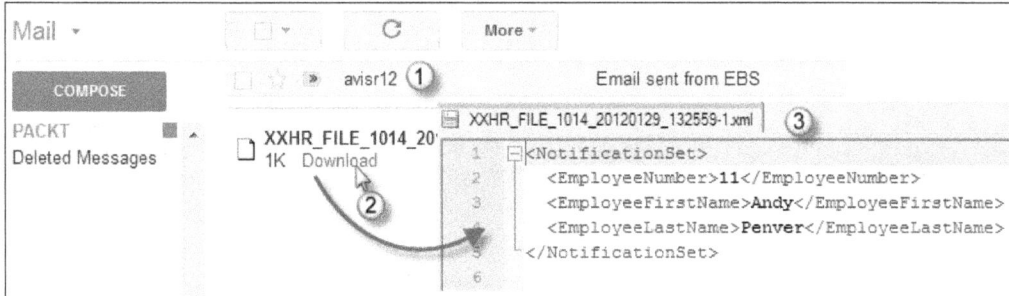

How it works...

We have run the concurrent program **XXHR Generate File and Email**, which in turn launched the **XXHR Email File** concurrent program. Both concurrent programs appear in the **Requests** screen. The file was generated on the database server and the host program picked up the file and e-mailed it to the e-mail address passed in as a parameter.

2
Oracle Forms

In this chapter, we will cover:

- ▸ Using forms builder for E-Business Suite
- ▸ Installing the database objects
- ▸ Getting started with forms
- ▸ Creating a master block and container objects
- ▸ Modifying the template code
- ▸ Adding a detail block to a form
- ▸ Adding insert, update, and delete events
- ▸ Deploying forms
- ▸ Adding buttons, list, and checkbox items
- ▸ Adding a query screen to a form
- ▸ Passing parameters to a form

Introduction

The **E-Business Suite (EBS)** user interface developed with **Oracle Forms Builder** is known as the *Professional User Interface*. The core modules have all been built using this development tool. However, the user interface for new modules is now developed using **JDeveloper** and is known as the *Self Service User Interface*.

Oracle provides a **TEMPLATE** form to get us started with developing forms. It has some referenced objects that allow us to develop forms in a consistent manner using the same standards and look and feel as all of the other forms within EBS. The referenced objects contain property classes and visual attributes, the standard toolbar, and the standard calendar. It also comes with code already written in triggers and program units. These help us to provide hooks to events that occur at runtime. This in turn ensures that any forms developed using the TEMPLATE.fmb conforms to Oracle standards and behaviors. Also, it makes it much easier for developers knowing that forms have been developed using the same standards.

When we develop a form we will always start by using the **TEMPLATE** form provided by Oracle. We will go through this in the coming chapter. Once we have developed our form we will then transfer the forms binary file (.fmb) over to the application tier. We then need to compile the form which will generate an executable (.fmx) file. It is the executable that Oracle will search for during runtime. When we create a new form we need to register the form in Oracle EBS. The form is registered with an application and it is this that determines the directory where Oracle will search for the executable. After we have registered the form we create a function that calls the form. We can then assign the function to a menu which is accessible to a menu associated with a responsibility. We will discuss the **TEMPLATE** form and where to get it from once we start building a new form.

Using forms builder for E-Business Suite

We are going to briefly look at forms builder before we start developing a new form. E-Business Suite does not use some features of the forms developer IDE such as alerts or reports. There are also some functions in EBS that replace some of the standard Oracle Forms built-ins. We will look at some of these in the coming chapters. Let's start by looking at the interface and discussing the features that need to be highlighted before we get started. The following screenshot shows us the forms developer once we have opened the **TEMPLATE** form:

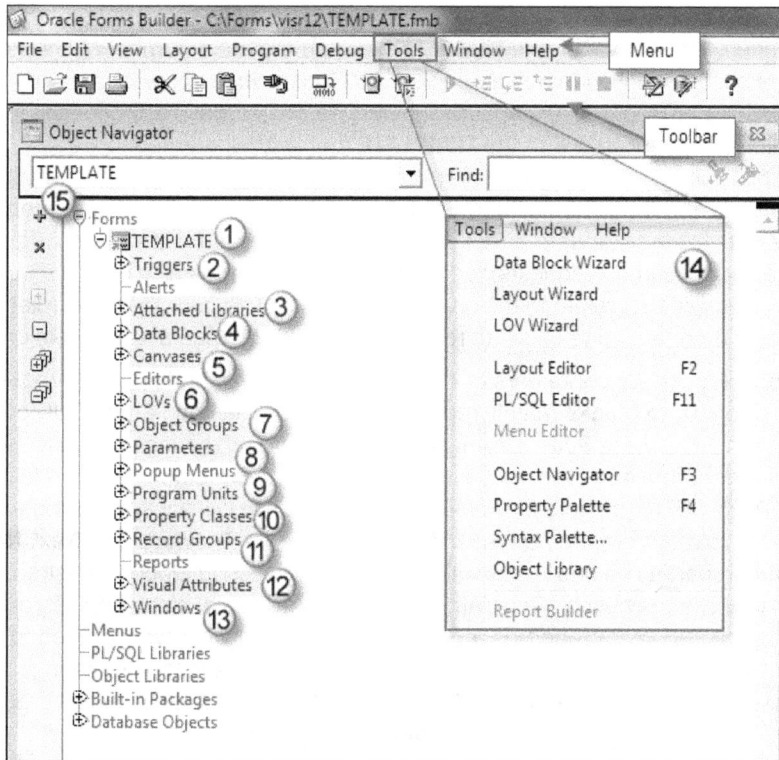

We will discuss the IDE and the features available before we get going:

1. **Module**: We need to change its properties from **TEMPLATE** to the name of our form. The name must be the same as the name of the form. We always need to set the property class (**Subclass Information**) to **MODULE**. We also need to set the **Console Window** and the **First Navigable Block** properties.

2. **Triggers**: The form level **Triggers** come with some code already in them. We have to modify a number of the triggers. You will notice that there is a call to `APP_STANDARD.EVENT` in most of the triggers. You must never remove this. If adding code to the `KEY-CLRFRM` trigger, then add code after the call to `APP_STANDARD.EVENT`. If we need to add code to the `POST-FORM` trigger, then add it after the call to the `APP_STANDARD.EVENT` call. There is a form-level trigger called `QUERY_FIND`. If we add a **QUERY_FIND** window, then we will create a block-level trigger to override the form-level trigger. If we create any new triggers, then the default execution hierarchy is set to override. We need to change it to `BEFORE` for *NEW* triggers, to `AFTER` for *POST* triggers, and to `OVERRIDE` for both *KEY* and *QUERY_FIND* triggers.

3. **Attached Libraries**: The **TEMPLATE** form comes with a number of libraries already attached. When we open the **TEMPLATE** form, there are a number of libraries that forms builder will look for locally on your PC. These can be copied from the `$AU_TOP/resource` directory on the application tier. We do not make any changes to any of the libraries that come with the **TEMPLATE** form with one exception, and that is the `CUSTOM` library. The `APPCORE` library contains packages that relate to application standards and the toolbar. The `CUSTOM` library is where we can write custom code that is used to extend standard forms. `FNDSQF` has code that relates to flexfields, profiles, currency, concurrent requests, record history, and the message dictionary. `APPDAYPK` has packages that relate to the calendar. `APPFLDR` has packages that relate to folders. There are quite a few more but the ones mentioned are the main ones.

4. **Blocks**: Blocks are containers of objects such as items, buttons, checkboxes, lists, and so on. **Data blocks** mainly represent logical entities and are usually based upon a view in E-Business Suite. Basing a block upon a view reduces network traffic as data is denormalized. This means we do not have to write additional code in PRE and POST-QUERY triggers for non-database fields. We will always use the `BLOCK` or `BLOCK_DIALOG` property classes. We need to set the **Previous** and **Next Navigation Block** properties so that users will navigate from block to block as desired. We would normally use the new block wizard when we create a new block and set/organize the layout and item properties afterwards. If we use a view, we will need to create `ON-INSERT`, `ON-UPDATE`, `ON-DELETE`, and `ON-LOCK` triggers to manage transactions with the database. We will also add `PRE-INSERT` and `PRE-UPDATE` triggers to add standard calls to set audit data in our blocks.

5. **Canvases**: **Canvases** are containers of objects that are displayed to the user. A canvas can be a content canvas, a stacked canvas, or a tabbed canvas. Therefore, we always set the property class to one of `CANVAS`, `CANVAS_STACKED`, `CANVAS_STACKED_FIXED`, or `TAB_CANVAS`. We need to define the **Window** property to associate a window with the canvas. In EBS, there are a few points to remember when creating objects in the **Layout Editor**. If we define more than one button, then the default button is the leftmost one. The **Alignment** property needs to be set to **Start**. We need to navigate through items from left-to-right and top-to-bottom. Unless the **Next** and **Previous Navigation Item** properties are defined, the navigation is defined as the order of the items in the **Object Navigator**. Oracle EBS has some look and feel guidelines when we are developing forms, such as leaving one character cell to the left and right of the canvas and one at the top and bottom of the canvas. When you double-click a canvas, the **Layout Editor** will open by default. To view the properties of a canvas, right-click the canvas and select **Property Palette** from the pop-up menu.

6. **LOVs**: **LOVs** are used for items that allow users to select predefined values from a list. A list of values uses the `LOV` property class and is usually based upon a record group. In Oracle E-Business Suite, there is a dummy list of values called `ENABLE_LIST_LAMP`. This shows the **LOV** button at runtime and allows developers to code `LOV` behavior in the `KEY-LISTVAL` trigger.

7. **Object Groups**: **Object Groups** are objects that have been defined in other forms and are inherited in the form. In Oracle E-Business Suite, all of the property classes and visual attributes are inherent in the **TEMPLATE** form. The property classes inherited should always be used when defining new objects within forms. It ensures that the objects look and feel the same as the object in standard forms and also that forms behave in the same manner. In addition to the property classes and visual attributes, the toolbar, and the standard calendar are also inherited.

8. **Parameters**: These are as the name suggests. Developers can define parameters that can be passed into the form and used to change behavior.

9. **Program Units**: These are used to write additional PL/SQL code. If you are writing large blocks of code, then it is best to create a package or procedure and put the code in there.

10. **Property Classes**: These are referenced objects that should be used whenever new objects are created. They set properties for items with values that conform to Oracle's development standards.

11. **Record Groups**: These are basically queries that are used to get the data for lists of values.

12. **Visual Attributes**: These are referenced and they are referenced in the property classes that are also referenced objects.

13. **Windows**: These are container objects relating to the Forms window. A window can be **modal** or **non-modal**. A modal window requires the WINDOW_DIALOG property class and is used for windows such as pop-up windows. Items within modal windows are based upon blocks that use the property class BLOCK_DIALOG. These windows are designed to not allow users to interact with other forms until the modal window is closed. The KEY triggers are disabled and we need to add code to close the window. You also need to define **OK** and **Cancel** buttons and can set the window properties using the APP_WINDOW package. A non-modal window uses the WINDOW property class and a window should contain at least one object.

14. **Tools menu**: The **Tools** menu has been highlighted as forms are context based. This means that if you double-click on an item in **Data Blocks**, the **Property Palette** will open. However, if you double-click on a canvas, the **Layout Editor** will open. From the **Tools** menu, you will be able to open the **Properties** window, **Layout Editor**, and **PL/SQL Editor** as required. You can also launch all of the built-in wizards from here. In addition, you can right-click on **objects** in the **Object Navigator** and launch the desired function in the same manner as using **Tools** from the menu.

15. **Left-hand toolbar**: This is used for creating and deleting objects within the navigator. In the recipes, we will refer to the left-hand toolbar on numerous occasions to add and remove objects. It is also used for expanding and collapsing nodes. However, it's much easier to click an object's **+** or **−** symbol to do the same.

Creating a custom schema

When we create new forms or other new objects, they need to be put in a custom schema. A custom schema has the same directory structure, under the PRODUCT_TOP, as a standard schema. Each custom schema is prefixed by *XX*. So, for example, if we are extending the HR module, then we would create a custom schema called *XXHR*. If we were extending the AP module, we would create a new schema called *XXAP*, and so on. The examples in this chapter are based upon a **Vision instance** and have been registered with a custom schema called *XXHR*. There are further details in the *Creating a custom schema* recipe in *Chapter 6, Utilities*.

Installing the database objects

Create the database objects for this chapter before you start by using a script provided called `4842_02_01.sh`. We are going to create a table, a view, and a synonym for the new block we will create. We will also create a package that will handle all of the database transactions such as insert, update, and delete. Finally, we will create a sequence that will be used to generate a unique number for new records. The following recipe provides details of how to run the script.

How to do it...

To create the database objects required for this chapter, perform the following tasks:

1. Create a local directory `c:\packt\scripts\ch2` where the scripts are downloaded and extracted to.

2. Open **Putty** and connect to the application tier user.

3. Create a new directory on the application tier under `$XXHR_TOP/install` using the following commands:

   cd $XXHR_TOP/install

   mkdir ch2

4. Navigate to the new directory `cd ch2` using the following command:

   cd ch2

5. Open **WinSCP** and FTP the files from `c:\packt\scripts\ch2` to `$XXHR_TOP/install/ch2`, as shown in the following screenshot:

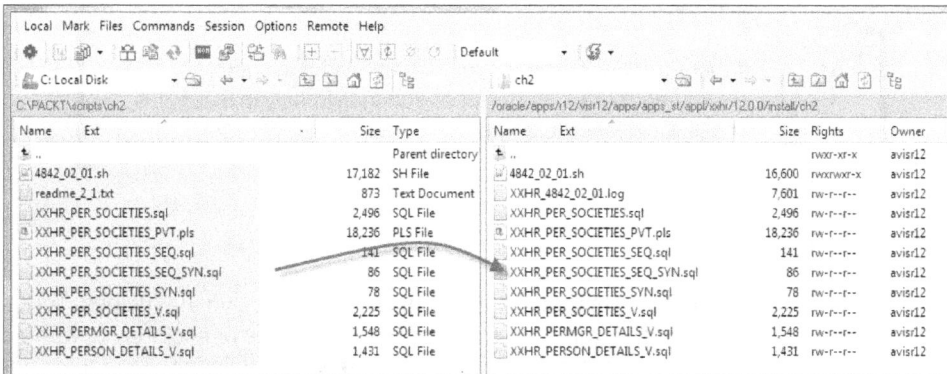

6. In **Putty**, change the permissions of the script with the following command:

   ```
   chmod 775 4842_02_01.sh
   ```

7. Run the following script to create all of the objects by issuing the following command:

   ```
   ./4842_02_01.sh apps/apps
   ```

8. The script checks whether all of the files are present in your $XXHR_TOP/install/ch2 directory and will prompt you to continue if they are all there, so type Y and press *Enter*.

9. After the script has completed, check the XXHR_4842_02_01.log file for errors. (It will be created in the same directory $XXHR_TOP/install/ch2).

10. Run the following query to check whether all of the objects have been created successfully:

```
SELECT OWNER, OBJECT_NAME, OBJECT_TYPE, STATUS
  FROM ALL_OBJECTS
 WHERE OBJECT_NAME LIKE 'XXHR_PER_SOC%'
ORDER BY 1, 2
```

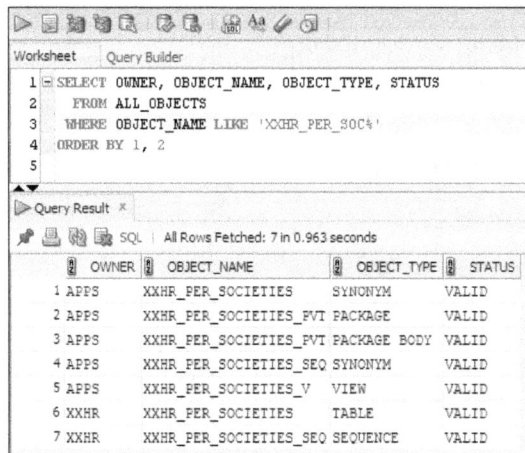

> If there are any problems running the script in your environment the scripts can be run individually in SQL*Plus or SQL Developer to create the objects.

How it works...

We have created a number of objects that we are going to use in the coming recipes. The table `XXHR_PER_SOCIETIES` table will store details relating to clubs or societies that the employee belongs to. We have created a synonym to the **APPS** user as all of our objects need to be accessed by this user. The table will store the raw data and so we have also created a view which has the meanings and descriptions visible to the user as well. We will use the views when we create the form and we will get into that a little bit later. The sequence we have created will generate a unique number each time a new record is created. Finally, the package we have created stores all of the procedures and functions relating to database activity within the form such as inserting, updating, or deleting records.

Getting started with forms

In this recipe, we are going to look at getting everything started so that we can build forms to be used in E-Business Suite. We are going to be using Oracle Forms Builder version 10g and we are also going to be using **WinSCP**.

In this recipe, we are going to perform the following tasks:

- Installing Oracle Developer Suite
- Creating the forms builder desktop shortcut
- Adding a TNS names entry
- Setting runtime parameters in the environment file
- FTP forms and libraries
- Opening the **TEMPLATE** form
- Renaming the **TEMPLATE** form

Installing Oracle Developer Suite

We need to install Oracle Developer Suite on our local PCs. We can develop the forms locally but will need to transfer the forms over to the application server and compile them there to run the form in the application. We will look at deploying and testing the forms later on but for now we will install the development tool.

How to do it...

To install the Oracle Developer Suite, perform the following steps:

1. Create three directories on your C drive as follows:
   - ❑ `C:\Install\Disk1`
   - ❑ `C:\Install\Disk2`
   - ❑ `C:\Forms\visr12`

2. Download **Oracle Developer Suite 10g (10.1.2.0.2)** from `http://www.oracle.com/technetwork/developer-tools/developer-suite/downloads/index.html`.

> The version of developer suite required is dependent upon the version of Oracle EBS that is installed. Always refer to the Oracle support site to find the correct version required for the EBS version that you are on.

3. You will need to download both files (**disk1** and **disk2**), as shown in the following screenshot:

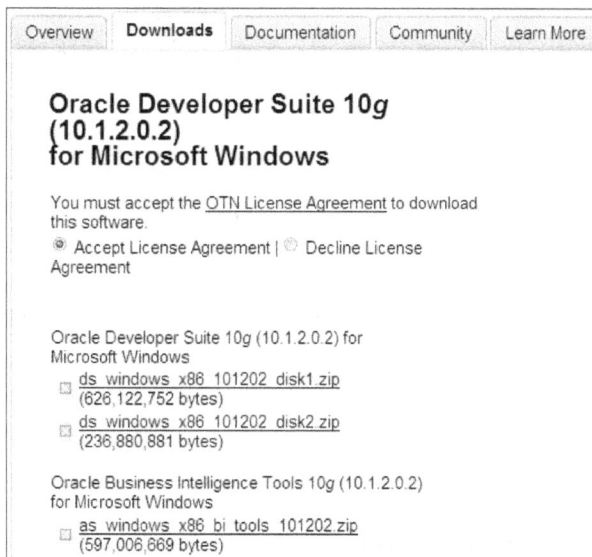

4. Unzip **ds_windows_x86_101202_disk1.zip** into `C:\Install\Disk1`.

5. Unzip **ds_windows_x86_101202_disk2.zip** into `C:\Install\Disk2`.

6. Navigate to `C:\Install\Disk1` and launch `setup.exe`.

7. Install the complete developer suite (includes forms and reports of size 1.1 GB). **Note**: If you are installing on Windows 7 OS, you may get the following message:

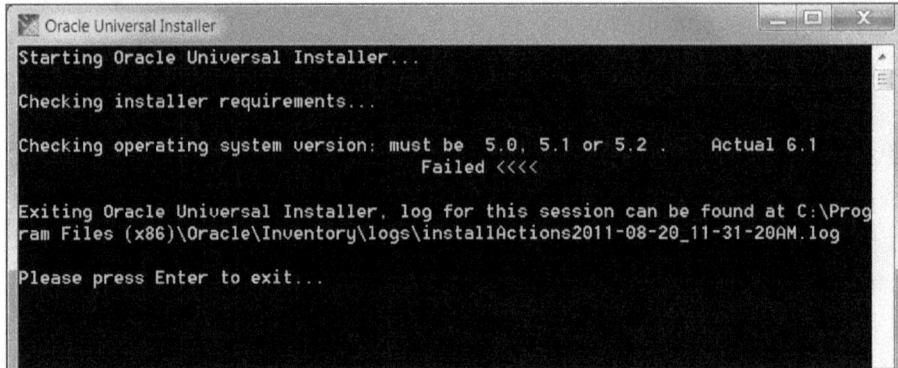

8. Press *Enter* and you will get a pop-up screen, as shown in the following screenshot. Select **Reinstall using recommended settings**:

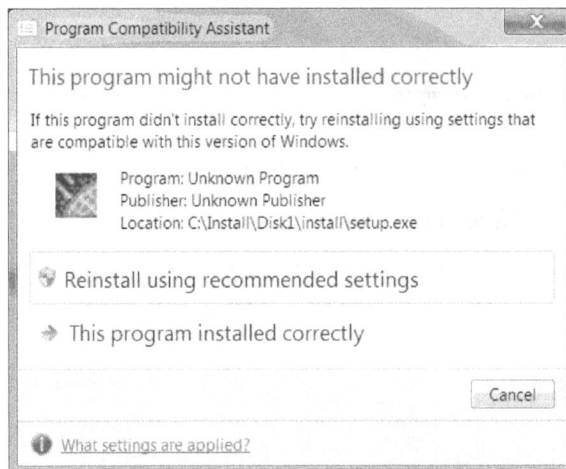

> You may also get an error complaining about the swap space. This is because the **Virtual Memory** setting on your PC has the **Automatically manage paging file size for all drives** checkbox checked. If so, navigate to **System Properties | Advanced** tab. Click on the **Change** button and set the **Virtual Memory** to a **Custom size** which has a minimum of `1535` MB.

9. To change the virtual memory setting on your PC carry out the steps shown in the following screenshot:

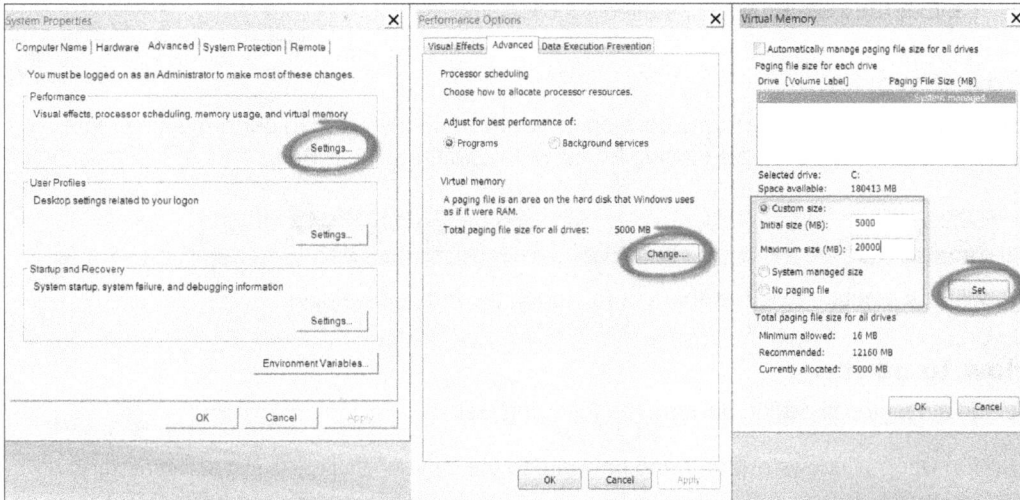

10. When asked to specify the **Destination**, set the **Name** to `DevSuiteHome` and the **Path** to `C:\DevSuiteHome` (if you decide to install in another directory, then bear this in mind when following the recipes):

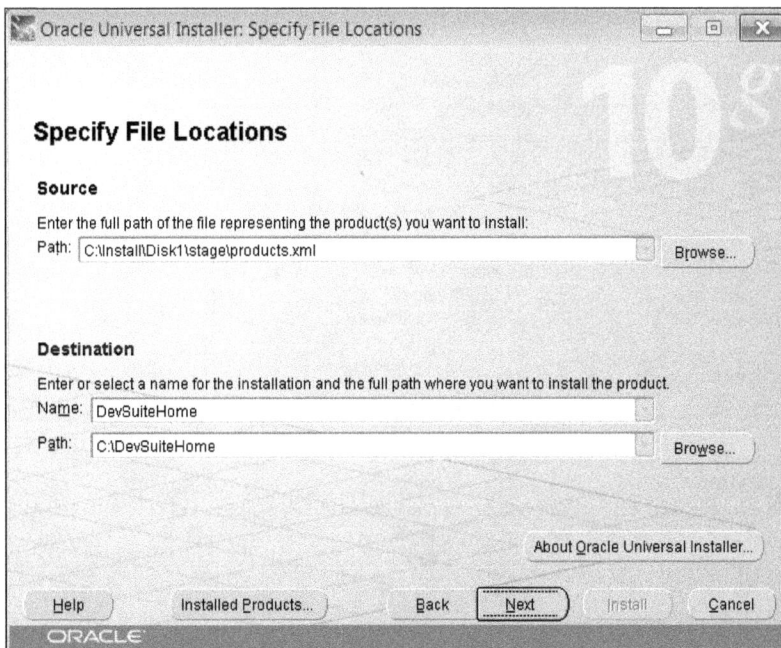

11. Click on **Next**.

12. When prompted to enter the **SMTP** mail server, just leave it blank and continue.

13. **Exit** the installer once installed successfully.

How it works...

We have now installed the forms developer. However, we still need to perform some more tasks before we can start developing forms for Oracle E-Business Suite.

Creating the forms builder desktop shortcut

We will now create a desktop shortcut to launch the forms developer.

How to do it...

To add a desktop shortcut, perform the following tasks:

1. Open Windows explorer and navigate to the `C:\DevSuiteHome\BIN` directory.

2. Right-click on `frmbld.exe` to create a shortcut on the desktop, as shown in the following screenshot:

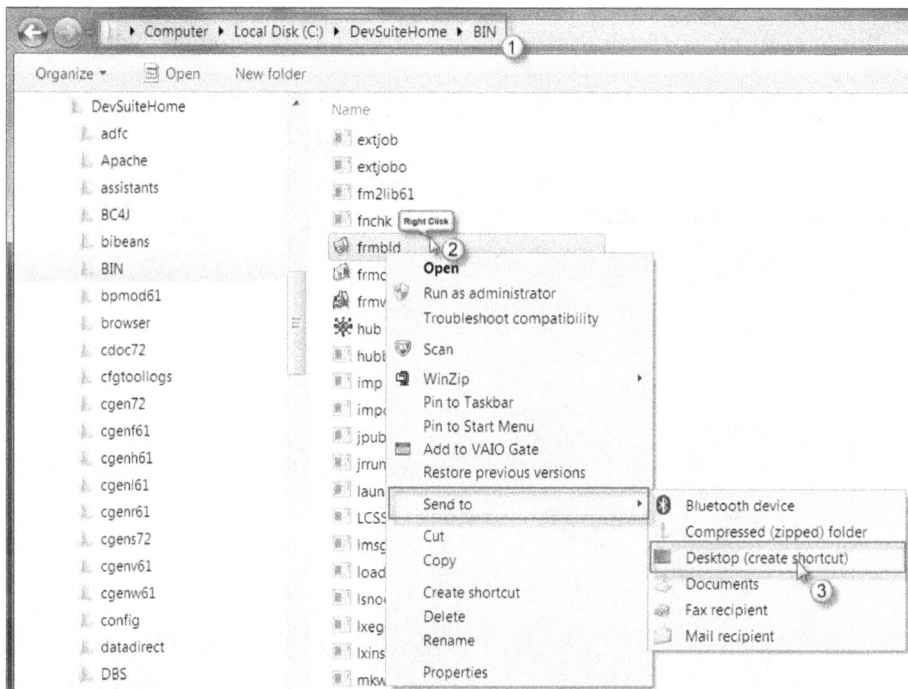

3. Navigate to the desktop.

4. Right-click on the `frmbld` icon on the desktop to set the shortcut properties.

5. Set the value in the **Target:** field to `C:\DevSuiteHome\BIN\frmbld.exe userid=apps/apps@visr12`.

> You can add the **userid** parameter to connect to your database when opening forms developer. The connection details will be specific to your environment but defined as `<username>/<password>@<SID>`.

6. Set the value in the **Start in:** field to **C:\Forms\visr12** (this is *important* as this is where *forms builder* searches for all of the reference forms and libraries):

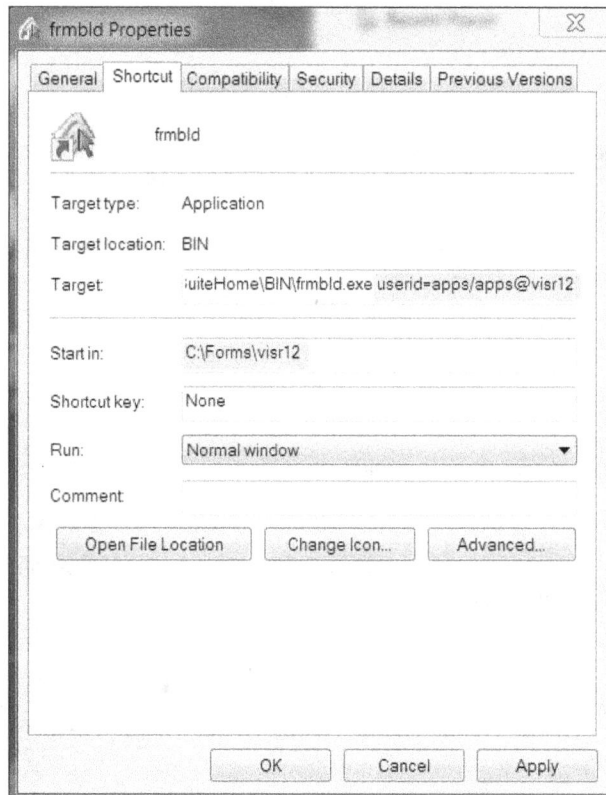

If you are using Windows 7, navigate to the **Compatibility** tab and check the **Run this program in compatibility mode for** checkbox and set the list of values to **Windows XP (Service Pack 3)**, as shown in the following screenshot:

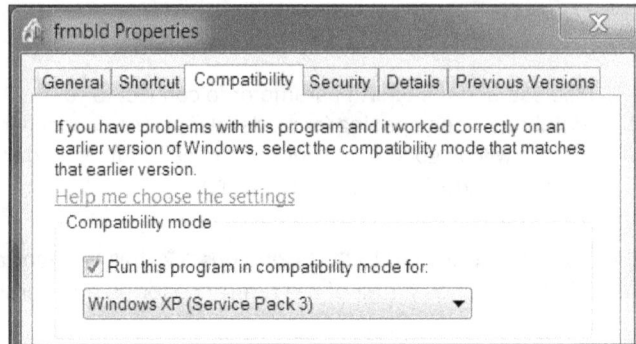

How it works...

We have now created a shortcut on our desktop, which will automatically connect to the database when we open the forms developer. We do however need to add the **Start in:** value. This is the directory path where we will transfer all of the reference forms and libraries that the **TEMPLATE** form requires.

Adding a TNS names entry

We also need to add a TNS names entry for connecting to the database.

How to do it...

To add a TNS names entry, perform the following tasks:

1. Navigate to the `C:\DevSuiteHome\NETWORK\ADMIN` directory.

2. Open the file `tnsnames.ora` in a text editor (for example, Notepad) and add a TNS names entry, as shown in the following example:

```
e.g. VISR12=
  (DESCRIPTION=
      (ADDRESS_LIST =
      (ADDRESS = (PROTOCOL=TCP)(HOST=<server name>)
      (PORT=<port number>))
   )
   (CONNECT_DATA=
      (SERVICE_NAME=VISR12)
   )
  )
```

Note: The *<server name>* and the *<port number>* are specific to your installation.

The `HOST` entry is the name of the server of the application tier. This will depend upon your instance of E-Business Suite and therefore, you will need to type the name of your application server here. The name of the server should also exist in your host file in the `C:\Windows\System32\drivers\etc` directory.

How it works...

Setting the TNS names entry allows the forms developer to connect to the database. If you are unsure of your TNS names entry for the environment you are using, then open a **Putty** session. Navigate to the `$TNS_ADMIN` directory by typing `cd $TNS_ADMIN` at the command prompt. In this directory will be the `tnsnames.ora` file. Open it up by typing `view tnsnames.ora` (case sensitive). Scroll down until you find the TNS names entry for your environment and you will see the server and port number you need to put in the forms developer `tnsnames.ora` file locally on your PC.

Setting runtime parameters in the environment file

In the older versions of forms builder, we would need to set the runtime parameters in the registry. However, in version 10g, the runtime parameters are set in an environment file located in the `<DevSuiteHome>\forms\server\default.env` file. However, this step is optional as we never run the E-Business Suite forms locally. They are always moved over to the server and run through the application.

How to do it...

To add the runtime variables to your environment, perform the following tasks:

1. Open the `default.env` file with Notepad.

2. Locate the `FORMS_PATH` environment variable and add the directory where all of the forms are located. For example, `C:\Forms\visr12`.

How it works...

We have now set the variable in the environment file.

FTP forms and libraries

When we create forms in Oracle E-Business Suite, we need to use the **TEMPLATE** form that Oracle provides. In the following recipe, we will be transferring the **TEMPLATE** form and associated referenced forms and libraries from the application tier.

Getting ready

The forms and libraries are available in the $AU_TOP directory on the application tier of your environment. You will need to FTP the forms and libraries to your local PC to be able to start developing a new form. All of the forms have attached libraries and objects referenced in other forms. Therefore, you will not be able to copy just the form you need as you will not be able to open it without getting errors. I prefer to FTP all of the libraries (.pll) files and all of the forms (.fmb) files but this will take a while depending on your network speed. However, to just develop a new form using the **TEMPLATE** form, you will only need to FTP the following forms and libraries associated with it to the directory defined in the desktop shortcut, for example, the C:\Forms\visr12 directory.

Forms (FMB files)

The **TEMPLATE** form and the forms referenced in the TEMPLATE.fmb form can be found in the $AU_TOP/forms/US directory. Therefore, the forms that we need to transfer to our local PC are TEMPLATE and APPSTAND.

Libraries (PLL files)

The libraries referenced in the TEMPLATE.fmb form can be found in the $AU_TOP/resource directory. We only require the .pll files. The libraries are APPCORE, FNDSQF, GLOBE, JE, JL, JA, VERT, GHR, APPCORE2, HRKPI, PQH_GEN, PSAC, PSB, PSA, GMS, FV, IGILUTIL, IGILUTIL2, IGI_CBC, CUSTOM, IGI_CC, IGI_CIS, IGI_DOS, IGI_EXP, IGI_IAC, IGI_MHC, IGI_SIA, IGI_STP, OPM, VERT1, VERT2, VERT3, VERT4, VERT5, FNDMOAC, and APPDAYPK.

How to do it...

To transfer the files from the application tier to a local directory, perform the following tasks:

1. Open **WinSCP** (or your preferred FTP client).
2. Log on to the application server of your E-Business Suite environment.
3. Navigate to the $AU_TOP\resource directory.
4. Select the library (.pll) files you wish to FTP and copy them to the C:\Forms\visr12 directory on your local PC.

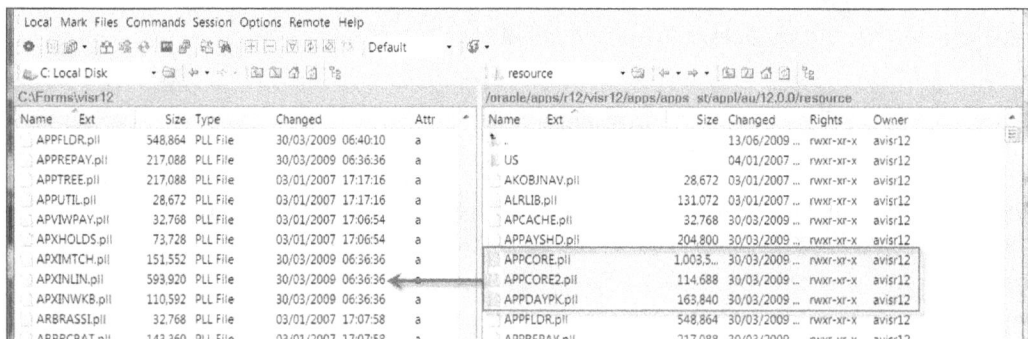

5. Navigate to the `$AU_TOP\forms\US` directory.

6. Select the form (`.fmb`) files you wish to FTP and *copy* them to the `C:\Forms\visr12` directory on your local PC.

How it works...

The libraries and forms referenced by the `TEMPLATE.fmb` are now on the your local PC. Now, when we open the `TEMPLATE.fmb` form in the forms builder, it will find the referenced objects and the form will open without any missing objects.

Opening the TEMPLATE form

The first thing we need to do when we develop a new form is to rename the **TEMPLATE** form.

How to do it...

To rename the **TEMPLATE** form, perform the following tasks:

1. Open Forms 10g by clicking on the `frmbld` shortcut we created on the desktop.

2. When forms builder opens for the first time, you will be prompted to use the forms builder wizard. Select the **Build a new form manually** radio button and uncheck the **Display at startup** checkbox.

3. Select **File | Open** from the menu bar.

4. Select `TEMPLATE.fmb` from the `C:\Forms\visr12` directory.

> If you get any of the following messages when you open the **TEMPLATE** form, then either you have not set the **Start in:** directory in the desktop shortcut or all of the forms and libraries referenced in the **TEMPLATE** form have not been transferred across to your local PC from the application server. Do not continue until you have opened the `TEMPLATE.fmb` without either of the following messages appearing and *NEVER* save the **TEMPLATE** form if this occurs. Close the form without saving and transfer the missing forms or libraries to your local PC. Then try to open the **TEMPLATE** form. You need to repeat this until the form opens without complaining about missing objects.

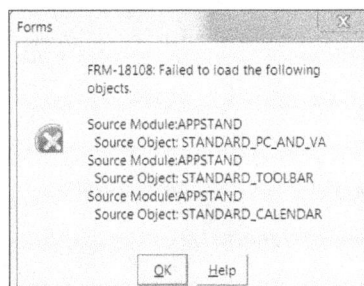

```
Forms                                                    X

            FRM-18108: Failed to load the following
            objects.

            Source Module:APPSTAND
             Source Object: STANDARD_PC_AND_VA
            Source Module:APPSTAND
             Source Object: STANDARD_TOOLBAR
            Source Module:APPSTAND
             Source Object: STANDARD_CALENDAR


                    OK        Help
```

The following is the message that is displayed if there are any missing forms or libraries when we open a form:

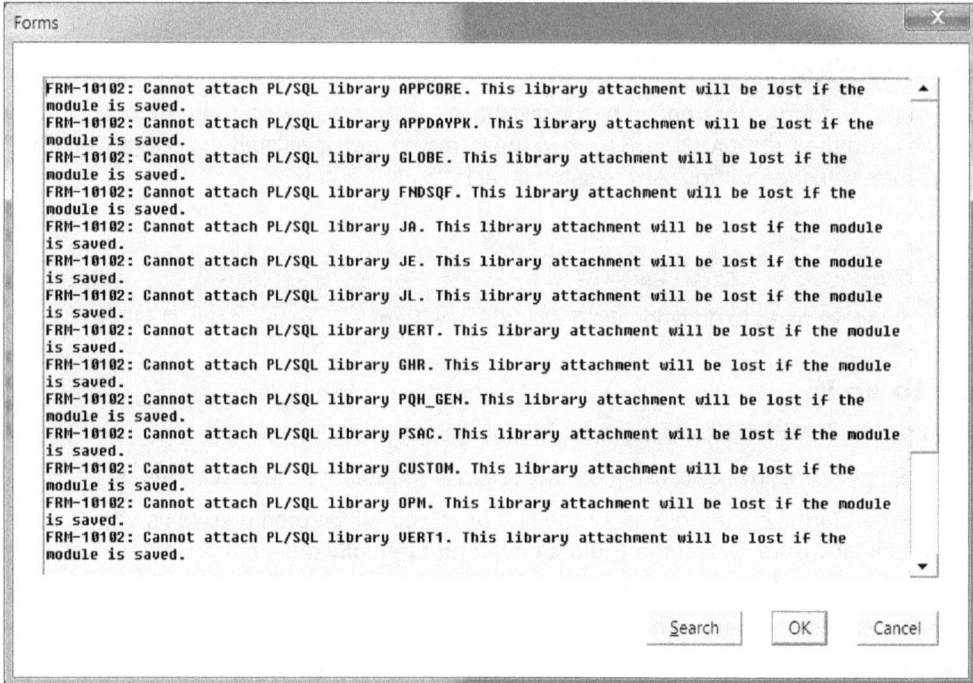

```
Forms                                                                    X

FRM-10102: Cannot attach PL/SQL library APPCORE. This library attachment will be lost if the
module is saved.
FRM-10102: Cannot attach PL/SQL library APPDAYPK. This library attachment will be lost if the
module is saved.
FRM-10102: Cannot attach PL/SQL library GLOBE. This library attachment will be lost if the
module is saved.
FRM-10102: Cannot attach PL/SQL library FNDSQF. This library attachment will be lost if the
module is saved.
FRM-10102: Cannot attach PL/SQL library JA. This library attachment will be lost if the module
is saved.
FRM-10102: Cannot attach PL/SQL library JE. This library attachment will be lost if the module
is saved.
FRM-10102: Cannot attach PL/SQL library JL. This library attachment will be lost if the module
is saved.
FRM-10102: Cannot attach PL/SQL library VERT. This library attachment will be lost if the module
is saved.
FRM-10102: Cannot attach PL/SQL library GHR. This library attachment will be lost if the module
is saved.
FRM-10102: Cannot attach PL/SQL library PQH_GEN. This library attachment will be lost if the
module is saved.
FRM-10102: Cannot attach PL/SQL library PSAC. This library attachment will be lost if the module
is saved.
FRM-10102: Cannot attach PL/SQL library CUSTOM. This library attachment will be lost if the
module is saved.
FRM-10102: Cannot attach PL/SQL library OPM. This library attachment will be lost if the module
is saved.
FRM-10102: Cannot attach PL/SQL library VERT1. This library attachment will be lost if the
module is saved.

                                           Search        OK        Cancel
```

Once the **TEMPLATE** form has opened without displaying any of the previous messages, then we need to rename the form.

How it works...

We have transferred the **TEMPLATE** form and associated forms and libraries to our local PC. When we can open the form without any messages about missing forms or libraries, we know we can save the form with a different name so that we can start developing our custom form.

Renaming the TEMPLATE form

Once we have opened the **TEMPLATE** form in forms builder we now need to save it with a new form name.

How to do it...

To rename the **TEMPLATE** form, perform the following steps:

1. Select **File | Save As** from the menu bar.

2. Set the filename to XXHRSOCC.fmb in the C:\Forms\visr12 directory, as shown in the following screenshot:

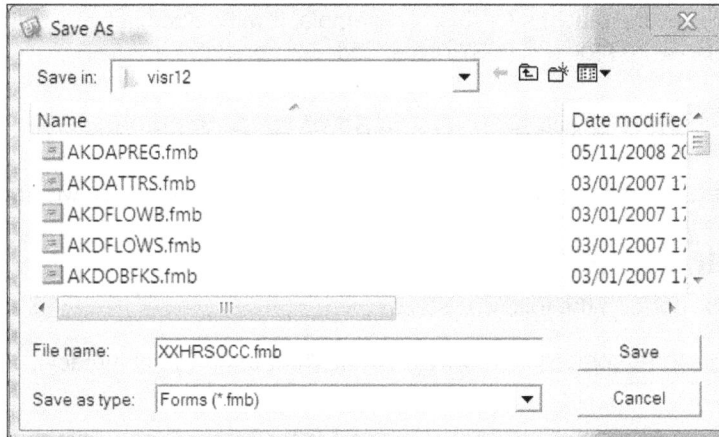

How it works...

We need to rename the **TEMPLATE** form and once this is done we can start developing our new form.

Creating a master block and container objects

In this recipe, we are going to start on the basics of a master detail form. There are several tasks that we will need to do:

 ▸ Creating a block using the block wizard
 ▸ Setting the block properties
 ▸ Setting the item properties
 ▸ Setting the canvas properties
 ▸ Setting the window properties
 ▸ Setting the module properties
 ▸ Creating a dummy item
 ▸ Removing unwanted objects
 ▸ Renaming prompts
 ▸ Resizing the viewport

We have already created two views to base our form on at the beginning of this chapter. The views are called XXHR_PERMGR_DETAILS_V and XXHR_PERSON_DETAILS_V. It is always better to base the block on a view, especially for more complex blocks that use multiple tables. There are several reasons for this; for example, it will reduce network traffic and we will not need to write PRE and POST trigger code for non-database fields.

Creating a block using the block wizard

We will first create the master block for the societies form using the block wizard.

How to do it...

To create a block, perform the following steps:

1. Open the XXHRSOCC form in **Oracle Forms Builder** (if it's not already).

> We shouldn't need to connect to the database as we have already connected in our forms builder shortcut. However, if the connection is lost reconnect with steps 2 and 3.

2. Select **File | Connect** and enter the connection details for the **APPS** user.

3. Click on the **Connect** button.

4. In the **Object Navigator**, click on the **Data Blocks** node, as shown in the following screenshot:

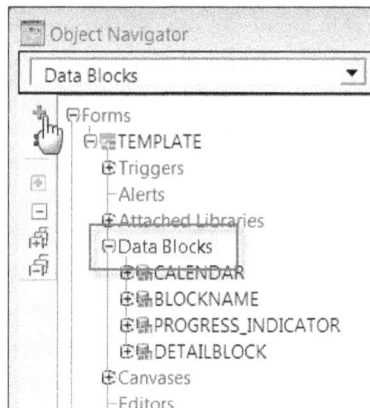

5. Click the green plus **+** sign to launch the **Data Block Wizard**.

6. Select the **Use the Data Block Wizard** radio button when prompted in the **New Data Block** window and click **OK**.

7. Click **Next** on the **Data Block Wizard** welcome page (uncheck the **Display this page next time** checkbox).

8. Select **Table or view** for the type of data block.

9. Enter XXHR_PERMGR_DETAILS_V in the **Table or view** field and press the *Tab* key. The available columns will appear, as shown in the following screenshot:

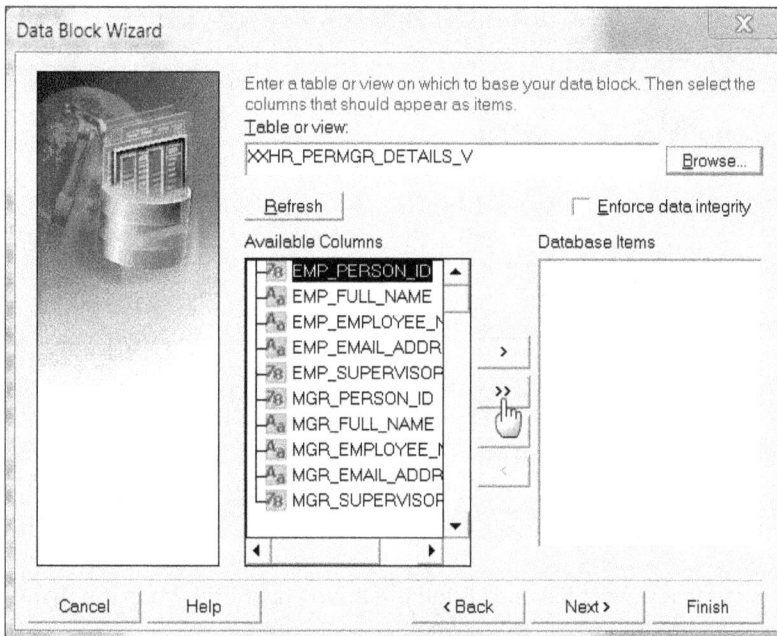

10. Click the **>>** button to shift all of the columns to the **Database Items** side.

11. Click on the **Finish** button and the **Layout Wizard** will appear.

12. If the **Welcome to the Layout Wizard** page appears, uncheck the **Display this page next time** checkbox and click on **Next**.

13. Select **(New Canvas)** for the **Canvas** field from the drop-down list.

14. Select **Content** for the **Type** field.

15. Click on the **Next** button as shown in the following screenshot:

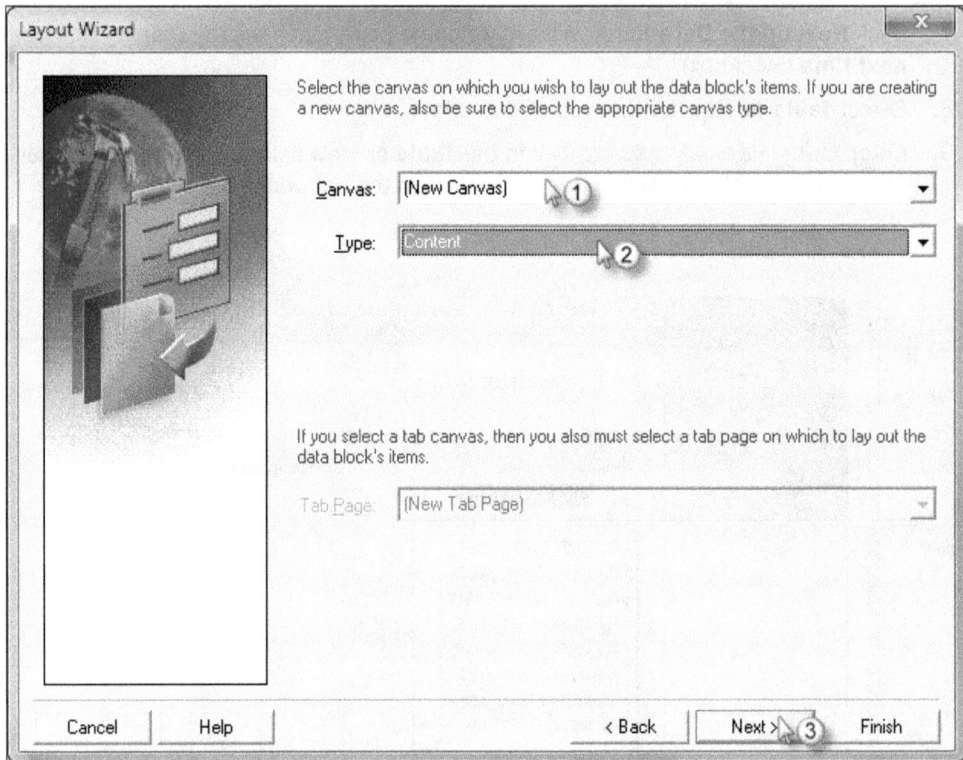

16. Select the following fields and click the **>** button to shift them to the **Displayed Items** side, as shown in the next screenshot:

- EMP_FULL_NAME
- EMP_EMPLOYEE_NUMBER
- EMP_EMAIL_ADDRESS
- MGER_FULL_NAME
- MGR_EMPLOYEE_NUMBER
- MGR_EMAIL_ADDRESS

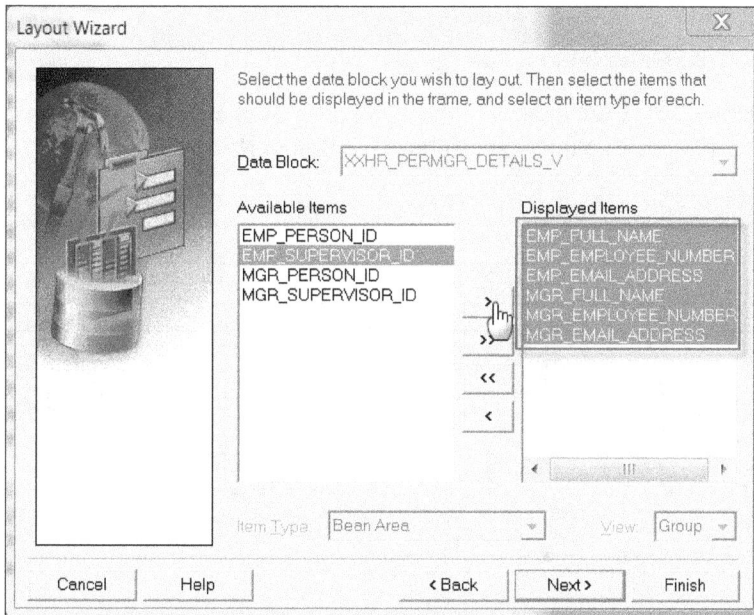

You can select multiple items from the **Available Items** region by holding down the *Ctrl* key and clicking on multiple items. Then click the **>** button to shift them across to the **Displayed Items** region.

17. Click on the **Next** button and set the **Prompt** and **Width** for each item as follows:

Name	Prompt	Width
EMP_FULL_NAME	**Employee Name**	2
EMP_EMPLOYEE_NUMBER	**Employee Number**	1.5
EMP_EMAIL_ADDRESS	**Employee Email**	2.5
MGR_FULL_NAME	**Manager Name**	2
MGR_EMPLOYEE_NUMBER	**Manager Employee Number**	1.5
MGR_EMAIL_ADDRESS	**Manager Email**	2.5

We do not need to set the **Height** just yet as this will be done later when we set the property class of each item.

18. Click on the **Next** button.

19. Select **Form** as the layout style.
20. Click on the **Finish** button.

The **Layout Editor** window will open with the items on it, as shown in the following screenshot. For now, close the window so that you just have the **Object Navigator** open.

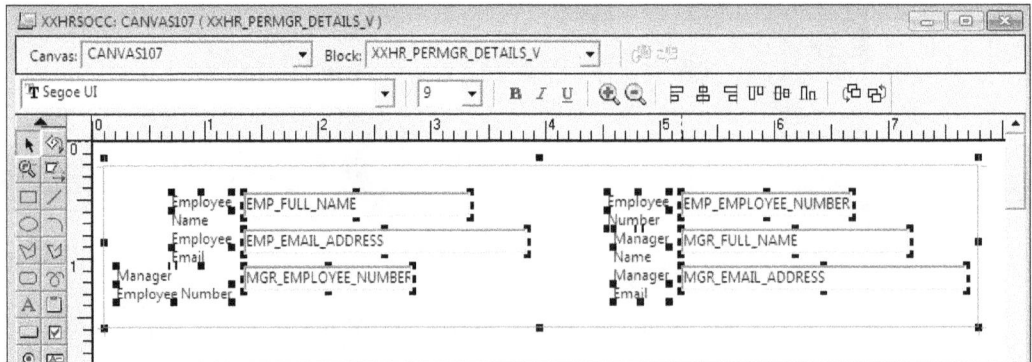

How it works...

The block wizard allows us to quickly create a block based upon a database object. It will generate a canvas and allow us to select items that we want to be displayed to the user. We don't need to worry about the layout too much at this stage as it will all be modified and tidied up later when we set the block and item properties.

Setting the block properties

We will now set the block properties of our master block. When we create any objects for use in Oracle E-Business suite, there are already many pre-defined property classes that we must use to conform to the GUI standards.

How to do it...

Now, we are going to set the properties of the objects we have just created:

1. In the navigator, right-click on the data block called XXHR_PERMGR_DETAILS_V and select **Property Palette** from the pop-up menu to display the **Property Palette**.

2. Change the following block properties as shown in the next screenshot:

   ❏ **Name**: PERMGR_DTLS

   ❏ **Subclass Information**: Property Class

   ❏ **Property Class Name**: BLOCK

   ❏ **Module**: TEMPLATE

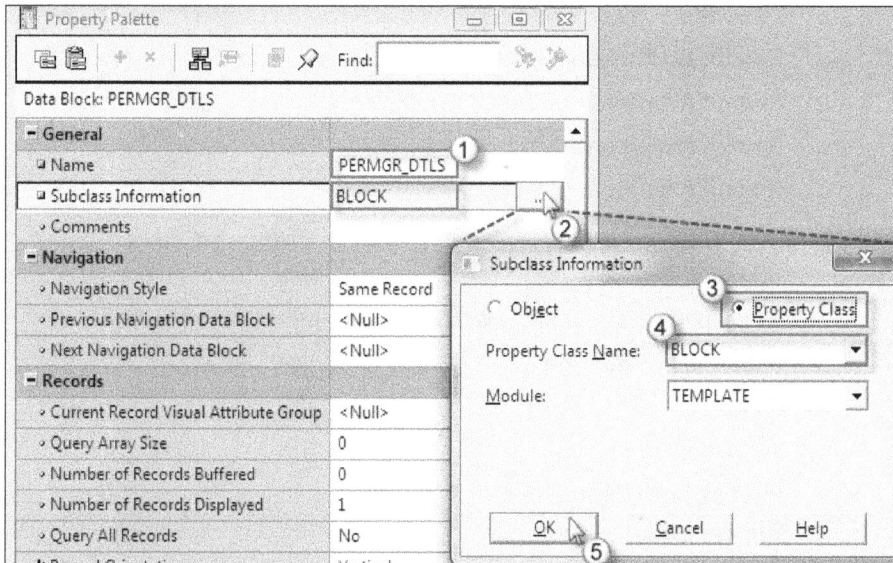

3. Click on the **OK** button.

How it works...

We have now set the property class to the BLOCK property class. Property classes for all objects are available from the **TEMPLATE** form, which is why we have used it. There are property classes for all of the different objects we will add to the form and we always use the property classes inherited from the **TEMPLATE** form. A property class sets a pre defined set of properties for each object. This allows us to develop forms that have the same behavior, look and feel as standard Oracle forms.

Setting the item properties

We will now set the properties of the items in our master block. Again, we will use the property classes that Oracle has provided us with.

How to do it...

To set the item properties, perform the following steps:

1. In the **Object Navigator**, right-click on **Data Blocks** | **PERMGR_DTLS** | **Items** | **EMP_FULL_NAME** and select **Property Palette** from the pop-up menu.

2. Change the properties of the EMP_FULL_NAME item to the following:

   ❑ **Subclass Information**: TEXT_ITEM_DISPLAY_ONLY

   ❑ **X Position**: 1.49

      ❑ **Y Position**: .244

      ❑ **Prompt Justification**: End

      ❑ **Prompt Attachment Edge**: Start

      ❑ **Prompt Alignment**: Center

      ❑ **Prompt Alignment Offset**: .1

3. In the **Object Navigator**, right-click on **Data Blocks | PERMGR_DTLS | Items | EMP_EMPLOYEE_NUMBER** and select **Property Palette** from the pop-up menu.

4. Change the properties of the EMP_EMPLOYEE_NUMBER item to the following:

      ❑ **Subclass Information**: TEXT_ITEM_DISPLAY_ONLY

      ❑ **X Position**: 1.49

      ❑ **Y Position**: .502

      ❑ **Prompt Justification**: End

      ❑ **Prompt Attachment Edge**: Start

      ❑ **Prompt Alignment**: Center

      ❑ **Prompt Alignment Offset**: .1

5. In the **Object Navigator**, right-click on **Data Blocks | PERMGR_DTLS | Items | EMP_EMAIL_ADDRESS** and select **Property Palette** from the pop-up menu.

6. Change the properties of the EMP_EMAIL_ADDRESS item to the following:

      ❑ **Subclass Information**: TEXT_ITEM_DISPLAY_ONLY

      ❑ **X Position**: 1.49

      ❑ **Y Position**: .76

      ❑ **Prompt Justification**: End

      ❑ **Prompt Attachment Edge**: Start

      ❑ **Prompt Alignment**: Center

      ❑ **Prompt Alignment Offset**: .1

7. In the **Object Navigator**, right-click on **Data Blocks | PERMGR_DTLS | Items | MGR_FULL_NAME** and select **Property Palette** from the pop-up menu.

8. Change the properties of the MGR_FULL_NAME item to the following:

      ❑ **Subclass Information**: TEXT_ITEM_DISPLAY_ONLY

      ❑ **X Position**: 5.606

      ❑ **Y Position**: .244

      ❑ **Prompt Justification**: End

      ❑ **Prompt Attachment Edge**: Start

□ **Prompt Alignment**: Center

□ **Prompt Alignment Offset**: .1

9. In the **Object Navigator**, right-click on **Data Blocks | PERMGR_DTLS | Items | MGR_EMPLOYEE_NUMBER** and select **Property Palette** from the pop-up menu.

10. Change the properties of the MGR_EMPLOYEE_NUMBER item to the following:

□ **Subclass Information**: TEXT_ITEM_DISPLAY_ONLY

□ **X Position**: 5.606

□ **Y Position**: .502

□ **Prompt Justification**: End

□ **Prompt Attachment Edge**: Start

□ **Prompt Alignment**: Center

□ **Prompt Alignment Offset**: .1

11. In the **Object Navigator**, right-click on **Data Blocks | PERMGR_DTLS | Items | MGR_EMAIL_ADDRESS** and select **Property Palette** from the pop-up menu.

12. Change the properties of the MGR_EMAIL_ADDRESS item to the following:

□ **Subclass Information**: TEXT_ITEM_DISPLAY_ONLY

□ **X Position**: 5.606

□ **Y Position**: .76

□ **Prompt Justification**: End

□ **Prompt Attachment Edge**: Start

□ **Prompt Alignment**: Center

□ **Prompt Alignment Offset**: .1

How it works...

We have set the item properties for the master block. Notice that they are display-only fields, which will prevent users from updating any of the values. For all of the items displayed, we have set the position on that canvas and the prompt position.

Setting the canvas properties

We are now going to set the canvas properties that our objects are going to be displayed on.

> When you double-click on a canvas, it will open the canvas editor. You must right-click the canvas and select **Property Palette** to view the properties of the canvas.

How to do it...

To set the canvas properties, perform the following tasks:

1. In the **Object Navigator**, right-click on **Canvases | CANVASxxx** and select **Property Palette** from the pop-up menu. The name will be something similar to CANVASxxx (this is a generated name we need to change and will be something like CANVAS103).

2. Set the following canvas properties of the automatically generated canvas:

    ❑ **Name**: SOCIETY_CNV

    ❑ **Subclass Information**: CANVAS

3. Navigate to **Canvases | SOCIETY_CNV | Graphics** and delete the FRAME. It will be called something similar to **FRAME104**, as shown in the following screenshot:

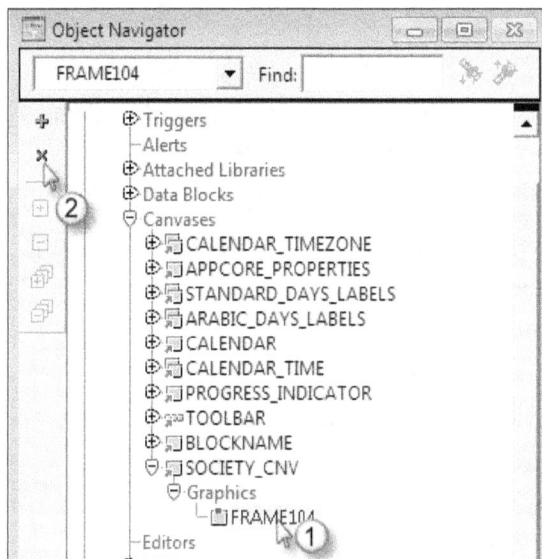

4. Click on the **OK** button when prompted, if you want to delete the object.

5. **Save** the form.

How it works...

We have now set the canvas properties and removed the frame that was generated automatically by the **Layout Wizard**. We can see that an item has had a property class set when it has a small red arrow next to the object.

Setting the window properties

We will now set the window properties of the form, which will determine the size of the window displayed to the user and the title displayed in the window title at the top of the form.

How to do it...

To set the window properties, perform the following tasks:

1. Right-click on **Windows | BLOCKNAME** in the **Object Navigator** and select **Property Palette** from the pop-up menu.

2. Set the properties to the following:

   - **Name**: SOCIETY_WND
   - **Subclass Information**: WINDOW
   - **Title**: Employee Societies Form
   - **Primary Canvas**: SOCIETY_CNV
   - **Width**: 8.5
   - **Height**: 5

How it works...

We have set the window properties of our form and associated the window with the SOCIETY_CNV canvas.

Setting the module properties

Now that we have created the primary objects in our form, we need to set the module properties.

How to do it...

To set the module properties, perform the following tasks:

1. Right-click on **Module** in the **Object Navigator** and select **Property Palette** from the pop-up menu.

2. Set the properties to the following:

   > The module name must be the same as the form name, without the .fmb extension.

   - **Name**: XXHRSOCC
   - **Subclass Information**: MODULE

- **Console Window**: SOCIETY_WND
- **First Navigation Data Block**: PERMGR_DTLS

How it works...

We have set the properties of module and set the form's primary window to our SOCIETY_WND window. We have also set the **First Navigation Data Block** to our master block. This means that when the form opens the default block it will navigate to will be the PERMGR_DTLS block.

Creating a dummy item

As we have created a master block that has no items that are navigable, we need to create a dummy item in the block that forms can navigate to. It will be a non-database item and will not be visible to the user.

How to do it...

To create a dummy item, perform the following tasks:

1. In the **Object Navigator**, expand **Data Blocks | PERMGR_DTLS | Items**.

2. Add an item to the PERMGR_DTLS block by clicking the green **+** icon in the left-hand toolbar, as shown in the following screenshot:

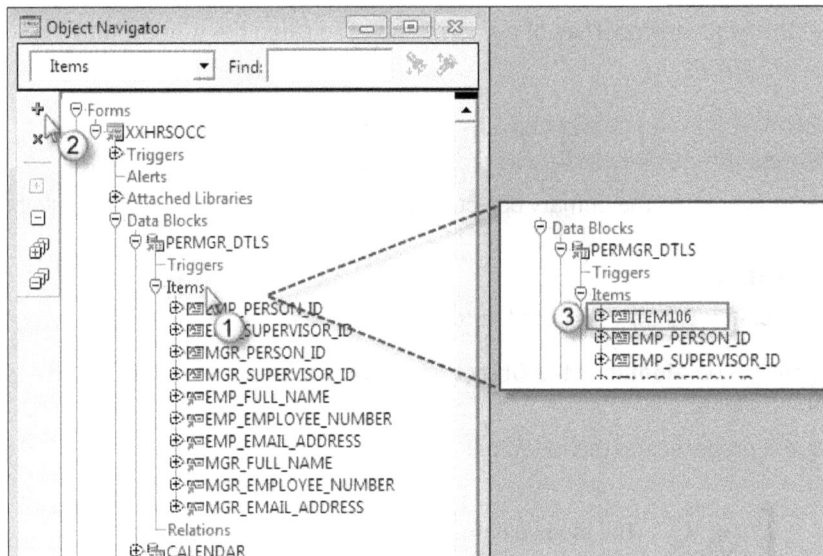

3. Right-click on the item that has been created and select **Property Palette** from the pop-up menu.

4. Set the following properties of the item we have added:

   ❑ **Name**: DUMMY

   ❑ **Subclass Information**: TEXT_ITEM

   ❑ **Database Item**: No

   ❑ **Visible**: Yes

   ❑ **Canvas**: SOCIETY_CNV

   ❑ **Width**: 0

   ❑ **Height**: 0

How it works...

The dummy item is an item that is navigable to forms and is in the PERMGR_DTLS block. Although we have set the **Visible** property to Yes, it is not visible to the user as we have set the **Height** and **Width** to 0. We need to navigate to this block when we enter the form and query the block to bring back the employee details but we do not want the user to be able to update any of the employee details as this is not the purpose of the block. Therefore, all of the items in this block are non-navigable but the block must have a navigable item in it.

Removing unwanted objects

We will now remove any unwanted objects left in the form as they are not required. The **TEMPLATE** form has two blocks by default called BLOCKNAME and DETAILBLOCK. We don't need these objects in our form so we are going to remove them. In addition, there is also a canvas called BLOCKNAME that we do not need.

How to do it...

To remove the objects from the form, perform the following tasks:

1. Navigate to **Data Blocks** in the **Object Navigator** and remove the following blocks. Highlight the objects and click the red **x** icon on the left-hand toolbar:

   ❑ BLOCKNAME

   ❑ DETAILBLOCK

2. When prompted to delete the objects select **Yes**.

3. Navigate to **Canvases** in the **Object Navigator** and remove the following canvas:

   ❑ BLOCKNAME

4. Select and drag the SOCIETY_CNV to the top of the list of **Canvases** (optional).

5. Navigate to **Windows** in the **Object Navigator** and drag the SOCIETY_WND to the top of the window's list (optional).

6. **Save** the form.

How it works...

We have just tidied up the form and removed any unwanted objects that are left in the **TEMPLATE** form. It is okay to delete these objects as they are not required. However, do not delete any other objects in the form.

Renaming prompts

We are now going to tidy up the prompts as you may notice that they are wrapped around.

How to do it...

To rename the prompts, perform the following tasks:

1. Navigate to **Canvases | SOCIETY_CNV** in the **Object Navigator** and double-click it to open the **Layout Editor**.

2. Right-click on the EMP_FULL_NAME item and select **Property Palette** from the pop-up menu.

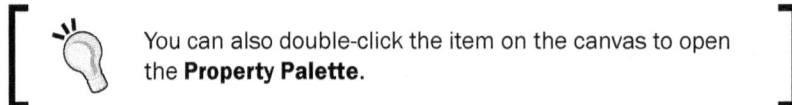

> You can also double-click the item on the canvas to open the **Property Palette**.

3. Scroll down to the **Prompt** property and click the **Editor** button.

4. Edit the text so that it is on one line, as shown in the following screenshot:

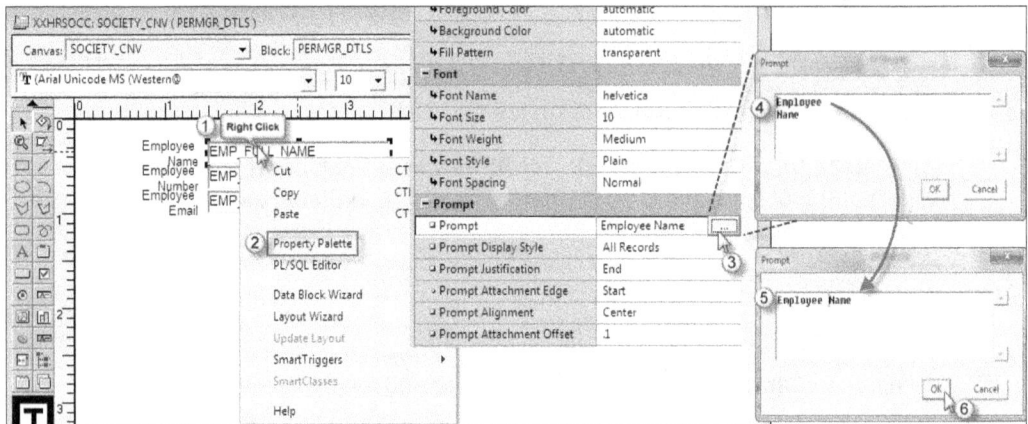

5. Click on the **OK** button.

6. Repeat for all of the other items in the **Layout Editor** so that the **Prompt** text is on one line.

The prompts for each item in the **Layout Editor** will now look similar to the following screenshot:

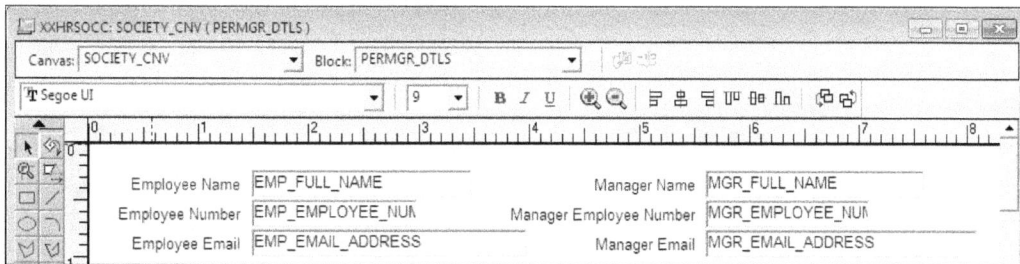

How it works...

We have tidied up the layout because when Forms 10g generates the layout from the wizard, the layout is not as we want it. Although the prompt text appears okay if you look at the text in the property palette, it is wrapped when displayed on the screen. If you open the editor for the prompt value, you can see that it is wrapped. We have deleted the carriage return so that the prompt is displayed on one line.

Resizing the viewport

We are now going to expand the viewport to the same size as the window.

How to do it...

1. Navigate to **Canvases | SOCIETY_CNV** in the **Object Navigator** and double-click it to open the **Layout Editor** if it is not already open.

2. Select **View** from the menu bar and ensure that **Show View** and **Show Canvas** are displayed as shown in the following screenshot:

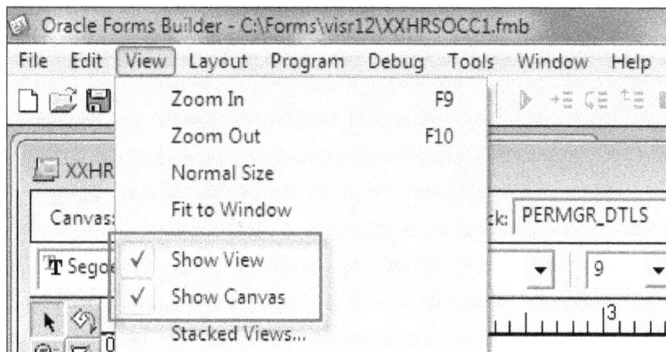

3. Click-and-drag the viewport line so that it is the same size as the canvas, as shown in the following screenshot:

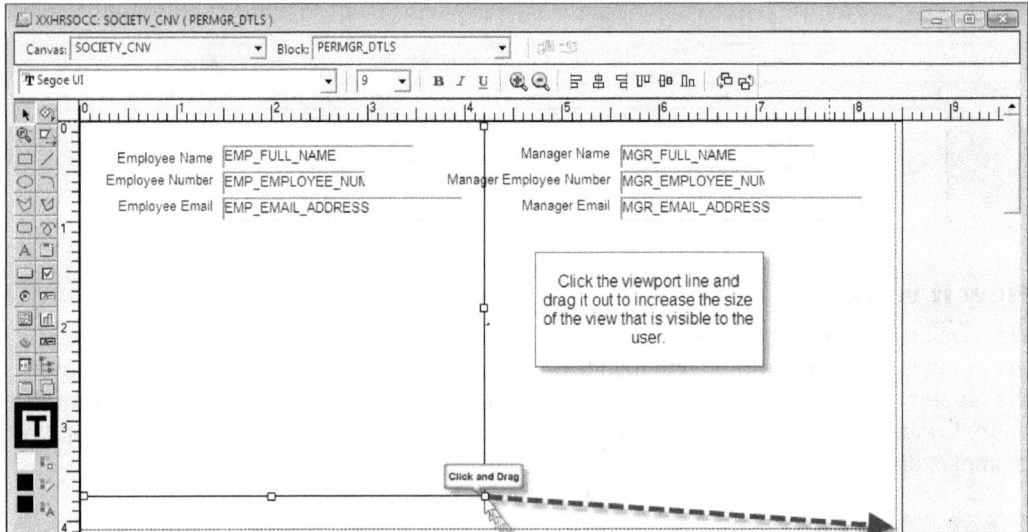

4. **Save** the form.

How it works...

We have set the object properties of our objects and tidied up the objects in the **Layout Editor**. One of the strong features of forms is that the layout is all drag-and-drop, so you can see exactly where objects are positioned and they can be edited as required and in accordance with Oracle's look and feel guidelines. After we have made the changes, the form will look like the following screenshot:

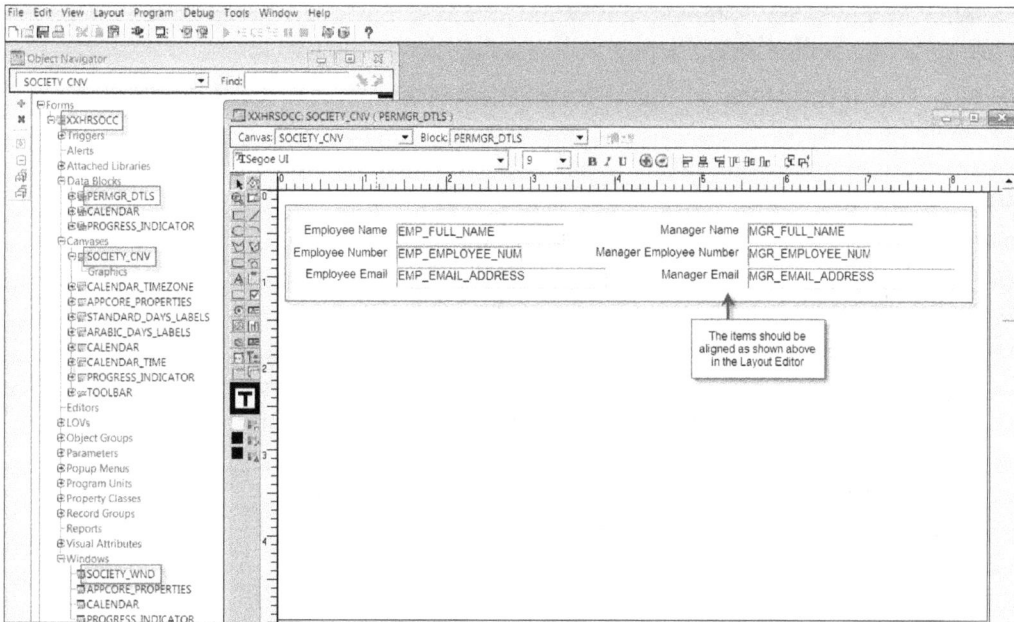

Open the Property Palette of the SOCIETY_WND window
and check whether the **Primary Canvas** property is still set
to SOCIETY_CNV. Also, open the **Property Palette** of the
SOCIETY_CNV window and check whether the **Window** property
of the SOCIETY_CNV canvas is still set to SOCIETY_WND.

Modifying the template code

In this recipe, we are going to modify the code in the TEMPLATE.fmb form. There are
certain triggers that need to be modified when creating a new form. The shell is there, we
just need to modify the code to make the form function properly. We need to modify code
in the following objects:

▸ Modifying the PRE-FORM trigger

▸ Modifying the WHEN-NEW-FORM-INSTANCE trigger

▸ Modifying the APP_CUSTOM procedure

Modifying the PRE-FORM trigger

The PRE-FORM trigger stores version information about the form and it also dictates the first window of the form.

How to do it...

To modify the PRE-FORM trigger, perform the following tasks:

1. Navigate to the form level PRE-FORM trigger and open it.

```
PL/SQL Editor                                                        _  □  ✕

  🖥 🗇   ↶↷   ⊞ ⊞   Name: PRE-FORM                                          ▾

 Type: Trigger              ▾  Object: (Form Level)           ▾

 FND_STANDARD.FORM_INFO('$Revision: 120.0
                         '$Date: 2005/05/06 23:25  $', '$Author: appldev $');
 app_standard.event('PRE-FORM');
 app_window.set_window_position('BLOCKNAME', 'FIRST_WINDOW');
```

2. Make the following changes to the FND_STANDARD.FORM_INFO parameters:

   ❑ Change the $Revision: number to 120.1 (change this each time a new version of the form is released)

   ❑ Change the $Date: to the current date

   ❑ Change the $Author: to your current username

3. Change the first parameter in the call to the procedure called app_window.set_window_position to the main window in our form called SOCIETY_WND.

> The built-in we have used here is not the native forms developer built-in. Oracle EBS has provided a replacement function. For more information, refer to the **Oracle Developer's Guide** from the Release 12 documentation library.

4. The PRE-FORM trigger will now look something similar to the following screenshot:

```
PL/SQL Editor

  🖥 🗇   ↶↷   ⊞ ⊞   Name: PRE-FORM

 Type: Trigger              ▾  Object: (Form Level)           ▾

 FND_STANDARD.FORM_INFO('$Revision: 120.1
                         '$Date: 2011/08/22 22:34  $', '$Author: apenver $');
 app_standard.event('PRE-FORM');
 app_window.set_window_position('SOCIETY_WND', 'FIRST_WINDOW');
```

5. Click on the **Compile** button.

6. Close down the **PL/SQL Editor** window.

How it works...

We need to amend the PRE-FORM trigger details to provide users with information about the form and to set the window properties. If the call to app_window.set_window_position is not changed, then the form will still compile. However, you will get a runtime error because the BLOCKNAME window does not exist in the form any more as we have changed it from the dummy value provided in the **TEMPLATE** form. The form will compile because the block name is surrounded by quotes and is a literal value. It is only at runtime that the literal value is interpreted and hence a runtime error occurs, as the window called BLOCKNAME no longer exists in the form.

Modifying the WHEN-NEW-FORM-INSTANCE trigger

The WHEN-NEW-FORM-INSTANCE trigger stores form and version information about the form and it also dictates the first navigable block of the form.

How to do it...

To modify the WHEN-NEW-FORM-INSTANCE trigger, perform the following tasks:

1. Navigate to the form level WHEN-NEW-FORM-INSTANCE trigger and double-click to open the **PL/SQL Editor**, as shown in the following screenshot:

2. Make the following changes to the FDRCSID parameter:

   ❑ Change the $Header: to XXHRSOCC.fmb

   ❑ Change the $Revision: number to 120.1 (change this each time a new version of the form is released)

   ❑ Change the $Date: to the current date

   ❑ Change the $author: to your current username

3. The `WHEN-NEW-FORM-INSTANCE` trigger will now look something similar to the following screenshot:

```
PL/SQL Editor
                     Name: WHEN-NEW-FORM-INSTANCE
Type: Trigger                    ▼   Object: (Form Level)               ▼
    FDRCSID('$Header: XXHRSOCC.fmb 120.1 2011/08/06 22:56  apenver ship
    APP_STANDARD.EVENT('WHEN-NEW-FORM-INSTANCE');
    --
    -- app_folder.define_folder_block('template test', 'folder_block', 'promp
    -- app_folder.event('VERIFY');
    --
```

4. Click on the **Compile** button.
5. Close down the **PL/SQL Editor** window.

How it works...

We have now updated the form information in the `WHEN-NEW-FORM-INSTANCE` trigger. We need to update the version and date information each time a new version of the form is released.

Modifying the APP_CUSTOM procedure

The `APP_CUSTOM` package consists of two procedures, `close_window` and `open_window`. The `close_window` procedure is called whenever the `WHEN_WINDOW_CLOSED` trigger is fired. The `open_window` procedure is called from the code within the form whenever it may result in a non-modal window being opened. We need to modify these procedures to add our window to the code.

How to do it...

To modify the `APP_CUSTOM` procedure, perform the following steps:

1. Navigate to **Program Units** in the **Object Navigator** and open the `APP_CUSTOM` package body.
2. Scroll down to the `close_window` procedure until you reach the following default code prompting for changes specific to our form:

3. Change the first line of the code that is highlighted in the previous screenshot:

```
if (wnd = '<your first window>') then
```

To the following:

```
if (wnd = 'SOCIETY_WND') then
```

4. Now, scroll down to the open_window procedure until you reach the following code:

5. Change the following line of code:

```
if (wnd = '<a window>') then
```

To the following:

```
if (wnd = 'SOCIETY_WND') then
```

6. Click on the **Compile** button.

7. Close down the **PL/SQL Editor** window.

8. **Save** the form.

How it works...

When we create our custom form, there is some code that is already written for us. We need to modify the code to determine the actions required when we navigate to a window specified here. As the code suggests, we are positioning the window, resetting any master detail relations, and specifying which block to navigate to. In addition, we can write code to perform other actions here as well when we navigate to a window.

Adding a detail block to a form

We are now ready to create a detail block to our form. The detail block is going to store information relating to societies the employee belongs to. The block is a detail block to the PERMGR_DTLS block we have already created. The foreign key is the PERSON_ID. In this recipe, we are going to perform the following tasks:

▶ Creating a lookup

▶ Creating a detail block

▶ Setting the block properties

▶ Setting the item properties

▶ Creating a relationship between the master and detail blocks

▶ Adding a record indicator to the block

> The following recipe assumes that you have created a custom schema called XXHR. If you do not have a custom schema, follow the recipe in *Chapter 6, Utilities* called *Creating a custom schema*. We have registered the custom application in *Chapter 1, Creating Concurrent Programs* but we need to create the directory structure on the applications tier. This is where we need to put our custom form.

We have already created a table called XXHR_PER_SOCIETIES to store the societies data in at the beginning of this chapter. The detail block is based upon a view called XXHR_PER_SOCIETIES_V. A synonym was created so that the table was accessible from the **APPS** user. I have assumed that the custom schema is XXHR.

Creating a lookup

If you look at the table definition, you will see that there is a column called **Code**. In the database, we will be storing the code of the society in this field. However, we want to be able to have a mechanism to be able to add new societies and clubs and also we want a more user friendly name to display in the form. To achieve this we will create a lookup which will allow us to add new values without having to modify the form.

How to do it...

To create a lookup, perform the following steps:

1. Log in to Oracle and select the **Application Developer** responsibility.
2. Navigate to **Application | Lookups | Application Object Library** and the **Application Object Library Lookups** window will open.
3. Populate the form header, as shown in the following table:

Field name	Value
Type	XXHR_SOCIETY_LOV
Meaning	List of Societies
Application	XXHR Custom Application
Description	List of Societies

4. Populate the detail block with the following data:

Code	Meaning	Description
CS01	Get Fit Sports Club	Get Fit Sports Club
CS02	Badminton Club	Badminton Club
CS03	Out and About Society	Out and About Society
CS04	Sports and Social Society	Sports and Social Society
CS05	Slimmer Club	Slimmer Club

5. The form should look similar to the following screenshot:

6. Click on the **Save** button in the toolbar (or press *Ctrl + S*) to save the record.
7. Exit the form.

How it works...

We have created a lookup that we will use in our form so that users must enter a value from a list. This is a common way of controlling what values are permitted to be entered by users. Free text fields are very difficult to report upon and you often get duplicate values. The downside is that the list needs to be maintained each time a new record is required.

Creating a detail block

Now that we have created the database objects, we can begin creating the detail block for recording details relating to societies and clubs that an employee may be a member of. The block will be a multi-record block that will be related to the master block via the PERSON_ID field.

How to do it...

To create a detail block, perform the following tasks:

1. Open the XXHRSOCC.fmb form in the forms builder.
2. Navigate to **Data Blocks** and highlight the PERMGER_DTLS block.
3. Click on the **+** button in the left toolbar to start the block wizard.
4. Select **Use the Data Block Wizard** from the **New Data Block** pop-up.
5. Click on the **OK** button.
6. In the **Data Block Wizard**, select **Table or view** and click on **Next**.

7. In the **Table or view** field, enter XXHR_PER_SOCIETIES_V and press *Tab*.

8. Click on **>>** to shift all of the fields over to the **Database Items** section, as shown in the following screenshot and click on **Next**:

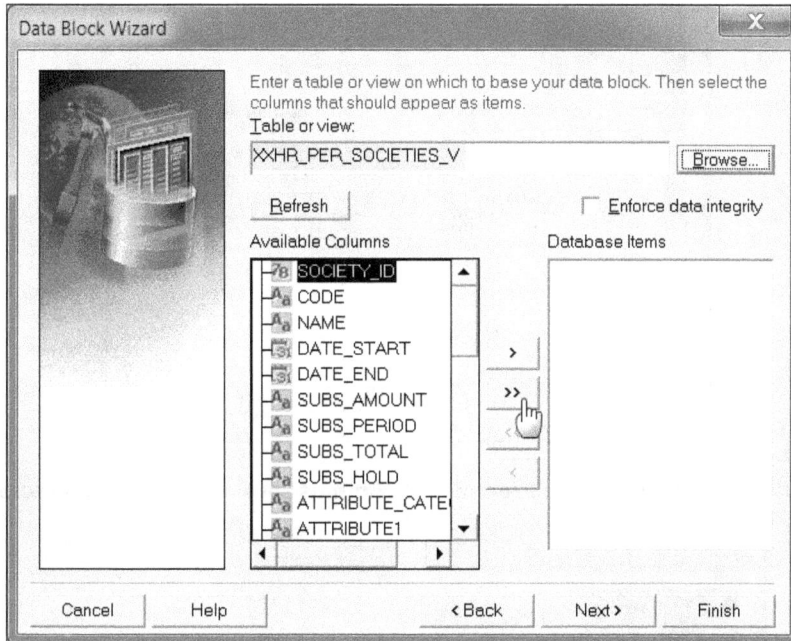

9. Click on **Next** on the **Create Relationship** screen.

10. Change the **Data Block** name to PER_SOCIETIES and click on **Next**.

11. Select **Create the data block, and then call the Layout Wizard** radio button and click on **Finish**.

12. In the **Layout Wizard**, if you get the **Welcome** screen click on **Next**.

13. Set the **Canvas** to SOCIETY_CNV (it may already default to this) and click on **Next**.

14. Select the following columns from the **Available Items** (click each item whilst holding down the *Ctrl* button):

   ❑ NAME

   ❑ DATE_START

   ❑ DATE_END

   ❑ SUBS_AMOUNT

   ❑ SUBS_PERIOD

   ❑ SUBS_TOTAL

   ❑ SUBS_HOLD

15. Click the **>** button to shift the selected fields to the **Displayed Items** side and click on **Next**, as shown in the following screenshot:

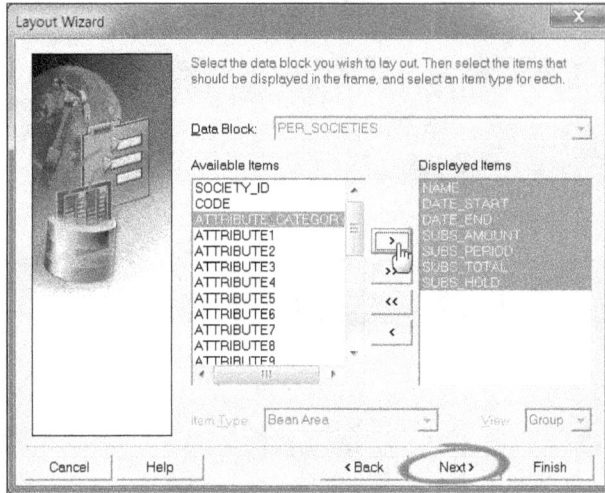

16. In the next screen, set the **Prompt** and **Width** as shown in the following screenshot:

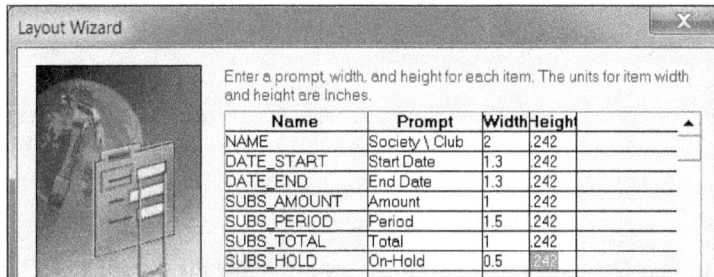

Name	Prompt	Width	Height
NAME	Society \ Club	2	.242
DATE_START	Start Date	1.3	.242
DATE_END	End Date	1.3	.242
SUBS_AMOUNT	Amount	1	.242
SUBS_PERIOD	Period	1.5	.242
SUBS_TOTAL	Total	1	.242
SUBS_HOLD	On-Hold	0.5	.242

17. Select **Tabular** as the **Layout Style** and click on **Finish**.

18. The **Layout Editor** will open, as shown in the following screenshot:

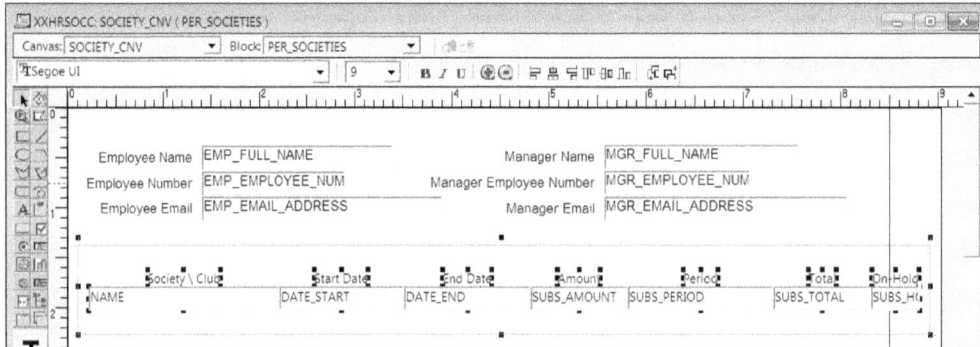

19. In the **Object Navigator**, expand **Canvases | SOCIETY_CNV | Graphics** and delete the **FRAME** automatically generated by the **Layout Wizard**.

20. **Save** the form.

How it works...

We have used the block wizard to create our detail block. This gives us a good place to start but we need to do a bit more before the detail block is complete.

Setting the block properties

We are now going to set the block properties of the PER_SOCIETIES block.

How to do it...

To set the block properties, perform the following tasks:

1. Open the **Property Palette** for the PER_SOCIETIES block.

2. Set the **Subclass Information** property to BLOCK, as shown in the following screenshot:

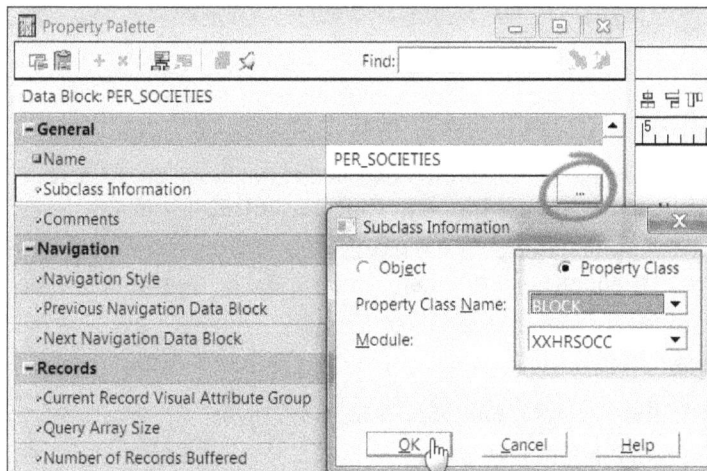

3. Set the following additional block properties:

    ❏ **Previous Navigation Data Block**: PERMGR_DTLS

    ❏ **Next Navigation Data Block**: PERMGR_DTLS

    ❏ **Number of Records Displayed**: 6

    ❏ **Show Scroll Bar**: Yes

    ❏ **Scroll Bar Canvas**: SOCIETY_CNV

    ❑   **Scroll Bar X Position**: 8.609

    ❑   **Scroll Bar Y Position**: 1.517

    ❑   **Scroll Bar Width**: .2

    ❑   **Scroll Bar Length**: 1.467

4. Open the **Property Palette** for the PERMGR_DTLS block and set the following properties:

    ❑   **Previous Navigation Data Block**: PER_SOCIETIES

    ❑   **Next Navigation Data Block**: PER_SOCIETIES

How it works...

We have set the block properties for our multi-record block. We are going to display six records and have set the navigation properties of the block. To show the scroll bar, the **Show Scroll Bar** property must be set to Yes.

Setting the item properties

We are now going to set all of the item properties as we did previously for the master block earlier in this chapter. We will always do this to maintain the look and feel.

How to do it...

To set the item properties, perform the following tasks:

1. We are now going to set the item properties of the items on the screen. In the **Object Navigator**, expand to **Data Blocks | PER_SOCIETIES | Items**.

2. Open the **Property Palette** for the NAME, SUBS_AMOUNT, SUBS_PEERIOD, SUBS_TOTAL, and SUBS_HOLD items and set the following properties:

    ❑   **Subclass Information**: TEXT_ITEM

    ❑   **Prompt Justification**: Start

    ❑   **Prompt Attachment Edge**: Top

    ❑   **Prompt Alignment**: Start

    ❑   **Prompt Attachment Offset**: 0

    ❑   **Prompt Alignment Offset**: .05

3. Open the **Property Palette** for the DATE_START and DATE_END items and set the following properties:

    ❑   **Subclass Information**: TEXT_ITEM_DATE

    ❑   **Prompt Justification**: Start

    ❑   **Prompt Attachment Edge**: Top

- ❑ **Prompt Alignment**: Start
- ❑ **Prompt Attachment Offset**: 0
- ❑ **Prompt Alignment Offset**: .05

4. Open the **Property Palette** for the **NAME** item and set the **Required** property to Yes.

> You can open up the **Layout Editor** and open the **Property Palette** from there. You need to right-click the items in the **Layout Editor** and select **Property Palette** from the pop-up menu or just double-click the item. You can also select multiple items and set the properties in the **Property Palette** in one go. To do this, open the **Property Palette** and then select multiple items (keep the *Ctrl* key pressed and click on each item). When multiple items are selected and the property differs you will see ***** in the property value.

How it works...

We have now set the item properties for the PER_SOCIETIES block. We have set the **Subclass Information** to inherit the properties of each type of item.

Creating a relationship between the master and detail blocks

Now we are going to create a relationship between the master and detail block. This will automatically create associated triggers and code that will query the detail block when the master block is queried.

How to do it...

To create a relationship between the master block and the detail block, perform the following tasks:

1. In the **Object Navigator**, expand the **Data Blocks | PERMGR_DTLS** nodes.
2. Click on the **Relations** node and click the **+** button in the left toolbar to create a new relationship.

3. Complete the wizard with the following details:

   ❑ **Detail Block**: PER_SOCIETIES

   ❑ **Join Condition**: EMP_PERSON_ID = PERSON_ID

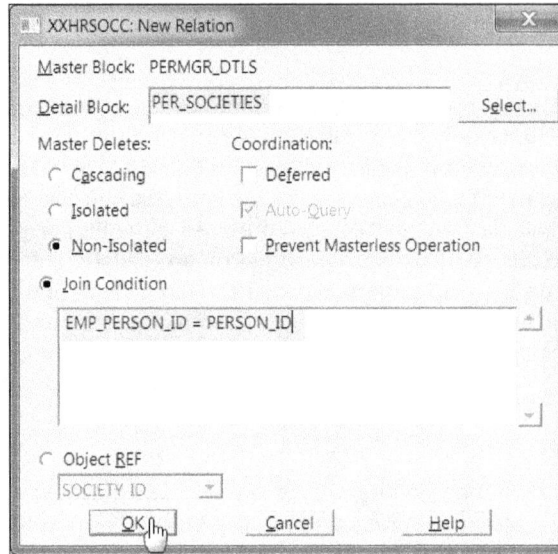

4. Click on the **OK** button.
5. **Save** the form.

How it works...

Creating a relationship between blocks will automatically generate code that will maintain a link between the two blocks. The **Join Condition** allows forms builder to create the code that will automatically query detailed records when master records are queried back.

Adding a record indicator to the block

Finally, to complete the basics of our form before we need to do some coding, we need to add a record indicator to the PER_SOCIETIES multi-record block. There is is a little bar on the left-hand side, which shows the current record the cursor is on.

How to do it...

To add a record indicator to the detail block, perform the following tasks:

1. In the **Object Navigator**, expand the **Data Blocks | PER_SOCIETIES | Items** nodes.

2. Click on the item before the **NAME** item and click the **+** icon from the left-hand toolbar to add an item.

3. Open the **Property Palette** for the item that has just been created and set the following properties:

   - ❑ **Name**: CURRENT_RECORD_INDICATOR
   - ❑ **Subclass Information**: CURRENT_RECORD_INDICATOR
   - ❑ **Canvas**: SOCIETY_CNV
   - ❑ **X Position**: .1
   - ❑ **Y Position**: 1.5

4. After the item properties have been set, move the items close to one another as shown in the following screenshot. The TEXT_ITEM_DATE property class changes the width of date items. To get precision when moving items, select the item and use the *up* and *down* arrow keys to move it around.

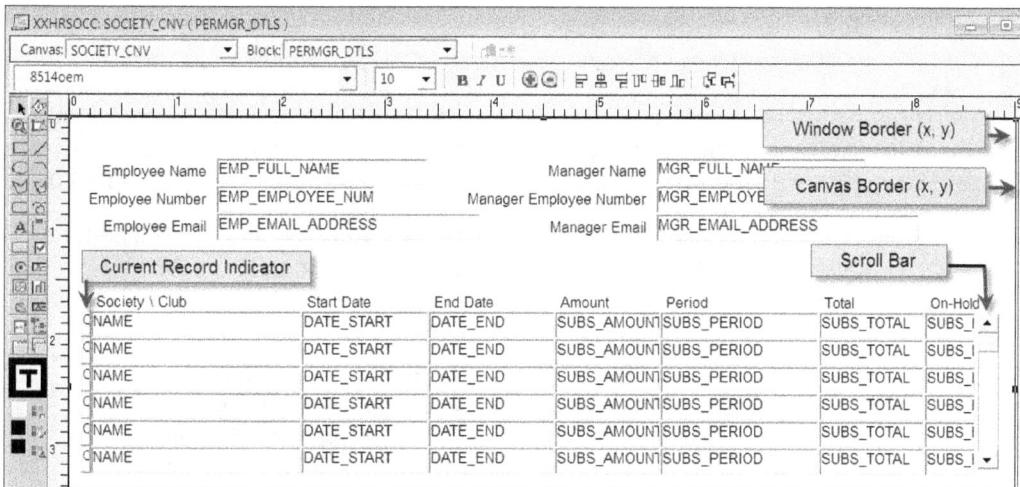

5. **Save** the form.

How it works...

We have added the current record indicator to the detail block and a scroll bar. Ensure that all of the items are within the canvas border. If they are not, drag the canvas and window borders so that the screen is similar to the one above. If any items are not on the canvas, the form will show an error when you attempt to compile it.

Adding insert, update, and delete events

Now that we have created the forms objects, it is time to start adding some code. We need to add code to perform inserts, updates, and deletes. As we have based the form on views, we need to trigger the events and then we need to write code to call database procedures to transact data. There are four triggers we need to create on each block where we need to perform transactions. In this example, the only block where we want to do any transactions is the PER_SOCIETIES block. When we insert data, we will also need to increment a sequence number for the SOCIETY_ID column. We will need to perform the following tasks to trigger and code database transactions within our form:

- ▶ Creating a program unit package specification
- ▶ Creating a program unit package body
- ▶ Creating ON-INSERT, ON-UPDATE, ON-DELETE, and ON-LOCK triggers
- ▶ Creating PRE-INSERT and PRE-UPDATE triggers to set the WHO columns

We have created a sequence as we need to generate a unique SOCIETY_ID before we can perform an insert. The sequence was created at the start of the chapter called XXHR_PER_ SOCIETIES_SEQ and a synonym was also created so that it was accessible to the **APPS** user.

We also created a database package called XXHR_PER_SOCIETIES_PVT that will perform the database transactions. Packages that we create are always owned by the **APPS** user and we will call it from our form.

> Oracle has created many APIs for transactions to its own standard tables. If we ever need to perform actions against Oracle's standard tables, we must always use the APIs that Oracle provides. If you do not, then the application will become unsupported by Oracle so this is an extremely important point to remember. Oracle's own APIs often perform transactions against multiple tables and the database integrity will be compromised if their APIs are not used. However, as our block is based upon a custom table, we must create our own API.

Creating a program unit package specification

We need to create program units in the form to call our APIs. Generally in forms a majority of code will reside in program units or libraries. If you need to write more than one or two lines of code in a trigger, it probably needs to be written as a procedure and called from the trigger.

How to do it...

To create a new program unit, perform the following tasks:

1. In the **Object Navigator**, click on **Program Units**.

2. Click on the + button in the left-hand toolbar to create a new package specification.

3. In the **Name** field, type PER_SOCIETIES and select **Package Spec**, as shown in the following screenshot:

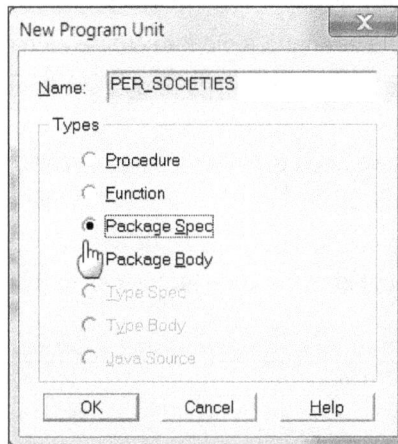

4. In **PL/SQL Editor**, we need to add four procedures as follows:

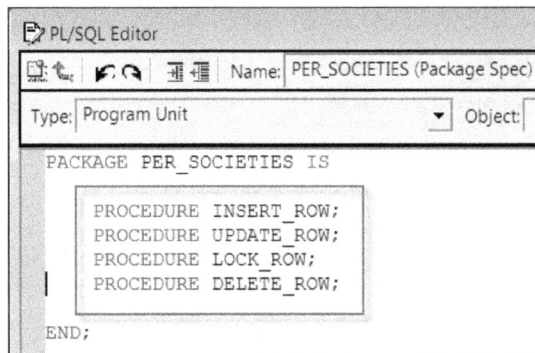

5. **Save** the form.

How it works...

We need to create code that will perform the insert, update, delete, and lock functions. We will call database procedures to perform the database activities but will perform validation and set some value attributes before we make the database call. The usual naming convention would be to call the procedure by the same name as the block it performs actions on.

Creating a program unit package body

Now we need to create the package body.

How to do it...

To add the package body, perform the following tasks:

1. In the **Object Navigator**, click on **Program Units**.

2. Click the **+** button in the left-hand toolbar to create a new package body.

3. In the **Name** field, type PER_SOCIETIES and select **Package Body** as shown in the next screenshot.

4. In the **PL/SQL Editor**, we need to write the code to call the database package XXHR_PER_SOCIETIES_PVT. The code is in the completed form in the download bundle for the book.

   The following screenshot is of the code for the call to the database package to insert a record:

```
1    PACKAGE BODY PER_SOCIETIES IS
2      PROCEDURE INSERT_ROW IS
3      BEGIN
4        xxhr_per_societies_pvt.insert_row( p_SOCIETY_ID => :per_societies.society_id,
5          p_CODE => :per_societies.CODE,
6          p_SUBS_PERIOD => :per_societies.SUBS_PERIOD,
7          p_DATE_END => :per_societies.DATE_END ,
8          p_DATE_START => :per_societies.DATE_START,
9          p_SUBS_HOLD => :per_societies.SUBS_HOLD,
10         p_SUBS_AMOUNT => :per_societies.SUBS_AMOUNT,
11         p_SUBS_TOTAL => :per_societies.SUBS_TOTAL,
12         p_PERSON_ID => :per_societies.PERSON_ID,
13         p_ATTRIBUTE_CATEGORY => :per_societies.ATTRIBUTE_CATEGORY,
14         p_ATTRIBUTE1 => :per_societies.ATTRIBUTE1,
15         p_ATTRIBUTE2 => :per_societies.ATTRIBUTE2,
16         p_ATTRIBUTE3 => :per_societies.ATTRIBUTE3 ,
17         p_ATTRIBUTE4 => :per_societies.ATTRIBUTE4,
18         p_ATTRIBUTE5 => :per_societies.ATTRIBUTE5,
19         p_ATTRIBUTE6 => :per_societies.ATTRIBUTE6 ,
20         p_ATTRIBUTE7 => :per_societies.ATTRIBUTE7,
21         p_ATTRIBUTE8 => :per_societies.ATTRIBUTE8 ,
22         p_ATTRIBUTE9 => :per_societies.ATTRIBUTE9 ,
23         p_ATTRIBUTE10 => :per_societies.ATTRIBUTE10 ,
24         p_ATTRIBUTE11 => :per_societies.ATTRIBUTE11 ,
25         p_ATTRIBUTE12 => :per_societies.ATTRIBUTE12 ,
26         p_ATTRIBUTE13 => :per_societies.ATTRIBUTE13 ,
27         p_ATTRIBUTE14 => :per_societies.ATTRIBUTE14 ,
28         p_ATTRIBUTE15 => :per_societies.ATTRIBUTE15 ,
29         p_ATTRIBUTE16 => :per_societies.ATTRIBUTE16 ,
30         p_ATTRIBUTE17 => :per_societies.ATTRIBUTE17 ,
31         p_ATTRIBUTE18 => :per_societies.ATTRIBUTE18 ,
32         p_ATTRIBUTE19 => :per_societies.ATTRIBUTE19,
33         p_ATTRIBUTE20 => :per_societies.ATTRIBUTE20 ,
34         p_CREATION_DATE => :per_societies.CREATION_DATE ,
35         p_CREATED_BY => :per_societies.CREATED_BY,
36         p_LAST_UPDATE_DATE => :per_societies.LAST_UPDATE_DATE,
37         p_LAST_UPDATED_BY => :per_societies.LAST_UPDATED_BY ,
38         p_LAST_UPDATE_LOGIN => :per_societies.LAST_UPDATE_LOGIN);
39    END;
```

The following screenshot is of the code for the call to the database package to update a record:

```
41      PROCEDURE UPDATE_ROW IS
42      BEGIN
43          xxhr_per_societies_pvt.update_row( p_SOCIETY_ID => :per_societies.society_id,
44              p_CODE => :per_societies.CODE,
45              p_SUBS_PERIOD => :per_societies.SUBS_PERIOD,
46              p_DATE_END => :per_societies.DATE_END ,
47              p_DATE_START => :per_societies.DATE_START,
48              p_SUBS_HOLD => :per_societies.SUBS_HOLD,
49              p_SUBS_AMOUNT => :per_societies.SUBS_AMOUNT,
50              p_SUBS_TOTAL => :per_societies.SUBS_TOTAL,
51              p_PERSON_ID => :per_societies.PERSON_ID,
52              p_ATTRIBUTE_CATEGORY => :per_societies.ATTRIBUTE_CATEGORY,
53              p_ATTRIBUTE1 => :per_societies.ATTRIBUTE1,
54              p_ATTRIBUTE2 => :per_societies.ATTRIBUTE2,
55              p_ATTRIBUTE3 => :per_societies.ATTRIBUTE3 ,
56              p_ATTRIBUTE4 => :per_societies.ATTRIBUTE4,
57              p_ATTRIBUTE5 => :per_societies.ATTRIBUTE5,
58              p_ATTRIBUTE6 => :per_societies.ATTRIBUTE6 ,
59              p_ATTRIBUTE7 => :per_societies.ATTRIBUTE7,
60              p_ATTRIBUTE8 => :per_societies.ATTRIBUTE8 ,
61              p_ATTRIBUTE9 => :per_societies.ATTRIBUTE9 ,
62              p_ATTRIBUTE10 => :per_societies.ATTRIBUTE10 ,
63              p_ATTRIBUTE11 => :per_societies.ATTRIBUTE11 ,
64              p_ATTRIBUTE12 => :per_societies.ATTRIBUTE12 ,
65              p_ATTRIBUTE13 => :per_societies.ATTRIBUTE13 ,
66              p_ATTRIBUTE14 => :per_societies.ATTRIBUTE14 ,
67              p_ATTRIBUTE15 => :per_societies.ATTRIBUTE15 ,
68              p_ATTRIBUTE16 => :per_societies.ATTRIBUTE16 ,
69              p_ATTRIBUTE17 => :per_societies.ATTRIBUTE17 ,
70              p_ATTRIBUTE18 => :per_societies.ATTRIBUTE18 ,
71              p_ATTRIBUTE19 => :per_societies.ATTRIBUTE19,
72              p_ATTRIBUTE20 => :per_societies.ATTRIBUTE20 ,
73              p_CREATION_DATE => :per_societies.CREATION_DATE ,
74              p_CREATED_BY => :per_societies.CREATED_BY,
75              p_LAST_UPDATE_DATE => :per_societies.LAST_UPDATE_DATE,
76              p_LAST_UPDATED_BY => :per_societies.LAST_UPDATED_BY ,
77              p_LAST_UPDATE_LOGIN => :per_societies.LAST_UPDATE_LOGIN);
78      END;
```

The following screenshot is of the code for the call to the database package to lock and delete a record:

```
80      PROCEDURE LOCK_ROW IS
81      BEGIN
82          null;
83      END;
84
85      PROCEDURE DELETE_ROW IS
86      BEGIN
87          xxhr_per_societies_pvt.delete_row(P_SOCIETY_ID => :per_societies.society_id);
88      END;
89
90  END;
```

You may have noticed that the `ON-LOCK` trigger contains just a `null` statement. This is an example of how you can suppress default transaction processing by including the `null` statement in the appropriate `ON-EVENT` trigger. We have done this in the `ON-LOCK` trigger to suppress default locking. Oracle Forms will attempt to obtain locks as users query and update records. The `On-Lock` trigger fires whenever Oracle Forms requests a lock. You can write code that will explicitly handle locking such as:

```
DECLARE
   RESOURCE_BUSY EXCEPTION;
   PRAGMA EXCEPTION_INIT(RESOURCE_BUSY, -54);
   CURSOR c_Lock IS
     SELECT ID FROM XXHR_PER_SOCIETIES
         WHERE SOCIETY_ID=:PER_SOCIETIES.SOCIETY_ID
          FOR UPDATE OF ID NOWAIT;
   v_count NUMBER;
BEGIN
   OPEN c_Lock;
   FETCH c_Lock INTO v_count;
   CLOSE c_Lock;
EXCEPTION WHEN RESOURCE_BUSY THEN
   fnd_message.debug('The record cannot be locked at present');
     RAISE FORM_TRIGGER_FIALURE;
END;
```

5. **Compile** the code.
6. **Save** the form.

How it works...

We need to call the database package to perform the insert, update, and delete actions when they occur in the form.

Creating ON-INSERT, ON-UPDATE, ON-DELETE, and ON-LOCK triggers

We are going to add four triggers to our PER_SOCIETIES block to capture events when a user actions a COMMIT statement.

How to do it...

To add the triggers, perform the following tasks:

1. In the **Object Navigator**, expand the **Data Blocks | PER_SOCIETIES** node.
2. Click on **Triggers** and click on the **+** button in the left-hand toolbar to add a trigger.
3. From the list of available triggers select ON-INSERT.

4. In the **PL/SQL Editor**, type the following call to our program unit:

```
per_societies.insert_row;
```

5. Click on the **Compile** button to compile the code.

6. Close the editor.

7. Highlight **Triggers** and click on the **+** button in the left-hand toolbar to add a trigger.

8. From the list of available triggers select `ON-UPDATE`.

9. In **PL/SQL Editor**, type the following call to our program unit:

```
per_societies.update_row;
```

10. Click on the **Compile** button to compile the code.

11. Close the editor.

12. Highlight **Triggers** and click on the **+** button in the left-hand toolbar to add a trigger.

13. From the list of available triggers select `ON-DELETE`.

14. In **PL/SQL Editor**, type the following call to our program unit:

```
per_societies.delete_row;
```

15. Click on the **Compile** button to compile the code.

16. Close the editor.

17. Highlight **Triggers** and click on the **+** button in the left-hand toolbar to add a trigger.

18. From the list of available triggers select `ON-LOCK`.

19. In **PL/SQL Editor**, type the following call to our program unit:

```
per_societies.lock_row;
```

20. Click on the **Compile** button to compile the code.

21. Close the editor.

You should now see that there are four triggers created on the `PER_SOCIETIES` block, as shown in the following screenshot:

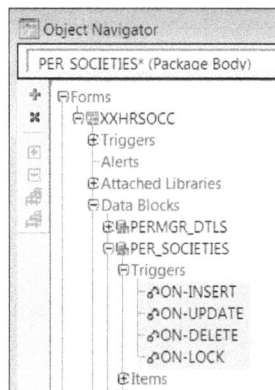

How it works...

When the form triggers an insert, update, lock or delete action, the corresponding ON trigger will fire. In the trigger, we will call our package in the **Program Units** to perform any validation and setting values before it calls the database package to perform the database activities.

Creating PRE-INSERT and PRE-UPDATE triggers to set the WHO columns

When we are performing inserts and updates, Oracle provides some standard fields to audit changes to a record and who made the changes. These are known as the **WHO** fields and they are CREATED_BY, CREATION_DATE, LAST_UPDATED_BY, LAST_UPDATE_DATE, and LAST_UPDATE_LOGIN. We can call a standard package that will set the data in these fields before the database transaction occurs. This is done in the PRE-INSERT and PRE-UPDATE triggers.

How to do it...

To add code to set the WHO data, perform the following tasks:

1. In the **Object Navigator**, expand the **Data Blocks | PER_SOCIETIES** block.
2. Highlight **Triggers** and click on the **+** button in the left-hand toolbar to add a trigger.
3. From the list of available triggers, select PRE-INSERT.
4. In the **PL/SQL Editor**, type the following call to our program unit:

    FND_STANDARD.SET_WHO;

5. Click on the **Compile** button to compile the code.
6. Close the editor.
7. Highlight **Triggers** and click on the **+** button in the left-hand toolbar to add a trigger.
8. From the list of available triggers, select PRE-UPDATE.
9. In the **PL/SQL Editor** type the following call to our program unit:

    FND_STANDARD.SET_WHO;

10. Click on the **Compile** button to compile the code.
11. Close the editor.

We have now created two triggers (PRE-INSERT and PRE-UPDATE) that call the Oracle FND_STANDARD API to set the WHO columns, as shown in the following screenshot:

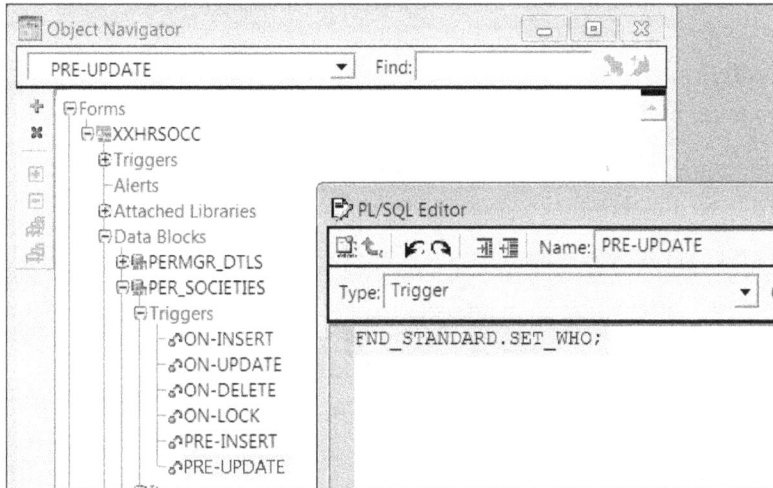

How it works...

The WHO columns record information about when a record was created and updated and by whom. We do not have to set the values for these fields as a call to the standard package will set the values for us. We always set the WHO columns in this way for our forms.

Deploying forms

Now we have created the form, we should test it. We cannot run the form locally on our PC, so we need to transfer it to the application tier and compile it. We also need to register the form and create a function for it. Then we can add the function to a menu. In this recipe, we are going to perform the following tasks:

- ▸ Registering a form
- ▸ Creating a function that calls a form
- ▸ Adding a form to a menu
- ▸ FTP the form to the application tier
- ▸ Compiling a form
- ▸ Testing a form

Registering a form

Before we can run the form, it needs to be registered in the application.

How to do it...

To register the form, perform the following tasks:

1. Log in to Oracle and select the **Application Developer** responsibility.
2. Navigate to **Application | Form** and the **Forms** window will open.
3. Add a record with the following data:

Item name	Item value
Form	XXHRSOCC
Application	XXHR Custom Application
User Form Name	Clubs and Societies Form
Description	Clubs and Societies Form

The screen should look similar to the following screenshot:

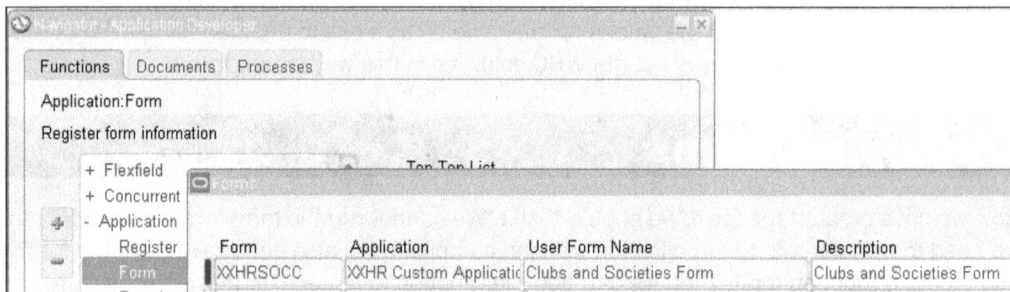

4. Click on the **Save** button in the toolbar (or press *Ctrl + S*) to save the record.

> The application defined here is what links the form executable on the server. This is where Oracle will search for the executable (.fmx) file at runtime. When we generate the form on the server, it must reside in the *top* directory associated with the application defined here.

5. **Exit** the form.

How it works...

We need to register the form before we can call it in Oracle. When we call a form, we actually call a function that calls the form. To create the function, we must have the form registered first.

Creating a function that calls a form

We will now create the function that calls the form.

How to do it...

To create the function, perform the following tasks:

1. Log in to Oracle and select the **Application Developer** responsibility.
2. Navigate to **Application | Function** and the **Form Functions** window will open.
3. Add a record with the following data:

Tab	Item name	Item value
Description	Function	XXHR_EMP_SOCIETY
Description	User Function Name	Employee Clubs and Societies
Description	Description	Employee Clubs and Societies
Properties	Type	Form
Form	Form	Clubs and Societies Form

4. Click on the **Save** button in the toolbar (or press *Ctrl + S*) to save the record.
5. **Exit** the form.

How it works...

The form function is what we call to launch the form. We add the function to a menu to make it available to a responsibility.

Adding a form to a menu

We will now add the form function to our responsibility.

How to do it...

To add the function to our responsibility, perform the following tasks:.

1. Log in to Oracle with the **Application Developer** responsibility.
2. Navigate to **Application | Menu** and the **Menus** window will open.

3. Press *F11* to enter a query.

4. Type XXHR_TEST_MENU in the menu and press *Ctrl + F11* to query back the menu we created in *Chapter 1, Creating Concurrent Programs*.

5. Enter data as in the following table for the detail records:

Seq	Prompt	Submenu	Function	Description
30	Societies Form		Employee Clubs and Societies	Employee Clubs and Societies

6. Click on the **Save** button in the toolbar (or press *Ctrl + S*) to save the record.

7. **Exit** the form.

How it works...

The form will now appear in the menu for our responsibility that has this menu assigned to it.

FTP the form to the application tier

Now we are going to compile the form on the server. We need to FTP the form from the local PC to the application tier.

How to do it...

To FTP the form, perform the following tasks:

1. Open **WinSCP** (or your preferred FTP client).

2. Copy the XXHRSOCC.fmb form to the $AU_TOP/forms/US directory, as shown in the following screenshot:

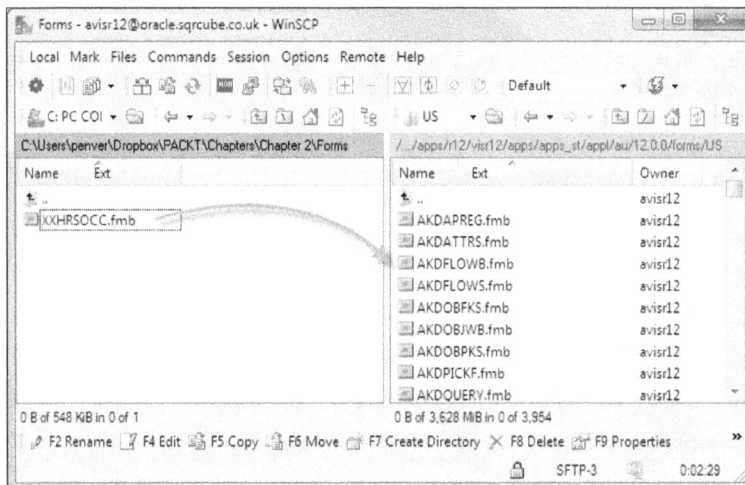

How it works...

All form binaries (.fmb) files are located in the $AU_TOP/forms/US directory (assuming that the language was US. If the installation is in a different language, then the directory US would be the two character acronym for the language that is installed). The executable files (.fmx) are located in the PRODUCTTOP directories. When we compile a form, we will specify the location where the executable will be generated. When the form is registered in Oracle, it will be registered with an **Application**. The directory for the **Application** is the PRODUCT_TOP where Oracle will look for the .fmx file. For example, if the **Application** the form is registered with is XXHR Custom Application, then at runtime Oracle will look for the executable in the $XXHR_TOP/forms/US directory. Also, it is worth bearing in mind that if any reference forms do not exist in the $AU_TOP/forms/<LANG> directory, then they will require the form's path environment variable in the environment file to be updated to contain the path of the referenced forms.

Compiling a form

We will now compile the form in the command line. We need to open a **Putty** session and connect to the application server to compile our forms.

How to do it...

To compile the form, perform the following tasks:

1. Open **Putty** and connect to the application tier.

2. Set the environment.

3. Navigate to $AU_TOP/forms/US directory.

4. Compile the form with the following command:

   ```
   frmcmp_batchmodule=$AU_TOP/forms/US/XXHRSOCC.fmb userid=apps/
   appsoutput_file=$XXHR_TOP/forms/US/XXHRSOCC.fmxcompile_all=special
   ```

> In Release 11*i* the command would be in the format f60gen module=<formname>.fmb userid=apps/<apps_pwd> output_file=$XX_TOP/forms/US/<formname>.fmx.

5. Navigate to $XXHR_TOP/forms/US and check to see that the XXHRSOCC.fmx file exists (if it already exists check the timestamp).

How it works...

The form will be compiled and the executable will be generated in the output_file directory specified in the command line. The APPL_TOP in the output file must be the same as the APPL_TOP for the application we registered the form with. For example, our form was registered with the XXHR Custom Application. This application is registered to the $XXHR_TOP directory on the application server.

Testing a form

We now want to perform a simple test to see if we can open the form.

How to do it...

To test the form, perform the following tasks:

1. Log in to Oracle with the **XXEBS Extending e-Business Suite** responsibility.
2. Navigate to the **Societies Form** and the societies and clubs form will open as shown in the following screenshot:

How it works...

We have tested that the form opens as expected, which means that we have generated the form in the correct directory on the application server.

Adding buttons, list, and checkbox items

Now that we have created the form and it is running, we want to add some buttons and change the types of fields that we have created in the form. In this recipe, we are going to perform the following tasks:

- Adding OK and Cancel buttons
- Modifying the layout
- Adding triggers to the buttons

- Creating an LOV for the society name field
- Configuring the date fields
- Creating a list item
- Creating a checkbox item
- Testing the form

Adding OK and Cancel buttons

We are going to add two buttons. We will add an **OK** button which will save and exit the form. We will also add a **Cancel** button which will exit the form without performing any validation. We are going to add the buttons to the PERMGR_DTLS block.

How to do it...

To add buttons to our form, perform the following tasks:

1. In the forms developer, navigate to **Data Blocks | PERMGR_DTLS | Items**.
2. Click on the **+** button twice to add two new items.
3. Set the following properties of the first item:
   - **Name**: OK_BTN
   - **Subclass Information (Property Class)**: BUTTON
   - **Label**: &OK
   - **Canvas**: SOCIETY_CNV
   - **X Position**: 6.358
   - **Y Position**: 3.525

> You will notice the & on the label of the button. This will underline the **O** so that it can be used as a shortcut key.

4. Set the following properties of the second item:
   - **Name**: CANCEL_BTN
   - **Subclass Information (Property Class)**: BUTTON
   - **Label**: &Cancel
   - **Canvas**: SOCIETY_CNV
   - **X Position**: 7.542
   - **Y Position**: 3.525

5. In the **Object Navigator**, select and drag the two buttons to the end of the block items, as shown in the following screenshot:

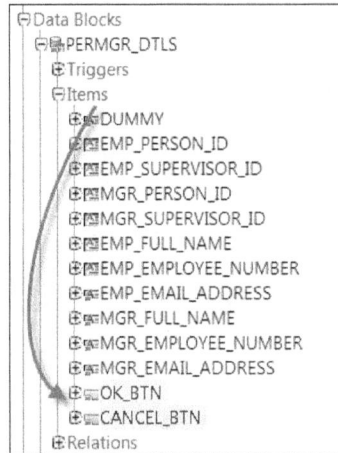

```
⊟Data Blocks
  ⊟⊞PERMGR_DTLS
    ⊞Triggers
    ⊟Items
      ⊞ DUMMY
      ⊞ EMP_PERSON_ID
      ⊞ EMP_SUPERVISOR_ID
      ⊞ MGR_PERSON_ID
      ⊞ MGR_SUPERVISOR_ID
      ⊞ EMP_FULL_NAME
      ⊞ EMP_EMPLOYEE_NUMBER
      ⊞ EMP_EMAIL_ADDRESS
      ⊞ MGR_FULL_NAME
      ⊞ MGR_EMPLOYEE_NUMBER
      ⊞ MGR_EMAIL_ADDRESS
      ⊞ OK_BTN
      ⊞ CANCEL_BTN
  ⊞Relations
```

How it works...

We have created two buttons for our form. We have also moved them to the bottom of the items list. If the **Next Navigation Item** and **Previous Navigation Item** properties are not set, Oracle will navigate through the items in the order in which they are placed in the items list. It is good practice to move items in the navigator in the order in which we want them to be navigated at runtime.

Modifying the layout

We are now going to modify the layout so that the items are aligned and there is spacing as per the Oracle look and feel guidelines.

How to do it...

To modify the layout, perform the following tasks:

1. Navigate to the **Canvases | SOCIETY_CNV** canvas and open the **Layout Editor**.

2. Select **View | Customize Ruler/Grid** from the menu bar and set the **Ruler Settings**, as shown in the following screenshot:

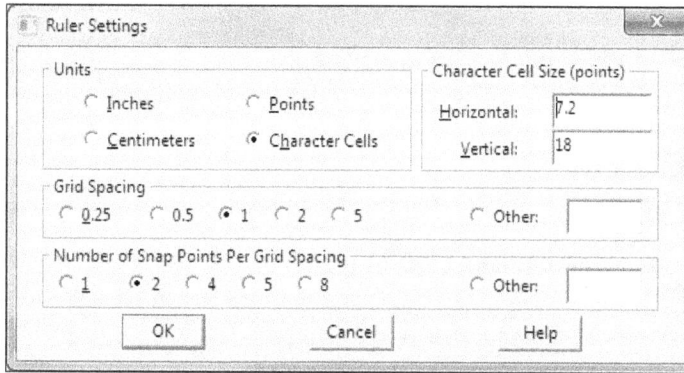

3. Select and drag the items on the canvas so that there is space at the top and bottom and as well as space on either side of the objects on the canvas, as shown in the following screenshot:

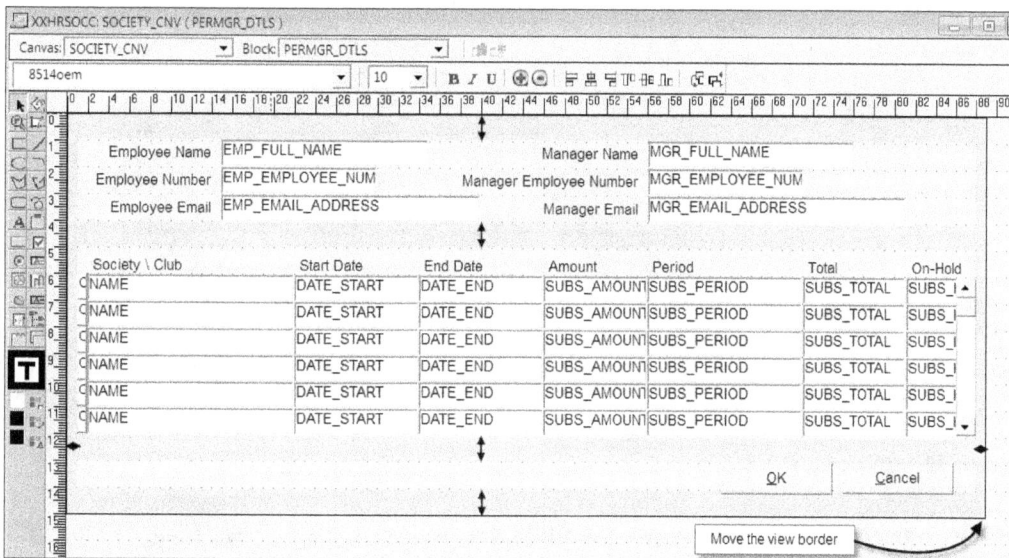

4. Resize the window and canvas borders so that the borders have a character space after the furthest items on the right and the buttons at the bottom.

5. **Save** the form.

How it works...

We have moved the items on the screen so that the layout conforms to Oracle's look and feel standards.

Adding triggers to the buttons

We now need to add triggers to the buttons which will fire when the buttons are clicked.

How to do it...

To add triggers to the buttons, perform the following tasks:

1. Navigate to the **Data Blocks | PERMGR_DTLS | Items | OK_BTN | Triggers** in the **Object Navigator**.

2. Click on the **+** icon to add a new WHEN-BUTTON-PRESSED trigger.

3. In the **PL/SQL Editor**, add the following code:

   ```
   DO_KEY('EXIT_FORM');
   ```

4. Expand the **Cancel** button and add a WHEN-BUTTON-PRESSED trigger.

5. In **PL/SQL Editor**, add the following code:

   ```
   EXIT_FORM(NO_VALIDATE);
   ```

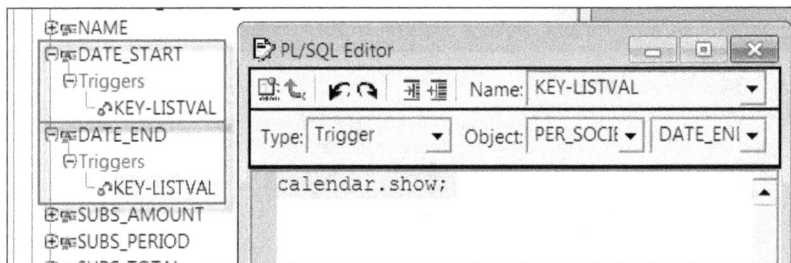

6. **Save** the form.

How it works...

We have added triggers to our buttons so that when they are clicked by the user our desired actions are performed. When the **OK** button is clicked, the form will trigger a standard KEY-EXIT trigger which will prompt the user to save if there are any changed records. The EXIT_FORM(NO_VALIDATE) code will execute if the **Cancel** button is clicked. This will exit the form regardless of the form status and will not prompt the user to save any changes.

Creating an LOV for the society name field

We are now going to create a **list of values (LOV)** for the name field so that the user will need to select a value from the list. To create an LOV, we first need to create a record group to base the list upon.

How to do it...

To create a list of values, perform the following tasks:

1. Navigate to **LOVs** in the **Object Navigator**.
2. Click on the **+** icon on the left-hand toolbar to add a new list of values.
3. Select **Use the LOV Wizard** from the **LOV Wizard** and click **OK**.
4. On the next screen, select **New record group based on a query**.
5. Click **Next**.
6. Click on the **Connect** button and enter the **Password** and **Database** values for the **APPS** user.
7. Click on **Connect**.
8. In the SQL query statement field, type the following query:

   ```
   SELECT lookup_code, meaning, description
   FROM fnd_lookup_typesflt, fnd_lookup_valuesflv
   WHERE flt.lookup_type = flv.lookup_type
   AND flt.lookup_type = 'XXHR_SOCIETY_LOV'
   AND enabled_flag = 'Y'
   ```

9. Click on **Next**.
10. Shift all of the columns across by clicking **>>** and click on **Next**.
11. Set the following properties:

Column	Title	Width	Return value
LOOKUP_CODE	Lookup_Code	0	PER_SOCIETIES.CODE
MEANING	Society \ Club	2	PER_SOCIETIES.NAME
DESCRIPTION	Description	5	

> To select the return values, click on the LOOKUP_CODE **Return value** field and click on the **Look up return item** button. Then select the PER_SOCIETIES.CODE item from the list. Do the same for the MEANING column **Return value** and set it to PER_SOCIETIES.NAME, as shown in the following screenshot.

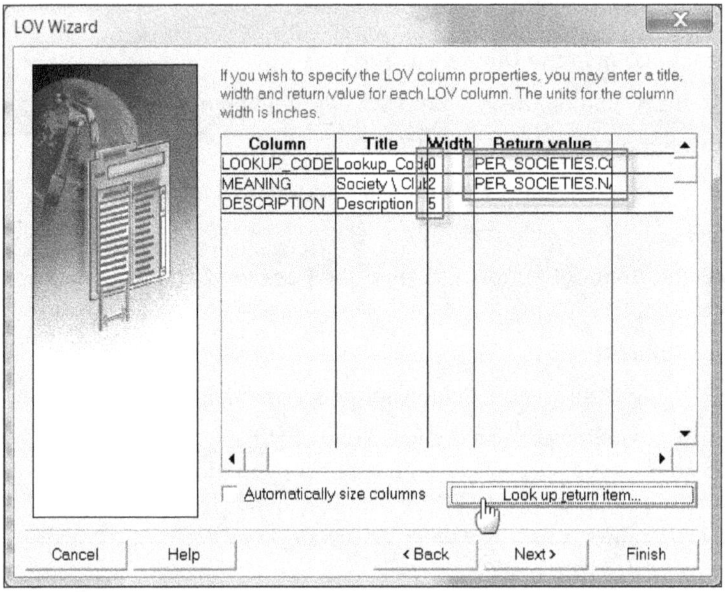

12. Click on **Next**.

13. Set the **Title** of the LOV to Societies \ Clubs List and click on **Next**.

14. Click on **Next** again.

15. When prompted to assign the LOV select PER_SOCIETIES.NAME and shift it across to **Assigned Items** by clicking **>**, as shown in the following screenshot:

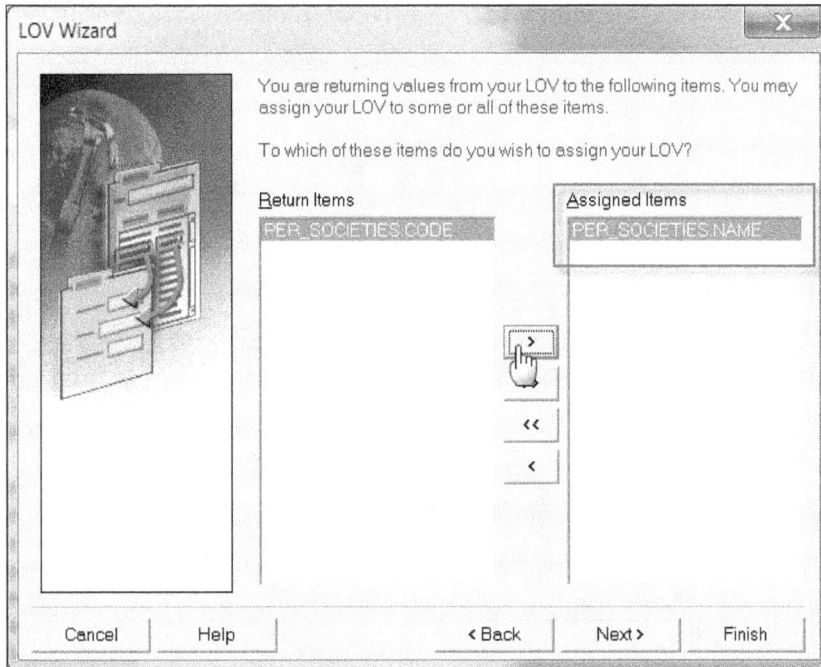

We only want to assign the LOV to the name field as this is the item that is displayed to the user. The return values will go into the code and name field. The code field is not displayed as we set the width to 0 when we set the properties.

16. Click on **Finish**.

17. Navigate to **Record Groups** in the **Object Navigator** and open the **Property Palette** of the record group that was generated from the **LOV Wizard**.

18. Set the **Name** property of the record group to SOCIETIES_RG.

19. Navigate to **LOVs** in the **Object Navigator** and open the **Property Palette** of the LOV that was generated from the **LOV Wizard**.

20. Set the **Name** property of the generated LOV to SOCIETIES_LOV.

21. Set the **Subclass Information** to LOV, as shown in the following screenshot:

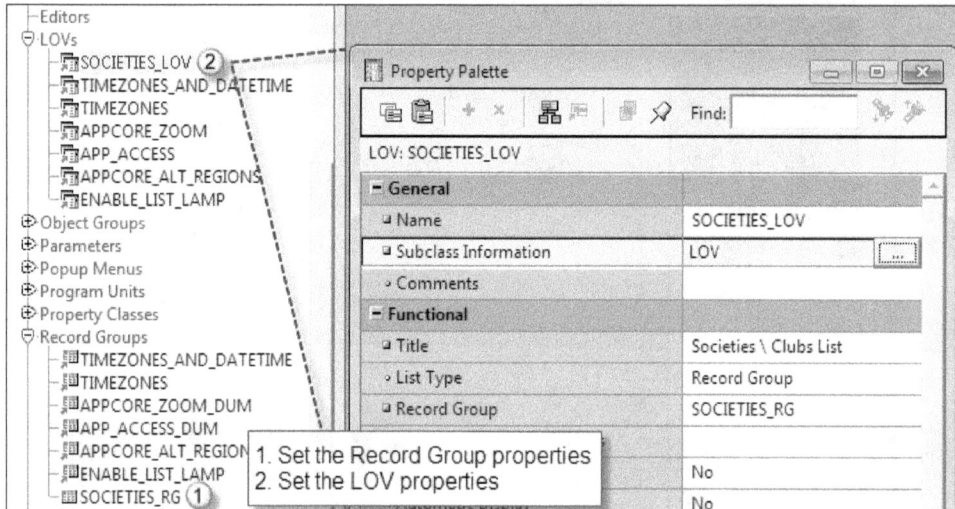

22. **Save** the form.

How it works...

We have now created a list of values. The list of values retrieves values from the XXHR_SOCIETY_LOV lookup that we created earlier. This is to control the values that the user can enter in this field.

Configuring the date fields

We now need to configure the date fields to use the standard list of values for the date fields. We need to set the date fields to use a dummy list of values called enable list lamp and then code the KEY-LISTVAL trigger.

How to do it...

To configure the date fields, perform the following tasks:

1. Navigate to **Data Blocks | PER_SOCIETIES | Items** in the **Object Navigator**.

2. Open the **Property Palette** for the DATE_START item.

3. Set the **LOVs** property to ENABLE_LIST_LAMP.

> The ENABLE_LIST_LAMP LOV is a dummy list of values. It ensures that the LOV icon appears in the field when the user navigates to the item at runtime. We are going to code a KEY-LISTVAL trigger to call the standard date calendar for the user to enter a date.

4. Open the **Property Palette** for the DATE_END item.

5. Set the **LOVs** property to ENABLE_LIST_LAMP.

6. Expand the DATE_START field and highlight **Triggers**.

7. Add a new KEY-LISTVAL trigger to the DATE_START field.

8. In the **PL/SQL Editor**, type calendar.show;.

9. Add a new KEY-LISTVAL trigger to the DATE_END field.

10. In **PL/SQL Editor**, type calendar.show; as shown in the following screenshot:

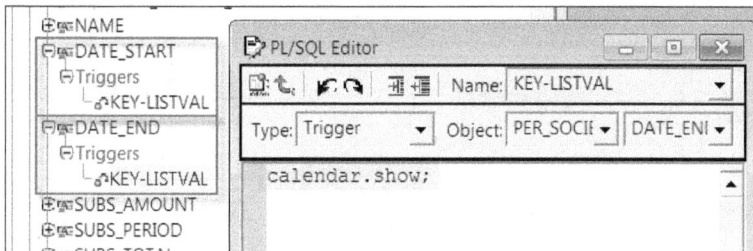

11. **Save** the form.

How it works...

We have added a dummy list of values to the date fields. When the user clicks on the date fields, the KEY-LISTVAL trigger will be fired. In the trigger, we have written code to call the standard calendar, which is a GUI widget showing a calendar. It allows the user to select a date and this is returned into the field the trigger fires from.

Creating a list item

We now want to change the period field to be a static list. These are only really used when the list is small and is unlikely to change very often. Elements in the list can be created dynamically but you would normally use an LOV if the list is likely to change. We want a list to have two values, annual and monthly. We will store A and M in the database.

How to do it...

To add a pop-up list to the period field, perform the following tasks:

1. Navigate to **Data Blocks | PER_SOCIETIES | Items | SUBS_PERIOD** in the **Object Navigator**.

2. Open the **Property Palette**.

3. Set the **Subclass Information** property to LIST.

4 Click on the **Elements in List** property and you will be prompted to enter elements. Fill in the elements as follows:

List Element	List Item Value
Annually	A
Monthly	M

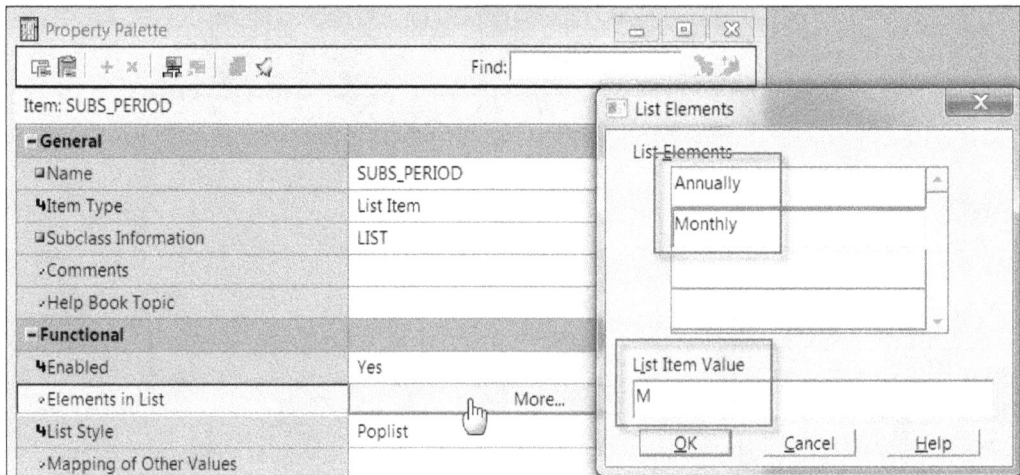

> The **List Elements** is the value that is displayed to the user and the **List Item Value** is the value that is stored in the database.

5 **Save** the form.

How it works...

The list property is mainly used for fairly static lists which are not usually more than a few elements. The list element is the value displayed to the user and the list item value is the value that is stored in the database.

Creating a checkbox item

We are now going to change the SUBS_HOLD item to a checkbox.

How to do it...

To change the SUBS_HOLD item to a checkbox, perform the following tasks:

1. Navigate to **Data Blocks | PER_SOCIETIES | Items | SUBS_HOLD** in the **Object Navigator**.

2. Open the **Property Palette** and set the properties to the following:

   - ❑ **Subclass Information**: CHECKBOX
   - ❑ **Value when Checked**: Y
   - ❑ **Value when Unchecked**: N
   - ❑ **Check Box Mapping of Other Values**: Unchecked
   - ❑ **Width**: .216
   - ❑ **Prompt Alignment**: Center

3. Navigate to **Canvases | SOCIETY_CNV** and open the **Layout Editor**.

4. Move the checkbox so that it is aligned as shown in the following screenshot:

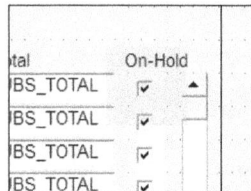

5. **Save** the form.

How it works...

We have added a checkbox that stores the values Y when the checkbox is checked and N if the checkbox is unchecked.

Testing the form

We now want to perform a simple test to see if we can open the form and see the changes that we have made.

How to do it...

To test the form, perform the following tasks:

1. FTP the form to `$AU_TOP/forms/US`.

2. **Compile** the form with the following command:

   ```
   frmcmp_batch module=$AU_TOP/forms/US/XXHRSOCC.fmb userid=apps/apps
   output_file=$XXHR_TOP/forms/US/XXHRSOCC.fmx compile_all=special
   ```

3. Log in to Oracle with the **XXEBS Extending e-Business Suite** responsibility.

4. Navigate to the **Societies Form** and the societies and clubs form will open, as shown in the following screenshot:

5. Navigate to the **Society \ Club** field and click on the **LOV** button to see if a list of values is displayed.

6. Navigate to the **Start Date** and **End Date** fields and click the **LOV** button to see if the standard calendar is displayed.

7. Navigate to the **Period** field and click the list to see if the list displays the elements we entered earlier.

8. Navigate to the **On-Hold** field and click it to see if we can check the box and uncheck it.

9. Click on the **Cancel** button to exit the form.

How it works...

We have tested the form to ensure that the changes we have added are present in the latest version of our form.

Adding a query screen to a form

As part of the **TEMPLATE** form, we get a standard mechanism to create a query screen. This usually is the first screen that is present when the form opens if no data is passed to the form via parameters. This allows the user to search for specific records. In our form, we want to create a query form that allows us to search for an employee. We want the user to be able to search by their name or their employee number. There are a number of steps required to implement a **QUERY_FIND** window. In this recipe, we are going to perform the following tasks:

- Adding code to the WHEN-NEW-FORMS-INSTANCE trigger
- Copying the QUERY_FIND object group
- Setting the block, canvas, and window properties
- Editing the button triggers on the QUERY_FIND block
- Creating items in the query block
- Resizing the objects on the canvas
- Creating a PRE-QUERY trigger
- Creating a QUERY_FIND trigger

Adding code to the WHEN-NEW-FORMS-INSTANCE trigger

Firstly, we are going to add some code to the WHEN-NEW-FORM-INSTANCE trigger to automatically query on entry to the form.

How to do it...

To add code to the WHEN-NEW-FORM-INSTANCE trigger, perform the following tasks:

1. Navigate to **Triggers | WHEN-NEW-FORM-INSTANCE** in the **Object Navigator**.
2. Open the **PL/SQL Editor** and enter the following code *after* the existing code:

   ```
   EXECUTE_TRIGGER('QUERY_FIND');
   ```

3. **Save** the form.

How it works...

We have added code to the WHEN-NEW-FORM_INSTANCE trigger to call the **QUERY_FIND** window when the form opens.

Copying the QUERY_FIND object group

When we code a **QUERY_FIND** window, we need the QUERY_FIND objects from APPSTAND. We can then edit them to create our own query window.

How to do it...

To copy the QUERY_FIND objects, perform the following tasks:

1. In **Forms Developer**, open the APPSTAND.fmb form.

2. In the APPSTAND form navigate to **Object Groups | QUERY_FIND**.

3. Click-and-drag the QUERY_FIND object group to the **XXHRSOCC | Object Groups** node, as shown in the following screenshot:

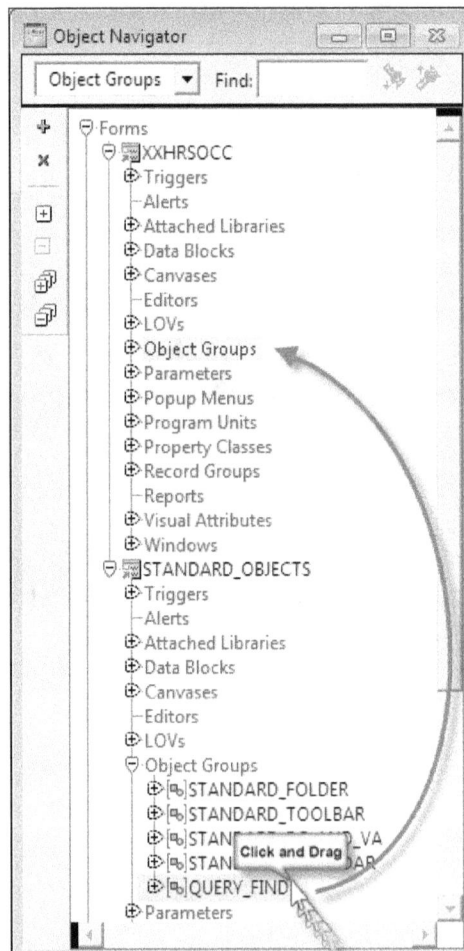

4. When prompted to **Copy the object or subclass it?** select **Copy**.

5. Now delete the QUERY_FIND object group that we have just copied. This will delete the object group but keep the block, canvas, and window in the form, as shown in the following screenshot:

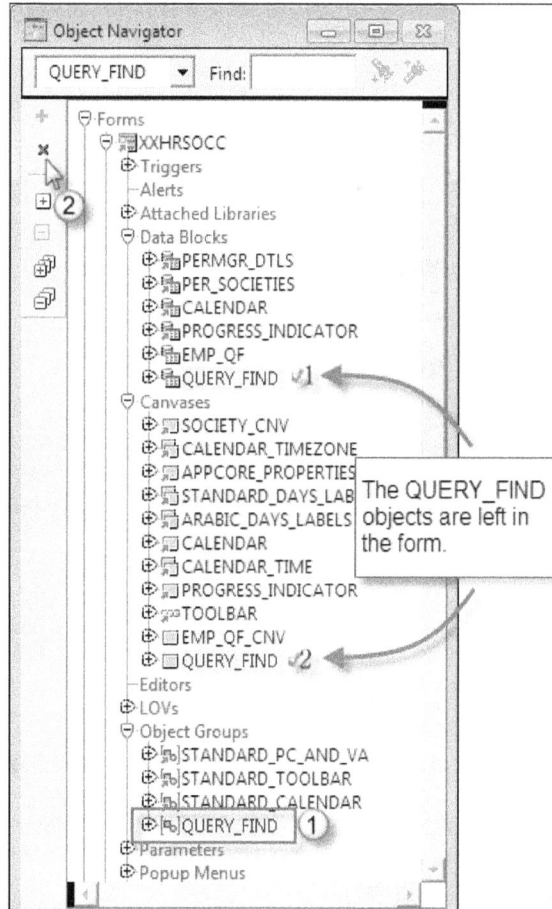

How it works...

Copying the QUERY_FIND object group has copied the block and canvas to our form. We do not want the object group any more so it can be deleted.

Setting the block, canvas, and window properties

We will now need to set the properties of the container objects.

How to do it...

To set the properties of the container objects, perform the following tasks:

1. Navigate to **Data Blocks** | **QUERY_FIND** and open the **Property Palette**:

2. Set the following properties of the QUERY_FIND block:
   - **Name**: EMP_QF
   - **Query Allowed**: No
   - **Previous Navigation Data Block**: PERMGR_DTLS
   - **Next Navigation Block**: PERMGR_DTLS

3. Navigate to **Canvases** | **QUERY_FIND** and open the **Property Palette**.

4. Set the following properties of the **QUERY_FIND** canvas:
   - **Name**: EMP_QF_CNV

5. Navigate to **Windows** | **QUERY_FIND** and open the **Property Palette**.

6. Set the following properties of the **QUERY_FIND** canvas:
   - **Name**: EMP_QF_WND
   - **Title**: Find Employees

How it works...

We have now set the properties of the QUERY_FIND objects we have copied into our form.

Editing the button triggers on the QUERY_FIND block

We now need to edit the button triggers in the EMP_QF block to determine the behavior when the buttons are pressed.

How to do it...

To code the EMP_QF block, perform the following tasks:

1. Navigate to **Data Blocks** | **EMP_QF** | **Items** | **NEW** | **Triggers** | **WHEN-BUTTON-PRESSED** and open the **PL/SQL Editor**.

2. Modify the code from:

   ```
   app_find.new('Your blockname here');
   ```

To the following:

```
app_find.new('PERMGR_DTLS');
```

> This will take the user into the form without executing a query.

3. Navigate to **Data Blocks | EMP_QF | Items | FIND | Triggers | WHEN-BUTTON-PRESSED** and open the **PL/SQL Editor**.

4. Modify the code from:

```
app_find.find('Your blockname here');
```

To the following:

```
app_find.find('PERMGR_DTLS');
```

> This will take the user into the form and will execute a query on the block PERMGR_DTLS.

5. Navigate to **Data Blocks | EMP_QF | Triggers | KEY-NXTBLK** and open the **PL/SQL Editor**.

6. Modify the code from:

```
app_find.find('Your blockname here');
```

To the following:

```
app_find.find('PERMGR_DTLS');
```

How it works...

We have coded the triggers in our QUERY_FIND block to ensure that the dummy coded is changed to the block name in our form.

Creating items in the query block

Now, we need to create the items that we want the users to be able to search with. It is easier to copy items from the destination block and change the properties.

How to do it...

To create items in the query block, perform the following steps:

1. Navigate to **Data Blocks | PERMGR_DTLS | Items**.

2. Highlight (*Ctrl* and click) the EMP_PERSON_ID, EMP_FULL_NAME, and EMP_EMPLOYEE_NUMBER items.

3. Select **Edit | Copy** from the menu (or *Ctrl + C*).

4. Navigate to **Data Blocks | EMP_QF | Items**.

5. Select **Edit | Paste** from the menu (or *Ctrl + V*), as shown in the following screenshot:

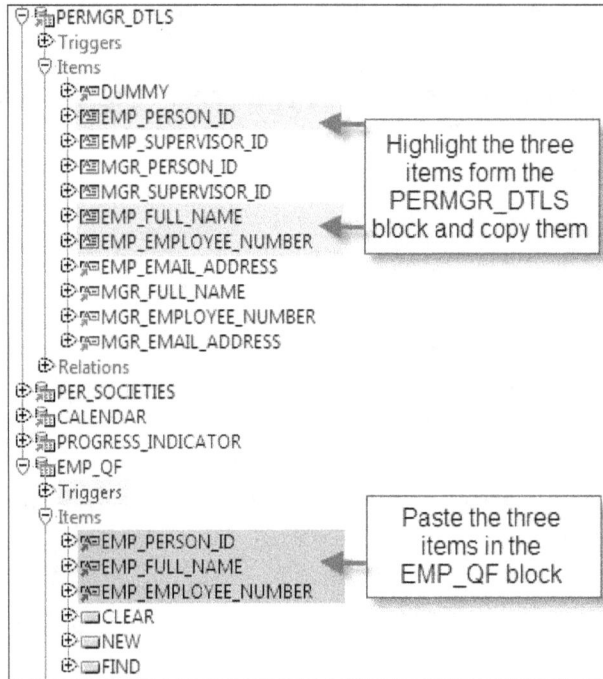

6. Set the following properties for the EMP_FULL_NAME and EMP_EMPLOYEE_NUMBER items in the EMP_QF block:

   ❑ **Subclass Information**: TEXT_ITEM

   ❑ **Required**: No

   ❑ **Database Item**: No

   ❑ **Canvas**: EMP_QF_CNV

How it works...

We have copied the QUERY_FIND items from our PERMGR_DTLS block to create the find items in our QUERY_FIND block. We have made them non-database items and defined which canvas they will be displayed on.

Resizing the objects on the canvas

We now need to resize the objects on the EMP_QF_CNV canvas to size and align the items on the **QUERY_FIND** canvas.

How to do it...

To resize the QUERY_FIND items, perform the following tasks:

1. Navigate to **Canvases | EMP_QF_CNV** and open the **Layout Editor**.

2. Check whether the **Ruler Settings** are still set to the following (**View | Customize Ruler/Grid**):

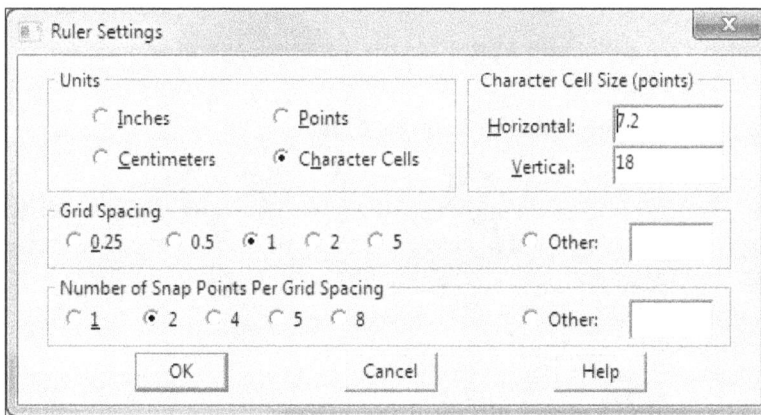

3. Drag the items, window, buttons, and canvas in the **Layout Editor** so that the layout looks something like the following screenshot:

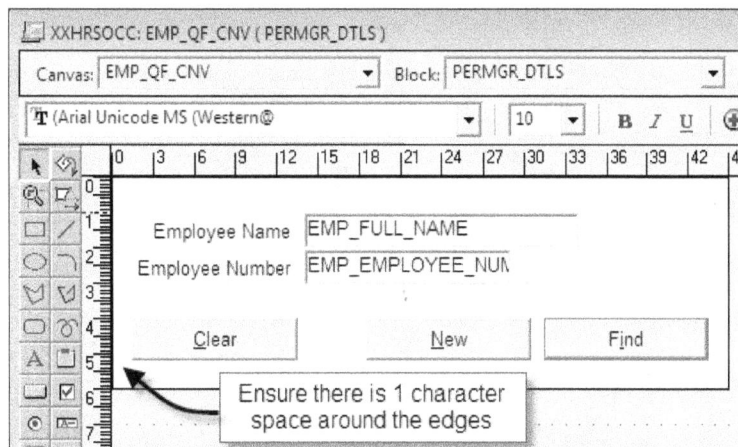

How it works...

We have now created the query parameters for the **QUERY_FIND** screen.

Creating a PRE-QUERY trigger

We need to create a PRE-QUERY trigger in the PERMGR_DTLS block to pass the details from the EMP_QF to the PERMGR_DTLS block before the query is executed. We are limiting the records returned when the query is executed with values from our **QUERY_FIND** window.

How to do it...

To copy the values in the **QUERY_FIND** window to the PERMGR_DTLS block before the query is executed, perform the following tasks:

1. Navigate to **Data Blocks | PERMGR_DTLS | Triggers** and add a new PRE-QUERY trigger.

2. In the **PL/SQL Editor**, type the following code:

```
IF :parameter.G_query_find = 'TRUE' THEN
  COPY(:EMP_QF.EMP_PERSON_ID,'PERMGR_DTLS.EMP_PERSON_ID');
  COPY(:EMP_QF.EMP_FULL_NAME,'PERMGR_DTLS.EMP_FULL_NAME');
  COPY(:EMP_QF.EMP_EMPLOYEE_NUMBER,
 'PERMGR_DTLS.EMP_EMPLOYEE_NUMBER');
  :parameter.G_query_find := 'FALSE';
END IF;
```

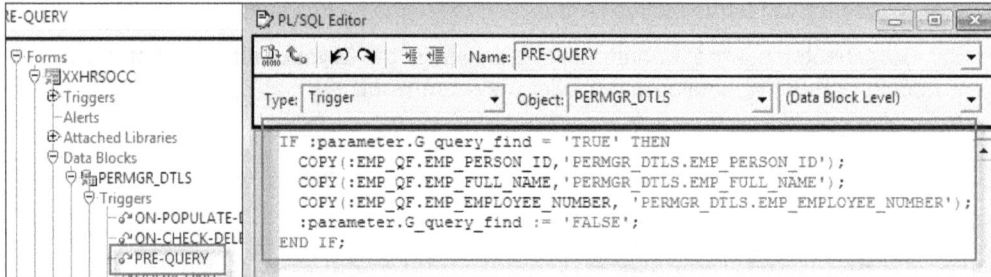

How it works...

The trigger will copy the values in the QUERY_FIND items to the PERMGR_DTLS block. This is done before the query is executed so that only values present in the QUERY_FIND items will be returned in the block.

Creating a QUERY_FIND trigger

We now need to create a `QUERY_FIND` trigger on the `PERMGR_DTLS` results block. This means that whenever the user clicks the enter query icon in the form, the **QUERY_FIND** window will open.

How to do it...

To create a `QUERY_FIND` trigger, perform the following tasks:

1. Navigate to **Data Blocks | PERMGR_DTLS | Triggers**.

2. Add a new trigger and select **User-named** from the list of values.

3. Set the **Name** property of the trigger created to `QUERY_FIND`.

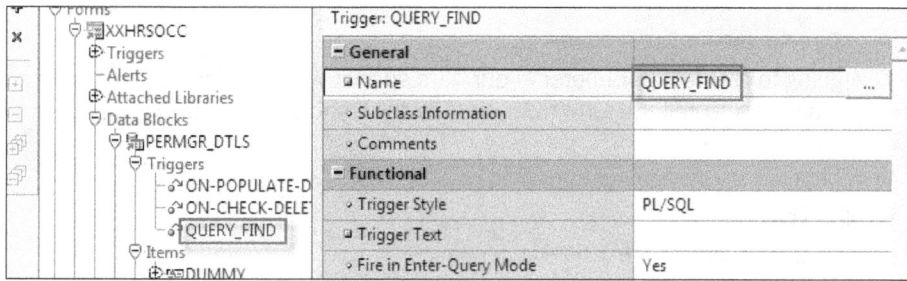

4. Open the **PL/SQL Editor** and add the following code:

```
APP_FIND.QUERY_FIND('SOCIETY_WND', 'EMP_QF_WND', 'EMP_QF');
```

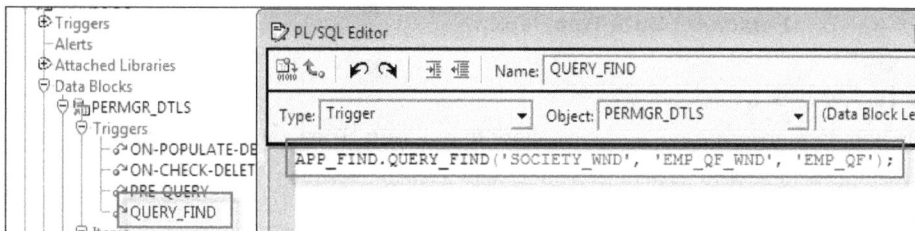

How it works...

The call to `APP_FIND.QUERY_FIND` will open the **QUERY_FIND** parameter screen whenever the user wants to perform a query when in the `PERMGR_DTLS` block.

Passing parameters to a form

We can pass parameters to a form to pass data that can help us to perform actions based upon that data. In this case, we want to add a parameter which passes in the PERSON_ID. If the parameter is populated with a value, we do not want to call the query screen. In this recipe, we are going to perform the following tasks:

- ▶ Creating a parameter
- ▶ Bypassing the query find screen
- ▶ Testing the form
- ▶ Testing the form with the PERSON_ID parameter passed in

Creating a parameter

We are now going to create a parameter in our form so that we can pass PERSON_ID into the form. This will allow us to call the form from another form and automatically query back an employee record.

How to do it...

To create a parameter, perform the following tasks:

1. Navigate to **Parameters** in the **Object Navigator**.
2. Set the following parameter properties:

   - ❏ **Name**: P_PERSON_ID
   - ❏ **Parameter Data Type**: Number

How it works...

We can add as many parameters as we want in our form. They can be used to pass information into our form.

Bypassing the query find screen

When we enter the form, we want to bypass the **QUERY_FIND** window if we are passing a PERSON_ID into the form. If this is the case, we do not want to call the **QUERY_FIND** window. We want to set the block property WHERE clause so that only the employee that is passed in can be queried. We also want to execute a query automatically.

How to do it...

To bypass the **QUERY_FIND** window if a PERSON_ID is passed into the form, perform the following tasks:

1. Navigate to **Data Blocks | PERMGR_DTLS | Triggers | QUERY_FIND** and open the **PL/SQL Editor**.

2. Add the following code to check if a parameter P_PERSON_ID is passed into the form and set the block property WHERE clause if the parameter contains a value. If the parameter contains a value, we want to add execute_query; to automatically query the record back.

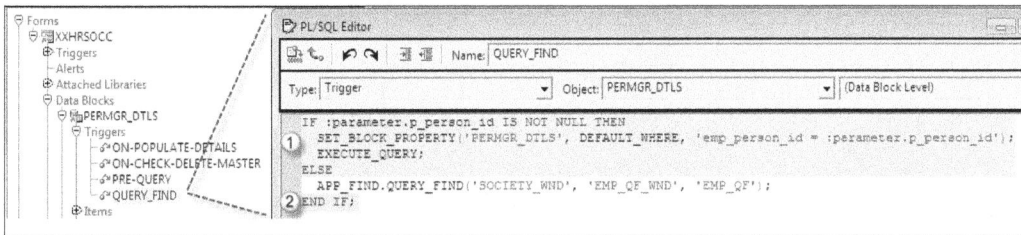

3. Compile the code in **PL/SQL Editor**.

4. **Save** the form.

How it works...

We have added code to bypass the **QUERY_FIND** window if the PERSON_ID is passed into the form. We set the default WHERE clause property for the PERMGER_DTLS block so that the user cannot query back other employees as we have opened the form for a specific employee.

Testing the form

We now need to test the form. We need to test that the unchanged parts of the form behaves as they did before we added the code. Then we need to test that the form bypasses the **QUERY_FIND** screen and automatically queries an employee record when a parameter is passed into the form. We can test this by setting the default value of the parameter to a valid PERSON_ID.

How to do it...

To test the form, perform the following tasks:

1. Open **WinSCP** and transfer the form over to the $AU_TOP/forms/US directory in the application tier.

2. Open **Putty** and connect to the application server.

3. Navigate to `$AU_TOP/forms/US` directory.

4. Compile the form with the following command:

```
frmcmp_batch module=$AU_TOP/forms/US/XXHRSOCC.fmb userid=apps/apps
output_file=$XXHR_TOP/forms/US/XXHRSOCC.fmx compile_all=special
```

5. Log in to Oracle with the **XXEBS Extending e-Business Suite** responsibility.

6. Navigate to **Societies Form** and the form will open, as shown in the following screenshot, showing the **QUERY_FIND** window:

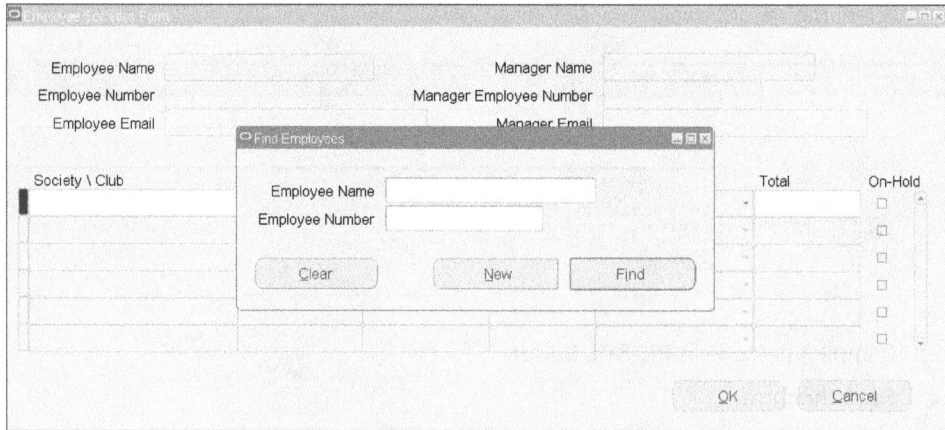

7. Enter an employee number in the **Employee Number** field and click on the **Find** button.

8. Add a record on the **Societies** block, as shown in the following screenshot:

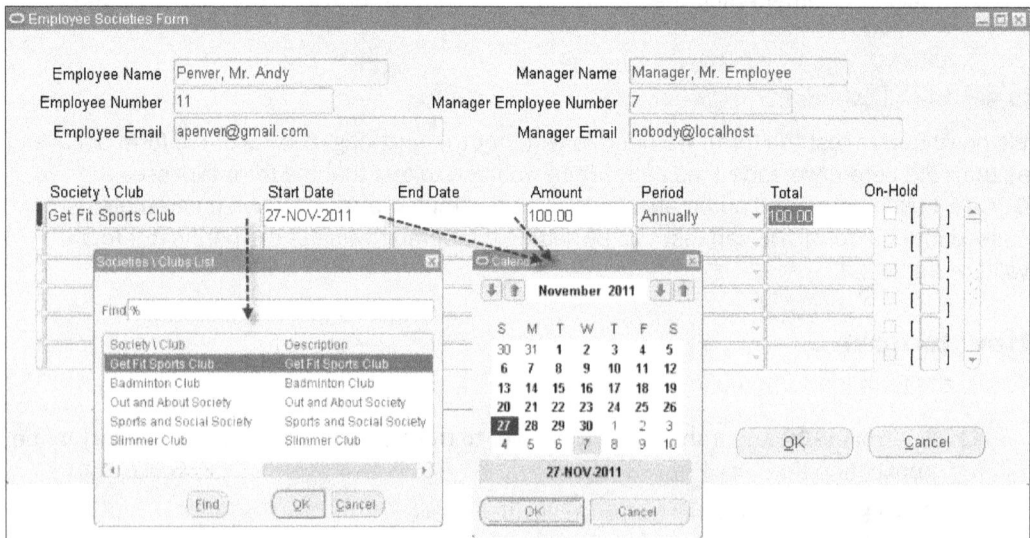

9. **Save** the record.

10. Before we exit the form, we want to get `PERSON_ID` for the next test.

11. Navigate to **Help | Diagnostics | Examine** from the menu bar.

12. Enter the **APPS** password if prompted.

13. In the **Examine field and Variable Values** window select `EMP_PERSON_ID` from the list of values.

14. Make a note of the **Value** that is returned, as shown in the following screenshot:

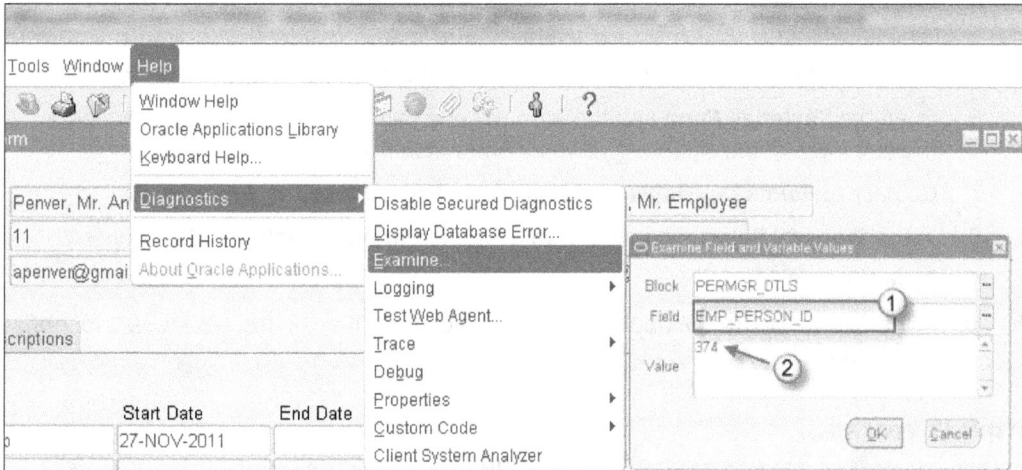

In this case, `PERSON_ID` is `374`. It may well be different in your environment.

How it works...

We have tested that we can open the form from the main menu. The **QUERY_FIND** screen appears and we can query an employee back by entering an employee number. We can also add a new record, testing that the list of values appears for the **Society \ Club** field and also the standard calendar appears for the two date fields. When we save the form, we can check whether the record has been saved to the database by exiting the form and then re-open it querying back the same employee record.

Testing the form with the PERSON_ID parameter passed in

Now we are going to test the form whilst passing in a parameter for the `PERSON_ID`. The **QUERY_FIND** window should not appear and the employee record should automatically query back a record.

How to do it...

To test the form passing in the `PERSON_ID` parameter, perform the following steps:

1. Go back to **Forms Developer** and navigate to **Parameters | P_PERSON_ID**.

2. In the **Property Palette**, set the **Parameter Initial Value** property to the `PERSON_ID` we have retrieved form from the **Help | Diagnostics | Examine** in the previous test. In this case it is `374`.

3. **Save** the form.

4. FTP the form over to the application tier and compile it again (repeat steps 1 to 7 of the previous test).

5. Log in to Oracle with the **XXEBS Extending e-Business Suite** responsibility.

6. Open the **Societies Form** and the form will open and will automatically query back the employee of the `PERSON_ID` value entered in the parameter `P_PERSON_ID`.

7. Go back to **Forms Developer** and navigate to **Parameters | P_PERSON_ID**.

8. In the **Property Palette**, delete the value in the **Parameter Initial Value** property.

9. **Save** the form.

10.. FTP the form over to the application tier and compile it again (repeat steps 1 to 7 of the previous test).

How it works...

We have performed a test to see if the **QUERY_FIND** window is bypassed if there is a parameter passed in the `P_PERSON_ID` parameter. We have tested this by setting a default value. The form has opened and automatically queried back the record. After we have performed the test, we must go back and clear the initial value from the `P_PERSON_ID` parameter. It would be quite easy to forget to do this and this would mean the parameter is defaulted to a `PERSON_ID` which is what we do not want. We have just done this to test the form.

3
Advanced Oracle Forms

In this chapter, we will cover:

- ▸ Installing the database objects
- ▸ Using messages from the message dictionary
- ▸ Creating tabs within a form
- ▸ Creating program units
- ▸ Adding lookups, date fields, and lists
- ▸ Controlling menu items
- ▸ Creating pop-up menu items
- ▸ Adding flexfields to forms
- ▸ Creating triggers for flexfield events
- ▸ Adding a zoom using the custom library
- ▸ Adding a spreadtable to a form
- ▸ Capturing events for a spreadtable

Introduction

In the previous chapter, we created a form which has a master and detail blocks. We created objects and became familiar with the user interface and how it is used within e-Business Suite. In this chapter, we are going to add to the form we have already created and also look at extending an Oracle standard form.

In this chapter, we will continue from the recipes we developed in *Chapter 2, Oracle Forms*. We will be adding some more advanced features to the form. We will learn how to add messages to our forms from the message dictionary.

We will also add a tabbed region to our form. We can use tabs to show related data to the header block, which is common among professional forms. We will look at how we can control menus, both the pop up and the toolbar menus. We will add custom menu items and can capture the event when the menu item is selected.

A common feature in Oracle is the use of flexfields, so we will also add a flexfield and go through the process of registering the database table and the flexfield. We will configure a DFF in our form so that the user can enter additional data relating to a society they belong to.

Later in the chapter we will use the custom library to create a zoom. We will show how we can zoom to a form and pass parameters, automatically querying back data in the form. Finally, we will learn how to add a spreadtable to a form, which is like a java bean used to display a multi- record block.

Installing the database objects

Create the database objects for this chapter before you start by using a script provided. The code comes with the following readme file: `readme_3_1.txt`.

We are going to create a table, view, and synonym for the new block we will create. We will also create a package that will handle all of the database transactions such as insert, update, and delete. Finally, we will create a sequence that will be used to generate a unique number for new records. For all of the database objects there is a script provided called `4842_03_01.sh`. The following section provides details of how to run the script.

How to do it...

To create the database objects, perform the following steps:

1. Create a local directory `C:\packt\scripts\ch3` where the scripts are downloaded to.

2. Open Putty and connect to the application tier user.

3. Create a new directory on the application tier under `$XXHR_TOP/install` with the following commands:

```
cd $XXHR_TOP/install


mkdir ch3
```

4. Navigate to the new directory with the following command:

   cd ch3

5. Open WinSCP and transfer the files from `C:\packt\scripts\ch3` to `$XXHR_TOP/install/ch3` as shown in the following screenshot:

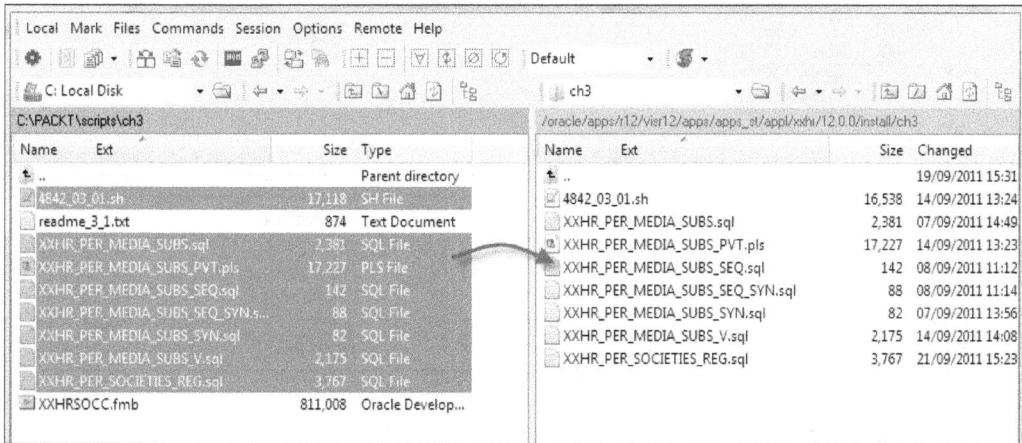

6. In Putty, change the permissions of the script with the following command:

   chmod 775 4842_03_01.sh

7. Run the following script to create all of the objects by issuing the following command:

   ./4842_03_01.sh apps/apps

8. The script checks that all of the files are present in your `$XXHR_TOP/install/ch3` directory and will prompt you to continue if they are all there, so type Y and press **Return**.

9. After the script has completed check the `XXHR_4842_03_01.log` file for errors. (It will be created in the same directory, `$XXHR_TOP/install/ch3`.)

10. Run the following query to check that all of the objects have been created successfully:

```
SELECT OWNER, OBJECT_NAME, OBJECT_TYPE, STATUS
  FROM ALL_OBJECTS
 WHERE OBJECT_NAME LIKE 'XXHR_PER_MEDIA_SUBS%'
ORDER BY 1, 2
```

OWNER	OBJECT_NAME	OBJECT_TYPE	STATUS
APPS	XXHR_PER_MEDIA_SUBS	SYNONYM	VALID
APPS	XXHR_PER_MEDIA_SUBS_PVT	PACKAGE	VALID
APPS	XXHR_PER_MEDIA_SUBS_PVT	PACKAGE BODY	VALID
APPS	XXHR_PER_MEDIA_SUBS_SEQ	SYNONYM	VALID
APPS	XXHR_PER_MEDIA_SUBS_V	VIEW	VALID
XXHR	XXHR_PER_MEDIA_SUBS	TABLE	VALID
XXHR	XXHR_PER_MEDIA_SUBS_SEQ	SEQUENCE	VALID

7 rows selected

How it works...

We have created the database objects required for this chapter. The table, view, and sequence are going to be used to add a tab to our form. The synonym allows access to the **apps** user to our table as the table is created in the XXHR schema. The package is called from the form when we want to insert, update, or delete records to our database table.

Using messages from the message dictionary

We can add messages in the form to display information to the user. There are debug messages and there are messages that we can call from the message dictionary. Debug messages can be triggered by a call to `fnd_messages.debug(<debug message>);`. However, if we want to call a message that the user will see we need to add it to the message dictionary and then call the message from within our form. The message dictionary is a central repository that stores messages displayed to the user. The reason we would use the message dictionary is so that we do not have to hard code messages in our form. Also, the message can be re-used in other forms and will maintain a consistent look and feel when messages are displayed. We can also insert dynamic text into a message from data within our form at runtime. There are a number of steps we need to perform to utilize a message dictionary:

▶ Creating a message directory
▶ Creating a message

- Creating a message file
- Coding logic to display messages
- Compiling the form
- Testing the form

Creating a message directory

We need to create a special directory under our custom top which will store the message dictionary files. If you have created the custom schema for the previous chapter then you will already have the message directory defined. The directory is created in the $XXHR_TOP directory and the directory is named mesg. If the directory does not already exist then create the directory as follows.

How to do it...

To create a message directory, perform the following tasks:

1. Open Putty.
2. Connect to the application server.
3. Navigate to $XXHR_TOP by typing:

   cd $XXHR_TOP

4. Type pwd to check the directory you are in.
5. Check if there is a folder called mesg by typing the following command:

   ls

6. If there is no directory called mesg create one in steps 5 and 6.
7. Create the directory by typing the following:

   mkdir mesg

8. Check the folder has been created by typing the following:

   ls

How it works...

Now we have created a directory in `$XXHR_TOP` directory which will be used to store a message file we create later in this chapter.

Creating a message

We will now define a message in Oracle. Each message by default displays the following text before each message: 'APP:<application short name>-<Number>, unless the number field is null or 0. When specifying tokens in a message you need to start the token with & and the token name must be specified in UPPER case.

How to do it...

To create a message, perform the following steps:

1. Log in to Oracle with the **Application Developer** responsibility.

2. Navigate to **Application | Messages** and the **Messages** window will open.

3. Enter the following data:

Item names	XXHR_ON_HOLD_WARNING
Language	US
Application	XXHR Custom Application
Number	0
Current Message Text	You are about to place the subscription for &NAME on hold.

4. Save the form.

The form should look like the following screenshot:

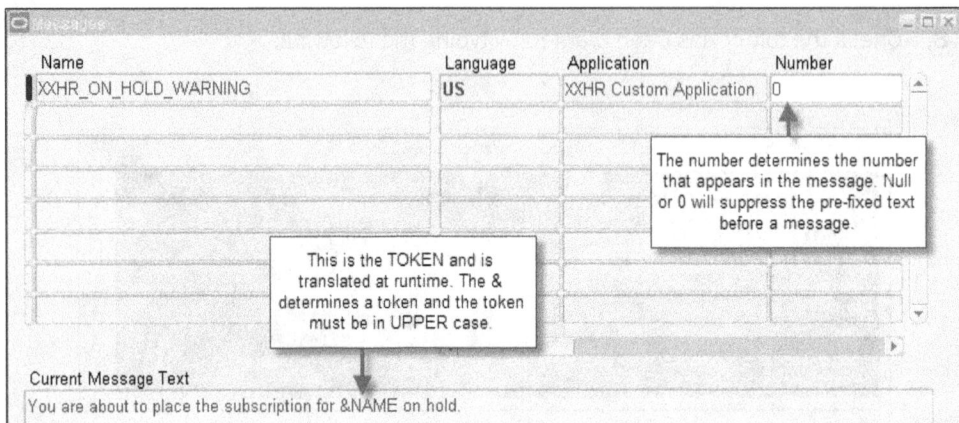

How it works...

We have now configured our message. The message has a number of 0 which will suppress the number when the message is displayed. We have also added a token to the message, which will be populated at runtime when we call the message.

Creating a message file

We will now create the message file which is generated by running a standard concurrent program.

How to do it...

To create the message file, perform the following steps:

1. Log in to Oracle with the **Application Developer** responsibility.
2. Select **View | Requests** from the menu.
3. Click the **Submit a New Request** button.
4. Select **Single Request** and click **OK**.
5. From the **Name LOV** select **Generate Messages** concurrent program.
6. Enter the following parameters for the concurrent program and click **OK**:

Language	US
Application	XXHR Custom Application
Mode	DB_TO_RUNTIME

**Leave the remaining field blank.

1. Click the **Submit** button to submit the concurrent program.
2. Click **No** to the 'Submit another request' pop up message.
3. In the **Find Requests** window click the **Find** button.
4. Press *Ctrl + F11* to query the form and repeat until the concurrent program has completed as shown in the following screenshot:

5. Once completed exit the form.

How it works...

The concurrent program has generated a message file. The application we entered when we ran the concurrent program means the message file will be created in the TOP directory associated with it. In this case, it is `$XXHR_TOP/mesg` as shown in the following screenshot:

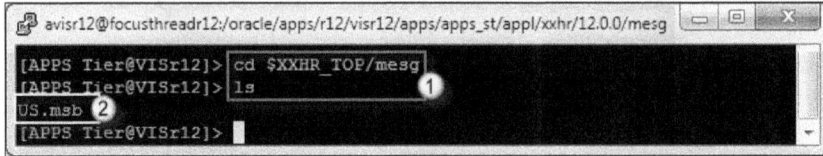

Coding logic to display messages

We will now code the message in the form to display when the **On Hold** checkbox is checked. There are three calls we need to make to the standard `FND_MESSAGE` package to call our message, which are as follows:

▸ Set the name of the message we want to display

▸ Set any tokens in the message

▸ Display the message

How to do it...

To call the message from the form, perform the following steps:

1. Open the `XXHRSOCC.fmb` form in **Forms Developer**.
2. Navigate to **Data Blocks | PER_SOCIETIES | Items | SUBS_HOLD | Triggers**.
3. Click the **+** on the left-hand toolbar to create a new trigger.
4. Select **WHEN-CHECKBOX-CHANGED** from the LOV.
5. In the **PL/SQL Editor**, add the following code:

```
IF :per_societies.subs_hold = 'Y' THEN
      FND_MESSAGE.SET_NAME('XXHR', 'XXHR_ON_HOLD_WARNING');
      FND_MESSAGE.SET_TOKEN('NAME', :PER_SOCIETIES.NAME);
      FND_MESSAGE.SHOW;
END IF;
```

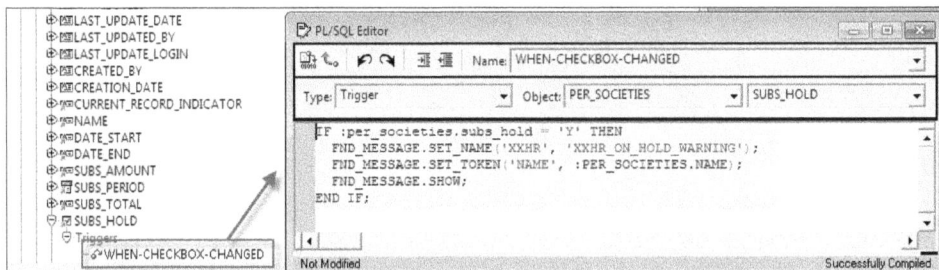

> First we get the message from the message dictionary. Then we assign a value to the token named &NAME. Finally, we show the message. There are other options available so take a look at the FND_MESSAGE package.

6. Compile the code.
7. Save the form.

How it works...

We have added code to a trigger in the form, so that when the **On-Hold** checkbox is checked a message will be displayed to the user. The message will warn the user that they are about to put the subscription on hold.

Compiling the form

Now we need to compile the form to display the message.

How to do it...

To compile the form, perform the following tasks:

1. Open WinSCP and transfer the form from your local directory to the $AU_TOP/forms/US in the application server.

2. Open Putty and connect to the application server.

3. Navigate to $AU_TOP/forms/US directory.

4. Compile the form with the following command:

```
frmcmp_batchmodule=$AU_TOP/forms/US/XXHRSOCC.fmb userid=apps/apps
output_file=$XXHR_TOP/forms/US/XXHRSOCC.fmx compile_all=special
```

How it works...

Now that we have compiled the form on the server, the changes that we have made to the form will be present in the form when we use the form within the application.

Testing the form

Now we need to test the form to display the message.

How to do it...

To test the form, perform the following tasks:

1. Log in to Oracle with the **XXEBS Extending e-Business Suite** responsibility.
2. Navigate to **Societies Form** and the societies and clubs form will open.
3. Enter an employee number in the query find window and click **Find**.
4. If there are no records returned in the **Societies** tab then enter some data as follows:

Society \ Club	Get Fit Sports Club
Start Date	27-NOV-2011
End Date	
Amount	10.00
Period	Monthly
Total	120.00

Society \ Club	Badminton Club
Start Date	27-NOV-2011
End Date	
Amount	100.00
Period	Annually
Total	100.00

5. Save the records.
6. Now check the **On-Hold** checkbox for the first record and a message will appear as shown in the following screenshot as we have triggered the **WHEN-CHECKBOX-CHANGED** trigger:

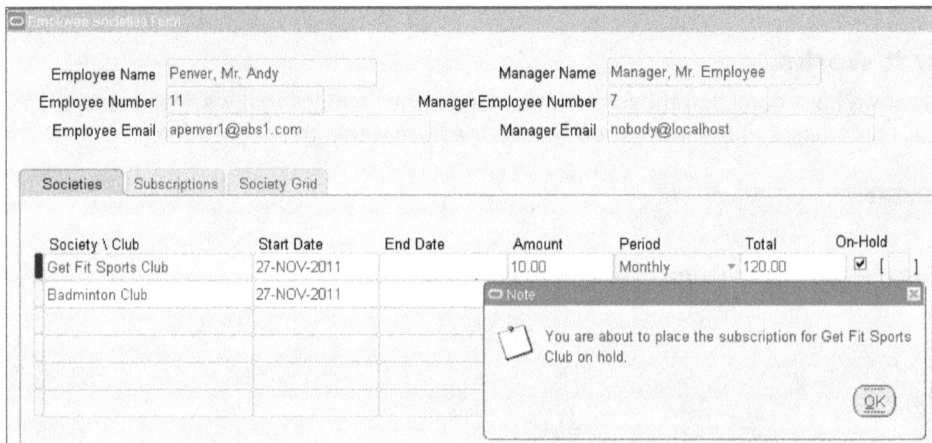

7. Click **OK** and then the **Cancel** button to exit the form.

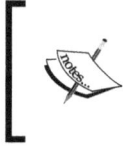

> If you update the message text in Oracle you will need to re-run the **Generate Messages** concurrent program. You may also need to exit Oracle and log in again to pick up any changes that have been made.

How it works...

We have now tested that the message we created appears when the **On-Hold** checkbox is checked. It is to warn the user that they are about to place the subscription on hold.

Creating tabs within a form

We are now going to add a tabbed region in the form. The new tab relates to media subscriptions and preferences. The tab will store details such as newsletter subscriptions and so on. The tab will be based upon data in a table called **XXHR_PER_MEDIA_SUBS**, and we will base the block in our form on a view called **XXHR_PER_MEDIA_SUBS_V**. Creating the tab will require a number of stages as follows:

- ▸ Creating a tabbed region
- ▸ Resizing objects on a canvas
- ▸ Creating a new block
- ▸ Setting block properties
- ▸ Setting item properties
- ▸ Creating program units to call database packages
- ▸ Creating a relationship between the master and detail blocks
- ▸ Adding a record indicator to a block
- ▸ Sizing and positioning items on a tabbed canvas
- ▸ Aligning a stacked canvas on a content canvas
- ▸ Adding a form level trigger to show a tabbed canvas
- ▸ Adding code to manage a tabbed canvas

Creating a tabbed region

Now we are going to create a tabbed canvas and move all of the items from the **PER_SOCIETIES** detail block from the content canvas to the new tabbed canvas.

How to do it...

To create a tabbed region, perform the following steps:

1. Open the XXHRSOCC.fmb form in **Forms Developer**.

2. Navigate to **Canvases** and click the **+** icon in the left-hand toolbar to create a new canvas.

3. Right-click the new canvas and open the property palette.

4. Set the following canvas properties:

    ❑ **Name**: SUBS_TAB_CNV

    ❑ **Subclass Information**: TAB_CANVAS

5. Navigate to **Canvases | SUBS_TAB_CNV | Tab Pages** and create two new tab pages.

6. Right-click the first new tab page and set the following properties:

    ❑ **Name**: SOC_TAB_PG

    ❑ **Subclass Information**: TAB_PAGE

    ❑ **Label**: Societies

7. Right-click the second new tab page and set the following properties:

    ❑ **Name**: SUBS_TAB_PG

    ❑ **Subclass Information**: TAB_PAGE

    ❑ **Label**: Subscriptions

8. Navigate to **Canvases | SUBS_TAB_CNV** and double-click it to open the **Layout Editor**.

9. Resize the canvas to 9.2 inches wide and 3 inches high. (Ensure that **View | Show View** and **View | Show Canvas** are ticked in the menu as shown in the following screenshot):

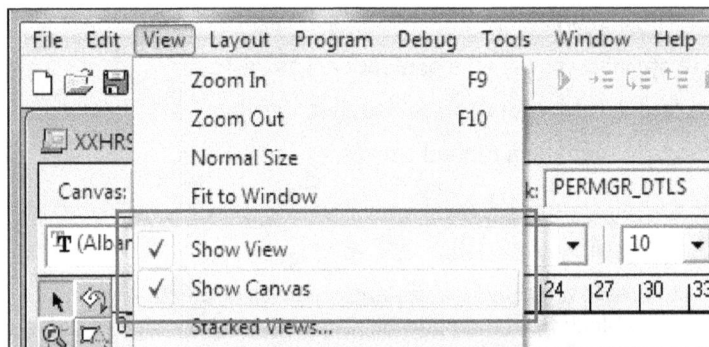

10. Navigate to **Data Blocks | PER_SOCIETIES | Items** and set the following properties of the **CURRENT_RECORD_INDICATOR, NAME, DATE_START, DATE_END, SUBS_AMOUNT, SUBS_PERIOD, SUBS_TOTAL,** and **SUBS_HOLD** items:

   ❑ **Canvas:** SUBS_TAB_CNV

   ❑ **Tab Page:** SOC_TAB_PG

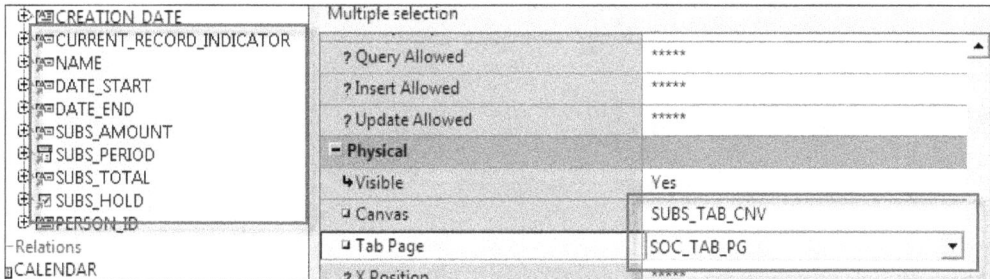

11. Navigate to **Data Blocks | PER_SOCIETIES** and set the following block properties:

   ❑ **Scroll Bar Canvas:** SUBS_TAB_CNV

   ❑ **Scroll Bar Tab Page:** SOC_TAB_PG

12. Save the form.

How it works...

We have now created our tabbed canvas and placed the detail block items on it for the **PER_SOCIETIES** block. We will now need to position the items so that they are within the view window and canvas.

Resizing objects on a canvas

We are now going to resize and position the objects on the canvases. The detail blocks are now on a tabbed canvas. First we will organize all of the items on the tabbed canvas and then we will position the objects on the main canvas.

How to do it...

To position the items on the canvas, perform the following steps:

1. Navigate to **Canvases | SUBS_TAB_CNV** and double-click to open the **Layout Editor.**

2. Select **View | Customize Ruler/ Grid** from the menu bar and set the **Ruler Settings** to the following:

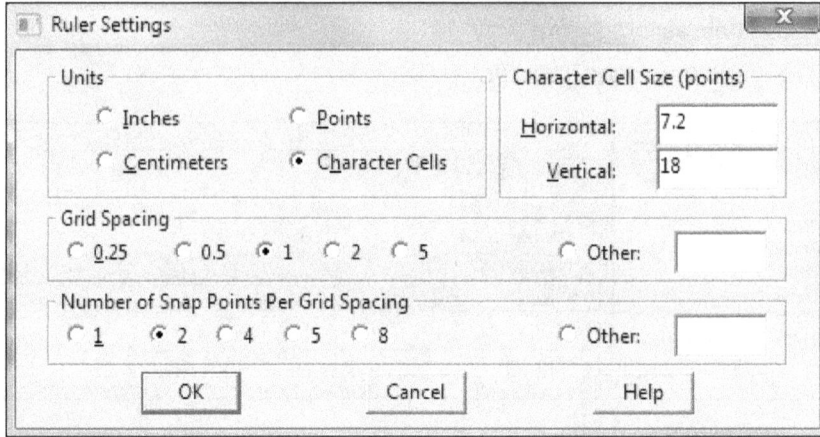

3. Click and drag all of the items and move them so that there is a space at the top and bottom, and a space at the left and right hand side of the canvas as shown in the following screenshot:

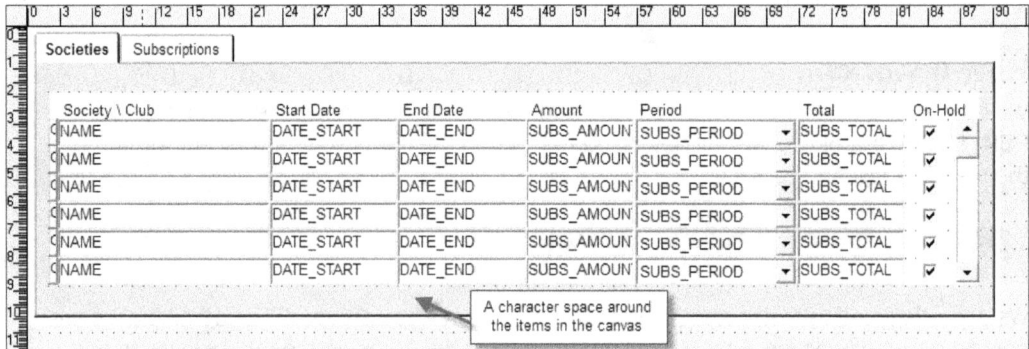

4. Double-click the **Canvases | SOCIETY_CNV** canvas to open the **Layout Editor**.

5. Select **View** from the menu and ensure **Show View, Show Canvas, Rulers, Ruler Guides**, and **Grid** are selected.

6. Move the **OK** and **Cancel** buttons and the **View** and **Window** borders as shown in the following screenshot.

7. Select **View | Stacked Views** from the menu bar.

8. Select **SUBS_TAB_CNV** from the list and click **OK**.

9. Move the stacked canvas.

10. Resize the window and canvas.

The activities we have just performed are shown as follows:

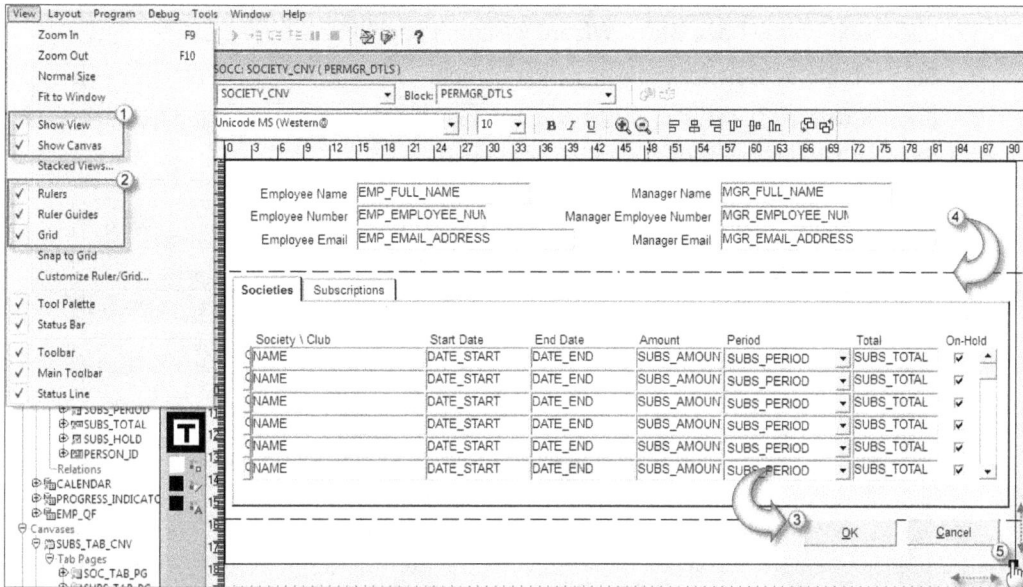

How it works...

We have positioned the items on the tabbed canvas first of all. We then positioned the tabbed canvas on the main canvas of the form. The tabbed canvas is a stacked canvas and that means it has a parent-child relationship with a content canvas. This is the canvas on which it will be displayed. We set the **Window** property of the tabbed canvas to the **SOCIETY_WND** window. The **SOCIETY_WND** window has the **Primary Canvas** property of **SOCIETY_CNV**. Therefore, we know that the stacked canvas we created will be stacked on the **SOCIETY_CNV** canvas.

Creating a new block

Now we are going to create a new block to add items on our **Subscriptions** tab.

How to do it...

To create a detail block on the **Subscriptions** tab, perform the following steps:

1. Open the XXHRSOCC.fmb form in **Forms Developer**.
2. In the **Object Navigator** click on **Data Blocks**.
3. Click the green plus (+) sign to launch the data block wizard.

4. Select the **Use the Data Block Wizard** radio button when prompted in the **New Data Block** window and click **OK**.

5. Click **Next** on the **Data Block Wizard** welcome page (if this appears).

6. Select **Table or View** for the type of data block.

7. Enter **XXHR_PER_MEDIA_SUBS_V** and press *Tab*. The available columns will appear as shown in the following screenshot:

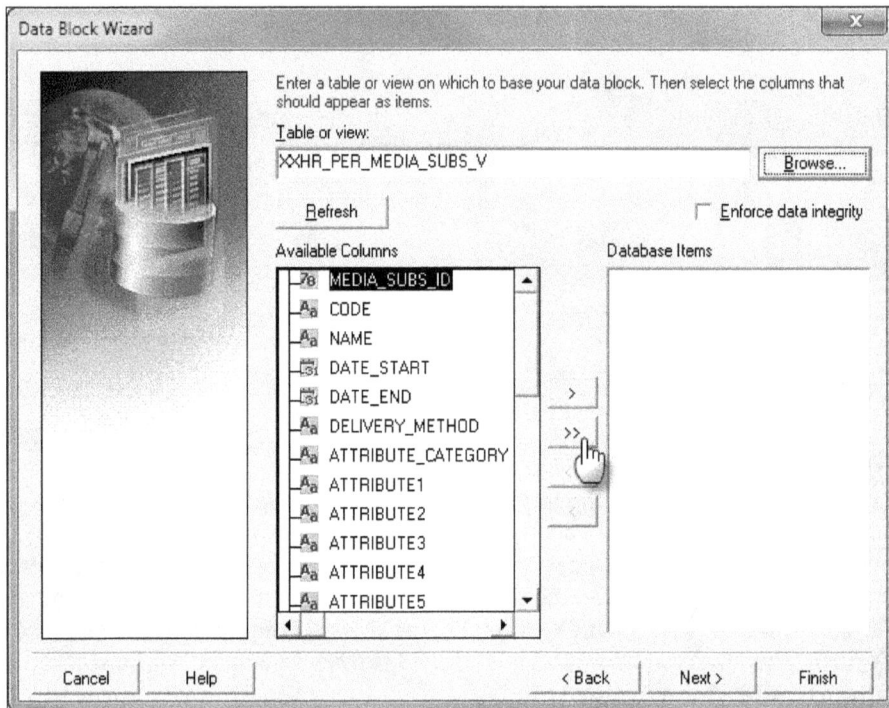

8. Click the **>>** button to shift all of the columns to the **Database Items** side.

9. Click **Finish**.

10. The **Layout Wizard** will appear and click **Next** on the welcome page.

11. Select **SUBS_TAB_CNV** for the **Canvas** field from the drop-down list.

12. Select **SUBS_TAB_PG** for the **Tab Page** field from the drop-down list.

13. Click **Next**.

14. Select the following fields and click the **>** button to shift them to the **Displayed Items** side:

    - **NAME**
    - **DATE_START**

❏ **DATE_END**

❏ **DELIVERY_METHOD**

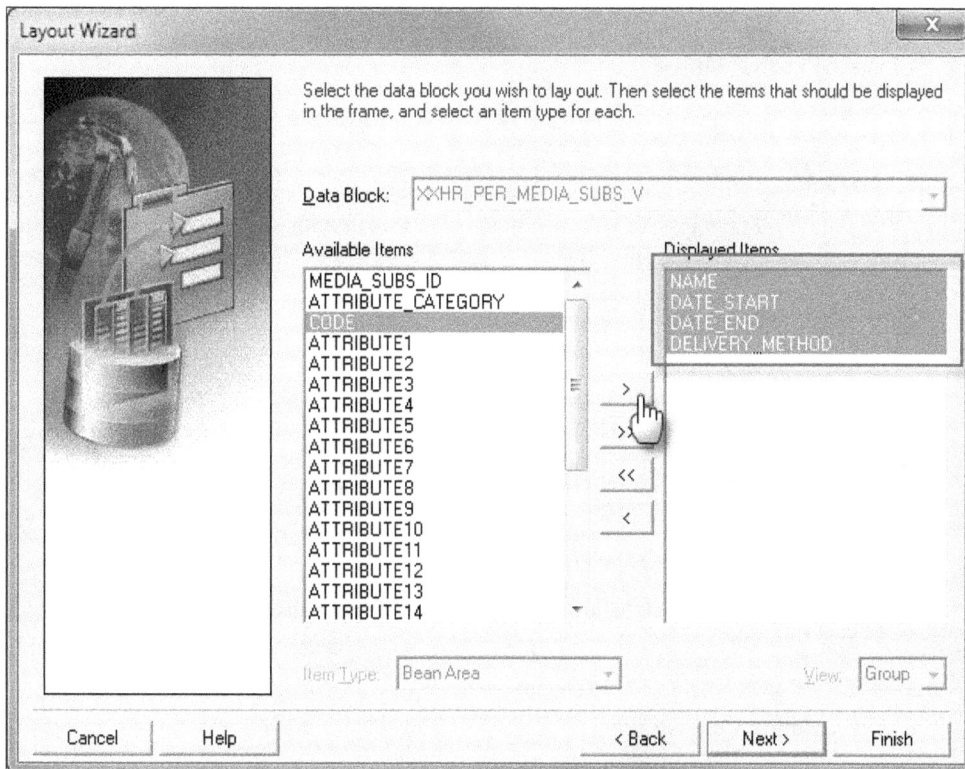

15. Click on **Next** and set the prompt and width for each item as follows:

Name	Prompt	Width
NAME	Subscription	5
DATE_START	Start Date	1.2
DATE_END	End Date	1.2
DELIVERY_METHOD	Delivery Method	2

16. Click **Next** and select **Tabular** as the layout style.

17. Click **Finish**.

Note: The canvas window will open with the items on it.

18. In the **Layout Editor**, click on the **Subscriptions** tab.

19. Highlight the FRAME around the new items and delete it. (Press delete on the keyboard. The frame was generated automatically by the **Layout Wizard** and we don't want it.)

20. Close the **Layout Editor**.

21. Save the form.

How it works...

We have now created a new block using the block wizard. The block is a detail block on the **Subscriptions** tab we created earlier.

Setting block properties

Now we will set the block and item properties for the new block that we have created.

How to do it...

To set the block properties, perform the following steps:

1. In the **Object Navigator** click on **Data Blocks**.

2. Right-click the data block called **XXHR_PER_MEDIA_SUBS_V** and open the **Property Palette**.

3. Change the following block properties:
    - **Name**: PER_SUBS
    - **Subclass Information**: Property Class
    - **Property Class Name**: BLOCK
    - **Number of Records Displayed**: 6
    - **Show Scroll Bar**: Yes
    - **Scroll Bar Canvas**: SUBS_TAB_CNV
    - **Scroll Bar Tab Page**: SUBS_TAB_PG
    - **Scroll Bar X Position**: 8.583
    - **Scroll Bar Y Position**: .502
    - **Previous Navigation Data Block**: PER_SOCIETIES
    - **Next Navigation Data Block**: PER_SOCIETIES

4. Right-click the data block called **PER_SOCIETIES** and open the **Property Palette**.

5. Change the following block properties:

   ❑ **Previous Navigation Data Block**: PER_SUBS

   ❑ **Next Navigation Data Block**: PER_SUBS

6. In the **Object Navigator**, click and drag the **PER_SUBS** block until it is below the **PER_SOCIETIES** block as shown in the following screenshot:

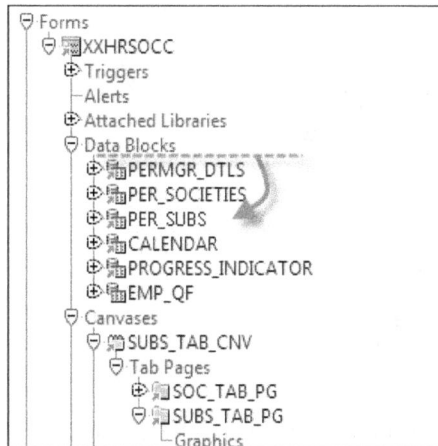

7. Save the form.

How it works...

We have now set the block properties for our detail **Subscriptions** block. We have also moved it below the **PER_SOCIETIES** block in the navigator because this is the default navigation path forms will use, unless there are block properties set specifically defining the next and previous navigation blocks.

Setting item properties

We will now set the properties of the items in the **PER_SUBS** block.

How to do it...

To set the properties of the items in the **PER_SUBS** block, perform the following steps:

1. In the **Object Navigator**, expand to **Data Blocks | PER_SUBS | Items**.

2. Open the **Property Palette** for the **NAME** and **DELIVERY_METHOD** items and set the following properties:

   ❑ **Subclass Information**: TEXT_ITEM

   ❑ **Prompt Justification**: Start

❑ **Prompt Attachment Edge**: Top

❑ **Prompt Alignment**: Start

❑ **Prompt Attachment Offset**: 0

❑ **Prompt Alignment Offset**: .05

3. Open the **Property Palette** for the **DATE_START, DATE_END** items and set the following properties:

❑ **Subclass Information**: TEXT_ITEM_DATE

❑ **Prompt Justification**: Start

❑ **Prompt Attachment Edge**: Top

❑ **Prompt Alignment**: Start

❑ **Prompt Attachment Offset**: 0

❑ **Prompt Alignment Offset**: .05

4. Set the **Required** property of the **NAME** item to **Yes**.

How it works...

We have now set the properties of the items in the **PER_SUBS** block.

Creating a relationship between the master and detail blocks

Now we are going to create a relationship between the master and detail block. This will automatically create associated triggers and code that will query the detail block when the master block is queried.

How to do it...

To create a relationship, perform the following tasks:

1. In the **Object Navigator** expand the **Data Blocks | PERMGR_DTLS** nodes.

2. Click on the **Relations** node and click the **+** on the left side toolbar to create a new relationship.

3. Complete the wizard with the following details:

❑ **Detail Block**: PER_SUBS

❑ **Join Condition**: EMP_PERSON_ID = PERSON_ID

4. Click on **OK**.

5. Save the form.

How it works...

We have created a relationship to link the detail block with the master block. Forms developer will automatically create triggers and code to automatically query the detail block whenever the master block returns or navigates to a new record.

Adding a record indicator to a block

We are now going to add a record indicator to the **PER_SUBS** multi record block. This is the little bar on the left-hand side which shows the current record the cursor is on.

How to do it...

To add a record indicator, perform the following tasks:

1. In the **Object Navigator**, open the **Data Blocks | PER_SUBS | Items** nodes.
2. Scroll down to the item before the **NAME** item and click the **+** icon from the left-hand toolbar to add an item.
3. Open the **Property Palette** for the item that has just been created and set the following properties:
   - **Name**: CURRENT_RECORD_INDICATOR
   - **Subclass Information**: CURRENT_RECORD_INDICATOR
   - **Canvas**: SUBS_TAB_CNV
   - **Tab Page**: SUBS_TAB_PG
4. Save the form.

How it works...

The current record indicator is a dummy item that sits to the left-hand side of a multi-record block. It highlights the record the form currently has focus on and is a feature among all multi-record blocks in professional forms.

Sizing and positioning items on a tabbed canvas

We are now going to position the items on the **Subscriptions** tab. Some property classes fix the width of the items as it is inherited from the property class. Examples of this are date fields and the current record indicator fields. The width of these fields should be left alone as the property is inherited to conform to Oracle standards. The width of the text items, however, largely depends upon how much space is available and the maximum size of the field.

How to do it...

To size and position the items, perform the following:

1. In the **Object Navigator**, set the properties of the following items:

Item name	Width	X position	Y position
CURRENT_RECORD_INDICATOR	.1	.115	.502
NAME	4.48	.229	.502
DATE_START	1.2	4.708	.502
DATE_END	1.2	5.906	.502
DELIVERY_METHOD	1.48	7.104	.502

2. In the **Object Navigator**, open the **Layout Editor** for the **Canvases | SUBS_TAB_CNV** canvas.

3. Click on the **Subscriptions** tab.

4. Resize the tab canvas so that there is only one character to the right and one space underneath the items within it. The screen should look similar to the following screenshot:

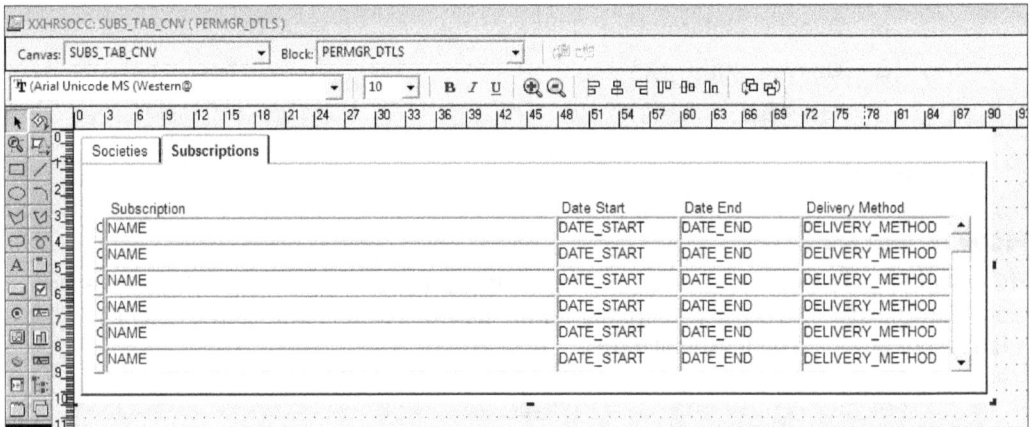

How it works...

The items on the canvas need to conform to Oracle standards but apart from that it is important to utilize space as much as possible.

Aligning a tabbed canvas on a content canvas

If changes are made to the size of the stacked canvas it will need to be repositioned. This is because the properties of the stacked canvas are set back to 0 so it will appear in the top-left hand corner of the main canvas. Therefore, perform the following steps to ensure that the layout is still as desired.

How to do it...

To move the stacked canvas, perform the following steps:

1. Navigate to **Canvases | SOCIETY_CNV** and open the **Layout Editor**.

2. Drag the stacked canvas down and across, so that there is one line above and below and one character space on either side of the stacked canvas as shown in the following screenshot:

> Note: You may have to resize the canvas and the view as well. The following screenshot shows the canvas with the **View | Show Canvas** unchecked from the main menu.

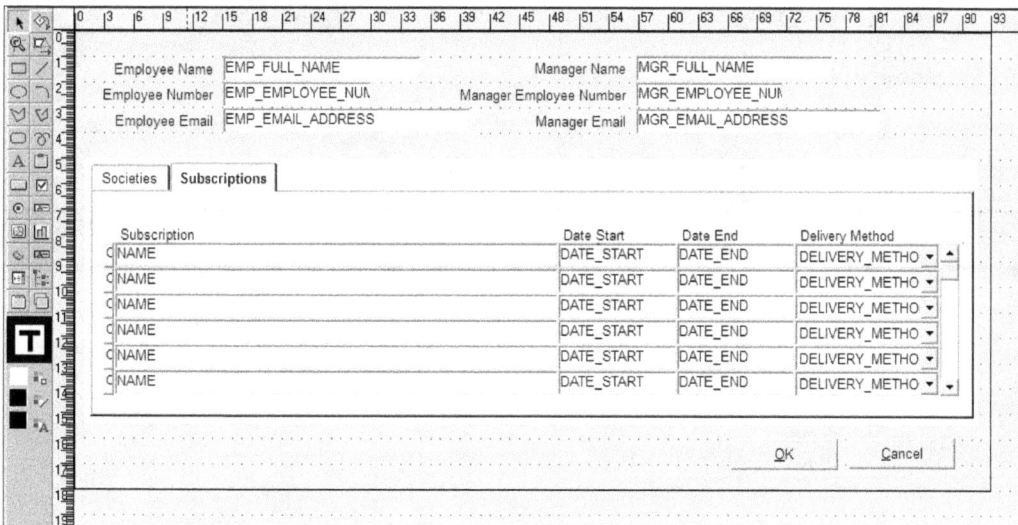

How it works...

We have now moved items and the stacked canvas so that they appear on the screen to conform to GUI standards. Also, it is important that no items are overlapping the window and canvas borders (when using tab pages you are not permitted to move objects outside the tab borders) so they must be resized accordingly.

> Objects must always be within the canvas window; otherwise you will get a compilation error. However, you can have items outside a view window and use a scrollbar to view items outside the window. However, if it makes sense it is better to use multiple tabs.

Adding a form level trigger to show a tabbed canvas

We need to show the view when the form is opened. We will therefore add some code to the **WHEN-NEW-FORM-INSTANCE** trigger to show the tabbed canvas.

How to do it...

To add a new form level trigger, perform the following steps:

1. Navigate to **Triggers | WHEN-NEW-FORM-INSTANCE** and double-click to open the **PL/SQL Editor**.

2. Before the line `EXECUTE_TRIGGER('QUERY_FIND');` type the following code as shown in the following screenshot:

   ```
   set_canvas_property('SUBS_TAB_CNV', TOPMOST_TAB_PAGE, 'SOC_TAB_
   PG');
   show_view('SUBS_TAB_CNV');
   ```

3. Compile the trigger code.

4. Save the form.

How it works...

We have added code to the **WHEN-NEW-FORM-INSTANCE** trigger so that the first tab displayed when the form opens is the **Societies** tab. We need to code some functionality to manage the events when a user clicks on a tab. We are going to do this next and put the code into a package.

Adding code to manage a tabbed canvas

Oracle provides code to handle tabs. There are two files; one is `fndtabs.txt` to handle tabbed regions where there is no scrolling or fixed fields and in cases where there is scrolling but no fixed fields. The second file is called `fndtabff.txt` and is for tabbed regions where there are fixed fields. In our case, we have independent tabs with no scrolling or fixed fields so we need the `fndtabs.txt` file. It can be located in `$FND_TOP/resource`.

How to do it...

To add a procedure to manage the tabbed pages, perform the following steps:

1. Open WinSCP and log onto the application server.
2. Navigate to `$FND_TOP/resource`.
3. Open the file `fndtabs.txt` and copy all of the text in the file.
4. In **Forms Developer**, navigate to **Program Units** and click **+** to create a new procedure.
5. Create a new procedure called **SUBS_TAB_CNV**.
6. Copy the code from `fndtabs.txt` into the procedure.

7. Modify the code as is shown in the following screenshot:

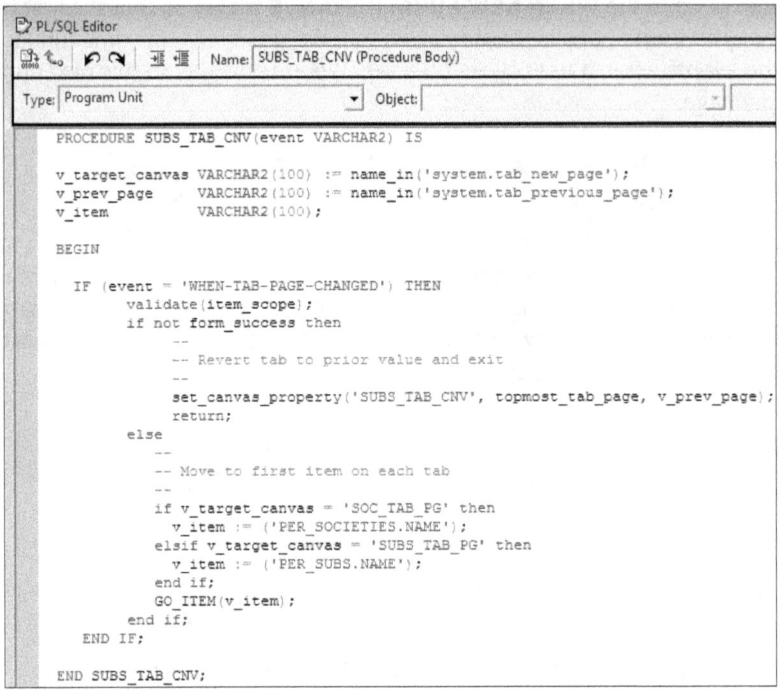

8. Compile the procedure.

9. Navigate to **Triggers (Form Level)** and click the green **+** icon to create a new **WHEN-TAB-PAGE-CHANGED** trigger.

10. Add the code to call our **SUBS_TAB_CNV** procedure as shown in the following screenshot:

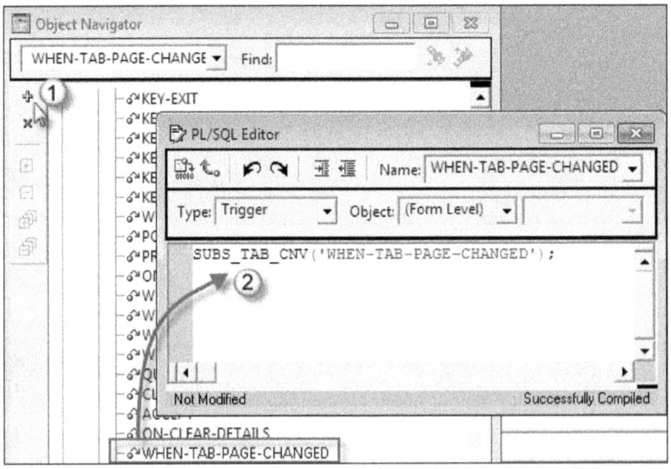

11. Compile the code.

12. Save the form.

How it works...

The trigger will fire whenever the user clicks on the tab of the tab page region we created. The procedure we created handles which page to display and which block to navigate to.

Creating program units

We are going to create a program unit within the form to write code that will handle various tasks within the form. We will be performing the following in the coming recipe:

- ▶ Creating a new package to handle database transactions
- ▶ Adding triggers to capture transactional events on a block
- ▶ Creating triggers to set the WHO columns

Creating a new package to handle database transactions

We are now going to create a package to handle the database transaction for the **PER_SUBS** block. The package name will be **PER_SUBS** as it will manage the transactions for the **PER_SUBS** block.

How to do it...

To create the package specification, perform the following steps:

1. In **Forms Developer** navigate to **Program Units**.

2. Click the **+** on the left-hand toolbar to create a new package specification.

3. In the **Name** field type **PER_SUBS**.

4. Select **Package Spec** as shown in the following screenshot and click **OK**:

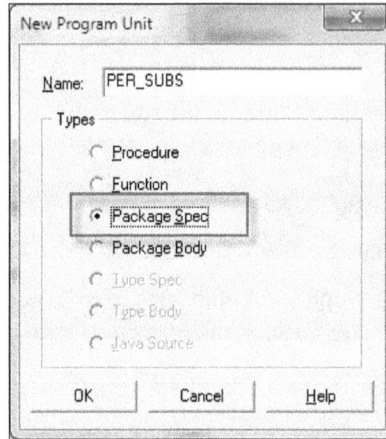

5. In the **PL/SQL Editor** we need to add four procedures as follows:

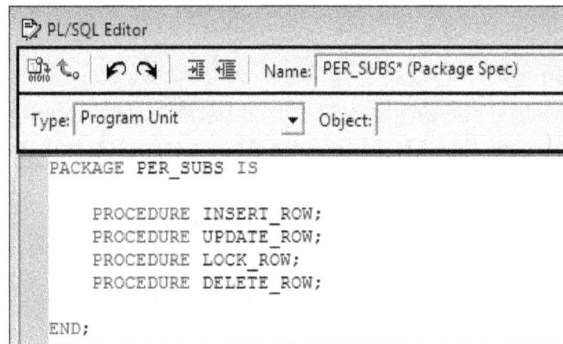

6. Compile the package specification.

7. In **Forms Developer** navigate to **Program Units**.

8. Click the **+** on the left-hand toolbar to create a new package body.

9. In the **Name** field type **PER_SUBS**.

10. Select **Package Body** and click **OK**.

11. In the **PL/SQL Editor** we need to write the code to call the database package **XXHR_PER_SOCIETIES_PVT**.

> Note: The code shown in the following image is available in a text file called Ch3 Form Code PER_SUBS.txt and is available in the download bundle.

The following code is the code for inserting a record:

```
PROCEDURE INSERT_ROW IS
BEGIN
  xxhr_per_media_subs_pvt.insert_row(
            p_MEDIA_SUBS_ID => :PER_SUBS.MEDIA_SUBS_ID,
            p_CODE => :PER_SUBS.CODE,
            p_DATE_END => :PER_SUBS.DATE_END ,
            p_DATE_START => :PER_SUBS.DATE_START,
            p_DELIVERY_METHOD => :PER_SUBS.DELIVERY_METHOD,
            p_PERSON_ID => :PER_SUBS.PERSON_ID,
            p_ATTRIBUTE_CATEGORY => :PER_SUBS.ATTRIBUTE_CATEGORY,
            p_ATTRIBUTE1 => :PER_SUBS.ATTRIBUTE1,
            p_ATTRIBUTE2 => :PER_SUBS.ATTRIBUTE2,
            p_ATTRIBUTE3 => :PER_SUBS.ATTRIBUTE3 ,
            p_ATTRIBUTE4 => :PER_SUBS.ATTRIBUTE4,
            p_ATTRIBUTE5 => :PER_SUBS.ATTRIBUTE5,
            p_ATTRIBUTE6 => :PER_SUBS.ATTRIBUTE6 ,
            p_ATTRIBUTE7 => :PER_SUBS.ATTRIBUTE7,
            p_ATTRIBUTE8 => :PER_SUBS.ATTRIBUTE8 ,
            p_ATTRIBUTE9 => :PER_SUBS.ATTRIBUTE9 ,
            p_ATTRIBUTE10 => :PER_SUBS.ATTRIBUTE10 ,
            p_ATTRIBUTE11 => :PER_SUBS.ATTRIBUTE11 ,
            p_ATTRIBUTE12 => :PER_SUBS.ATTRIBUTE12 ,
            p_ATTRIBUTE13 => :PER_SUBS.ATTRIBUTE13 ,
            p_ATTRIBUTE14 => :PER_SUBS.ATTRIBUTE14 ,
            p_ATTRIBUTE15 => :PER_SUBS.ATTRIBUTE15 ,
            p_ATTRIBUTE16 => :PER_SUBS.ATTRIBUTE16 ,
            p_ATTRIBUTE17 => :PER_SUBS.ATTRIBUTE17 ,
            p_ATTRIBUTE18 => :PER_SUBS.ATTRIBUTE18 ,
            p_ATTRIBUTE19 => :PER_SUBS.ATTRIBUTE19,
            p_ATTRIBUTE20 => :PER_SUBS.ATTRIBUTE20 ,
            p_CREATION_DATE => :PER_SUBS.CREATION_DATE ,
            p_CREATED_BY => :PER_SUBS.CREATED_BY,
            p_LAST_UPDATE_DATE => :PER_SUBS.LAST_UPDATE_DATE,
            p_LAST_UPDATED_BY => :PER_SUBS.LAST_UPDATED_BY ,
            p_LAST_UPDATE_LOGIN => :PER_SUBS.LAST_UPDATE_LOGIN);
END;
```

The following code is the code for updating a record:

```
PROCEDURE UPDATE_ROW IS
BEGIN
xxhr_per_media_subs_pvt.update_row(
            p_MEDIA_SUBS_ID => :PER_SUBS.MEDIA_SUBS_ID,
            p_CODE => :PER_SUBS.CODE,
            p_DATE_END => :PER_SUBS.DATE_END ,
            p_DATE_START => :PER_SUBS.DATE_START,
            p_DELIVERY_METHOD => :PER_SUBS.DELIVERY_METHOD,
            p_PERSON_ID => :PER_SUBS.PERSON_ID,
            p_ATTRIBUTE_CATEGORY => :PER_SUBS.ATTRIBUTE_CATEGORY,
            p_ATTRIBUTE1 => :PER_SUBS.ATTRIBUTE1,
            p_ATTRIBUTE2 => :PER_SUBS.ATTRIBUTE2,
            p_ATTRIBUTE3 => :PER_SUBS.ATTRIBUTE3 ,
            p_ATTRIBUTE4 => :PER_SUBS.ATTRIBUTE4,
            p_ATTRIBUTE5 => :PER_SUBS.ATTRIBUTE5,
            p_ATTRIBUTE6 => :PER_SUBS.ATTRIBUTE6 ,
            p_ATTRIBUTE7 => :PER_SUBS.ATTRIBUTE7,
            p_ATTRIBUTE8 => :PER_SUBS.ATTRIBUTE8 ,
            p_ATTRIBUTE9 => :PER_SUBS.ATTRIBUTE9 ,
            p_ATTRIBUTE10 => :PER_SUBS.ATTRIBUTE10 ,
            p_ATTRIBUTE11 => :PER_SUBS.ATTRIBUTE11 ,
            p_ATTRIBUTE12 => :PER_SUBS.ATTRIBUTE12 ,
            p_ATTRIBUTE13 => :PER_SUBS.ATTRIBUTE13 ,
            p_ATTRIBUTE14 => :PER_SUBS.ATTRIBUTE14 ,
            p_ATTRIBUTE15 => :PER_SUBS.ATTRIBUTE15 ,
            p_ATTRIBUTE16 => :PER_SUBS.ATTRIBUTE16 ,
            p_ATTRIBUTE17 => :PER_SUBS.ATTRIBUTE17 ,
            p_ATTRIBUTE18 => :PER_SUBS.ATTRIBUTE18 ,
            p_ATTRIBUTE19 => :PER_SUBS.ATTRIBUTE19,
            p_ATTRIBUTE20 => :PER_SUBS.ATTRIBUTE20 ,
            p_CREATION_DATE => :PER_SUBS.CREATION_DATE ,
            p_CREATED_BY => :PER_SUBS.CREATED_BY,
            p_LAST_UPDATE_DATE => :PER_SUBS.LAST_UPDATE_DATE,
            p_LAST_UPDATED_BY => :PER_SUBS.LAST_UPDATED_BY ,
            p_LAST_UPDATE_LOGIN => :PER_SUBS.LAST_UPDATE_LOGIN);
END;
```

The following code is the code for locking and deleting a record:

```
PROCEDURE LOCK_ROW IS
BEGIN

    null;
END;

PROCEDURE DELETE_ROW IS
BEGIN
    xxhr_per_subs_pvt.delete_row(p_MEDIA_SUBS_ID => :PER_SUBS.MEDIA_SUBS_ID);
END;
```

12. Compile the code.
13. Save the form.

How it works...

We have created the code in the form that will perform the database transactions. The database package that we created at the beginning of the chapter is called and passed the values from the **PER_SUBS** block.

Adding triggers to capture transactional events on a block

We now need to add four triggers to our **PER_SUBS** block to capture events when a user performs a commit action. We will call the procedures we have just created to perform an insert, update, or delete.

How to do it...

To add the triggers on the **PER_SUBS** block, perform the following steps:

1. Open the **Object Navigator** and expand the **Data Blocks | PER_SUBS** block.
2. Highlight **Triggers** and click the **+** on the left-hand toolbar to add a trigger.
3. From the list of available triggers select **ON-INSERT**.
4. In the **PL/SQL Editor** type the following call to our program unit:

   ```
   per_subs.insert_row;
   ```

5. Click on the compile button to compile the code.
6. Close the **PL/SQL Editor**.
7. Highlight **Triggers** and click the **+** on the left-hand toolbar to add a trigger.
8. From the list of available triggers select **ON-UPDATE**.

9. In the **PL/SQL Editor** type the following call to our program unit:

```
per_subs.update_row;
```

10. Click on the compile button to compile the code.

11. Close the **PL/SQL Editor**.

12. Highlight **Triggers** and click the **+** on the left-hand toolbar to add a trigger.

13. From the list of available triggers select **ON-DELETE**.

14. In the **PL/SQL Editor** type the following call to our program unit:

```
per_subs.delete_row;
```

15. Click on the compile button to compile the code.

16. Close the **PL/SQL Editor**.

17. Highlight **Triggers** and click the **+** on the left-hand toolbar to add a trigger.

18. From the list of available triggers select **ON-LOCK**.

19. In the **PL/SQL Editor** type the following call to our program unit:

```
per_subs.lock_row;
```

20. Click on the compile button to compile the code.

21. Close the **PL/SQL Editor**.

22. Save the form.

How it works...

We have now added the triggers that will call our **PER_SUBS** procedures whenever a user performs an insert, update, or delete.

Creating triggers to set the WHO columns

When we are performing INSERTS and UPDATES Oracle provides some standard fields to audit changes to a record and who made the changes. These are known as the WHO fields and they are **CREATED_BY**, **CREATION_DATE**, **LAST_UPDATED_BY**, **LAST_UPDATE_DATE**, and **LAST_UPDATE_LOGIN**. We can call a standard package that will set the data in these fields before the database transaction occurs. This is done in the **PRE-INSERT** and **PRE-UPDATE** triggers.

How to do it...

To add the triggers to set the WHO columns, perform the following steps:

1. Open the **Object Navigator** and expand the **Data Blocks | PER_SUBS** block.

2. Highlight **Triggers** and click the **+** on the left-hand toolbar to add a trigger.

3. From the list of available triggers select **PRE-INSERT**.

4. In the **PL/SQL Editor**, type the following call to our program unit:

   ```
   FND_STANDARD.SET_WHO;
   ```

5. Click on the compile button to compile the code.

6. Close the **PL/SQL Editor**.

7. Highlight **Triggers** and click the **+** on the left-hand toolbar to add a trigger.

8. From the list of available triggers select **PRE-UPDATE**.

9. In the **PL/SQL Editor**, type the following call to our program unit:

   ```
   FND_STANDARD.SET_WHO;
   ```

10. Click on the compile button to compile the code.

11. Close the **PL/SQL Editor**.

12. Save the form.

How it works...

We have now created two triggers (**PRE-INSERT** and **PRE-UPDATE**) that call the Oracle FND_STANDARD API to set the WHO columns. The **PER_SUBS** block will now contain the six block-level triggers as shown in the following screenshot:

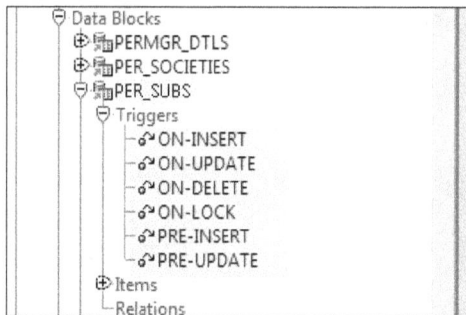

Adding lookups, date fields, and lists

We will now change the properties of some of the items in our new block to create a new lookup, configure date fields, and add a list item. To do this we will perform the following tasks:

- Creating a lookup
- Creating a new LOV based upon a record group
- Configuring date fields
- Creating a list item

Creating a lookup

If you look at the table definition you will see that there is a column called CODE. In the database we will be storing the code of the society in this field. However, we need to have a mechanism to be able to add new societies and clubs and also we need a more user-friendly name to display in the form. To achieve this we will create a lookup, which will allow us to add new values without having to modify the form.

How to do it...

To create a lookup, perform the following steps:

1. Log in to Oracle and select the **Application Developer** responsibility.

2. Navigate to **Application | Lookups | Application Object Library** and the **Application Object Library Lookups** window will open.

3. Populate the form header as shown in the following table:

Field name	Value
Type	XXHR_SUBS_LOV
Meaning	List of Subscriptions
Application	XXHR Custom Application
Description	List of Subscriptions

4. Populate the detail block with the following data:

Code	Meaning	Description
SUB01	Working Together	Working together weekly
SUB02	Out and About	Out and About monthly newsletter
SUB03	Help at Home	Help at Home monthly newsletter
SUB04	Badminton Club News	Badminton Club News monthly
SUB05	Company News	Company News weekly

The form should look like the following:

Code	Meaning	Description	Tag	From	To	Enabled [ ]
SUB01	Working Together	Working together weekly		14-SEP-2011		✔
SUB02	Out and About	Out and About monthly		14-SEP-2011		✔
SUB03	Help at Home	Help at Home monthly n		14-SEP-2011		✔
SUB04	Badminton Club News	Badminton Club News n		14-SEP-2011		✔
SUB05	Company News	Company News weekly		14-SEP-2011		✔

Application Object Library Lookups

Type XXHR_SUBS_LOV
Meaning List of Subscriptions
Application XXHR Custom Application
Description List of Subscriptions

Access Level
• User
○ Extensible
○ System

Effective Dates

5. Click the **Save** button in the toolbar (or *Ctrl + S*) to save the record.

6. Exit the form.

How it works...

We have created a new lookup that we will use in our form for a list of subscriptions. We create a lookup so that we can control the quality of data that the user is permitted to enter. If we can reduce the number of free text fields then the better the quality of the data will be. Of course there will be certain fields that should be free text such as notes or descriptions and so on.

Creating a new LOV based upon a record group

We are now going to create a list of values (LOV) for the NAME field using the lookup that we have just created. This is so that the user will need to select a value from the list. To create an LOV we first need to create a record group to base the list upon.

How to do it...

To create an LOV using the LOV wizard, perform the following steps:

1. In **Forms Developer** navigate to **LOVs** and click the **+** icon on the left-hand toolbar to add a new LOV.

2. Select **Use the LOV Wizard** from the LOV wizard and click **OK**.

3. On the next screen select **New record group based on a query**.

4. Click **Next**.

5. In SQL Query Statement, type the following query:

```
SELECT lookup_code, meaning, description
FROM fnd_lookup_types flt, fnd_lookup_values flv
WHERE flt.lookup_type = flv.lookup_type
AND flt.lookup_type = 'XXHR_SUBS_LOV'
AND enabled_flag = 'Y'
```

6. Click **Next**.

7. Shift all of the columns across by clicking **>>** button and click **Next**.

8. Set the following properties:

Column	Title	Width	Return value
LOOKUP_CODE	Lookup_Code	0	PER_SUBS.CODE
MEANING	Subscription	2	PER_SUBS.NAME
DESCRIPTION	Description	0.5	

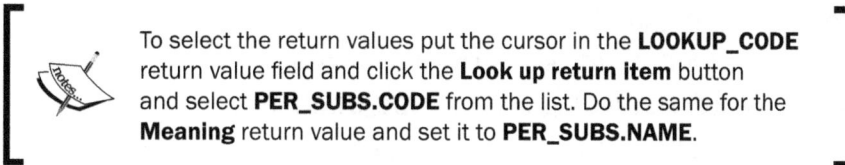

> To select the return values put the cursor in the **LOOKUP_CODE** return value field and click the **Look up return item** button and select **PER_SUBS.CODE** from the list. Do the same for the **Meaning** return value and set it to **PER_SUBS.NAME**.

9. Click **Next**.

10. Set the title of the LOV to **Subscriptions** and click **Next**.

11. Click **Next** and **Next** again.

12. When prompted to assign the LOV select **PER_SUBS.NAME** and shift it across to **Assigned Items** by clicking **>**.

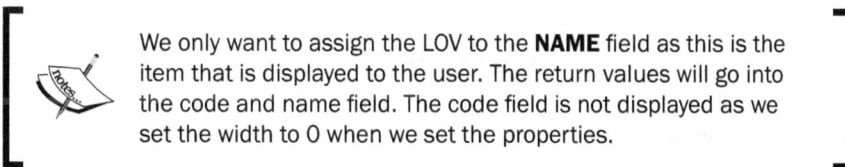

> We only want to assign the LOV to the **NAME** field as this is the item that is displayed to the user. The return values will go into the code and name field. The code field is not displayed as we set the width to 0 when we set the properties.

13. Click **Finish**.

14. Navigate to **Record Groups** and set the **Name** property of the generated record group to SUBS_RG.

15. Navigate to **LOVs** and set the **Name** property of the generated LOV to SUBS_LOV.

16. Set the **Subclass Information** to **LOV**.

17. Save the form.

How it works...

We have used the LOV wizard to create an LOV. The LOV wizard allows us to enter a query to base our LOV upon and will automatically create a record group for us. We assign the items in the form that the LOV is assigned to so that the LOV icon appears when the user navigates to the form.

Configuring date fields

We now need to configure the date fields to use the standard list of values for date fields. We need to set the date fields to use a DUMMY LOV called enable list lamp and then code the **KEY-LISTVAL** trigger.

How to do it...

To create a list of values for the date fields, perform the following:

1. In **Forms Developer** navigate to **Data Blocks | PER_SUBS | Items**.
2. Set the **List of Values** property for the **DATE_START** and **DATE_END** fields to **ENABLE_LIST_LAMP**.
3. Expand the **DATE_START** field and highlight **Triggers**.
4. Add a new **KEY-LISTVAL** trigger to the **DATE_START** field.
5. In the **PL/SQL Editor**, type `calendar.show;`
6. Add a new **KEY-LISTVAL** trigger to the **DATE_END** field.
7. In the **PL/SQL Editor**, type `calendar.show;`

How it works...

We have added triggers to the date fields to call the standard calendar for the date fields.

Creating a list item

We now want to change the **DELIVERY_METHOD** field to be a static list. We only use LIST items for relatively small lists that are likely to be pretty static. The list in our form is small and is unlikely to change so we will use a list. The benefit of a list is that it tends to reduce mouse clicks but a disadvantage is that the values in the list require more effort to add or remove.

How to do it...

To create a LIST item, perform the following steps:

1. In **Forms Developer** navigate to **Data Blocks | PER_SUBS | Items | DELIVERY_METHOD**.
2. Set the **Subclass Information** property to **LIST**.

3. In the **Property Palette** click on the **Elements In List** property and you will be prompted to enter elements. Fill in the elements as follows:

List element	List item value
Email	E
White mail	W
SMS	S

4. Save the form.

How it works...

We have created a list item that will allow the user to select the delivery method for any correspondence to the subscription.

Controlling menu items

In this recipe, we will show how standard menu items can be controlled. We are going to disable the standard 'New' menu item in the **PERMGR_DTLS** block as this action cannot be performed in this block. We are also going to create a new menu item and capture the event when the user selects the item from the menu or toolbar. There are specific issues with managing standard menu items as they are controlled by standard events in the triggers. Therefore, you may try to disable a menu item only to find that upon running the form it is enabled:

▸ Copying the standard menu from the application server and opening it in forms

▸ Disabling an existing menu item

▸ Adding a new menu item

▸ Adding a trigger to capture new menu item event

▸ Compiling the form

Copying the standard menu from the application server and opening it in forms

The first task we are going to perform is to copy over the menu from the application server. This will give us the menu items that we can reference when we are dealing with menu items.

How to do it...

To copy the menu from the application server, perform the following:

1. Open WinSCP and connect to the application tier.

2. Navigate to $AU_TOP/resource/US.

3. Copy the `FNDMENU.mmb` file to a local directory, for example, `C:\Forms\visr12` as shown in the following screenshot:

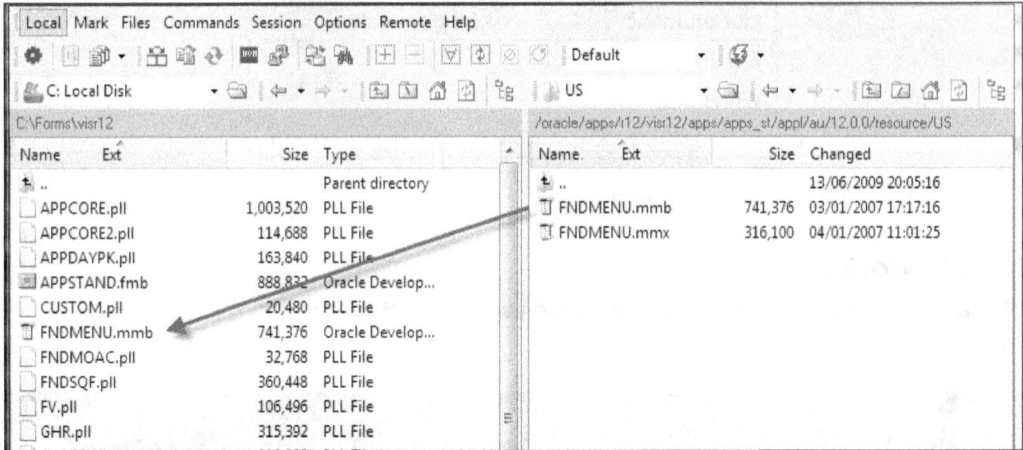

4. In **Forms Developer** open the `FNDMENU.mmb` file.

> We can open the menu to view the menu items. If we refer to a menu item in our code we will reference the menu item as it appears in the menu with a dot separating the menu hierarchy. For example, we would refer to the `NEW` item as `FILE.NEW`, as shown in the following screenshot. Please note that we must never modify the `FNDMENU`. We are opening the menu purely to view the menu item names and the structure.

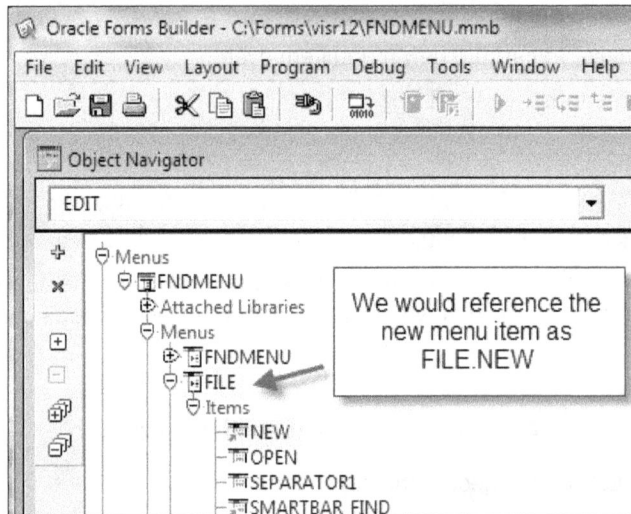

How it works...

We have copied the standard menu from the application server, so that we can see the structure of the menu items. We need to see these if we need to reference a menu item.

Disabling an existing menu item

We will disable a standard menu item that allows users to create a new record in the `PERMGR_DTLS` block as we do not want to allow users to create new records in this block.

How to do it...

To disable the "new record" menu item, perform the following steps:

1. Open the **XXHRSOCC** form in **Forms Developer**.

2. Navigate to **Data Blocks | PERMGR_DTLS | Triggers**.

3. Create a **WHEN-NEW-BLOCK-INSTANCE** block-level trigger.

4. When the **PL/SQL Editor** opens, type the lines of code shown in the following screenshot:

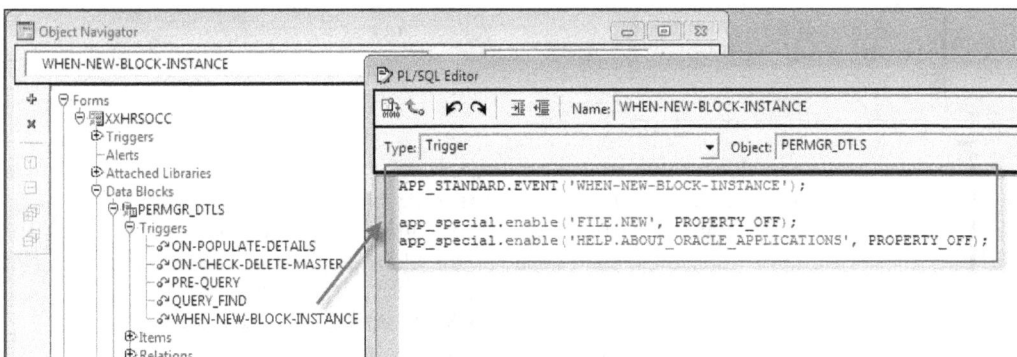

5. Right-click the **WHEN-NEW-BLOCK-ITEM** trigger and open the property palette.

6. Set the **Execution Hierarchy** property to **Override**.

> We need to set the override property as there is also a form level **WHEN-NEW-BLOCK-INSTANCE** trigger. If we do not set the property to override then the code in the form level trigger and the block-level trigger will be executed.

7. Save and transfer the form to `$AU_TOP/resource/US`.

8. Compile the form using the following command:

```
frmcmp_batch module=$AU_TOP/forms/US/XXHRSOCC.fmb userid=apps/apps
output_file=$XXHR_TOP/forms/US/XXHRSOCC.fmx compile_all=special
```

9. Log in to Oracle with the **XXEBS Extending e-Business Suite** responsibility.

10. Navigate to **Societies Form** and the societies and clubs form will open.

11. Enter an employee number in the query find window and click **Find**.

If we now look at our form it has the **New** and the **About Oracle Applications** menu items disabled.

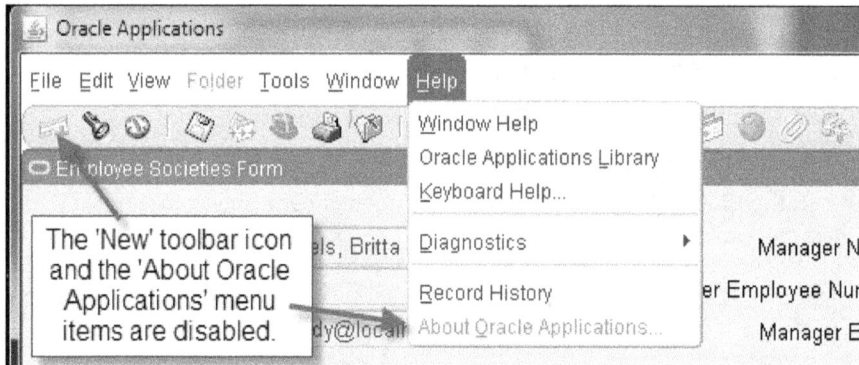

We can also disable toolbar buttons through setting properties. For example, we can disable the insert record icon on this block by setting the block properties. The 'New' toolbar button is managed by the standard application code based on the block properties. Try removing the `app_special.enable('FILE.NEW', PROPERTY_OFF);` line of code in the **WHEN-NEW-BLOCK-INSTANCE** trigger and setting the **Insert Allowed, Update Allowed, Delete Allowed** properties of the **PERMGER_DTLS** block to **No**. If you now recompile and re-run the form you will notice that the 'New' and 'Delete' toolbar items in the header block are disabled. The point to note is that there are several ways of achieving the same thing. We need to choose the easiest and in this case it would be setting the block properties.

How it works...

We have disabled the 'create record' menu item so that the user is prevented from inserting new records.

Adding a new menu item

In the next recipe, we will add a new menu item. We will add the label to the menu item and also define the icon that will be displayed on the toolbar for the menu item.

How to do it...

To add a menu item, perform the following steps:

1. In **Forms Developer** open the **XXHRSOCC** form.
2. Navigate to **Triggers** and open the **PL/SQL Editor** of the **PRE-FORM** trigger.
3. At the end of the code add the following line as shown in the following image:

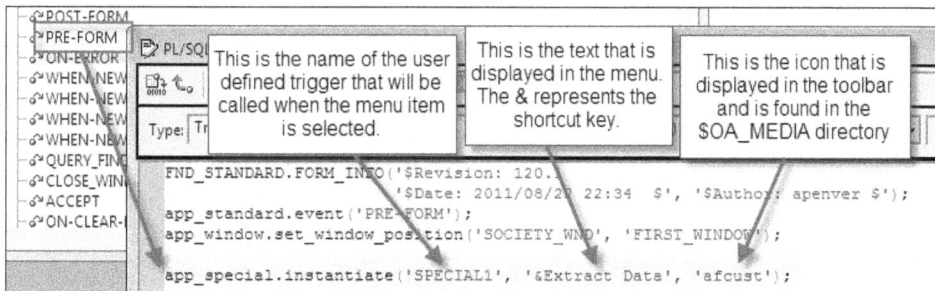

4. Compile the trigger.
5. Save the form.

How it works...

The **PRE-FORM** trigger fires first when the form is opened. We would normally perform any actions that need to be set before the form is opened. We have called the `app_special` package to initiate a menu item.

Adding a trigger to capture new menu item events

Now we need to create a form level user-defined trigger called `SPECIAL1`. The code in this trigger will be executed when the menu item or toolbar is selected.

How to do it...

To create a user defined trigger, perform the following steps:

1. In **Forms Developer** open the **XXHRSOCC** form.
2. Navigate to **Triggers** and create a new user-named form level trigger (Select <user-named> from the Triggers list of values).

3. Click **OK** and type the following code in the trigger's **PL/SQL Editor**:

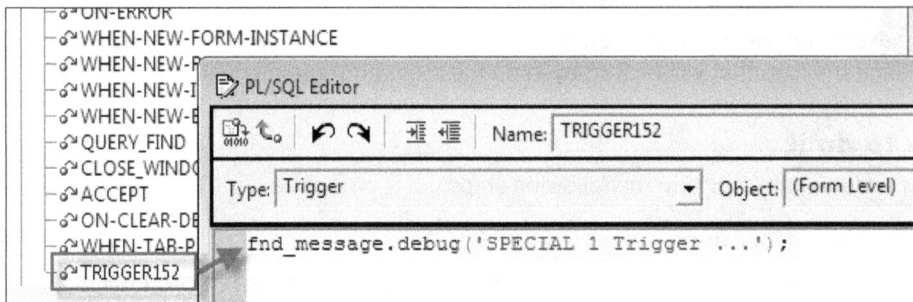

4. Compile the trigger.
5. In the **Object Navigator** open the property palette for the trigger and set the **Name** property to SPECIAL1.
6. Save the form.

How it works...

We have created a user-defined trigger called SPECIAL1. This trigger will only ever be executed when the menu item is selected.

There's more...

Oracle allows developers to customize the menu with user-defined menu entries. The menu supports up to 45 menu entries, which trigger form level user-defined triggers from the form that have the naming format SPECIALn. If we are extending a standard form we use the highest available SPECIAL trigger and work backwards. This will prevent us from clashing with Oracle's use of special triggers.

Compiling the form

We will now compile the form so that we can test the menu is visible to the user in Oracle EBS. When the user selects the menu item or toolbar button associated with the SPECIAL1 trigger we will get a message, 'SPECIAL 1 Trigger ...' displayed.

How to do it...

To test the form, perform the following steps:

1. Open WinSCP and transfer the form over to the $AU_TOP/forms/US in the application tier.
2. Open Putty and connect to the **apps** tier.

3. Navigate to the $AU_TOP/forms/US directory.

4. Compile the form with the following command:

```
frmcmp_batch module=$AU_TOP/forms/US/XXHRSOCC.fmb userid=apps/apps
output_file=$XXHR_TOP/forms/US/XXHRSOCC.fmx compile_all=special
```

5. Log in to Oracle with the **XXEBS Extending e-Business Suite** responsibility.

6. Navigate to **Societies Form** and the societies and clubs form will open.

7. Enter an employee number in the query find window and click **Find**.

8. Select **Tools | Extract Data** and the message will appear as shown in the following screenshot:

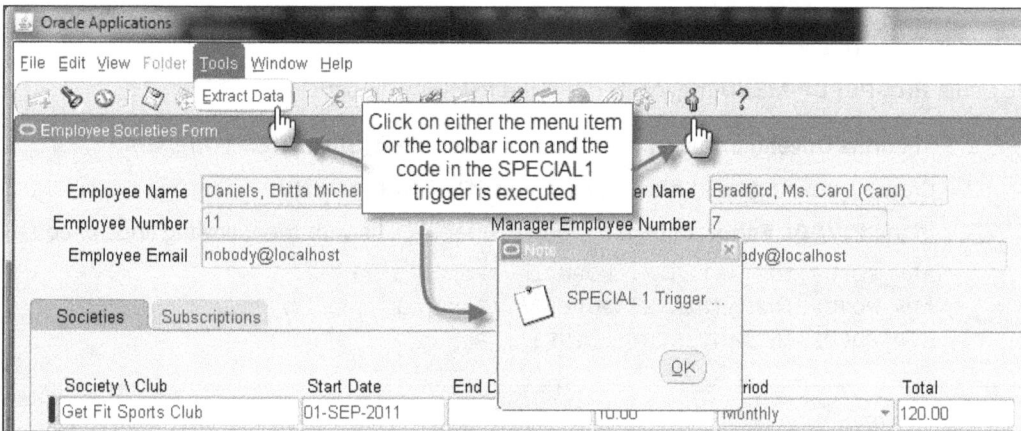

How it works...

We can see that the menu item displays a message to the user when the menu item is selected or the user clicks on the toolbar button. The toolbar triggers the code associated with the menu item. The toolbar icons are essentially a shortcut for the menu items.

Creating pop-up menu items

We are going to add some entries to the default pop-up menu. This is standard in all forms and is activated by right-clicking the mouse. We are going to add three different types of pop-up menu items as follows:

- A pop-up menu item
- A pop-up menu item with a line separator
- A pop-up menu item that is disabled

To achieve this we need to perform the following tasks:

- ▸ Adding items to a pop-up menu
- ▸ Compiling the form
- ▸ Capturing pop-up menu events

Adding items to a pop-up menu

We are going to modify the pop-up menu, which is activated by a right mouse click when in the block. We therefore need to create the additional pop-up menu items in a PRE-POP-UP trigger at block level.

How to do it...

To add a **PRE-POPUP-MENU** trigger, perform the following steps:

1. In **Forms Developer** navigate to **Data Blocks | PER_SOCIETIES | Triggers**.
2. Create a new trigger at block level called **PRE-POPUP-MENU**.
3. In the **PL/SQL Editor**, initiate the pop-up menu items with the following lines of code:

```
APP_POPUP.INSTANTIATE('POPUP1','Popup 1');
APP_POPUP.INSTANTIATE('POPUP2','Popup 2', TRUE, 'LINE');
APP_POPUP.INSTANTIATE('POPUP3','Popup 3', FALSE);
```

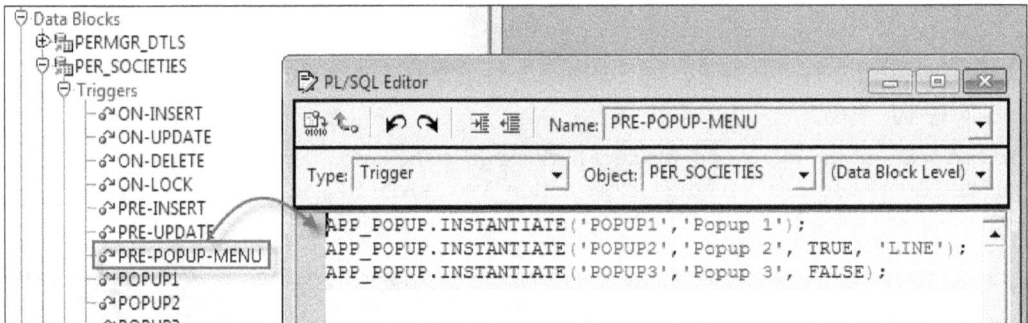

How it works...

This is going to add three items to the pop-up menu. The first item, that is, Pop-up 1 will be added to the next item in the pop-up menu. The second item, that is, Popup 2 will appear next in the pop-up menu but with a line above the menu entry. The third item will be next in the menu but will appear disabled.

Compiling the form

We are now going to compile the form so that we can see the pop-up menu in EBS.

How to do it...

To test the form, perform the following steps:

1. Open WinSCP and transfer the form over to the `$AU_TOP/forms/US` in the application tier.

2. Open Putty and connect to the **apps** tier.

3. Navigate to the `$AU_TOP/forms/US` directory.

4. Compile the form with the following command:

   ```
   frmcmp_batch module=$AU_TOP/forms/US/XXHRSOCC.fmb userid=apps/apps
   output_file=$XXHR_TOP/forms/US/XXHRSOCC.fmx compile_all=special
   ```

5. Log in to Oracle with the **XXEBS Extending e-Business Suite** responsibility.

6. Navigate to **Societies Form** and the societies and clubs form will open.

7. Enter an employee number in the query find window and click **Find**.

8. Click in the **Societies** tab and right-click the mouse and the pop-up menu will be displayed as follows:

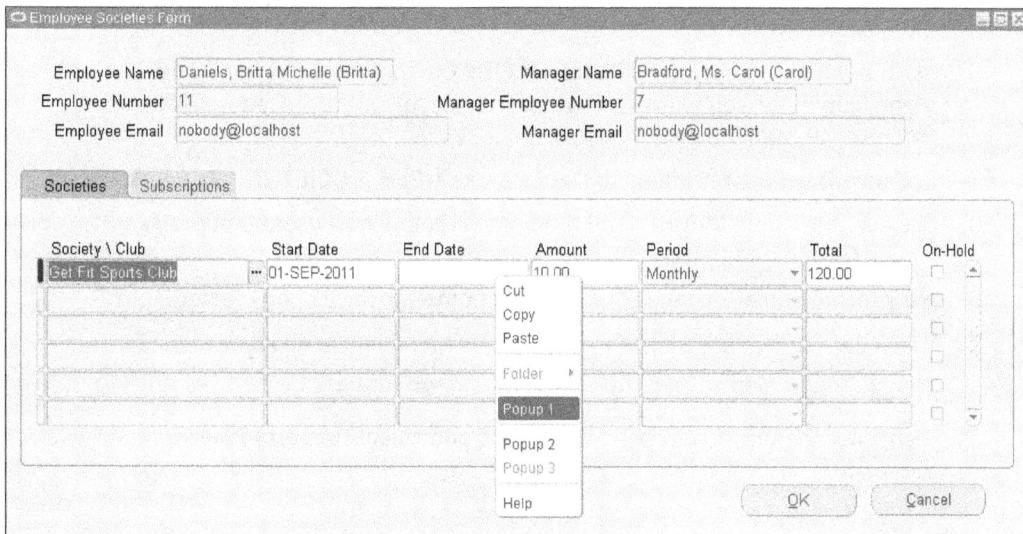

How it works...

The pop-up menu is displayed when the user right-clicks the mouse. We can add items to the pop-up menu as desired. The menu items we have added simply display a message but we can perform any PL/SQL code here to perform the actions we wish to perform.

Adding a trigger to capture pop-up events

Now that we have created the pop-up menu we need to capture the events when they are selected by the user. For this we need to create a user named trigger corresponding to the name we supplied the initialize statement for each of the pop-up menu items.

How to do it...

To add a pop-up menu item, perform the following steps:

1. In **Forms Developer** navigate to **Data Blocks | PER_SOCIETIES | Triggers**.
2. Click on the **+** from the left hand toolbar to create a new user-named trigger (select (User-named) from the list of values).
3. A trigger with an automatically generated name will have been created.
4. When the **PL/SQL Editor** opens write the following line of code:

    ```
    fnd_message.debug('Popup 1 code can go here ....');
    ```

5. Right-click the trigger we have just created and select **Property Palette** from the menu.
6. Set the **Name** property to **POPUP1**. (**POPUP1** is the name of the pop-up menu item in the call to the APP_POPUP.INSTANTIATE procedure in the **PRE-POPUP-MENU** trigger.)
7. In **Forms Developer** navigate to **Data Blocks | PER_SOCIETIES | Triggers**.
8. Click on the **+** from the left hand toolbar to create a new user-named trigger. (select (User-named) from the list of values).
9. A trigger with an automatically generated name will have been created.
10. When the **PL/SQL Editor** opens write the following line of code:

    ```
    fnd_message.debug('Popup 2 code can go here ....');
    ```

11. Right-click the trigger we have just created and select **Property Palette** from the menu.

12. Set the **Name** property to **POPUP2**.

13. In **Forms Developer** navigate to **Data Blocks | PER_SOCIETIES | Triggers**.

14. Click on the **+** from the left hand toolbar to create a new user-named trigger (select (User-named) from the list of values).

15. When the **PL/SQL Editor** opens put the following line of code:

```
fnd_message.debug('Popup 3 code can go here ....');
```

16. Right-click the trigger we have just created and select **Property Palette** from the menu.

17. Set the **Name** property to **POPUP2**.

How it works...

We have now added three triggers to capture the events when a user selects a menu item from a pop-up menu. Now save, transfer, and re-compile the form as we have done previously and we can see the results of the coding. Open the form in EBS and query back a record. Right-click in the **Societies** block. When **Popup 1** is selected from the menu the debug message appears showing that the message we coded is being executed:

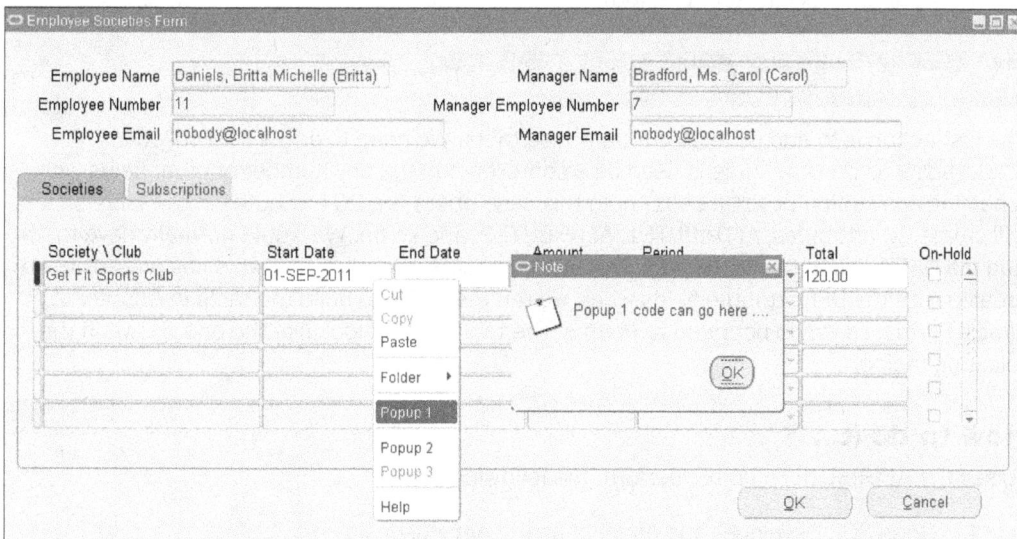

Adding flexfields to forms

Flexfields are generic data items that allow you to be able to store additional information. There are key flexfields (KFF) and Descriptive Flexfield (DFF). **Key flexfields** are collections of data that represent business entities. An example would be inventory items, that is, if you can imagine that an item is defined by four different sub fields. In this example, the key flexfield may be defined as the description code, the size, the color, and the manufacturer. So if we had a black Sony 42 inch monitor it may well be represented as LED-42-BLK-SONY. A **Descriptive Flexfield (DFF)** is a way of being able to add additional data items to an entity. So if a screen does not have all of the items that the business requires then DFFs allow users to be able to store additional information relating to an entity. We need to perform the following tasks to create a new DFF:

 ▸ Adding flexfield items to a table
 ▸ Registering a table within EBS
 ▸ Registering a Descriptive Flexfield
 ▸ Enabling a flexfield value
 ▸ Adding a flexfield item to a form

Adding flexfield items to a table

The first action is to add fields to our database table. We need to add a field called ATTRIBUTE_CATEGORY (this is used as a context field) and any number of other fields with a naming convention of ATTRIBUTEn. In this case, there are 20 attributes in our table so we will create 20 attributes, ATTRIBUTE1, ATTRIBUTE2, and so on. We would normally have to add the DFF fields to the XXHR_PER_SOCIETIES table. However, the table has already been created with the DFF attribute fields when we ran the script to build the table in *Chapter 2, Oracle Forms*, so we do not need to do this. The table should look like the one shown in the following recipe.

How to do it...

To see the ATTRIBUTE columns, perform the following steps:

1. Open SQL Developer and connect as the **apps** user.
2. Type the command desc XXHR_PER_SOCIETIES; to view the table definition as shown in the following screenshot:

```
desc XXHR_PER_SOCIETIES
Name                  Null       Type
------------------    --------   -------------
SOCIETY_ID            NOT NULL   NUMBER
CODE                  NOT NULL   VARCHAR2(20)
DATE_START                       DATE
DATE_END                         DATE
SUBS_AMOUNT                      VARCHAR2(20)
SUBS_PERIOD                      VARCHAR2(20)
SUBS_TOTAL                       VARCHAR2(20)
SUBS_HOLD                        VARCHAR2(10)
ATTRIBUTE_CATEGORY               VARCHAR2(30)
ATTRIBUTE1                       VARCHAR2(150)
ATTRIBUTE2                       VARCHAR2(150)
ATTRIBUTE3                       VARCHAR2(150)
ATTRIBUTE4                       VARCHAR2(150)
ATTRIBUTE5                       VARCHAR2(150)
ATTRIBUTE6                       VARCHAR2(150)
ATTRIBUTE7                       VARCHAR2(150)
ATTRIBUTE8                       VARCHAR2(150)
ATTRIBUTE9                       VARCHAR2(150)
ATTRIBUTE10                      VARCHAR2(150)
ATTRIBUTE11                      VARCHAR2(150)
ATTRIBUTE12                      VARCHAR2(150)
ATTRIBUTE13                      VARCHAR2(150)
ATTRIBUTE14                      VARCHAR2(150)
ATTRIBUTE15                      VARCHAR2(150)
ATTRIBUTE16                      VARCHAR2(150)
ATTRIBUTE17                      VARCHAR2(150)
ATTRIBUTE18                      VARCHAR2(150)
ATTRIBUTE19                      VARCHAR2(150)
ATTRIBUTE20                      VARCHAR2(150)
LAST_UPDATE_DATE                 DATE
LAST_UPDATED_BY                  NUMBER(15)
LAST_UPDATE_LOGIN                NUMBER(15)
CREATED_BY                       NUMBER(15)
CREATION_DATE                    DATE
PERSON_ID                        NUMBER(10)
```

How it works...

When we create our custom tables in EBS we should always build them with the WHO columns and additional fields for DFF attributes. This will allow additional attributes to be stored if a solution requires extending at a later date.

Registering a table within EBS

Now that the table has the fields defined in the database we need to register the table in EBS. We need to do this as Oracle needs the table defined in EBS as it is required for lists of values when we configure the DFF later on. We will run the script to register the PER_SOCIETIES table and all of its columns.

How to do it...

To run the script to register the **PER_SOCIETIES** table, perform the following steps:

1. Start SQL Developer and open the XXHR_PER_SOCIETIES_REG.sql file available from the download bundle.

2. Click the run as script toolbar icon to run the script.

> You can run the script in SQL*Plus or other development tool such as TOAD if you prefer.

How it works...

To register the table we must use the AD_DD package that is provided by Oracle as the form does not allow users to enter records. The script has been provided and this has been run to register the database table. Let's have a look at the syntax. An example of the code is shown as follows:

```
EXECUTE ad_dd.register_table('XXHR', 'XXHR_PER_SOCIETIES', 'T');
```

The parameters are as follows:

Parameter	Meaning
p_appl_short_name	The application short name of the table. This is our custom application XXHR.
p_tab_name	Table name (this needs to be in uppercase).
p_tab_type	Type of table. We will nearly always use 'T'.

Likewise we have added each item and we did this by calling the ad_dd.register_column procedure for each column.

An example would be as follows:

```
EXECUTE ad_dd.register_column('XXHR', 'XXHR_PER_SOCIETIES',
'SOCIETY_ID',1, 'NUMBER', 38, 'N', 'N');
```

The parameters are as follows:

Parameter	Meaning
p_appl_short_name	The application short name of the table. This is our custom application XXHR.
p_tab_name	Table name (this needs to be in uppercase).
p_col_name	Type of table. We will nearly always use 'T'.
p_col_seq	This is a unique number of the columns.
p_col_type	This parameter is the type of column, for example, NUMBER or DATE and so on.
p_col_width	This parameter specifies the width of the column.
p_nullable	This parameter is a 'Y', 'N' parameter to determine if NULL values are allowed.
p_translate	This parameter is a 'Y', 'N' parameter to determine if the values will be translated by Oracle.

Viewing the table registration in EBS

We have run the script and now we can check to see that the table has been registered in EBS.

How to do it...

To check that the table has been registered in EBS, perform the following steps:

1. Log in to Oracle with the **Application Developer** responsibility.

2. Navigate to **Database | Table** and the **Messages** window will open:

How it works...

We can see that the table has been registered within Oracle as expected and the database fields will now be available in the list of values when we create the DFF attributes.

Registering a Descriptive Flexfield

We now need to register the Descriptive Flexfield in Oracle. This will define the table and application that we wish to configure the DFF for.

How to do it...

To register the DFF, perform the following steps:

1. Log in to Oracle with the **Application Developer** responsibility.

2. Navigate to **Flexfield | Descriptive | Register** and the **Descriptive Flexfields** window will open.

3. Enter the following data:

Application	XXHR Custom Application
Name	XXHR_PER_SOCIETIES
Title	Additional Society Information
Description	Additional Society Information
Table Application	XXHR Custom Application
Table Name	XXHR_PER_SOCIETIES
Structure Column	ATTRIBUTE_CATEGORY
Context Prompt	Context Value
Protected	<Unchecked>
DFV View Name	

4. Save the form, which should look like the following:

If we click on the columns button we can see that the attribute fields are already enabled:

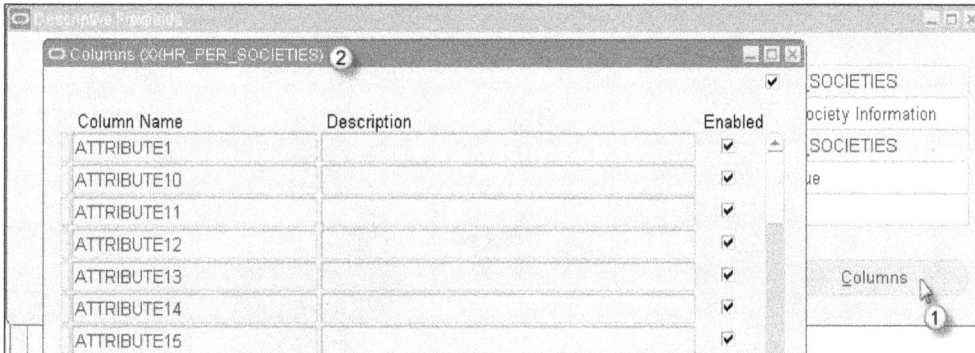

How it works...

We have now defined the DFF and associated it with the table we want to add additional attributes to.

Enabling a flexfield value

We want to enable a flexfield value so that we can test the form. We will create a free text field and assign it to **ATTRIBUTE1**.

How to do it...

To enable a DFF attribute, perform the following steps:

1. Log in to Oracle with the **Application Developer** responsibility.
2. Navigate to **Flexfield | Descriptive | Segments** and the **Descriptive Flexfields Segments** window will open.
3. Press *F11* to enter a query.
4. When in ENTER-QUERY mode type **Additional Society Information** in the **Title** field and press *Ctrl + F11* to execute the query.
5. If the **Freeze Flexfield Definition** is checked, uncheck it.
6. Click **OK** when the warning message appears.

7. Uncheck the **Required** and **Displayed** checkboxes in the **Context Field** region as shown in the following screenshot and then click the **Segments** button:

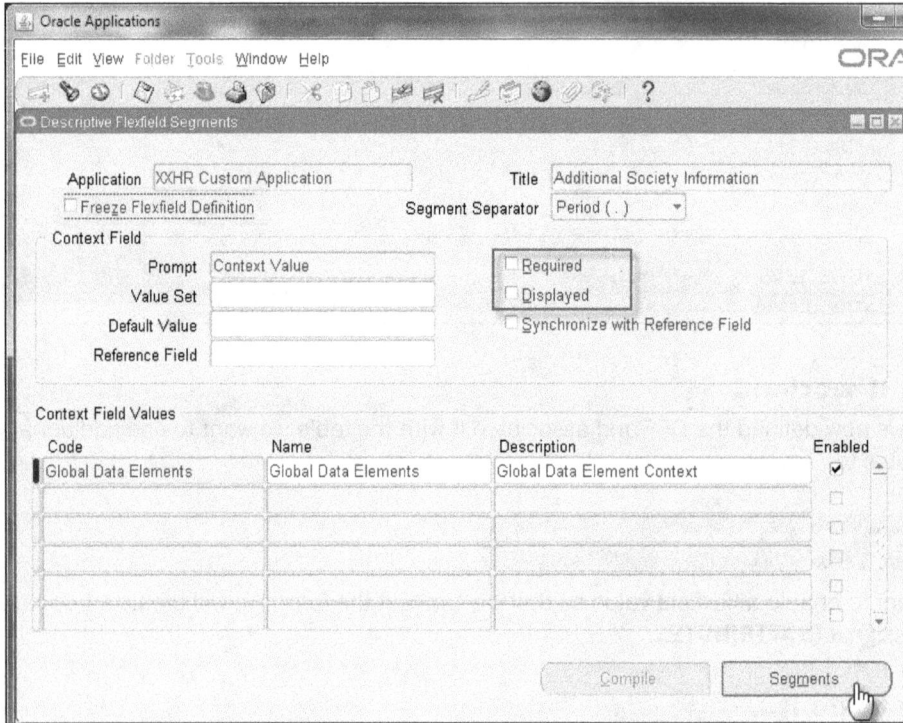

8. Enter the following data in the **Segments Summary** screen:

Number	Name	Window Prompt	Column	Value Set	Displayed	Required
10	Test DFF	Test DFF	ATTRIBUTE1		☑	☑

9. Click the **Open** button.

10. Enter the following data:

Name	Test DFF
Description	Test DFF
Enabled	☑
Displayed	☑
Required	☒
Display Size	10

Description Size	10
Concatenated Description Size	25
List of Values	Test DFF
Window	Test DFF

11. When you change the **Display Size** field click **OK** when the warning appears.

12. Click **Save**.

13. Close the **Segments** screen.

14. Close the **Segments Summary** screen.

15. Check the **Freeze Flexfield Definition** checkbox to recompile the flexfield definition.

16. Click **OK** when the warning appears.

17. Click **Save** and **OK** when a note message appears.

18. Exit the form.

How it works...

Okay, we have now defined our Descriptive Flexfield. We must now develop the DFF in our form.

Adding a flexfield item to a form

When we add a Descriptive Flexfield we must create an item called **DESC_FLEX** in the **PER_SOCIETIES** block.

How to do it...

To add a DFF item, perform the following steps:

1. In **Forms Developer** navigate to **Data Blocks | PER_SOCIETIES | Items | SUBS_HOLD**.

2. Click on the **+** from the left hand toolbar to create a new item.

3. Set the following properties of the item:

   - **Name**: DESC_FLEX
   - **Subclass Information**: TEXT_ITEM_DESC_FLEX
   - **Database Item**: No
   - **List of Values**: ENABLE_LIST_LAMP
   - **Canvas**: SUBS_TAB_CNV
   - **Tab Page**: SOC_TAB_PG
   - **Validate from List**: No

4. Navigate to **Canvases | SUBS_TAB_CNV | Tab Pages | SOC_TAB_PGand** and open the **Layout Editor**.

5. Reduce the width of the **SUBS_AMOUNT** field and click and drag the **DESC_FLEX** item in line with the other items.

6. Click the A icon on the left-hand toolbar and create the [' and '] boilerplate text around the DFF item, as shown in the following screenshot:

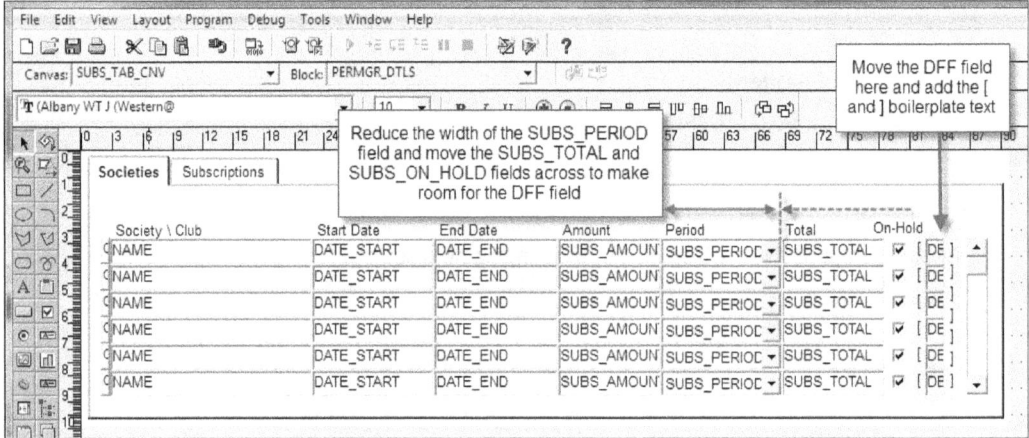

How it works...

The DFF item is a special item on the form. When a user navigates to the item a window will pop up for the user to enter values for any DFF attributes that have been enabled. We have enabled one of our DFF attributes so when we test the form we will see the item pop up in its own DFF window.

Creating triggers for flexfield events

Now we need to add some triggers to manage the Descriptive Flexfield. We are going to call the standard package to define the Descriptive Flexfield when a user enters the form. We are also going to add a **WHEN-NEW-ITEM-INSTANCE** trigger on the **DESC_FLEX** item to automatically pop up the DFF when a user navigates to the item. We will perform the following tasks:

▶ Adding a **WHEN-NEW-FORM-INSTANCE** event

▶ Adding a **WHEN-NEW-ITEM-INSTANCE** event

▶ Testing the form

Adding a WHEN-NEW-FORM-INSTANCE event

Before we add the code to the **WHEN-NEW-FORM-INSTANCE** trigger we will write the code in the **PER_SOCIETIES** package to define the Descriptive Flexfield and then call the procedure from the trigger.

How to do it...

To add a **WHEN-NEW-FORMS-INSTANCE** trigger, perform the following steps:

1. In **Forms Developer** navigate to **Program Units | PER_SOCIETIES | Package Spec**.
2. Add a new procedure by adding the following code:

   ```
   PROCEDURE DESC_FLEX(event VARCHAR2);
   ```

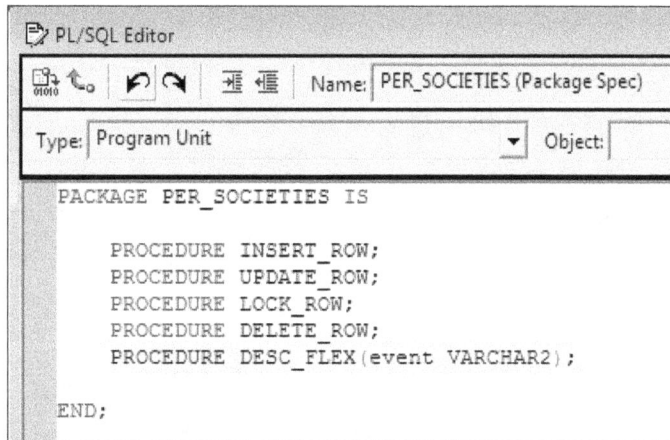

```
PACKAGE PER_SOCIETIES IS

    PROCEDURE INSERT_ROW;
    PROCEDURE UPDATE_ROW;
    PROCEDURE LOCK_ROW;
    PROCEDURE DELETE_ROW;
    PROCEDURE DESC_FLEX(event VARCHAR2);

END;
```

3. Now open the **PER_SOCIETIES** package body and add the following procedure:

```
PROCEDURE DESC_FLEX(event VARCHAR2) IS
BEGIN
  IF event = 'WHEN-NEW-FORM-INSTANCE' THEN
    fnd_descr_flex.define( block => 'PER_SOCIETIES'
                         , field => 'DESC_FLEX'
                         , appl_short_name => 'XXHR'
                         , desc_flex_name => 'XXHR_PER_SOCIETIES');
  END IF;

END;
```

4. Navigate to the form level **WHEN-NEW-FORMS-INSTANCE** trigger and in the **PL/SQL Editor** add a call to the procedure we have just added passing in the event, which is **WHEN-NEW-FORM-INSTANCE** as shown in the following screenshot:

```
PL/SQL Editor
                        Name: WHEN-NEW-FORM-INSTANCE
Type: Trigger                      ▼   Object: (Form Level)                    ▼

   FDRCSID('$Header: XXHRSOCC.fmb 120.1 2011/08/06 22:56  apenver ship
   APP_STANDARD.EVENT('WHEN-NEW-FORM-INSTANCE');
   --
   -- app_folder.define_folder_block('template test', 'folder_block', 'prompt_bl
   -- app_folder.event('VERIFY');
   --
   set_canvas_property('SUBS_TAB_CNV', TOPMOST_TAB_PAGE, 'SOC_TAB_PG');
   show_view('SUBS_TAB_CNV');

   PER_SOCIETIES.DESC_FLEX('WHEN-NEW-FORM-INSTANCE');

   EXECUTE_TRIGGER('QUERY_FIND');
```

5. Compile and save the form.

How it works...

The call to our procedure will initiate the Descriptive Flexfield when the form is opened.

Adding a WHEN-NEW-ITEM-INSTANCE event

We now need to add a **WHEN-NEW-ITEM-INSTANCE** trigger to the **DESC_FLEX** item. This will trigger the standard code that will create a DFF window, which will display any enabled DFF attributes.

How to do it...

To add a **WHEN-NEW-ITEM-INSTANCE** trigger on a **DFF_DESC** item, perform the following steps:

1. In **Forms Developer** navigate to **Data Blocks | PER_SOCIETIES | Items | DESC_FLEX | Triggers**.

2. Click on the **+** icon on the left-hand toolbar to add a trigger.

3. Select a **WHEN-NEW-ITEM-INSTANCE** trigger from the list of values.

4. In the **PL/SQL Editor**, type the following line of code:

   ```
   FND_FLEX.EVENT('WHEN-NEW-ITEM-INSTANCE');
   ```

5. Compile the code and save the form.

How it works...

We have now created the trigger so that the DFF window will automatically open when a user navigates to the item.

Testing the form

Now we will test that the DFF field displays the attribute we have enabled and that the correct DFF is called when we navigate to the DFF item.

How to do it...

To test the form with a DFF item, perform the following steps:

1. Open WinSCP and transfer the form to the `$AU_TOP/forms/US` directory on the application tier.

2. Compile the form as we have done previously.

3. Log in to Oracle with the **XXEBS Extending e-Business Suite** responsibility.

4. Open the **Societies** form and query back a record in the query find screen.

5. Navigate to the Descriptive Flexfield and the DFF screen will pop up as shown in the following screenshot:

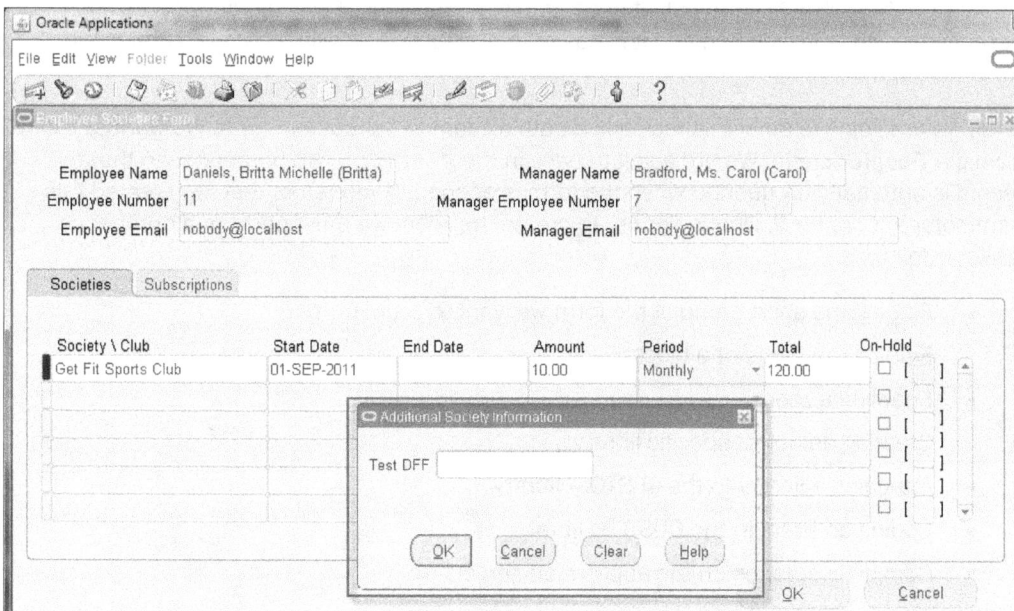

6. You can add some free text in the **Test DFF** field and click **OK**.

7. Save the record.

How it works...

We have tested that the DFF has been added to the form and allows us to save additional details. If the solution requires extending in future we can enable additional attributes to the form without having to make changes to the underlying form.

Adding a zoom using the CUSTOM library

We can use the CUSTOM library to add or modify functionality without making code changes to the standard form. All of the standard forms have calls to the custom library from specific events that occur at runtime. We can add code to the CUSTOM library to capture the events (such as **WHEN-NEW-FORM-INSTANCE, ZOOM**, and so on) and then add code to perform additional functionality. If you need to see which events are fired on any particular form you can navigate to **Help | Diagnostics | Custom Code | Show Custom Events** from the menu and you will see a message appear each time an event is triggered (you may be prompted for the **apps** password when you do this). The message will show the event that was triggered.

The CUSTOM library is shipped with e-Business Suite and can be found in the $AU_TOP/ resource directory. It is recommended that you do not put all of your code in the CUSTOM library. It is a good practice to create a sub library per form and put your code in there. Then just write the call to the sub library in the CUSTOM library. The sub library must be attached to the CUSTOM library. The reason this is done is that there may well be several developers working on the CUSTOM library all at once. If this model is followed then developers can develop their code in isolation and it is easier to maintain. This will become clearer when we go through the recipe.

What we are going to do in this recipe is create a zoom to our custom form. We want to zoom from the **People** screen. We are going to pass in the P_PERSON_ID parameter so that the record is automatically queried when the form is opened. If you remember, we created this parameter in *Chapter 2, Oracle Forms*. To create the zoom we must perform a number of tasks as follows:

- ▶ Finding the short name of the form we want to zoom from
- ▶ Finding the name of a block
- ▶ Enabling a zoom
- ▶ Creating an object-specific library
- ▶ Attaching a library to the CUSTOM library
- ▶ Coding an event in the CUSTOM library
- ▶ Compiling libraries on the application server
- ▶ Adding a function to a menu
- ▶ Test the zoom

Finding the short name of the form we want to zoom from

We will use the **Help** | **About** feature in Oracle constantly as a developer to gain information about the name and version of the form we are in. In this instance, we are going to determine the name of the form that we want to enable a zoom from by using the **Help** | **About** menu item.

How to do it...

To find out the item names from within EBS, perform the following steps:

1. Log in to Oracle with the **UK HRMS Administrator** responsibility.

2. Navigate to **People** | **Enter and Maintain** and the **People** window will open.

3. Click the **New** button to exit the query find window.

4. Select **Help** | **About Oracle Applications** from the menu.

5. Scroll down to the **Current Form** section and you will see the form name and the version, as shown in the following screenshot:

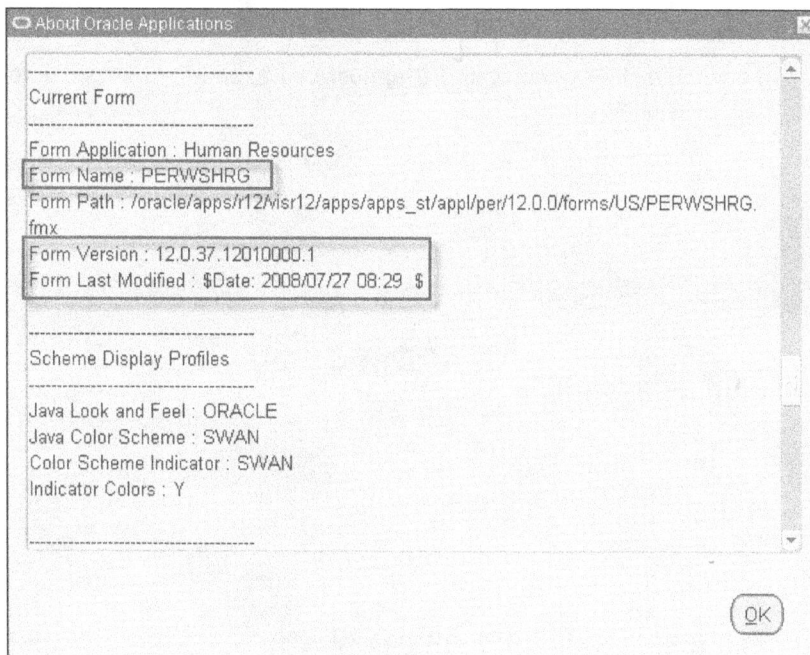

How it works...

You will often need to determine details about a form when we are extending EBS. If you are ever dealing with Oracle Support they may well ask for the form and version if you are experiencing a problem with a professional form and this is where you will get the information from.

Finding the name of a block

We need to find the block name of the form we want to enable the zoom in. To do this we need to open the form and navigate to the block we need to enable the zoom in. We will do this by navigating to the **Help | Diagnostics** menu item. Remember we may need the **apps** password to be able to access this feature, but as a developer it is essential to have access to this menu item.

How to do it...

To find the name of the block, perform the following:

1. Log in to Oracle with the **UK HRMS Administrator** responsibility.

2. Navigate to **People | Enter and Maintain** and the **People** window will open.

3. Click the **New** button to exit the query find window.

4. From the menu toolbar select **Help | Diagnostics | Examine** as shown in the following screenshot:

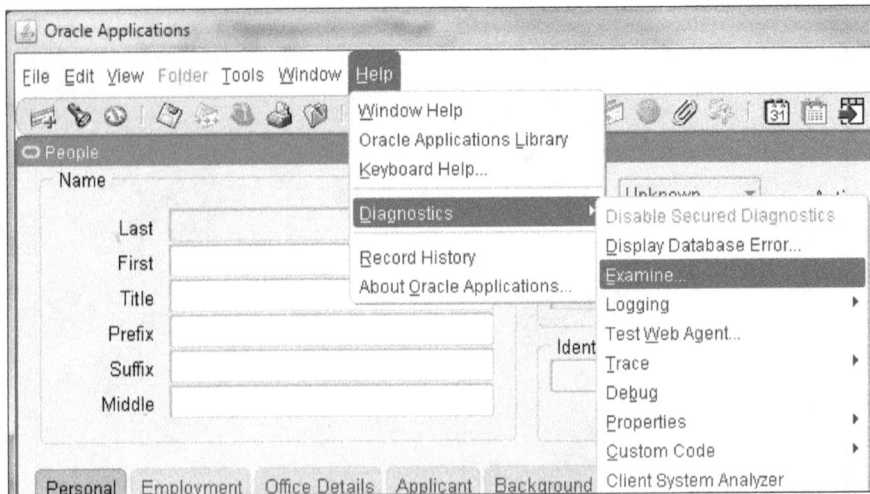

5. If prompted for the **apps** password then enter the **apps** password and click **OK**.

6. The details of the block, field, and value are displayed as shown in the following screenshot:

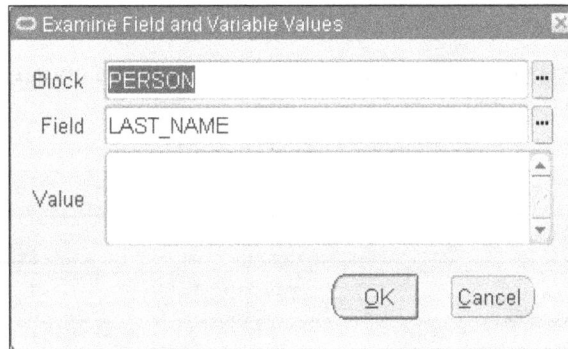

```
┌─────────────────────────────────────────────────┐
│ ⊂ Examine Field and Variable Values          [×] │
│                                                   │
│  Block  [PERSON                            ] [...]│
│                                                   │
│  Field  [LAST_NAME                         ] [...]│
│                                                   │
│         ┌──────────────────────────────┐ [▲]    │
│  Value  │                              │ [ ]    │
│         │                              │ [▼]    │
│         └──────────────────────────────┘        │
│                                                   │
│                        ( OK )  ( Cancel )        │
└─────────────────────────────────────────────────┘
```

7. The name of the block we need to zoom from is called PERSON.

How it works...

We have been able to determine the block name that we want to zoom from, that is, the PERSON block.

Enabling a zoom

In the custom library, there is a procedure that will enable the zoom button in the toolbar. We need to add code to enable the zoom.

How to do it...

To enable the zoom button using the CUSTOM library, perform the following:

1. In **Forms Developer** open the CUSTOM.pll library.

2. Navigate to **PL/SQL Libraries | CUSTOM | Program Units | CUSTOM (Package Body)**.

3. In the **PL/SQL Editor**, scroll down to the `zoom_available` procedure and edit the code to add the form name as `PERWSHRG` and block name as `PERSON`, as shown in the following screenshot:

> Most of the code is already commented in the library already – you can copy and paste it and amend it as necessary.

```
PL/SQL Editor

Name: CUSTOM* (Package Body)@

Type: Program Unit          ▼   Object:

    --
    -- Real code starts here
    --
    form_name   varchar2(30) := name_in('system.current_form');
    block_name  varchar2(30) := name_in('system.cursor_block');
begin
    -- If the form is the Person form and the block is the PERSON block
    -- then enable the zoom icon
    if (form_name = 'PERWSHRG' and block_name = 'PERSON') then
        return TRUE;                (1)                      (2)
    else
        return FALSE;
    end if;
end zoom_available;
```

> Note: When we code in libraries we cannot reference items in a form using the : (colon) notation. The two built-in functions NAME_IN and COPY are used. NAME_IN is effectively getting the value that is stored in the variable passed in. The COPY built-in function copies the variable from one variable to another, for example, COPY (NAME_IN (source) , destination);

4. Compile the code.

5. Save the library.

How it works...

The standard code in a form makes calls to the CUSTOM library when certain triggers are executed at runtime. We need to add code to the CUSTOM library to capture the form and the block that we want to perform an action on.

Creating an object-specific library

We want to now create sub custom library. We will do this to limit the code in the custom library so this step is really just good practice. You can create a sub library that stores all of the module-specific custom code or to be even more granular, create a sub library specific to the form. We are going to create one sub library specific to the module.

> The library XXHRCUST.pll and CUSTOM.pll are both available in the download bundle if you cannot get your library to compile or you want to refer to them.

How to do it...

To create a sub CUSTOM library, perform the following:

1. Open forms developer and click on **PL/SQL Libraries** in the navigator.

2. Click the **+** icon from the left hand toolbar to add a new library.

3. Forms developer will generate a new library and give it a name (such as LIB_001 for example).

4. The CUSTOM library has an attached library called FNDSQF. We will be using functions from the FNDSQF library so we must also attach this library to our **XXHRCUST** custom library.

5. Click the **+** icon from the left hand toolbar to attach the FNDSQF library.

6. In the **Attach Library** window, select the FNDSQF library.

7. Click the **Attach** button.

8. When prompted to remove the path click **Yes**.

> This is important as we do not want the full path referenced in the attachment. The library will be transferred to the application tier and recompiled. If the path is referenced there will be compilation errors.

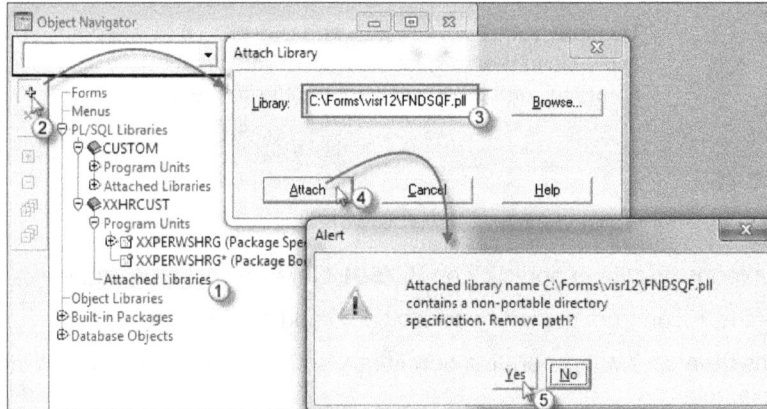

9. Save the library.

10. Navigate to **PL/SQL Libraries | XXHRCUST | Program Unit**s.

11. Click the **+** icon on the left hand toolbar to create a new package.

12. Set the name to **XXPERWSHRG** and select **Package Spec** from the list of types as shown in the following screenshot:

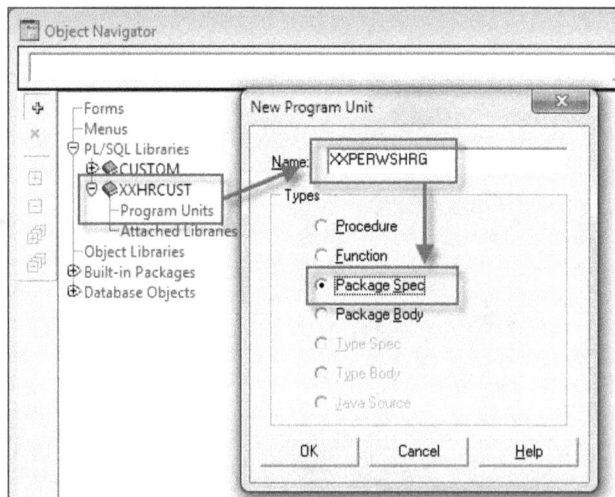

13. In the **PL/SQL Editor** add a new procedure called `event` as shown in the following screenshot:

14. Compile the package specification.

15. Close the **PL/SQL Editor**.

16. Navigate to **PL/SQL Libraries | XXHRCUST | Program Units**.

17. Click the **+** icon on the left hand toolbar to create a new package body.

19. Set the name to **XXPERWSHRG** and select **Package Body** from the list.

20. In the **PL/SQL Editor**, type the following code:

> Note: The OTHER_PARAMS parameter that is passed in the call to
> fnd_function.execute is surrounded by double quotes. If we were
> hard-coding the parameter, the line would look like the following:
>
> ```
> OTHER_PARAMS=>'P_PERSON_ID="1234"');
> ```

21. Compile the program unit.
22. Save the library.

How it works...

We have created our own CUSTOM library for zooming from the **Person** screen. This will allow us to modularize the code. It can be as granular as required. For example, if there is a small development team we can create a sub-custom library that is module-specific, that is, HR, PAY. If the development team is large with lots of extensions then it's probably better to have a sub-custom library per form.

Attaching a library to the CUSTOM library

We now want to attach our sub-custom library to the CUSTOM.pll.

How to do it...

To add the **XXHRCUST** library to the CUSTOM library, perform the following:

1. In **Forms Developer** open the CUSTOM.pll library.
2. Navigate to **PL/SQL Libraries | CUSTOM | Attached Libraries**.
3. Click the **+** icon on the left-hand toolbar to attach a library.
4. Select XXHRCUST.pll from the **Attach Library** pop-up and click the **Attach** button.
5. When prompted to remove the path select **Yes**.
6. Save the library.

The navigator will now look like the following:

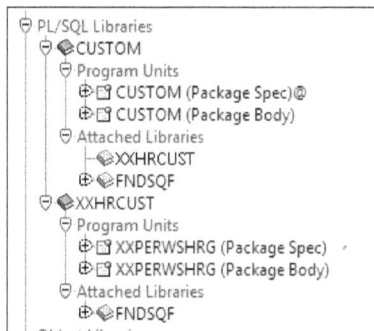

How it works...

We need to attach our sub-custom library to the CUSTOM.pll as it will call the program unit for the zoom that we have created.

Coding an event in the CUSTOM library

In the CUSTOM library, there is a procedure that will enable the zoom button in the toolbar. We need to add code to enable the zoom.

How to do it...

To enable the zoom button using the CUSTOM library, perform the following:

1. In **Forms Developer** open the CUSTOM.pll library.

2. Navigate to **PL/SQL Libraries | CUSTOM | Program Units | CUSTOM (Package Body)**.

3. In the **PL/SQL Editor** scroll down to the zoom_available procedure and add the code as shown in the following screenshot (most of the code is already commented in the library – you can copy and paste it and amend it as necessary):

4. Compile the code.

How it works...

In the `event` procedure in the CUSTOM library, we need to make a call to our procedure to capture the ZOOM event. Whenever the user clicks on the zoom button in the **Person** screen the **Societies** form will open, passing in the `PERSON_ID` as a parameter. The form will automatically query back the employee in the **Person** screen we zoomed from.

Compiling libraries on the application server

We now need to transfer the two libraries to the application server and compile them. All libraries are in the `$AU_TOP/resource` directory. Oracle will first attempt to find the `.plx` file (the executable) and then will look for the `.pll` file. The command for compiling libraries is similar to that of forms.

How to do it...

To test the zoom, perform the following:

1. Open WinSCP and connect to the application tier.

2. Navigate to the `$AU_TOP/resource` directory and rename the existing `CUSTOM.pll` (to back it up).

3. Transfer the `XXHRCUST.pll` and `CUSTOM.pll` libraries to the `$AU_TOP/resource` directory.

4. Open Putty and change directory to `$AU_TOP/resource`.

5. Compile XXHRCUST.pll with the following command (for the `userid` parameter you need to enter the **apps** password for your environment by replacing <apps pwd>):

    ```
    frmcmp_batchmodule_type=library module=$AU_TOP/resource/XXHRCUST.
    pll userid=apps/<appspwd> output_file=$AU_TOP/resource/XXHRCUST.
    plx compile_all=special
    ```

6. Compile `CUSTOM.pll` with the following command:

    ```
    frmcmp_batchmodule_type=library module=$AU_TOP/resource/CUSTOM.
    pll userid=apps/<appspwd> output_file=$AU_TOP/resource/CUSTOM.plx
    compile_all=special
    ```

How it works...

We have compiled the two libraries. As the **XXHRCUST** library is a dependent of the CUSTOM library we must compile the **XXHRCUST** library first.

Adding a function to a menu

The form function needs to be added to the menu that we are zooming into. Therefore in this case, we need to add our custom form function **XXHR_EMP_SOCIETY** to the menu that is used by the **UK HRMS Manger** responsibility. If the function is not assigned to the menu that the responsibility uses the user will get the following error message when attempting to zoom:

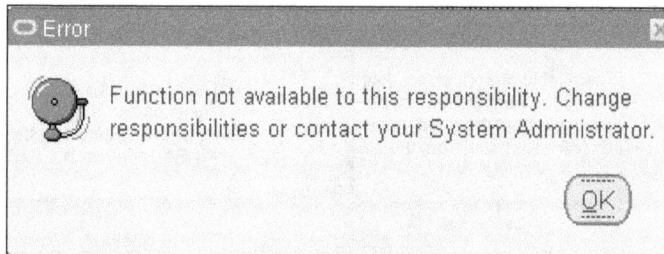

How to do it...

To add a function to the menu that is used by the **UK HRMS Manager** responsibility, perform the following:

1. Log in to Oracle with the **System Administrator** responsibility.
2. Navigate to **Security | Responsibility | Define** and the **Responsibilities** window will open.
3. Press *F11* to enter a query.
4. Enter **UK HRMS Manager** in the **Responsibility Name** field and press *Ctrl + F11*.
5. Copy the value that is in the **Menu** field (in this case it is **UK HRMS Navigator**).
6. Close the form.
7. Navigate to **Application | Menu** and the **Menus** window will open.
8. Press *F11* to enter a query.
9. Enter **UK HRMS Navigator** in the **User Menu Name** field and press *Ctrl + F11*.

10. In the detail block enter a new record with the following details:

Seq	Prompt	Submenu	Function	Description
800			Employee Clubs and Societies	

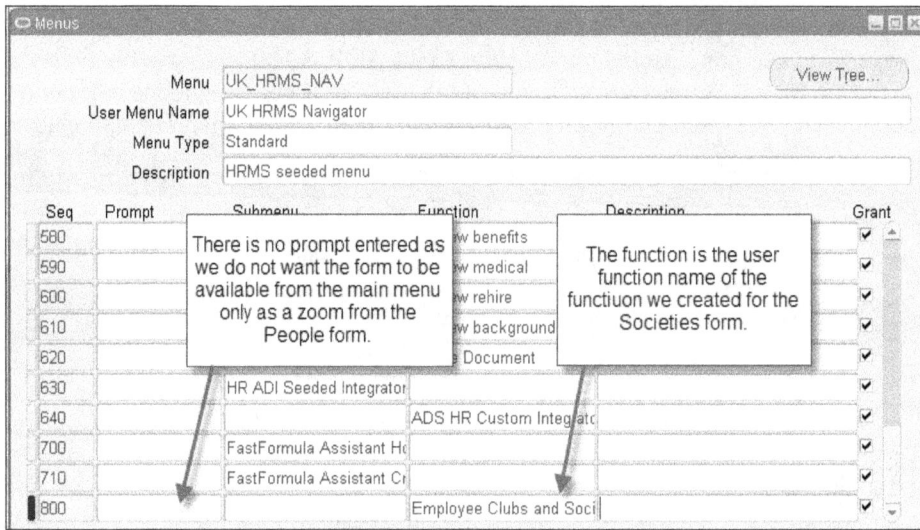

11. Save the form.

> Note that we have not entered any data in the **Prompt** field. This is because we do not want the **Societies** form available from the main menu. If we did then we would put a **Prompt** value in here and the form would open with the query find window as no parameter would be passed in.

How it works...

We have added the function to the menu used by the **UK HRMS Manager** responsibility. You will notice that there is no text in the **Prompt** field, which means that the user can zoom to the **Societies** form from this menu, but the **Societies** form is not available to the user from the navigator.

Testing the zoom

Now we can test how the zoom works. When we zoom to the **Societies** form we are passing the parameter P_PERSON_ID. Therefore, we would not expect to see the query find window as we coded this into the form in *Chapter 2, Oracle Forms*. The employee record should automatically query the employee that was in the **People** form that we zoomed from.

How to do it...

To test the zoom, perform the following:

1. Log in to Oracle with the **UK HRMS Manager** responsibility.
2. Navigate to **People | Enter and Maintain** and the **People** window will open.
3. Query back an employee record.
4. Click on the zoom button which will now be enabled.

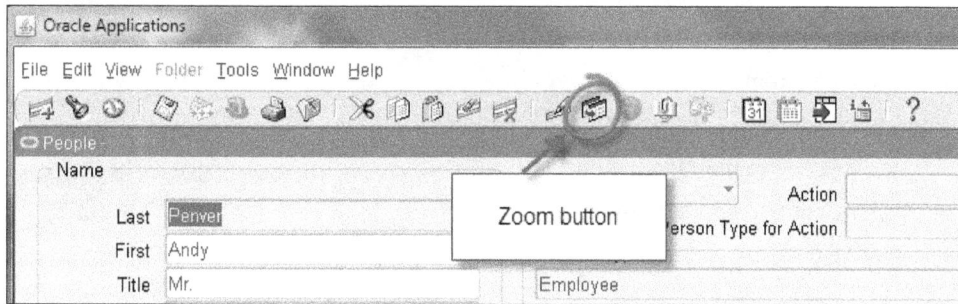

5. The **Employee Societies Form** will open and the employee record will be automatically queried back as shown in the following screenshot:

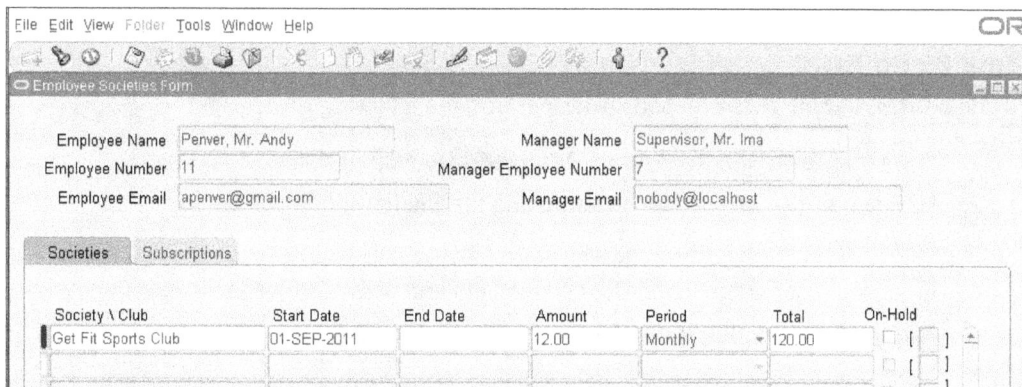

How it works...

We have tested that the user can now zoom from the **Person** screen when using the **UK HRMS Manager** responsibility. The record has automatically queried back data of the employee from the **Person** screen that we zoomed from.

Adding a spreadtable to a form

We are now going to add some more advanced features to our forms. In CRM there is a form that allows us to create spreadtables. To create a spreadtable we will need to complete the following tasks:

▸ Adding the **CRM Administrator** responsibility

▸ Configuring a spreadtable

▸ Adding a tab page

▸ Adding the **JTF_GRID** object group

▸ Adding a block

▸ Adding an item

▸ Adding a library

▸ Adding code to manage the grid

▸ Adding code to populate the grid

▸ Testing the form

Adding the CRM Administrator responsibility

The first thing we need to do is add a **CRM Administrator** responsibility. This is the responsibility that allows us to configure our spreadtable.

How to do it...

To add a **CRM Administrator** responsibility, perform the following:

1. Log in to Oracle with the **System Administrator** responsibility.
2. Navigate to **Security | User | Define** and the **Users** window will open.
3. Press *F11* to enter a query.
4. Enter your user name in the **User Name** field and press *Ctrl + F11*.
5. Add the **CRM Administrator, Vision Utilities** responsibility to your user.

> Note: It is not particularly important which **CRM Administrator** you choose as long as the responsibility provides access to the **Spreadtable | Metadata Administration** screen.

6. Save the record.

How it works...

We have provided access to a **CRM Administrator** responsibility which will allow us access to the **Metadata Administration** forms. This form allows us to configure our spreadtable.

Configuring a spreadtable

We are now going to configure our spreadtable.

How to do it...

To configure our spreadtable, perform the following:

1. Log in to Oracle with the **CRM Administration** responsibility that you added to your user.
2. Navigate to **Spreadtable | Metadata Administration** and the **Spreadtable Meta Data Administration** window will open.
3. Add a new spreadtable definition with the following details:

Datasource Name	XXHR_SOCIETIES_DS
Application	XXHR Custom Application
Title	Employee Societies
Relational View Name	XXHR_PER_SOCIETIES_V

The header will now look like the following:

4. Add new detail records using the **Database** and **Display** tabs with the following details (any attributes not defined here should be left as the default value):

Column Alias	PERSON_ID
View Column/Function	PERSON_ID
Datatype	Number
Query Sequence	10
Label	Person ID
Visible	☒
Display Sequence	10
Display Width	30

Column Alias	NAME
View Column/Function	NAME
Datatype	Char
Query Sequence	20
Label	Name
Visible	☑
Display Sequence	20
Display Width	200

Column Alias	DATE_START
View Column/Function	DATE_START
Datatype	Date
Query Sequence	30
Label	Start Date
Visible	☑
Display Sequence	30
Display Width	100

Column Alias	DATE_END
View Column/Function	DATE_END
Datatype	Date
Query Sequence	40
Label	End Date
Visible	☑
Display Sequence	40
Display Width	100

Column Alias	SUBS_AMOUNT
View Column/Function	SUBS_AMOUNT
Datatype	Char
Query Sequence	50
Label	Amount
Visible	☑
Display Sequence	50
Display Width	100

Column Alias	SUBS_PERIOD
View Column/Function	SUBS_PERIOD
Datatype	Char
Query Sequence	60
Label	Amount
Visible	☑
Display Sequence	60
Display Width	100

Column Alias	SUBS_TOTAL
View Column/Function	SUBS_TOTAL
Datatype	Char
Query Sequence	70
Label	Total
Visible	☑
Display Sequence	70
Display Width	60

Column Alias	SUBS_HOLD
View Column/Function	SUBS_HOLD
Datatype	Char
Query Sequence	80
Label	On-Hold
Visible	☑
Display Sequence	80
Display Width	100

The **Database** tab should now look like the following:

Column Alias	View Column/Function	Datatype	Query Sequence Fire Post Query	Sortable	Sort Column	Default Sort Order
PERSON_ID	PERSON_ID	Number	10 ☐	✔		Ascending
NAME	NAME	Char	20 ☐	✔		Ascending
DATE_START	DATE_START	Date	30 ☐	✔		Ascending
DATE_END	DATE_END	Date	40 ☐	✔		Ascending
SUBS_AMOUNT	SUBS_AMOUNT	Char	50 ☐	✔		Ascending
SUBS_PERIOD	SUBS_PERIOD	Char	60 ☐	✔		Ascending
SUBS_TOTAL	SUBS_TOTAL	Char	70 ☐	✔		Ascending
SUBS_HOLD	SUBS_HOLD	Char	80 ☐	✔		Ascending

Tabs: Database | Display | Alignments and Formatting | Custom Format Masks and Mappings | Query | Sort Order | Test

The **Display** tab should now look like the following:

Tabs: Database | Display | Alignments and Formatting | Custom Format Masks and Mappings | Query | Sort Order | Test

Column Alias	Label	Visible	Freeze Visible Property	Display Sequence	Display Width
PERSON_ID	Person ID	☐	☐	10	30
NAME	Name	✔	☐	20	200
DATE_START	Start Date	✔	☐	30	100
DATE_END	End Date	✔	☐	40	100
SUBS_AMOUNT	Amount	✔	☐	50	100
SUBS_PERIOD	Period	✔	☐	60	100
SUBS_TOTAL	Total	✔	☐	70	60
SUBS_HOLD	On-Hold	✔	☐	80	100

5. Navigate to the **Alignments and Formatting** tab and for the **SUBS_HOLD** record set the **Display Typelist** to **Checkbox**.

6. Navigate to the **Custom Format Masks and Mappings** tab and for the **SUBS_HOLD** record set the following fields:

   ❑ **Checked**: Y

   ❑ **Unchecked**: N

   ❑ **Other**: Unchecked

Database	Display	Alignments and Formatting	Custom Format Masks and Mappings

	Checkbox Value Mapping			Image Description Column	
Column Alias	Checked	Unchecked	Other		Form:
PERSON_ID			✓		
NAME			✓		
DATE_START			✓		
DATE_END			✓		
SUBS_AMOUNT			✓		
SUBS_PERIOD			✓		
SUBS_TOTAL	①	②	✓		
SUBS_HOLD	Y	N	③		

7. Save the form.

How it works...

We have configured our spreadtable defining the fields we want displayed to the users.

Adding a tab page

Now we are going to add a tab to our form to put our bean object on it.

How to do it...

To add a tab to our form, perform the following:

1. Open the XXHRSOCC.fmb form in **Forms Developer**.
2. Navigate to **Canvases | SUBS_TAB_CNV | Tab Pages** and create a new tab page.
3. Right-click the new tab page and set the following properties:
   - ❑ **Name**: CS_GRID_PG
   - ❑ **Subclass Information**: TAB_PAGE
   - ❑ **Label**: Society Grid
4. Save the form.

How it works...

We have now created our tabbed canvas as a container for our bean item.

Adding the JTF_GRID object group

We need to copy the property classes into our form so that we have the property classes for grids in our form.

How to do it...

1. Open the XXHRSOCC.fmb form in **Forms Developer**.

2. Open the JTFSTAND.fmb form in **Forms Developer**.

3. In the **Object Navigator** click on **JTFSTAND | Object Groups | JTF_GRID**.

4. Drag the **JTF_GRID** object group from the **JTFSTAND** form to the **Object Groups** node in our **XXHRSOCC** form.

5. When prompted select **Copy the object group** as shown int he following screenshot:

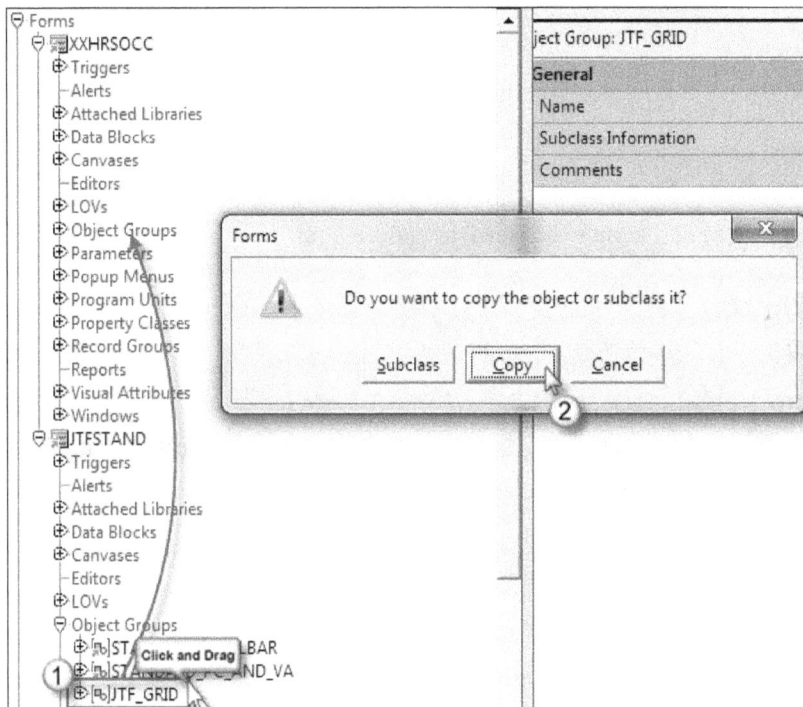

6. Save the form.

How it works...

We have copied the **JTF_GRID** object group from the **JTFSTAND** form to inherit the property classes and other objects used for defining a grid.

Adding a block

Now we are going to create a new block to add items on our **Society Grid** tab.

How to do it...

To create a detail block on the **Society Grid** tab, perform the following:

1. Open the XXHRSOCC.fmb form in **Forms Developer**.
2. In the **Object Navigator** click on **Data Blocks**.
3. Click the green plus (+) sign to launch the data block wizard
4. Select the **Build a new data block manually** radio button when prompted in the **New Data Block** window and click **OK**.
5. Set the following properties for the block:
   - **Name**: CS_GRID
   - **Subclass Information**: JTF_GRID_BLOCK
6. Save the form.

How it works...

We have now added a block for our grid item using the **JTF_GRID_BLOCK** property class we inherited from the **JTFSTAND** form.

Adding an item

We are now going to add our bean object to the block. The bean item is a container for the grid. We determine the spreadtable through the code that we will add later.

How to do it...

To create a detail block on the **Society Grid** tab, perform the following:

1. Open the XXHRSOCC.fmb form in **Forms Developer**.
2. In the **Object Navigator** click on **Data Blocks | CS_GRID | Items**.
3. Click the green plus (+) sign to add a new item.
4. Set the following properties for the item:
   - **Name**: ITEM_GRID
   - **Subclass Information**: JTF_GRID_ITEM
   - **Visible**: Yes

     ❑   **Canvas**: SUBS_TAB_CNV

     ❑   **Tab Page**: CS_GRID_PG

     ❑   **X Position**: 0.146

     ❑   **Y Position**: 0.156

     ❑   **Width**: 8.604

     ❑   **Height**: 1.854

   5.   Save the form.

How it works...

We have added the bean item which acts as a container for our grid. You may notice that the JTF_GRID_ITEM property class inherited the **Implementation Class** property and set it to oracle.apps.jtf.table.SpreadTableWrapper as shown in the following screenshot:

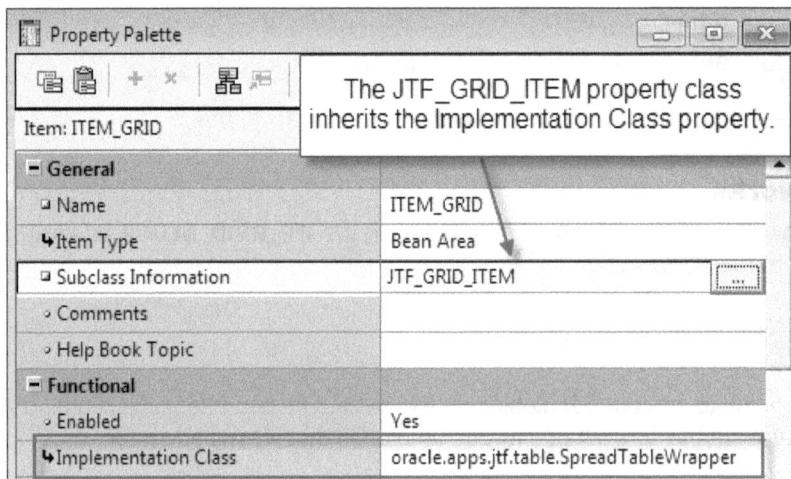

Adding a library

We now need to attach the **JTF_GRID** library which contains the procedures available for controlling a grid item.

How to do it...

To attach the **JTF_GRID** library, perform the following:

   1.   Open the XXHRSOCC.fmb form in **Forms Developer**.

   2.   Navigate to **Attached Libraries**.

   3.   Click the **+** icon on the left-hand toolbar to attach a library.

4. Select `JTF_GRID.pll` from the **Attach Library** pop-up and click the **Attach** button.

5. When prompted to remove the path select **Yes**.

6. Save the form.

How it works...

We have attached the **JTF_GRID** library to our form. This means we can call procedures to manage the grid in our form.

Adding code to manage the grid

We are now going to add code to the form to initialize the grid and to populate the grid. We are going to initialize the grid in the **WHEN-NEW-FORMS-INSTANCE** trigger. We are going to populate the grid when we navigate to the **Society Grid** tab.

How to do it...

1. Open the `XXHRSOCC.fmb` form in **Forms Developer**.

2. Navigate to **Triggers | WHEN-NEW-FORM-INSTANCE** to edit the trigger.

3. Add the following line of code: `cs_grid.init_grid('CS_GRID.ITEM_GRID');` into the **WHEN-NEW-FORM-INSTANCE** trigger as shown in the following screenshot:

4. Close the **PL/SQL Editor**.

5. Navigate to **Program Units | SUBS_TAB_CNV** to edit the procedure.

6. Scroll down to the end of the **SUBS_TAB_CNV** procedure and add a variable `v_item` and three lines of code to perform actions when navigating to the grid tab page as shown in the following screenshot:

   First add the line `v_item VARCHAR2(100);` to declare the variable `v_item`, shown as follows:

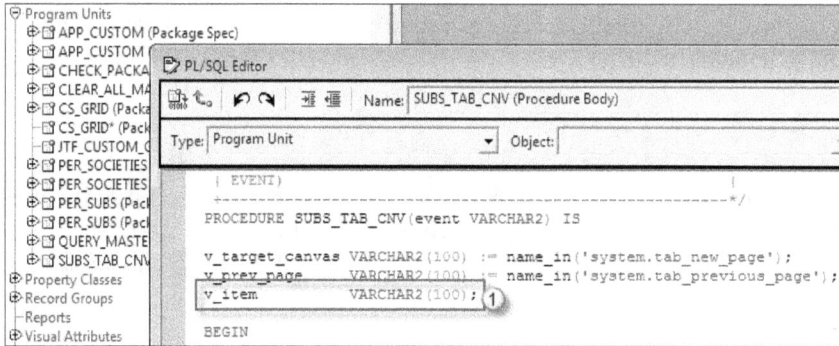

7. Now we are going to add the following three lines of code:

```
elsif v_target_canvas = 'CS_GRID_PG' then
v_item := ('CS_GRID.ITEM_GRID');
cs_grid.populate_grid('CS_GRID.ITEM_GRID');
```

8. to manage the actions when we navigate to the grid tab page as shown in the following screenshot:

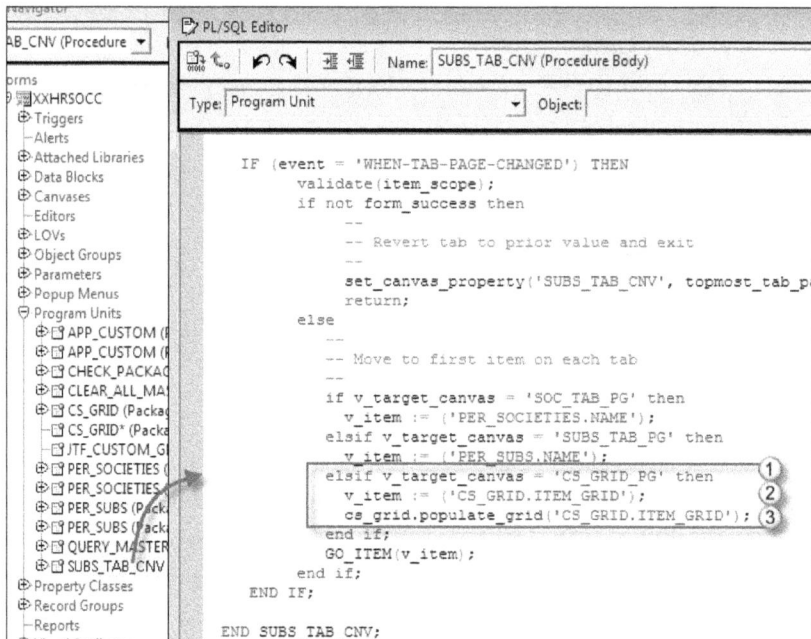

9. Save the form.

How it works...

We have added code to the **WHEN-NEW-FORM-INSTANCE** trigger to initialize the grid and we have also added code to the **SUBS_TAB_CNV** procedure to populate the grid when we navigate to the **Societies Grid** tab page.

Adding code to populate the grid

The code we have just added is used to make calls to the `cs_grid` package. We are now going to create this package with two procedures to initialize the grid and to populate the grid.

How to do it...

To create the package specification, perform the following:

1. In **Forms Developer** navigate to **Program Units**.
2. Click the **+** on the left-hand toolbar to create a new package specification.
3. In the **Name** field type **CS_GRID**.
4. Select **Package Spec** as shown in the following screenshot and click **OK**:

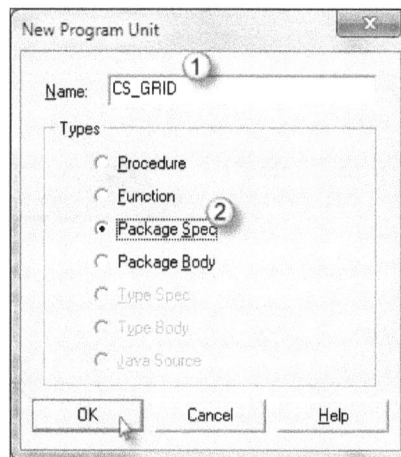

5. Add the following code to the **Package Spec**:

```
PACKAGE CS_GRID IS
   PROCEDURE init_grid (p_grid IN VARCHAR2);      (1)

   PROCEDURE populate_grid (p_grid IN VARCHAR2);  (2)
END;
```

PL/SQL Editor — Name: CS_GRID (Package Spec), Type: Program Unit

6. In **Forms Developer** navigate to **Program Units**.

7. Click the **+** on the left-hand toolbar to create a new package body.

8. In the **Name** field type **CS_GRID**.

9. Select **Package Body** and click **OK**.

10. In the **PL/SQL Editor** we need to write the code to call the database package body called **CS_GRID**.

> Note: The following code is available in a text file and is available in the download bundle.

PL/SQL Editor — Name: CS_GRID (Package Body), Type: Program Unit*

```
PACKAGE BODY CS_GRID IS

   /* Procedure to initialize the grid.
      The data set is the name of the spreadtable we defined in EBS */
   PROCEDURE init_grid (p_grid IN VARCHAR2) IS
      v_data_set VARCHAR2(100) := 'XXHR_SOCIETIES_DS';
   BEGIN
      jtf_grid.init(p_grid, v_data_set);
   END;

   /* Procedure to populate the grid.
      We need to set the WHERE clause of the grid to ass
      to the employee in the master block. Then we call
      populate the grid */
   PROCEDURE populate_grid (p_grid IN VARCHAR2) IS
      w_clause VARCHAR2(1000);
   BEGIN
      jtf_grid.removeAllBindVariables(p_grid);
      jtf_grid.setBindVariable(p_grid,':PERSON_ID', NAME_IN('PERMGR_DTLS.EMP_PERSON_ID'));
      w_clause := ('PERSON_ID = :PERSON_ID');
      jtf_grid.setCharProperty(p_grid, JTF_GRID_PROPERTY.WHERE_CLAUSE, w_clause);
      jtf_grid.populate(p_grid);
   END;
END;
```

We need to set a bind variable to use in our where clause. The bind variable is set to the PERSON_ID in the PERMGR_DTLS block. We can then set the where calse and populate the grid.

Navigator: (Package Body) — Data Blocks, Canvases, Editors, LOVs, Object Groups, Parameters, Popup Menus, Program Units (APP_CUST, APP_CUST, CHECK_P, CLEAR_AL, CS_GRID, CS_GRID, JTF_CUST, PER_SOCI, PER_SOCI, PER_SUBS, PER_SUBS, QUERY_M, SUBS_TAB), Property Classe, Record Groups, Reports, Visual Attribute, Windows*

11. Compile the code.

12. Save the form.

How it works...

We have now added the package to initialize the grid which we call from the **WHEN-NEW-FORM-INSTANCE** trigger. The package also has a procedure that populates the grid and is called from the **SUBS_TAB_CNV** procedure executed from the **WHEN-TAB-PAGE-CHANGED** trigger. We will now test the form to see the grid in EBS.

Testing the form

We are now going to test the form in EBS.

How to do it...

To test the form, perform the following:

1. Transfer the form over to the Application server and compile it as we have done previously.

2. Log in to Oracle with the **XXEBS Extending e-Business Suite** responsibility.

3. Navigate to **Societies Form** and the societies and clubs form will open.

4. Enter an employee number in the query find window and click **Find**.

5. Navigate to the **Society Grid** tab and the grid will be displayed as follows:

How it works...

We have tested the form after we have created a new tab that contains a spreadtable. The form will populate the spreadtable each time we navigate to the tab based upon the XXHR_SOCIETIES_DS spreadtable that we configured earlier in the chapter.

Capturing events for a spreadtable

We are now going to see how we can capture events from a spreadtable. You can capture events such as clicking on a hyperlink, navigating to a new row, or selecting multiple rows to name a few. We are going to add the triggers we require to capture the events and add code to show a message when the user clicks on a hyperlink. To do this we will perform the following actions:

 ▶ Configuring a hyperlink on a spreadtable

 ▶ Adding triggers to capture events for a grid

 ▶ Adding a custom trigger to capture an event

 ▶ Adding code to manage events from a grid

 ▶ Testing the form

Configuring a hyperlink on a spreadtable

First we will modify the definition of the spreadtable to make one of the fields a hyperlink.

How to do it...

To modify the spreadtable, perform the following:

1. Log in to Oracle with the **CRM Administration** responsibility that you added to your user.

2. Navigate to **Spreadtable | Metadata Administration** and the **Spreadtable Meta Data Administration** window will open.

3. Query back the XXHR_SOCIETIES_DS spreadtable.

4. Navigate to the **Alignments and Formatting** tab and change the **Display Type** for the **NAME** field to **Hyperlink**.

5. Save the record.

How it works...

We have changed the value in the **NAME** field for our spreadtable to a hyperlink. This means that it will appear in the grid with a line underneath it.

Adding triggers to capture events for a grid

We are now going to add a trigger on the bean item to capture all events that occur on the spreadtable.

How to do it...

To add the trigger, perform the following:

1. Open the XXHRSOCC.fmb form in **Forms Developer**.

2. In the **Object Navigator** click on **Data Block | CS_GRID | Items | ITEM_GRID | Triggers**.

3. Click the green plus (+) sign to add a new trigger.

4. Select (User-named) from the list of values.

5. Rename the trigger to **WHEN-CUSTOM-ITEM-EVENT**.

6. In the **PL/SQL Editor**, add the following line of code:

   ```
   jtf_grid.customEvent('CS_GRID.ITEM_GRID');
   ```

   The form should now look like the following:

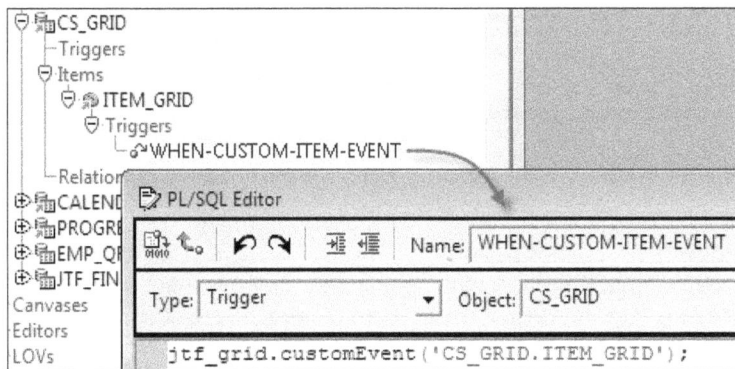

7. Save the form.

How it works...

We have now added a custom trigger to capture events on the bean item called **ITEM_GRID**.

Adding a custom trigger to capture an event

The **JTF_GRID** object group we referenced in should have added a form level trigger called **JTF_GRID_EVENT**.

How to do it...

To check the trigger exists, perform the following:

1. Open the XXHRSOCC.fmb form in **Forms Developer**.

2. In the **Object Navigator** click on **Triggers (Form Level)**.

3. Check that the trigger `JTF_GRID_EVENT` exists at form level.

4. In the **PL/SQL Editor**, check that the trigger contains the following line of code:

```
jtf_custom_grid_event
(jtf_grid.getCharProperty(jtf_grid_property.EVENT_GRID),
jtf_grid.getCharProperty(jtf_grid_property.EVENT_TYPE));
```

The form should now look like the following:

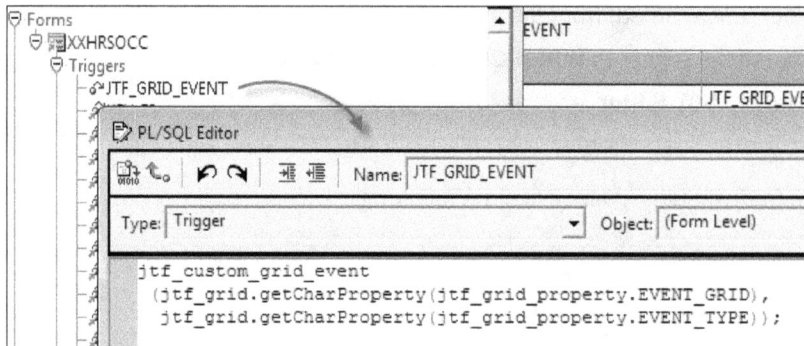

5. Save the form.

How it works...

We have now checked that there is a form level trigger that passes the event grid and event type to the procedure that we are just about to add in the next section.

Adding code to manage events from a grid

We are now going to add code to the form to initialize the grid and to populate the grid. We are going to initialize the grid in the **WHEN-NEW-FORMS-INSTANCE** trigger. We are going to populate the grid when we navigate to the **Society Grid** tab.

How to do it...

1. Open the `XXHRSOCC.fmb` form in **Forms Developer**.

2. Navigate to **Program Units** and add a new procedure called `JTF_CUSTOM_GRID_EVENT`.

3. We are now going to add the following code to the trigger:

```
PROCEDURE JTF_CUSTOM_GRID_EVENT (gridName in varchar2,
event_type in varchar2) IS
row_number NUMBER;
v_name VARCHAR2(200);
```

```
BEGIN

    /* First we capture the event
       Then we get the row number of the record in the grid.
       Then we capture the value of the item in the grid
       We then show a message with the name of the item clicked on
*/

    IF event_type = JTF_GRID_EVENTS.HYPERLINK_EVENT THEN
row_number := jtf_grid.getintproperty(gridName, jtf_grid_property.
rownumber);
v_name := jtf_grid.getColumnCharValue(gridName, row_number,
'NAME');
fnd_message.debug('Triggered a hyperlink event for '||v_name);
    END IF;

END;
```

First add the line `v_item VARCHAR2(200);` to declare the variable `v_item` as shown in the following screenshot:

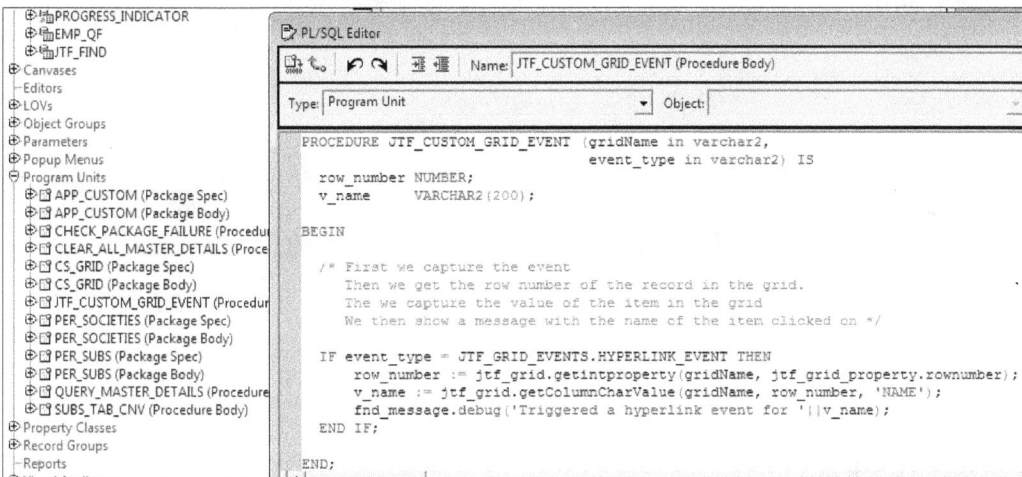

4. Save the form.

How it works...

We have now added the code to handle a hyperlink event. We capture the ID of the record and the item that the event occurred on. We will then display a message to the user.

Testing the form

We are now going to test the form in EBS.

How to do it...

To test the form, perform the following:

1. Transfer the form over to the Application server and compile it as we have done previously.

2. Log in to Oracle with the **XXEBS Extending e-Business Suite** responsibility.

3. Navigate to **Societies Form** and the societies and clubs form will open.

4. Enter an employee number in the query find window and click **Find**.

5. Navigate to the **Society Grid** tab and click on the **Get Fit Sports Club** hyperlink as follows:

How it works...

We have tested the form after we added code to capture events that occur in the grid. We have just shown a simple example but we have shown that we can capture the event and the record that the event was triggered on.

4
Forms Personalization

In this chapter, we will cover the following:

- ▸ Opening the personalization screen
- ▸ Installing the database objects
- ▸ Changing properties
- ▸ Adding a menu item to a form
- ▸ Performing a simple validation and displaying a message
- ▸ Launching a form
- ▸ Adding a toolbar icon to a form
- ▸ Performing complex validation
- ▸ Altering an LOV's record group

Introduction

Forms personalization was first introduced in the release 11.5.10 as a way of changing the way forms behave without having to modify the underlying form. Previously, the CUSTOM library was the only way to extend a form without customizing it. Generally, the CUSTOM library is still used to perform more complex logic, but forms personalization replaces much of the need to use the CUSTOM library. It is worth noting that extensions in forms personalization are executed first, followed by the code in the CUSTOM.pll.

It is much easier to configure and many actions can be performed without any coding. That being said, there are some pretty complex tasks that can be performed using personalization and it has some extremely powerful features. When we want to personalize a form, we have to navigate to the form before we launch the personalization screen. To prevent unauthorized use of the personalization screen, we can set the following profile options:

- **Utilities Diagnostics**: No
- **Hide Diagnostics**: No

In addition, the user is required to know the **apps** password before access to the screen is permitted.

Opening the personalization screen

We can open the personalization form by selecting **Help | Diagnostics | Custom Code | Personalize** from the menu bar, as shown in the following screenshot. The **Personalization** screen will open at this point. We may be prompted for the app's password the first time you open a menu item from **Diagnostics** in the **Help** menu.

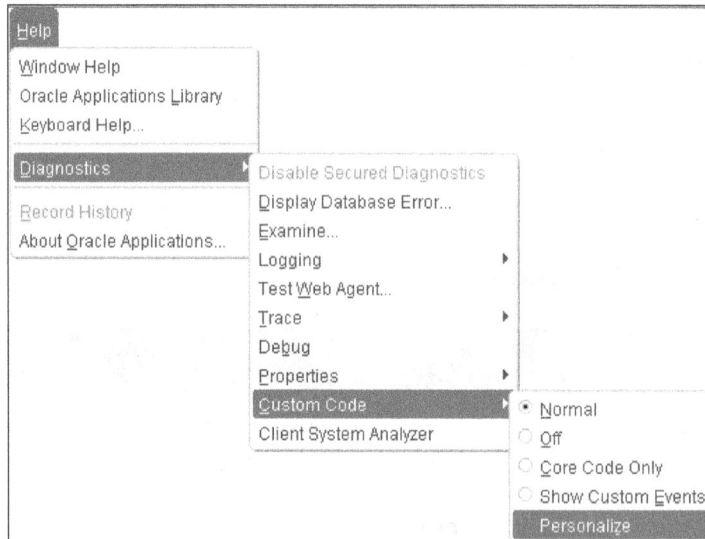

Getting started

If we want to see the custom events that are triggered in the form, we can select **Show Custom Events** from the menu. A pop-up message giving the name of the trigger that is fired will appear each time there is a triggering event in the form. It's a good idea to check that the event we wish to base our personalization upon fires in the form we want to personalize.

How it works...

We are now going to look at the **Personalization** screen in some more detail.

The Personalization screen

The **Personalization** screen has four main regions on the screen. These are the definition, the condition, the context, and the action, as shown in the following screenshot:

Definition

Let's start by looking at the definition region:

- ▶ The sequence (**Seq**) field is a number and determines the order in which a personalization is performed

- ▶ The **Description** is the name given to describe all of the actions that will be performed when the condition is met

- ▶ The **Level** can be set to be the **Function** or **Form**:

  - ❑ The **Function** is the function that launched the form

  - ❑ The **Form** performs the personalization when it is invoked, regardless of the function it was launched with

- ▶ The **Enabled** field allows us to turn the whole personalization on or off

Condition tab

The **Condition** tab allows us to define the conditions when the personalization will be performed. All Oracle forms are based upon the TEMPLATE library, which has hooks to raise events when they occur in the form. We can specify the triggering event and the object where the trigger was raised. The condition field allows us to specify a condition when the action can be performed. This can be left blank if the personalization should always be performed when a trigger is raised, such as a `WHEN-NEW-FORMS-INSTANCE`, or can contain fairly complex conditions, such as calling database functions.

Context region

The context region allows us to specify the level at which the personalization will be triggered. This is the same as profile options and can be restricted to Industry, Site, Responsibility, and User level. Bear in mind that the greater the level of granularity enforced, the greater the maintenance required.

Actions tab

The **Actions** tab is where we can perform an action each time the condition and context in the Condition tab evaluates to TRUE. There are four types of actions that we can perform:

- Property
- Message
- Builtin
- Menu

The **Actions** tab is context sensitive, meaning that the items on the right-hand side of the screen will change. This is dependent upon the action that is selected in the **Type** field. Following is a chart that shows each of the four action types and the actions that are available to each action type. The menu action type depends upon the triggers that are available in the form and the list of values will show the label of the `SPECIAL` triggers that have already been used by the form. We will go into this later in the chapter, but as a good practice, work from the last `SPECIAL` trigger as the standard forms will generally tend to use the special triggers in an ascending numerical order.

Property	Item	Message	Show	Builtin	Launch SRS Form	Menu	MENU1
	Window		Hint		Launch a Function		..
	Block		Error		Launch a URL		...
	Tab Page		Debug		DO_KEY		MENU15
	Canvas		Warn		Execute Procedure		SPECIAL1
	Radio Button				GO_ITEM		
	View				GO_BLOCK		..
	Global Variable				FORMS_DLL		...
	Parameter				RAISE FORM_TRIGGER_FAILURE		SPECIAL45
	Lov				EXECUTE_TRIGGER		
	Local Variable				SYNCHRONIZE		
					Call Custom Library		
					Create Record Group from Query		
					Set Profile Value in Cache		

Property

We can change properties of a number of different objects within the form. When the **Property** action is selected, there are four fields on the right-hand side of the screen—the **Object Type**, **Target Object**, **Property Name**, and **Value**.

Message

We can create messages to display to the user. If we look at the **Message** action type, we see that there are only two fields to the right-hand side of the screen, namely, **Message Type** and **Message Text**.

Builtin

The fields displayed when the **Builtin** action type is selected are context-sensitive.

Menu

The **Menu** action has five fields, namely, the **Menu Entry**, the **Menu Label**, the **Render line before menu** checkbox, the **Icon Name**, and the **Enabled in Block(s)** field. It allows us to add new menu items to a form.

How it works...

We have just discussed the key elements of the **Personalization** screen. In the coming recipes, we will create some personalization to demonstrate a little of what we can and cannot do with personalization.

Installing the database objects

Create the database objects for this chapter before you start by using a script provided. The code comes with the readme file, `readme_4_1.txt`.

We will be creating a database package that we will use in some of the following recipes in this chapter. Finally, we will create a sequence that will be used to generate a unique number for new records. For all the database objects, there is a script provided called `4842_04_01.sh`. The following recipe provides details on how to run the script.

How to do it...

To create the database objects, perform the following tasks:

1. Create a local directory, `C:\packt\scripts\ch4`, where the scripts are downloaded to.

2. Open **Putty** and connect to the application tier user.

3. Create a new directory on the application tier under `$XXHR_TOP/install` with the following commands:

   cd $XXHR_TOP/install

   mkdir ch4

4. Navigate to the new directory with the following command:

   cd ch4

5. Open `WinSCP` and `FTP` the files from `C:\packt\scripts\ch4` to `$XXHR_TOP/install/ch4`, as shown in the following screenshot:

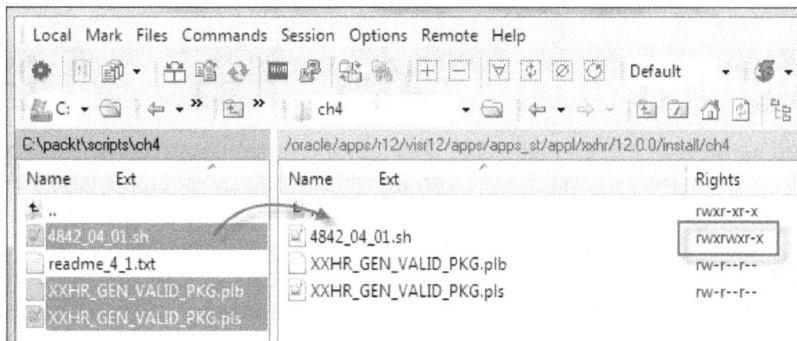

6. In **Putty**, change the permissions of the script with the following command:

   `chmod 775 4842_04_01.sh`

7. Run the following script to create all of the objects by issuing the following command:

   `./4842_04_01.sh apps/apps`

8. The script checks that all of the files are present in your `$XXHR_TOP/install/ch4` directory and will prompt you to continue if they are all there, so type *Y* and press **Return**.

9. After the script has completed, check the `XXHR_4842_04_01.log` file for errors. (It will be created in the same directory `$XXHR_TOP/install/ch4`.)

10. Run the following query to check that all of the objects have been created successfully:

```
SELECT OWNER, OBJECT_NAME, OBJECT_TYPE, STATUS
  FROM ALL_OBJECTS
 WHERE OBJECT_NAME LIKE 'XXHR_GEN%'
ORDER BY 1, 2
```

How it works...

We have created the database objects that we are going to use in this chapter. The `XXHR_GEN_VALID_PKG` package will be called to perform validation and will return a value based upon the validation performed.

Changing properties

To get started we are going to change some object properties through personalization. There are a number of properties we will change and we will start off by renaming labels of items on the screen. We will also change properties to hide and move or disable fields. We want to change the properties every time we enter the form or block and the triggers that fire on these events are the WHEN-NEW-FORMS-INSTANCE and WHEN-NEW-BLOCK-INSTANCE triggers. In the following recipes, we are going to perform several actions on a WHEN-NEW-FORM-INSTANCE trigger as follows:

- ▸ Changing prompts
- ▸ Disabling buttons
- ▸ Renaming tabs
- ▸ Hiding fields
- ▸ Moving fields
- ▸ Testing the form after applying personalization
- ▸ Fixing a personalization that doesn't seem to work

> Before we create a personalization, especially changing properties, it is important to check any profile options that may be available or see if there are any menu exclusions that are available for the form. There may well be some that perform the desired functionality required.

Changing prompts

We are firstly going to change the prompt of the **Birth Date** field in the **People: Enter and Maintain** screen in the HCM module. We will change the prompt to **Date of Birth** by writing a personalization when the form is opened. When we create a personalization, we need to navigate to the screen we want to personalize. Then we can open the personalization screen through the **Help** menu item. When we create personalization, we may need to know the **apps** password.

How to do it...

To change the **Birth Date** label, perform the following steps:

1. Log in to Oracle with the **UK HRMS Manager** responsibility.
2. Navigate to **People | Enter and Maintain**.
3. In the **Find Person** screen, click the **New** button.
4. Select **Help | Diagnostics | Custom Code | Personalize** from the menu.

> Depending on the version and configuration of your environment, you may be prompted to enter the **apps** password to enable diagnostics. You will only be prompted once the first time you enter a **Help | Diagnostics** screen.

5. Enter a new record and populate the following details:

Seq	10
Description	Property changes at form level
Level	**Form**
Enabled	☑

6. In the **Condition** tab, ensure that the trigger event is set to WHEN-NEW-FORM-INSTANCE, as displayed in the following screenshot:

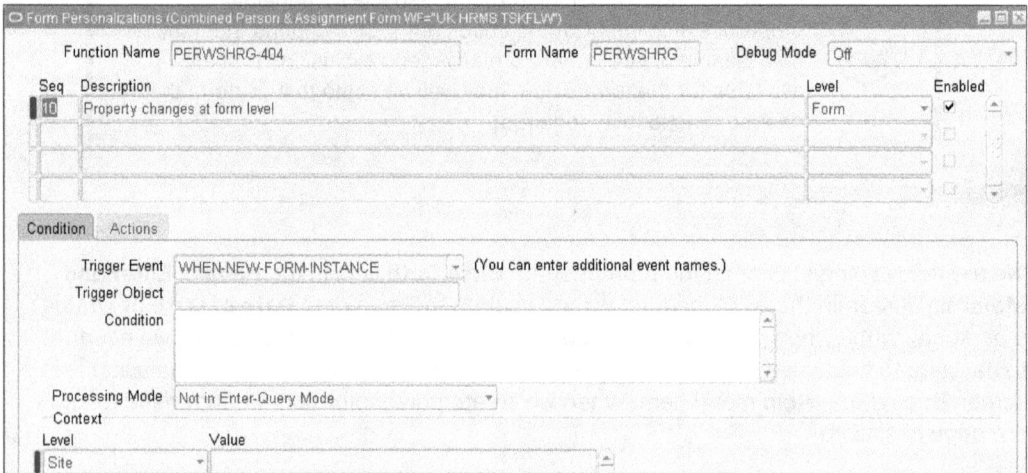

7. Navigate to the **Actions** tab and enter a new record with the following data:

Seq	10
Type	**Property**
Description	Birth Date
Language	**All**
Enabled	☑
Object Type	**Item**
Target Object	PERSON.DATE_OF_BIRTH
Property Name	PROMPT_TEXT
Value	Date of Birth

8. Save the record.

9. The **Actions** tab should look like the following screenshot:

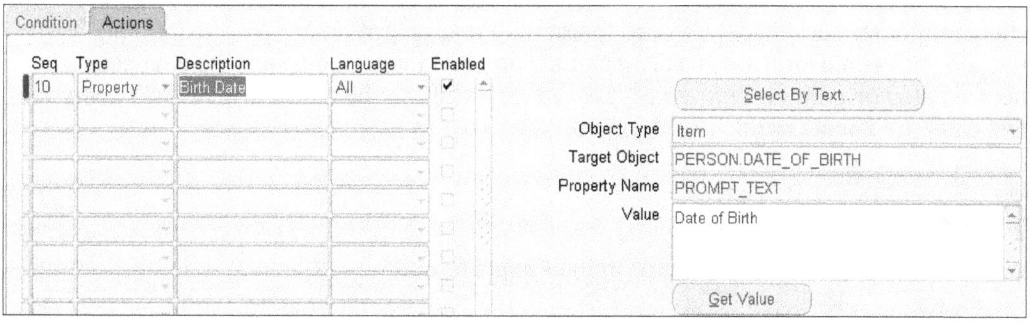

> To find the name of the field to enter in the **Target Object** field, you can put the cursor in the field you want and select **Help | Diagnostics | Examine** from the menu, as shown in the following screenshot. Alternatively, you can click the **Select By Text** button in the **Actions** tab and start typing the label of the item, that is, *Bi* (for **Birth Date**). The list will reduce as you type. Select **PERSON.DATE_OF_BIRTH** from the list.

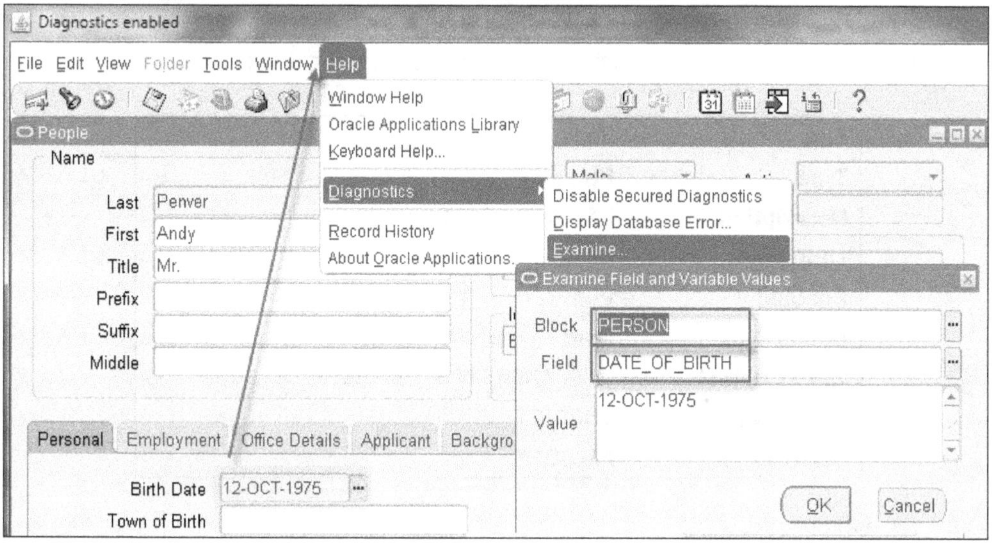

How it works...

We have added a personalization to change the label of the **Birth Date** field. To see any changes that we have made, we need to exit the **Personalization** and **People** form and then re-open the **People** form again. Follow steps 2 and 3 of the recipe again. The changes have been created on a WHEN-NEW-FORM-INSTANCE trigger, so the property will be set when we first enter the **People** form.

Disabling buttons

We are now going to disable a button in the **People** form.

How to do it...

To disable the **Picture** button, perform the following tasks. (If the **Personalization** screen is already open from the previous personalization, then jump straight to *step 6*.)

1. Log in to Oracle with the **UK HRMS Manager** responsibility.
2. Navigate to **People | Enter and Maintain**.
3. In the **Find Person** screen, click the **New** button.
4. Select **Help | Diagnostics | Custom Code | Personalize** from the menu.
5. Navigate to the **Property changes at form level** personalization.
6. In the **Actions** tab, enter a new record with the following data:

Seq	**20**
Type	**Property**
Description	Picture Button
Language	**All**
Enabled	☑
Object Type	**Item**
Target Object	CTL_PERWSEPI_NAV.NAV_BUTTON2
Property Name	ENABLED
Value	**FALSE**

7. Save the record.

8. The screen should look like the following screenshot:

Condition	Actions						
Seq	Type	Description	Language	Enabled			
10	Property ▾	Birth Date	All ▾	✔		Select By Text...	
20	Property ▾	Picture Button	All ▾	✔			
					Object Type	Item	▾
					Target Object	CTL_PERWSEPI_NAV.NAV_BUTTON2	
					Property Name	ENABLED	
					Value	FALSE	▾

How it works...

When we now enter the **People** form, the **Picture** button should be disabled, as we have set the property to **FALSE** upon entry to the form. We are going to change a few more properties first starting with renaming tab labels and then look at the results. We will get an unexpected result on one of the personalization we make which we will look into later.

Renaming tabs

We are now going to rename the label of the **Personal** tab page. We are going to change the label to **Info**.

How to do it...

To rename the **Personal** tab, perform the following tasks (if the **Personalization** screen is already open from the previous personalization, then jump straight to *step 6*):

1. Log in to Oracle with the **UK HRMS Manager** responsibility.
2. Navigate to **People | Enter and Maintain**.
3. In the **Find Person** screen, click the **New** button.
4. Select **Help | Diagnostics | Custom Code | Personalize** from the menu.
5. Navigate to the **Property changes at form level** personalization.
6. In the **Actions** tab, enter a new record with the following data:

Seq	**30**
Type	**Property**
Description	Personal Tab
Language	**All**
Enabled	☑
Object Type	**Item**
Target Object	**REGION_LIST.PER**
Property Name	LABEL
Value	Info

7. Save the record.

8. The screen should look like the following screenshot:

Condition	Actions				

Seq	Type	Description	Language	Enabled	
10	Property	Birth Date	All	✓	
20	Property	Picture Button	All	✓	
30	Property	Personal Tab	All	✓	

Select By Text...

Object Type: Tab Page
Target Object: REGION_LIST.PER
Property Name: LABEL
Value: Info

Get Value

How it works...

When we now enter the **People** form, the **Personal Tab** label will have been changed, as we have set the **Label** property to **Info** upon entry to the form.

Hiding fields

We are now going to hide the **Region of Birth** field, so when we enter the form, it is not visible to the user.

How to do it...

To hide the **Region of Birth** field, perform the following tasks (if the personalization screen is already open from the previous personalization, then jump straight to *step 6*):

1. Log in to Oracle with the **UK HRMS Manager** responsibility.

2. Navigate to **People | Enter and Maintain**.

3. In the **Find Person** screen, click the **New** button.

4. Select **Help | Diagnostics | Custom Code | Personalize** from the menu.

5. Navigate to the **Property changes at form level** personalization.

6. In the **Actions** tab, enter a new record with the following data:

Seq	40
Type	Property
Description	Region of Birth
Language	All
Enabled	☑
Object Type	Item

Target Object	PERSON.D_REGION_OF_BIRTH
Property Name	DISPLAYED (APPLICATIONS COVER)
Value	**FALSE**

Oracle Applications provide a cover routine to the Oracle Forms' built-in routine SET_ITEM_PROPERTY. This cover routine, APP_ITEM_PROPERTY.SET_PROPERTY, modifies or augments the native Oracle Forms' behaviors for specific properties. Therefore, any properties with an **(APPLICATIONS COVER)** should be used if you wish to adhere to the Oracle Applications' cover routines.

7. Save the record.
8. The screen should look like the following screenshot:

How it works...

The **Region of Birth** field will now be hidden to users when entering the form, as we have set the **Displayed** property of the field to **FALSE** upon entry to the form.

Moving fields

Now that we have hidden the **Region of Birth** field in the previous recipe, we are going to move the **Country of Birth** up to where the **Region of Birth** field was. We can use the same **Y Pos** property of the **Region of Birth** field. The left edge is already aligned, so we will not need to change the **X Pos** property. The field will move position, as shown in the following screenshot:

How to do it...

To move the **Country of Birth** field, perform the following tasks (if the **Personalization** screen is already open from the previous personalization, then jump straight to *step 6*):

1. Log in to Oracle with the **UK HRMS Manager** responsibility.
2. Navigate to **People | Enter and Maintain**.
3. In the **Find Person** screen, click the **New** button.
4. Select **Help | Diagnostics | Custom Code | Personalize** from the menu.
5. Navigate to the **Property changes at form level** personalization.
6. In the **Actions** tab, enter a new record with the following data:

Seq	50
Type	Property
Description	Country of Birth
Language	All
Enabled	☑
Object Type	Item
Target Object	PERSON.D_COUNTRY_OF_BIRTH
Property Name	Y_POS
Value	.61

7. Save the record.

How it works...

We have now moved the **Country of Birth** field by setting the **Y_POS** property.

Testing the form after applying personalization

Now we will test the form to see the results of our personalization. The actions are performed on a WHEN-NEW-FORM-INSTANCE trigger, so we will need to exit the form to see the personalizations take effect. The personalization screen, with the five property changes we have just created, should look like the following screenshot:

How to do it...

To test our personalization, perform the following steps:

1. Close any open windows and ensure that you are currently in the **UK HRMS Manager** responsibility (it will work in any responsibility that has access to this form, as we have registered the personalization at form level).

2. Navigate to **People | Enter and Maintain**.

3. Query back an employee record and the form should now appear similar to the following screenshot:

We can compare it to the form before the personalization was applied:

How it works...

We can see that the personalization we have created has made changes in the form. However, you will notice our second personalization to disable the **Picture** button appears not to have worked. This is possibly because the item attributes are set dynamically in the code of the form. There are instances where there will be code in the form that sets properties and changes the way the form behaves. We need to be aware of this when we implement personalizations.

Fixing personalization that doesn't seem to work

Okay, now the **Picture** button is still enabled. When we create a personalization, it may well be that the forms code sets properties dynamically in the form. In this case, the property of the **Picture** button is set in the code after our personalization is executed. We can, in some cases, override this by performing our personalization with a triggering event after the property is set in the form. For example, we could create a new personalization that triggers on a WHEN-NEW-BLOCK-INSTANCE trigger, as shown in the following example.

How to do it...

To create a personalization at the block level, perform the following steps:

1. Log in to Oracle with the **UK HRMS Manager** responsibility.
2. Navigate to **People | Enter and Maintain**.
3. In the **Find Person** screen, click the **New** button.
4. Select **Help | Diagnostics | Custom Code | Personalize** from the menu.

5. Enter a new record and populate the following details:

Seq	**10**
Description	Property changes at block level
Level	**Form**
Enabled	☑

In the **Condition** tab, ensure that the trigger event is set to WHEN-NEW-BLOCK-INSTANCE and the block is set to **PERSON**, as displayed in the following screenshot:

6. In the **Actions** tab, enter a new record with the following data:

Seq	**10**
Type	**Property**
Description	Picture Button
Language	**All**
Enabled	☑
Object Type	**Item**
Target Object	CTL_PERWSEPI_NAV.NAV_BUTTON2
Property Name	**ENABLED**
Value	**FALSE**

7. Save the record.

8. Close the **Personalization** screen and the **People** screen.

    If we enter the form and query back our employee again, we can see that the button is now disabled, as shown in the following screenshot:

Info	Employment	Office Details	Applicant	Background	Rehire	Further Name	Medical	Other	Benefits

Date of Birth 12-OCT-1975	Age 36
Town of Birth	Status Married
Country of Birth United Kingdom	Nationality British
	Disabled No

Button is now disabled.

Effective Dates

From 10-DEC-2001   To   Latest Start Date 01-JAN-1987   [EN]

Address	Picture	Assignment	Special Info	Others...

How it works...

We can see that the button is now disabled in the form. We may often come across personalization that will not work because code in the form supersedes our personalization. It may be that the personalization cannot be applied in some cases. However, it is often the case that we need to perform the personalization at block or item level instead of at form level. Also, be aware that there are other options available, such as menu exclusions, which also perform actions such as hiding fields or disabling buttons. Menu exclusions are not discussed in detail in this book. However, these can be applied in the **Responsibilities** form and there are many menu exclusions that may well perform the actions you require.

Adding a menu item to a form

Our next step is to add a menu item. This can be used to call new forms or to trigger other business processes. We looked at adding menus in the previous chapter when we built our custom form. We will now add a menu item to a standard form using personalization. We will do the following tasks:

▸   Adding a menu item

▸   Testing the menu item that has been added

Adding a menu item

There are, by default, user named triggers called SPECIAL triggers in the standard forms, which range from SPECIAL1 to 45. We can use these triggers to add functionality to the menu bar. Oracle may occasionally use the SPECIAL triggers in a form, so we always start with the highest SPECIAL trigger available. In this next recipe we are going to enable the SPECIAL45 trigger and rename the label.

How to do it...

To add a menu item, we will perform the following tasks:

1. Log in to Oracle with the **UK HRMS Manager** responsibility.

2. Navigate to **People | Enter and Maintain**.

3. In the **Find Person** screen, click the **New** button.

4. Select **Help | Diagnostics | Custom Code | Personalize** from the menu.

5. Enter the following details in the header:

Seq	20
Description	Adding a menu item to a form
Level	Form
Enabled	☑

6. Enter the following details in the **Condition** tab:

Trigger Event	WHEN-NEW-FORM-INSTANCE

7. Save the form, as shown in the following screenshot:

8. In the **Actions** tab, enter the following details:

Seq	**10**
Type	**Menu**
Description	Enable Special 45
Language	**All**
Enabled	☑
Menu Entry	**SPECIAL45**
Menu Label	Societies

9. Save the record.

10. The **Actions** tab will look like the following screenshot:

How it works...

We have now enabled the menu item and renamed it to **Societies**. Later, we will need to create another personalization to perform an action, once it is selected by the user.

Testing whether the menu item has been added

Now we will test the form to see if the menu item we have added is present. The action is performed on a WHEN-NEW-FORM-INSTANCE trigger, so we will need to exit the form to see the personalization take effect.

How to do it...

To test if the new menu item appears, perform the following steps:

1. Close any open windows and ensure that you are currently in the **UK HRMS Manager** responsibility.

2. Navigate to **People | Enter and Maintain**.

3. Query back an employee record and select **Actions** from the menu bar. You will see the **Societies** menu item, as shown in the following screenshot (clicking on it will not do anything just yet, as we need to code the event when the menu item is triggered):

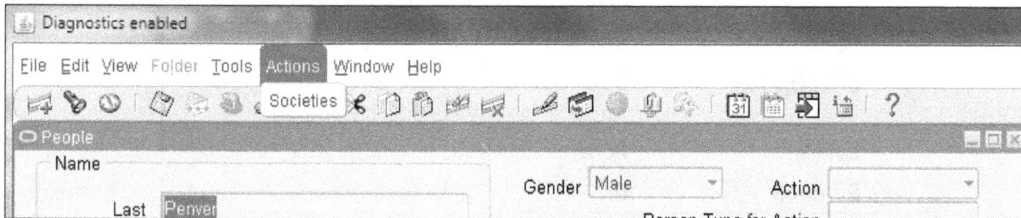

How it works...

As you can see, the menu item appears from the **Actions** menu. The menu displays a drop down list that has an item on it called **Societies**, which we named in the previous recipe.

Performing a simple validation and displaying a message

When certain actions are performed, we may need to do some validation and display a message to the users. Oracle may not display a message as standard functionality, but we can add messages too through personalization. In the next recipe, we are going to check that a record has been queried back before we can navigate to the **Societies** form. If there is no person record, then we are going to display a message to the user. We are going to perform the following tasks:

▸ Adding validation when an event is triggered
▸ Adding a message
▸ Testing the form

Adding validation when an event is triggered

We want to check that when we select the **Societies** menu, there is a person record in the current form. We are going to display a message and halt processing when there is no data in the PERSON_ID field in the form, that is, an employee has not been queried.

How to do it...

To display an error message, perform the following tasks:

1. Log in to Oracle with the **UK HRMS Manager** responsibility.
2. Navigate to **People | Enter and Maintain**.

3. Query back an employee record.

4. Select **Help | Diagnostics | Custom Code | Personalize** from the menu.

5. Enter the following details in the header:

Seq	30
Description	`Performing simple validation and displaying a message`
Level	**Form**
Enabled	☑

6. Enter the following details in the **Condition** tab:

Trigger Event	SPECIAL45
Condition	`:PERSON.PERSON_ID IS NULL`

7. Save the form.

How it works...

We have written the condition when we want the message to appear. When the `SPECIAL45` trigger is fired, we will check to see if a `person` record exists in the current form before we allow the call to launch the **Societies** form.

Adding a message

We now want to display a message if the condition we have just written evaluates to `TRUE`, that is, if there is no data in the `PERSON.PERSON_ID` field, we will not allow the user to navigate to the **Societies** form.

How to do it...

To add a message, perform the following tasks:

1. In the **Actions** tab, enter the following details:

Seq	10
Type	**Message**
Description	**Message to ensure a person record has been queried**
Language	**All**
Enabled	☑
Message Type	**Error**
Message Text	`Please query back a person record before opening the Societies form.`

2. Save the record.

3. The **Actions** tab will look like the following screenshot:

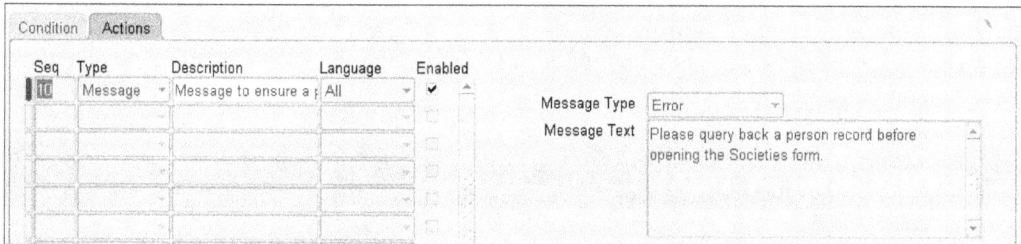

How it works...

The message has been added to the actions when the previous condition was met. When the message type is **Error,** a RAISE FORM_TRIGGER_FAILURE is also performed so that no additional _actions_ will be performed.

Testing the form

Now we will test the form to see the menu item we have added. The action is performed when the **Actions | Societies** menu item is selected. The trigger that will be fired will be the SPECIAL45 trigger.

How to do it...

To test that the message is displayed, perform the following tasks:

1. Close any open windows and ensure that you are currently in the **UK HRMS Manager** responsibility.

2. Navigate to **People | Enter and Maintain**.

3. In the query entry screen, select the **New** button.

4. Select **Actions | Societies** from the menu and the following message will appear:

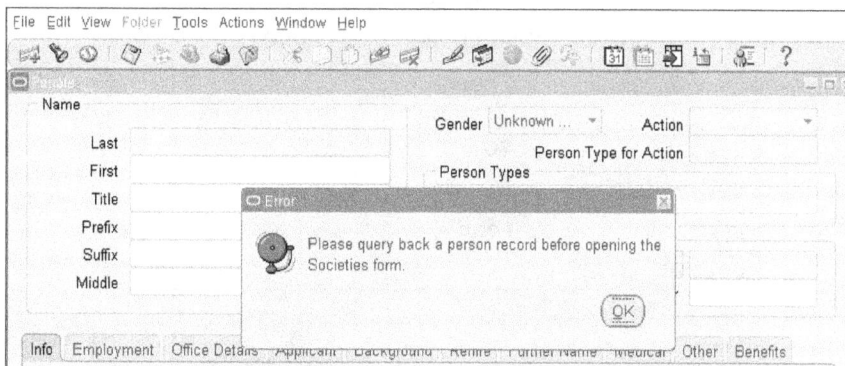

How it works...

We can see that the message is displayed as expected. There is no `PERSON_ID` as we did not query en employee record back. Therefore, the condition we created evaluated to `TRUE` and the error message appeared as expected. Next we will create a new action to launch a form. We will see that the message does not appear when an employee record is queried back and the condition evaluates to `FALSE`.

Launching a form

Now that we have created a menu item, we want to execute an action when the menu is selected. We are going to call the **Societies** form we have developed in the previous forms chapters (if you have not done so then you can install the completed form from the *Chapter 3, Advanced Oracle Forms* download bundle). This demonstrates how we can call a form using personalization. To launch a form we will need to perform the following tasks:

- ▶ Adding a condition
- ▶ Adding a builtin to launch a form
- ▶ Testing to see if the form is launched

Adding a condition

The first thing we need to do is add a custom trigger that will fire when we want to launch the form. In this case, whenever a `SPECIAL45` trigger is raised, we want to be able to launch the form. The `SPECIAL45` trigger is raised whenever we select **Societies** from the menu.

How to do it...

To launch a form, we will perform the following tasks:

1. Log in to Oracle with the **UK HRMS Manager** responsibility.
2. Navigate to **People | Enter and Maintain**.
3. In the query entry screen, select the **New** button.
4. Select **Help | Diagnostics | Custom Code | Personalize** from the menu.
5. Enter the following details in the header:

Seq	40
Description	`Launching a form`
Level	Form
Enabled	☑

> Remember that a personalization will be executed in sequence. Therefore, we must do the validation personalization with a sequence number less than the personalization we want performed after validation is done.

6. Enter the following details in the **Condition** tab:

Trigger Event	**SPECIAL45**
Condition	`:PERSON.PERSON_ID IS NOT NULL`

7. Save the form.

How it works...

We have now created the personalization and the condition in which it will perform the action associated with it. We only want to launch the form if there is a PERSON_ID in the form. We have already added a message if there is no PERSON_ID, but we want to add it here also in case the message personalization is disabled at any point.

Adding a builtin to launch a form

Now that we have created the condition, we need to add the action we want to perform when the condition is met. We will call a standard builtin to call a form function. The function we specify will call our **Societies** form. In addition, we will pass a parameter called P_PERSON_ID. This will utilize functionality we built into our custom form and will automatically query the person record when we enter the **Societies** form. If you remember from the previous chapter, we added the parameter to our **Societies** form. When a value is passed as a parameter when the form is called, the **QUERY_FIND** window is bypassed. Also, when there is a parameter value in P_PERSON_ID, the employee record is automatically queried back.

How to do it...

To call our **Societies** form and pass in a parameter, perform the following tasks:

1. In the **Actions** tab, enter the following details:

Seq	**10**
Type	**Builtin**
Description	`Call function to launch the societies form`
Language	**All**
Enabled	☑
Builtin Type	**Launch a Function**

Function Code	XXHR_EMP_SOCIETY
Function Name	Employee Clubs and Societies
Parameters	'P_PERSON_ID="'||${item.person.person_id.value}||'"'

> The syntax for the parameter can be obtained by selecting the **Insert Item Value** button. The syntax is similar to SPEL. Pay special attention to the single and double quotes. The syntax would be read out as **single quote**, P_PERSON_ID= **double quote, single quote** \|\|${item.person.person_id.value}\|\| **single quote, double quote, single quote**.

2. Save the record.

3. The **Actions** tab will look like the following image:

How it works...

We have now added an action that will call our **Societies** form. When we call the form, we will also pass the PERSON_ID in the P_PERSON_ID parameter.

Testing the form is launched

We will now test the personalization to see if the **Societies** form opens and automatically queries back the employee record. However, we are calling a function from the menu of the **UK HRMS Manager** responsibility we are using. This menu does not contain the function of the form we are calling and therefore we must add it. If we do not add the function to the menu, we will get the following error message:

> **Error** ✖
>
> Function not available to this responsibility. Change responsibilities or contact your System Administrator.
>
> OK

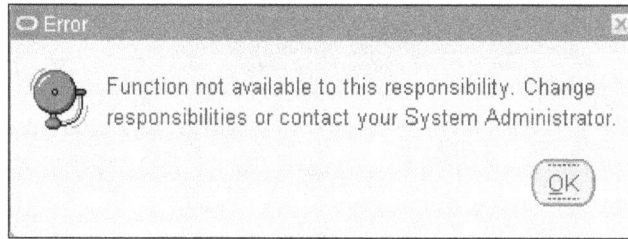

Getting started

Before we test the form, we must add the function to the **UK HRMS Manager** responsibility menu. To do this, perform the following steps:

1. Log in to Oracle with the **Application Developer** responsibility.
2. Navigate to **Application | Menu** and the **Menus** window will open.
3. Press *F11* to enter a query.
4. Type UK_HRMS_NAV in the menu field and press *Ctrl + F11* to query back the menu associated with the **UK HRMS Manager** responsibility.
5. Enter data as in the following table for the record details:

Seq	Prompt	Submenu	Function	Description
800			Employee Clubs and Societies	Employee Clubs and Societies

6. Click the **Save** button in the toolbar (or *Ctrl + S*) to save the record.
7. Exit the form.

We have now attached the function to the menu for the **UK HRMS Manager** responsibility. We will now test the personalization we created earlier.

How to do it...

To test the personalization, perform the following tasks:

1. Close any open window and ensure that you are currently in the **UK HRMS Manager** responsibility.
2. Navigate to **People | Enter and Maintain**.
3. In the query entry screen, select the **New** button.
4. Select **Actions | Societies** from the menu bar.

5. The **Societies** form will open and automatically query the person record from the **People** screen, as shown in the following screenshot:

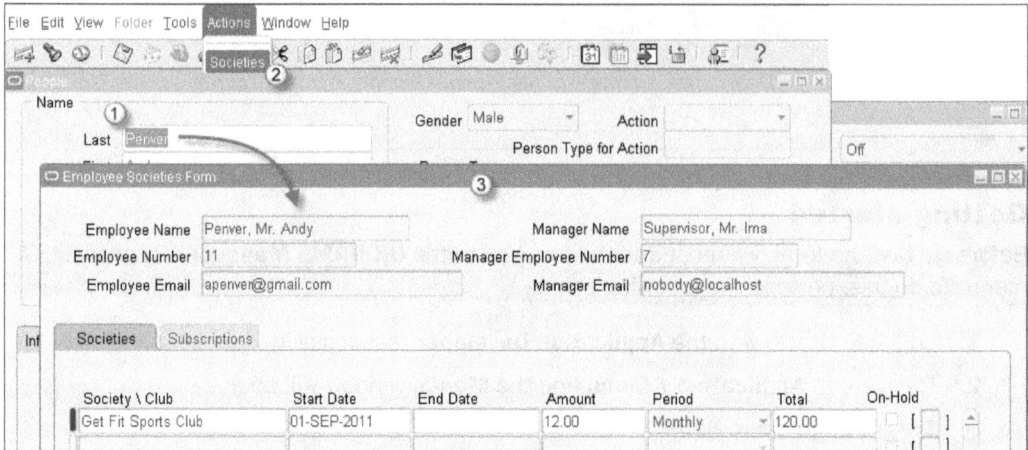

How it works...

We have tested that we can call the function to launch the **Societies** form. When the form is opened, the same employee record is returned that we queried back in the **People** form.

Adding a toolbar icon to a form

Our next step is to add a button to the toolbar. We have already added the menu item. We want to create an icon on the toolbar that will perform the same action as the user using the menu. In this recipe, we will accomplish the following:

▸ Adding an icon to the toolbar

▸ Testing to see if the toolbar icon is displayed

Adding an icon to the toolbar

We have added the menu to call the **Societies** form in the previous recipe. We are now going to add a toolbar icon as well.

How to do it...

To add a toolbar icon, perform the following tasks:

1. Log in to Oracle with the **UK HRMS Manager** responsibility.

2. Navigate to **People | Enter and Maintain**.

3. In the query entry screen, select the **New** button.

4. Select **Help | Diagnostics | Custom Code | Personalize** from the menu.

5. Navigate to the **Adding a menu item to a form** record.

6. Navigate to the **Actions** tab.

7. Check the **Render line before menu** checkbox.

8. Set the **Icon Name** value to **hrvwshlwas**, as shown in the following screenshot:

> The `.gif` file is an existing `.gif` that is stored in the `$OA_MEDIA` directory on the application server. Notice that the value does not need the `.gif` extension. If we want to use our own GIF, then we need to ftp it to the `$OA_MEDIA` directory.

9. Save the record.

10. The **Actions** tab will look like the following image:

How it works...

The **Societies** form can now be launched by selecting the menu item or by clicking on a toolbar button. The icon we specify must exist in the `$OA_MEDIA` directory on the applications tier, and we enter the icon name without the extension when we define the personalization.

Testing to see if the toolbar icon is displayed

We will now test whether the icon is displayed on the toolbar.

How to do it...

To check that the icon is displayed, perform the following tasks:

1. Close any open window and ensure that you are currently in the **UK HRMS Manager** responsibility.

2. Navigate to **People | Enter and Maintain**.

3. You can see the new icon is displayed in the toolbar and triggers the SPECIAL45 trigger when selected, as shown in the following screenshot:

> The icon we have added does not replace the menu item. The **Societies** menu item is still available from the toolbar menu.

How it works...

The icon performs the same action as selecting **Societies** from the menu.

Performing complex validation

We are now going to perform some more advanced validation. The scenario is that we need to check that the e-mail address entered for the employee belongs to a specific domain. We are going to validate this by checking the domain of an e-mail address to ensure that it contains a specified string. First we are going to create a lookup that will contain valid strings that we will check for in our personalization. Then we will create a database function that will check the e-mail address on a WHEN-VALIDATE-RECORD trigger. If the string does not exist in the e-mail address, then a warning message will be displayed. So we are going to perform the following tasks:

▸ Create a lookup

▸ Call a database function from a condition statement

▸ Add a warning message

▸ Test the validation

▸ Stop any further processing

▸ Check a database value against a form value

Creating a lookup

We are going to create a lookup that we can use to store valid strings that we will look for in the e-mail address entered.

How to do it...

To create the e-mail validation lookup, perform the following tasks:

1. Log in to Oracle and select the **Application Developer** responsibility.
2. Navigate to **Application | Lookups | Application Object Library**, and the **Application Object Library Lookups** window will open.
3. Populate the form header, as shown in the following table:

Type	XXHR_EMAIL_VALIDATION
Meaning	List of valid email domain strings
Application	XXHR Custom Application
Description	List of valid email domain strings

4. Populate the detail block with the following data:

Code	Meaning	Description
SEC	@secure	secure domain string
DOM	@dom	dom domain string

The form will now look similar to the following screenshot:

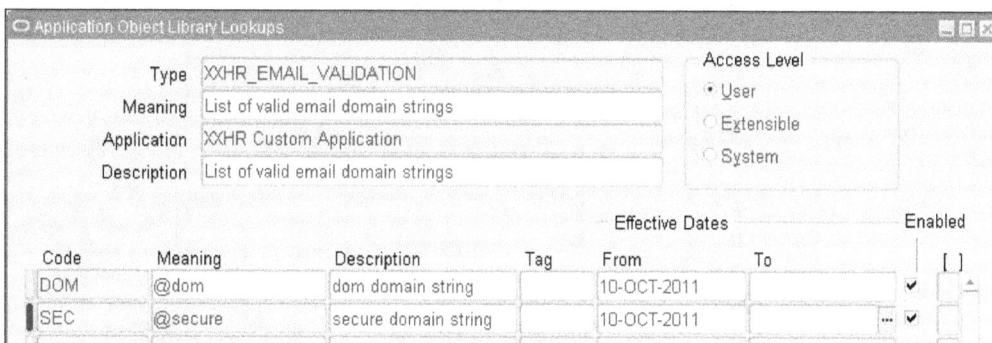

How it works...

The lookup will be used in our validation package that we will use later to validate an e-mail address.

Calling a database function in a condition statement

We will now call a database function in our condition statement. The function will return a VARCHAR2. If the value returned is N, then the e-mail address is not in the list of valid e-mail strings.

Getting ready

At the beginning of the chapter, we had created the database package called XXHR_GEN_ VALID_PKG. In the package, there is a function called Secure_Email_Address. There is a parameter passed into the function that is an e-mail address. We will then query the strings in the lookup and see if any of them exist in the e-mail address we need to validate. The function will return a Y if the string is included in the value (e-mail address) that was passed in. If there are none of the strings defined in the lookup in the string (e-mail address) passed in, then a value of N is returned.

How to do it...

To add a condition that calls a a database function when validating a record, perform the following tasks:

1. Log in to Oracle with the **UK HRMS Manager** responsibility.
2. Navigate to **People | Enter and Maintain**.
3. In the query entry screen, select the **New** button.
4. Select **Help | Diagnostics | Custom Code | Personalize** from the menu.
5. Enter the following details in the header:

Seq	**50**
Description	**Performing complex validation**
Level	**Form**
Enabled	☑

6. Enter the following details in the **Condition** tab. The condition is that if the e-mail address is not null or does not contain a string stored in our lookup, then the action is performed. We perform this validation whenever the WHEN-VALIDATE-RECORD trigger fires in the **PERSON** block.

Trigger Event	**WHEN-VALIDATE-RECORD**
Trigger Object	PERSON
Condition	:PERSON.EMAIL_ADDRESS IS NOT NULL AND XXHR_GEN_VALID_PKG.Secure_Email_Address (:PERSON.EMAIL_ADDRESS) = 'N'

7. The **Condition** tab will look like the following screenshot:

How it works...

When the WHEN-VALIDATE-RECORD trigger is executed, we will call the database function to validate the e-mail address.

Adding a warning message

We will add a message to be displayed if the e-mail address is not in the list of valid e-mail address strings in our XXHR_EMAIL_VALIDATION lookup.

How to do it...

To add an a warning, perform the following tasks:

1. In the **Actions** tab, enter the following details:

Seq	10
Type	**Message**
Description	Valid email message
Language	**All**
Enabled	☑
Message Type	**Warn**
Message Text	The email address is not a secure email address

2. Save the record.

3. The **Actions** tab will look like the following screenshot:

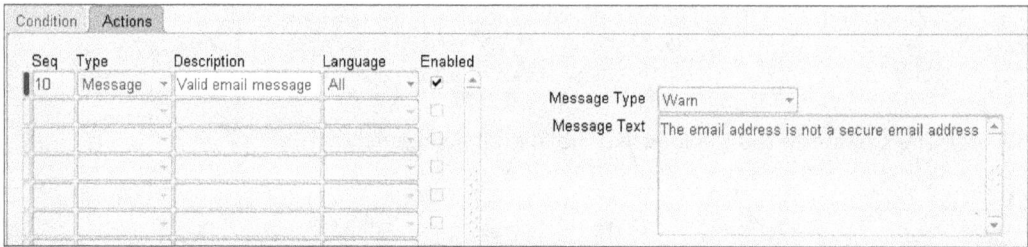

Condition	Actions						
Seq	Type	Description	Language	Enabled			
10	Message	Valid email message	All	☑		Message Type	Warn
				☐		Message Text	The email address is not a secure email address
				☐			
				☐			
				☐			

How it works...

We have added a warning message to be displayed when the e-mail address entered in the **People** form does not have a string that exists in the XXHR_EMAIL_VALIDATION lookup. The warning message will not perform a FORM_TRIGGER_FAILURE, as it is only a **Message Type** of **WARN**.

Testing the validation

We want to test that the message is displayed when an invalid e-mail address is entered.

How to do it...

To perform the test, follow the given steps:

1. Close any open window and ensure that you are currently in the **UK HRMS Manager** responsibility.

2. Navigate to **People | Enter and Maintain**.

3. Query back an employee record and navigate to the **Office Details** tab.

4. In the **Email** field, enter a dummy e-mail address that does not contain the string @*secure* or @*dom* from the XXHR_EMAIL_VALIDATION lookup, for example, dummyemail@ebs.com.

5. When prompted to update or correct the record, select the **Correction** button (without going onto an HR feature called **date tracking**, selecting **CORRECTION** is the same as saving the record in a form without data tracking).

6. Save the record.

7. The following message will appear to warn the user that the e-mail address entered does not contain a string from the XXHR_EMAIL_VALIDATION lookup we created:

| Info | Employment | Office Details | Applicant | Background | Rehire | Further Name | Medical | Other | Benefits |

Office				Email	dummyemail@ebs.com
Location		
Mailstop		

Caution ⊠

⚠ The email address is not a secure email address

[OK] [Cancel]

Effective Dates

From 10-DEC-2001   To   EN]

> Now update the e-mail address in the e-mail field and change the @*ebs*
> to @*secure*. When prompted to update or correct the record, select the
> **Correction** button. Save the record and notice that the message no longer
> appears, as the e-mail address contains a valid string.

How it works...

Each time the WHEN-VALIDATE-RECORD trigger is executed, the validation will be performed, and if the e-mail address is not valid, the warning message will appear.

Stop any further processing

The message we just added does not prevent the user from continuing with the form. We just display a warning message to the user. If we wanted to prevent the user from continuing, we could either make the message type, **Error**, or we could create a new action that implicitly raises a FORM TRIGGER FAILURE. We are going to add a new action to raise a FORM_TRIGGER_FAILURE, which will stop processing the **Message Type, Error.**

How to do it...

To add a FORM_TRIGGER_FAILURE builtin, perform the following tasks:

1. In the **Personalization** screen for the **People** form, navigate to the **Performing complex validation** personalization.

2. In the **Actions** tab, enter the following details:

Seq	**20**
Type	**Builtin**
Description	RAISE form_trigger_failure
Language	**All**
Builtin Type	**RAISE FORM_TRIGGER_FAILURE**

3. Save the record.

4. The **Actions** tab will look like the following screenshot:

How it works...

We have added an action to explicitly raise a FORM_TRIGGER_FAILURE builtin. This will prevent the form from continuing when the condition in the **Condition** tab evaluates to True. We could have achieved the same result by updating the message type from Warn to Error, as a message type of error will execute a FORM_TRIGGER_FAILURE when an *Error* message type is triggered.

Checking a database value against a form value

The problem we have is that the validation we have entered checks the validation every time the WHEN-VALIDATE-RECORD trigger is fired. We only want the e-mail to be validated when the e-mail address is changed. To do this, we are going to add an additional statement to the *condition* of the personalization that will check to see if the e-mail address stored in the database is different from the value in the form.

How to do it...

To check the database value, perform the following tasks:

1. Log in to Oracle with the **UK HRMS Manager** responsibility.

2. Navigate to **People | Enter and Maintain**.

3. In the query entry screen, select the **New** button.

4. Select **Help | Diagnostics | Custom Code | Personalize** from the menu.

5. Navigate to the **Performing complex validation** personalization.

6. Change the condition to the following:

Condition	NVL (:PERSON.EMAIL_ADDRESS, -1) != NVL (${item. PERSON.EMAIL_ADDRESS.database_value}, -1) AND XXHR_GEN_VALID_PKG.Secure_Email_Address (:PERSON.EMAIL_ADDRESS) = 'N'

7. The **Condition** tab will look like the following screenshot:

| 50 | Performing complex validation |

| Condition | Actions |

Trigger Event	WHEN-VALIDATE-RECORD ▾	(You can enter additional event names.)
Trigger Object	PERSON
Condition	NVL (:PERSON.EMAIL_ADDRESS, -1) != NVL (${item.PERSON.EMAIL_ADDRESS. database_value}, -1) AND XXHR_GEN_VALID_PKG.Secure_Email_Address (:PERSON. EMAIL_ADDRESS) = 'N'

8. Save the form.

> The syntax for checking the database value is `${item.<block_ name>.<item_name>.database_value}`.

How it works...

The condition now only triggers the message when the e-mail address in the form is different from the e-mail address that is stored in the database. This prevents the message from appearing each time the `WHEN-VALIDATE-RECORD` trigger fires when no changes to the e-mail address have been made.

There's more...

We need to test the personalization again to ensure that the changes we have made work as desired. Exit the **People** form and the **Personalization** screen and perform the following tests:

▶ Query back an employee record and change the e-mail address to a valid e-mail. Save the changes.

▶ Query back an employee record and change the e-mail address to an invalid e-mail. Save the changes.

▶ Query back an employee record and change the **Mail To** field to another value. Save the changes.

The message should now only be displayed on the second test when we enter an invalid e-mail address.

Altering an LOV's record group

In the next scenario, we are going to modify a query for a list of values through personalization. The **Person** screen has a field called **Country of Birth**. This has a list of values called COUNTRY_OF_BIRTH_LOV. We want to change the record group the LOV uses so that we can modify the meaning the user sees in the list. We are going to concatenate the country code to the meaning and then assign the new record group to the list of values. The following tasks will be performed:

- ▸ Creating a new record group
- ▸ Assigning a new record group to an LOV
- ▸ Testing whether a radio group has changed

Creating a new record group

We are going to create a new record group that we want the LOV to use.

How to do it...

To create the record group through personalization, perform the following steps:

1. Log in to Oracle with the **UK HRMS Manager** responsibility.
2. Navigate to **People | Enter and Maintain**.
3. Query back an employee record.
4. Select **Help | Diagnostics | Custom Code | Personalize** from the menu.
5. Enter the following details in the header:

Seq	60
Description	Altering an LOV's record group
Level	Form
Enabled	☑

6. Enter the following details in the **Condition** tab (this should already be defaulted):

Trigger Event	**WHEN-NEW-FORM-INSTANCE**

7. In the **Actions** tab, enter the following details:

Seq	**5**
Type	**Builtin**
Description	Create Country LOV
Language	**All**
Enabled	☑
Builtin Type	**Create Record Group from Query**
Argument	SELECT territory_short_name||' ('||TERRITORY_ CODE||')' territory_short_name, territory_code FROM fnd_territories_vl ORDER BY territory_short_name
Group Name	XXHR_COUNTRY_OF_BIRTH_LOV

8. The **Actions** tab will look like the following screenshot:

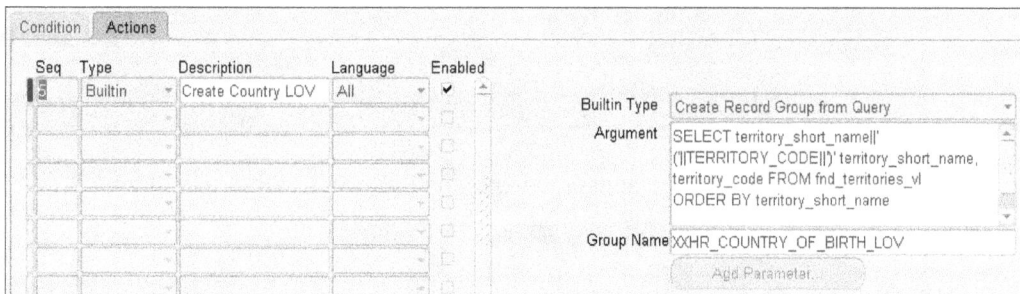

9. Save the record.

How it works...

We need to create a new query for the record group before we can replace the existing record group. Then at runtime we will replace the seeded record group query with our own. Bear in mind that the number of fields in the new query must be the same as the number of fields in the existing query. A common usage for this type of personalization is to restrict the list of values returned by adding conditions to the WHERE clause.

There's more...

The existing record group can be identified by opening the **PERWSHRG** form in Forms Developer. To find the LOV we want to change, we can look at the properties of the item through **Help | Diagnostics**, as shown in the following screenshot:

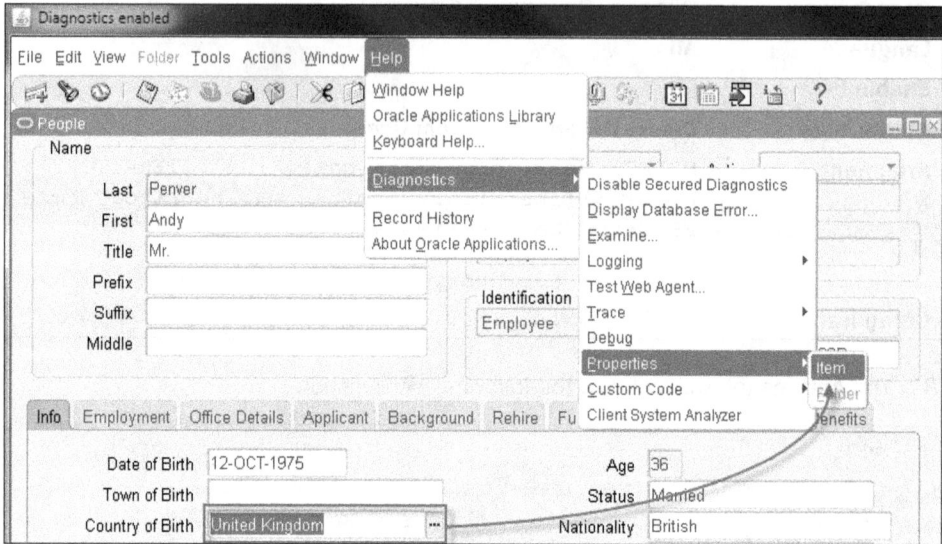

The following screenshot shows the item property of the country of birth display item:

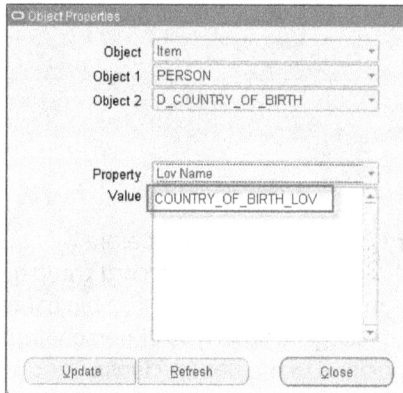

1. From the preceding screenshot, we can see that the LOV name is COUNTRY_OF_
   BIRTH_LOV. In the form, we can examine the properties of the LOV, as shown in the
   following screenshot:

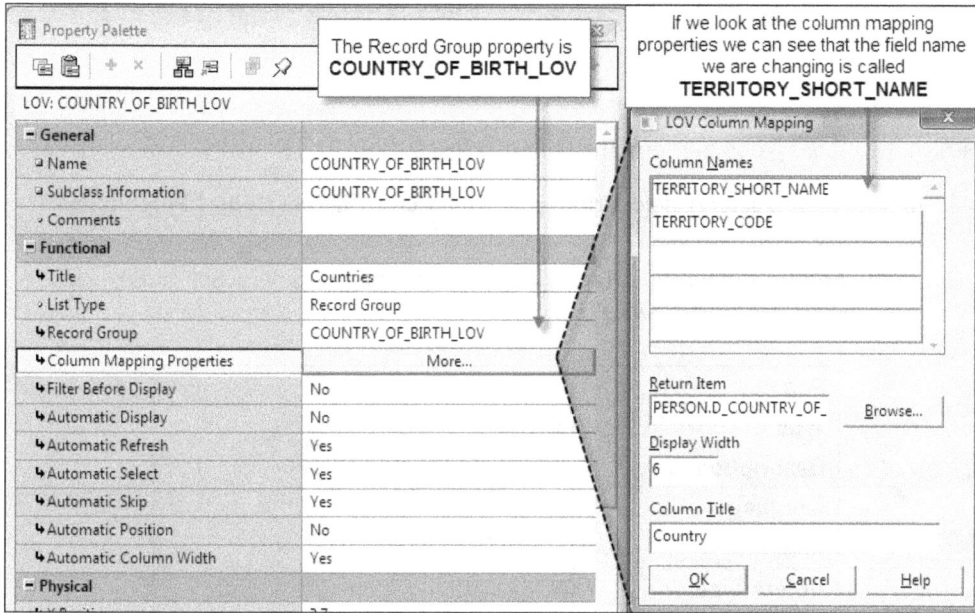

2. The existing query for COUNTRY_OF_BIRTH_LOV is

```
SELECT territory_short_name, territory_short_name, territory_code
FROM fnd_territories_vl
ORDER BY territory_short_name
```

3. We have amended the query to concatenate the territory_code to the
   territory_short_name, so that the user can see it in the LOV. The query
   now becomes

```
SELECT territory_short_name||' ('||territory_code||')'territory_
short_name, territory_code
FROM fnd_territories_vl
ORDER BY territory_short_name
```

4. We have concatenated the code to the territory_short_name with ||'
   ('||territory_code||')' territory_short_name. Notice that the name
   of the field has been specified as territory_short_name, so that the LOV in
   forms still maps to the territory_short_name field in the **LOV Column Mapping**
   properties, as we cannot change these mappings through personalization.

Assigning a new record group to an LOV

Now that we have created a new record group called XXHR_COUNTRY_OF_BIRTH, we need to change the LOV to use the new record group instead of the Oracle seeded one. We can do this by changing the property of the LOV in our personalization.

How to do it...

To assign the record group, perform the following tasks:

1. In the **Person** screen, select **Help | Diagnostics | Custom Code | Personalize** from the menu.

2. In the **Actions** tab for the **Altering an LOV's record group** personalization, create a new record with the following details:

Seq	**10**
Type	**Property**
Description	Change Country LOV RG
Language	**All**
Enabled	☑
Object Type	**LOV**
Target Object	**COUNTRY_OF_BIRTH_LOV**
Property Name	GROUP_NAME
Value	XXHR_COUNTRY_OF_BIRTH_LOV

3. The **Actions** tab will look like the following screenshot:

4. Save the record.

How it works...

The LOV is now using the new record group called XXHR_COUNTRY_OF_BIRTH_LOV, we created earlier, as we have changed the **Group_Name** property of the LOV.

Testing a radio group has changed

We are now going to test whether the LOV is using the new record group.

How to do it...

To test if the LOV is using the new record group or not, perform the following steps:

1. Close any open windows and ensure that you are currently in the **UK HRMS Manager** responsibility.

2. Navigate to **People | Enter and Maintain**.

3. Query back an employee record and navigate to the **Info** tab.

4. In the **Country of Birth** field, select the LOV as shown in the following screenshot:

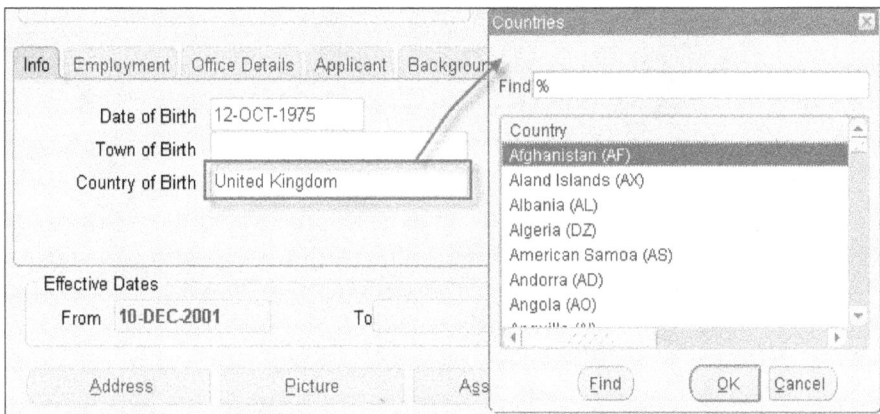

5. Select a country and click **OK** and **Save**.

6. If prompted, choose to update as a **CORRECTION**.

How it works...

We can see that the LOV has now picked up our new LOV and has concatenated the country code to the country name. Be aware that this is just an example and if the record was queried back, the value displayed to the user would not contain the *country_code*. Think very carefully before changing an LOV. If we want to restrict the list because values are no longer required we would add an end date to the unwanted values in the lookup rather than restrict the LOV than through forms personalization. We are only changing the description that is displayed to the user here, not the value that is stored in the database.

5
Workflow

In this chapter, we will cover the following:

- ▶ Introducing Workflow Builder
- ▶ Installing the database objects
- ▶ Creating an advanced queue
- ▶ Building a workflow
- ▶ Creating a business event
- ▶ Viewing a workflow status and monitoring progress
- ▶ Adding a function
- ▶ Creating a lookup
- ▶ Creating a subprocess
- ▶ Creating messages
- ▶ Sending notifications and processing responses
- ▶ Calling an API

Introduction

In this chapter, we are going to take a look at workflow. There is a fair bit to go through but by the end of this chapter you will have a good grasp of the concepts of developing workflows and how to monitor them. We will also delve into business events and advanced queues as they are fairly closely related, especially in Release 12. Workflow Builder can be downloaded from Oracle (follow note ID 261028.1 from Oracle Support).

In this chapter we are going to create a workflow that is triggered by a business event. We are going to create our own advanced queue and service component that will monitor the inbound XML messages for the recipes in this chapter.

We are going to build a solution for a scenario where a signed absence form is sent in to the office from an employee's manager. The document is scanned and an XML message is extracted from metadata in the absence form. The XML message is then en-queued onto the advanced queue. The message on the queue launches a workflow, triggered by a business event, that will perform a number of actions and will end up creating an absence. When we create the workflow we will progress the workflow throughout the chapter until we have a solution to the business scenario. We will be starting the process at the point where we put an XML message onto the inbound queue. There will be a number of features of workflow that will be demonstrated, which will include:

- Creating attributes
- Creating messages
- Creating lookups
- Branching
- Notifications
- Timeouts
- Events
- Processes and sub-processes

Introducing Workflow Builder

Workflow builder is a development tool we will use to develop our workflow processes. It has a navigator similar to Oracle forms which is used to define attributes, processes, notifications, functions, events, messages, and lookup types. We can create and use these objects to build our processes. It is assumed that you have it installed on your PC.

How to do it...

There is a feature called access protection in Workflow Builder and this allows objects within a workflow to be locked. This prevents seeded workflows from being modified. Nearly all objects within Oracle Workflow have an **Access** tab on the **Properties** window except lookup codes, function attributes, and message attributes which inherit access protection settings from their parent object. The level of access can be set in Workflow Builder and developers need to set access levels as defined in the following list:

- 0-9 is reserved for Oracle Workflow
- 10-19 is reserved for Oracle Application Object Library

- 20-99 is reserved for Oracle E-Business Suite
- 100-999 is reserved for customer specific extensions
- 1000 is reserved for public

An object will be locked to users that have a higher protection level than the object. You can see this as there is a padlock against objects that you do not have the access level to modify. The access level defaults to 100 and as an e-Business Suite developer, we always operate with an access level of 100. The access level can be modified by navigating to **Help | About Oracle Workflow Builder** as shown in the following screenshot:

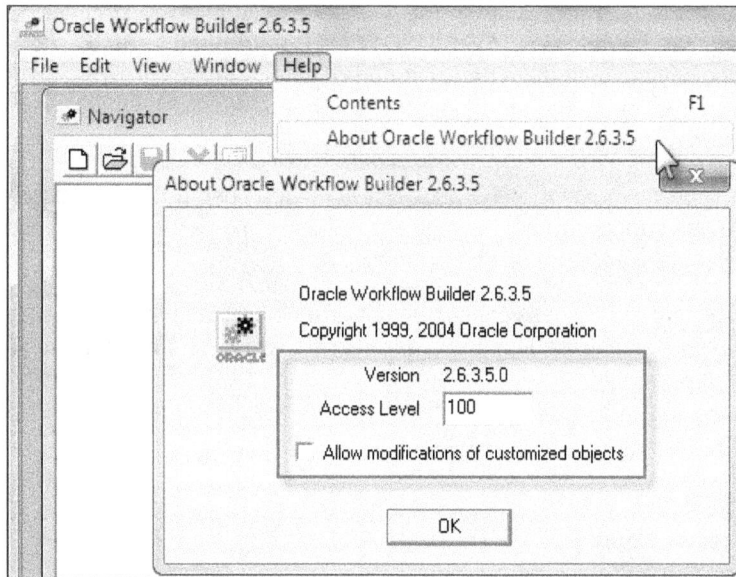

> Oracle does not support customizations to standard workflows that have a protection level less than 100. We should not alter an object's protection level if it is less than 100 and we should never change the access level with the intention of modifying an object.

How it works...

We have discussed access control and how it determines the objects that should not be modified. However, always refer to the product-specific user guide and documents available through Oracle Support for details relating to specific seeded workflows. The product specific documentation will detail what should *not* be modified. Oracle Support Services will not support extensions to any workflow processes that they specifically state should not be modified.

There's more...

In addition to what we have discussed relating to access, it is also important to understand what the workflow engine is and how we can create supplemental engines to process costly activities such as *Deferred* workflows through the **Workflow Background Process** concurrent program.

The **Workflow Engine** is a collection of server side PL/SQL tables, views, packages, and procedures embedded in the Oracle Applications database. It processes activities as they are executed at runtime and will process these through to completion provided each preceding activity completes successfully. When an activity gets stuck, deferred, or timed out, it will be left in that state to be processed by the **Workflow Background Engine** as these activity statuses are too costly to be maintained at runtime. When the background engine runs any stuck, deferred, or timed out activity statuses will be re-evaluated and the workflow will resume if logical conditions permit it.

The workflow engine will process all function activities and send out notifications automatically. It can support numerous logical conditions such as launching subprocesses, running parallel processes, looping, and branching.

The Workflow Background Process concurrent program is available in the **System Administrator** responsibility request group and can also be run from the **Oracle Applications Manager** screen. Generally, we will schedule a background engine concurrent program for specific item types to run periodically but there should be at least one background engine for each of the following:

- ▸ Timed out activities
- ▸ Deferred activities
- ▸ Stuck processes

There are a number of parameters for the concurrent program that allow us to restrict the process to handle activities for specific item types, and within specific cost ranges. We can select parameters to process any combination of deferred, timed out, or stuck activities. A separate background engine to check for stuck processes can be scheduled at less frequent intervals than those scheduled for deferred activities.

See also

For more information on Oracle Workflow refer to the *Oracle Workflow User Guide, Oracle Workflow Developers Guide,* and *Oracle Workflow API Reference Guide.*

Installing the database objects

Create the database objects for this chapter before you start by using a script provided. The code comes with the readme file, `readme_5_1.txt`.

We are going to create a number of objects that we will use throughout the chapter. For all the database objects, there is a script provided called `4842_05_01.sh`. The following recipe provides details of how to run the script.

How to do it...

To create an advanced queue, perform the following steps:

1. Create a local directory `C:\packt\scripts\ch5` where the scripts are downloaded to.

2. Open **Putty** and connect to the application tier user.

3. Create a new directory on the application tier under `$XXHR_TOP/install` with the following commands:

   ```
   cd $XXHR_TOP/install
   ```

   ```
   mkdir ch5
   ```

4. Navigate to the new directory with the following command:

   ```
   cd ch5
   ```

5. Open **WinSCP** and ftp the files from `C:\packt\scripts\ch5` to `$XXHR_TOP/install/ch5` as shown in the following screenshot:

C:\packt\scripts\ch5			/oracle/apps/r12/visr12/apps/apps_st/appl/xxhr/12.0.0/install/ch5		
Name	Ext	Size	Name	Ext	Size	Rights
↑ ..			↑ ..			rwxr-xr-x
4842_05_01.sh		17,073	4842_05_01.sh		16,494	rwxr-xr-x
AQ Query.sql		349	AQ Query.sql		349	rw-r--r--
CH5 Test Harness 1.sql		1,150	CH5 Test Harness 1.sql		1,150	rw-r--r--
CH5 Test Harness 2.sql		1,625	CH5 Test Harness 2.sql		1,625	rw-r--r--
CH5 Test Harness 3.sql		1,628	CH5 Test Harness 3.sql		1,628	rw-r--r--
XXHR_ABSENCE_IN_WF_PKG.pkb		26,954	XXHR_ABSENCE_IN_WF_PKG.pkb		26,954	rw-r--r--
XXHR_ABSENCE_IN_WF_PKG.pks		2,426	XXHR_ABSENCE_IN_WF_PKG.pks		2,426	rw-r--r--
XXHR_CREATE_ABS_AQ.sql		1,300	XXHR_CREATE_ABS_AQ.sql		1,300	rw-r--r--
XXHR_EVENT_ENQUEUE_S.sql		150	XXHR_EVENT_ENQUEUE_S.sql		150	rw-r--r--
XXHR_XML_WF_IN.sql		1,388	XXHR_XML_WF_IN.sql		1,388	rw-r--r--
XXHR_XML_WF_IN_SYN.sql		71	XXHR_XML_WF_IN_SYN.sql		71	rw-r--r--
XXHRIABS.wft		64,780	XXHRIABS.wft		64,780	rw-r--r--

6. In **Putty**, change the permissions of the script with the following command:

    ```
    chmod 775 4842_05_01.sh
    ```

7. Run the following script to create all of the objects by issuing the following command:

    ```
    ./4842_05_01.sh apps/apps
    ```

8. The script checks whether all of the files are present in your $XXHR_TOP/install/ ch5 directory and will prompt you to continue if they are all there, so type Y and press **Return**.

9. After the script has completed check the XXHR_4842_05_01.log file for errors. (It will be created in the same directory, $XXHR_TOP/install/ch5).

How it works...

We have now created all of the database objects for this chapter.

Creating an advanced queue

We will now create an advanced queue and the messages we put into the queue will trigger our workflow process later in the chapter. The creation of advanced queues is performed by calls to the dbms_aqadm package. Advanced queues are very different from normal database tables. For example, we cannot insert records directly into the advanced queue tables. We must enqueue and dequeue messages to the advanced queue. When we create an advanced queue we will perform the following tasks:

 ▸ Create queue table
 ▸ Create queue
 ▸ Start queue
 ▸ Grant ENQUEUE and DEQUEUE privileges to the **apps** user

Getting started

To perform these actions there is a script in the download bundle called XXHR_CREATE_ABS_ AQ.sql. We are going to use this script to create the queue in the APPLSYS schema.

How to do it...

To create the advanced queue, perform the following steps:

1. Ftp the SQL script XXHR_CREATE_ABS_AQ.sql to $XXHR_TOP/install/ch5.

2. Open a **Putty** session and change the directory to $XXHR_TOP/install/ch5 with the following command:

    ```
    cd $XXHR_TOP/install/ch5
    ```

3. Start an SQL*Plus session and log on as the **APPLSYS** user by typing the following command:

   `sqlplusapplsys/<apps password>`

   (Remember the **APPLSYS** password will be the same as the **apps** password.)

4. Run the SQL script with the following command:

   `SQL> @XXHR_CREATE_ABS_AQ.sql`

5. When the script has completed type `exit` to come out of SQL*Plus.

6. Now you can close the **Putty** session.

7. Run the following query to check that all of the objects have been created successfully:

```
SELECT OWNER, OBJECT_NAME, OBJECT_TYPE, STATUS
  FROM ALL_OBJECTS
 WHERE (OBJECT_NAME LIKE 'XXHR%ABS%'
    OR OBJECT_NAME LIKE 'XXHR%XML%')
ORDER BY 1, 2
```

	OWNER	OBJECT_NAME	OBJECT_TYPE	STATUS
1	APPLSYS	XXHR_ABS_DOC_IN	TABLE	VALID
2	APPS	XXHR_ABSENCE_IN_WF_PKG	PACKAGE BODY	VALID
3	APPS	XXHR_ABSENCE_IN_WF_PKG	PACKAGE	VALID
4	APPS	XXHR_XML_WF_IN	SYNONYM	VALID
5	XXHR	XXHR_XML_WF_IN	TABLE	VALID

Query...   SQL   All Rows Fetched: 5 in 0.125 seconds

How it works...

The advanced queue will be used to enqueue XML messages in this chapter. We will use a script to put XML messages onto the queue. The queue will be monitored by an agent listener so that any message will trigger a business event. We will subscribe to the business event to launch a workflow.

Building a workflow

We are going to start off by creating a simple workflow and then we will save it to the database. We need to do this before we create the business event subscription as we must select the workflow when we configure the business event subscription later in the chapter. To begin with, the workflow will have just a `start` and `end` function which all workflows *must* have. We will create some attributes which we will use later in the chapter to store the values passed in an XML payload.

To achieve this, we will need to complete a number of mini recipes as follows:

- ▶ Creating a new workflow
- ▶ Creating a new item type
- ▶ Creating a new process
- ▶ Creating a start function
- ▶ Creating an end function
- ▶ Creating attributes to store the event details
- ▶ Assigning the start event details
- ▶ Saving a workflow to the database

Creating a new workflow

We will start by creating a new workflow using a workflow template.

Getting ready

It is assumed that you have installed Workflow Builder locally on your PC.

How to do it...

To create a new workflow, perform the following steps:

1. Open Workflow Builder.
2. Browse to the **Workflow Home | wf | DATA | US directory** and select the `WFSTD.wft` template.
3. Select **File | Save As** from the toolbar and rename the workflow to `XXHRIABS`.

How it works...

When we create a new workflow we will use a template. This is because it already has all of the standard objects in it which we will use in our workflow.

Creating a new item type

To add new processes we must first create a new item type.

How to do it...

To create a new item type we need to add a new item type in the navigator and complete the item type properties. To create a new item type, perform the following steps:

1. Highlight XXHRIABS and right-click as shown in the following screenshot:

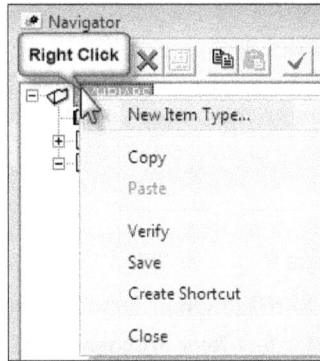

2. Select **New Item Type** from the pop-up menu.

3. Complete the item type property details as shown in the following table and click **OK**.

Internal Name	XXHRIABS
Display Name	XXHR Inbound Absence Item
Description	XXHR Inbound Absence Item
Persistence	**Temporary**
Number of Days	0
Selector	

How it works...

The **Item Type** is the definition of the workflow. The **Internal Name** is what is referred to when we search for the workflow. The **Internal Name** is in uppercase and is the short name for the workflow.

Creating a new process

We are going to add a new process to our workflow which will be triggered by a subscription to a business event. We will first create the process and then look at the start function in the next recipe.

How to do it...

We will now create our main process for the workflow by following the given steps:

1. Navigate to **XXHRIABS | XXHR Inbound Absence Item | Processes**.
2. Right-click **Processes** and select **New Process** from the pop-up menu.
3. Complete the properties of the new process with the details in the following table:

Internal Name	XXHR_INBOUND_ABSENCES
Display Name	XXHR Inbound Absences
Description	XXHR Inbound Absences
Icon	**PROCESS.ICO**
Runnable	☑

The properties will now be as shown in the following screenshot:

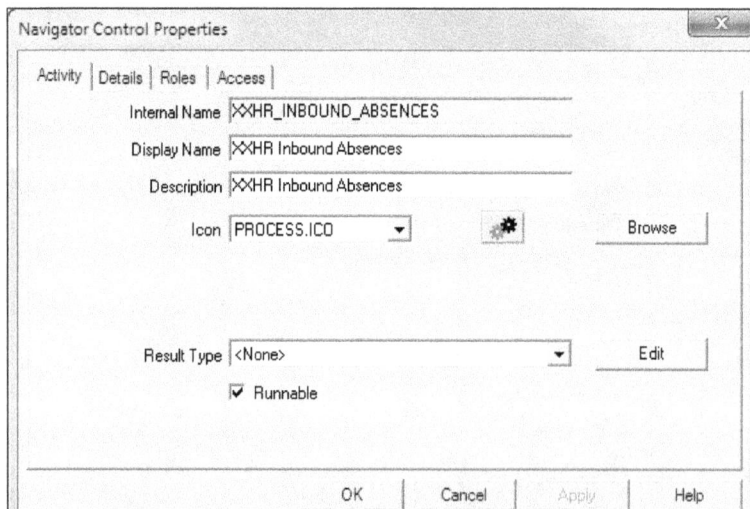

4. Click the **OK** button.

How it works...

The process diagram is a graphical representation of the workflow. It displays the logical steps that a process may follow. We can drag-and-drop our functions and notifications into the diagram and connect them together to represent the connection between activities.

Creating a start function

Every workflow has to have a **Start** function. It is a special function that is defined as a start process in the function properties.

How to do it...

To create the **Start** function, perform the following steps:

1. Navigate to **XXHRIABS | XXHR Inbound Absence Item | Processes**.
2. Double-click the **XXHR Inbound Absences** process and a blank process diagram window will open.
3. Click the **Business Event** icon on the toolbar and create a business event activity in the process diagram as shown in the following screenshot.

   You will notice that the cursor becomes a crosshair as you move the mouse in the process window as shown in the following screenshot. Click the mouse button while the cursor is a crosshair and the **Properties** window will open.

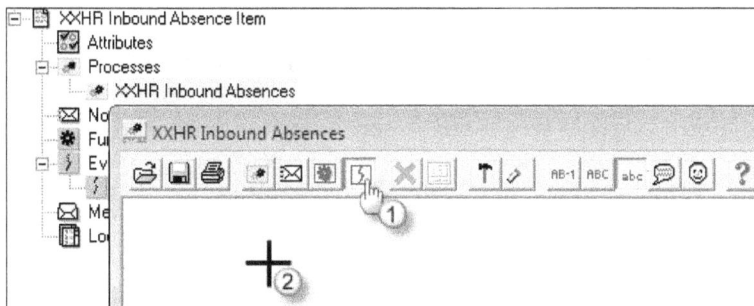

4. Complete the details of the **Event** tab as shown in the following table:

Item Type	XXHR Inbound Absence Item
Internal Name	ABSENCE_START_EVENT
Display Name	XXHR Inbound Absence
Description	XXHR Inbound Absence
Icon	EVENT.ICO

Event Action	Receive
Event Filter	`oracle.apps.xxhr.absence.inbound`
Cost	`0.00`

Navigator Control Properties

Event | Details | Roles | Access | Node | Event Details | Node Attributes

Item Type	XXHR Inbound Absence Item
Internal Name	ABSENCE_START_EVENT
Display Name	XXHR Inbound Absence
Description	XXHR Inbound Absence
Icon	EVENT.ICO
Event Action	Receive
Event Filter	oracle.apps.xxhr.absence.inbound
Cost	0.00

Edit | New | Browse

The event filter is the name of the business event that will trigger the workflow

OK | Cancel | Apply | Help

5. Click on the **Node** tab and set the **Start/End** property to **Start**.

Navigator Control Properties

Event | Details | Roles | Access | (Node) | Event Details | Node Attributes

Label	XXHR_INBOUND_ABSENCE
Start/End	Start
Comment	

6. Click on **OK** to accept the properties and the start object will appear as shown in the following screenshot:

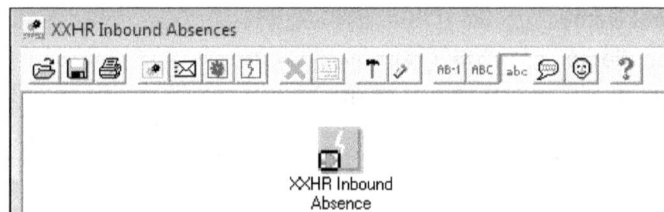

XXHR Inbound Absences

XXHR Inbound Absence

How it works...

All processes in a workflow have to have a **Start** and an **End** function. The **Start** function can be a standard function where it is initiated by PL/SQL for example or it can be an event where it is triggered as a result of a subscription to a business event.

Creating an end function

We will now create an end activity to complete the workflow.

How to do it...

To complete the workflow we must also create an end activity; perform the following steps:

1. Click on the **New Function** (🔲) icon on the toolbar in the **XXHR Inbound Absences** window.

2. When the cursor becomes a crosshair, click the mouse in the process window, somewhere to the right of the start event that we created.

3. When the **Properties** window opens complete the properties with the details from the following table:

Item Type	Standard
Internal Name	END

The function **Properties** window will look similar to the following screenshot:

4. Click on the **Node** tab and set the **Start/End** property to **End**.

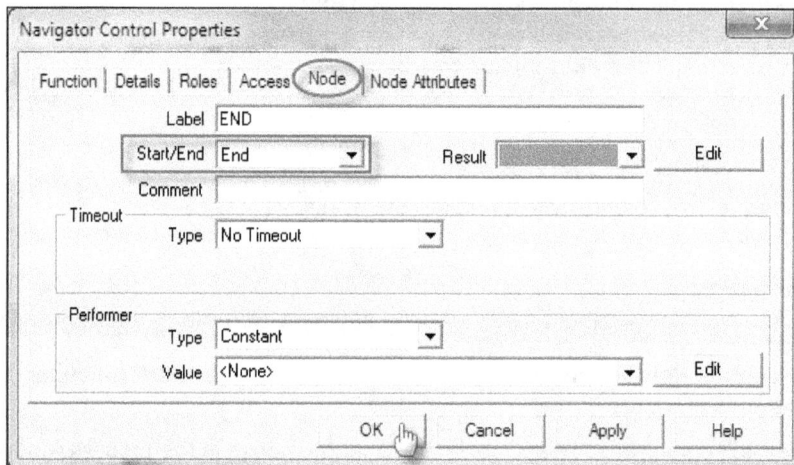

5. Click on **OK** to accept the changes and the **Properties** window will close as shown in the following screenshot:

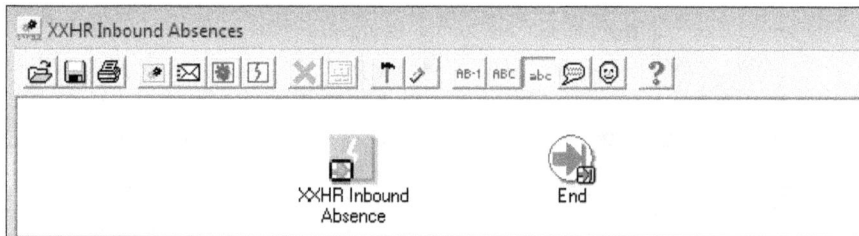

6. Link the **Start** and **End** together as shown in the following screenshot:

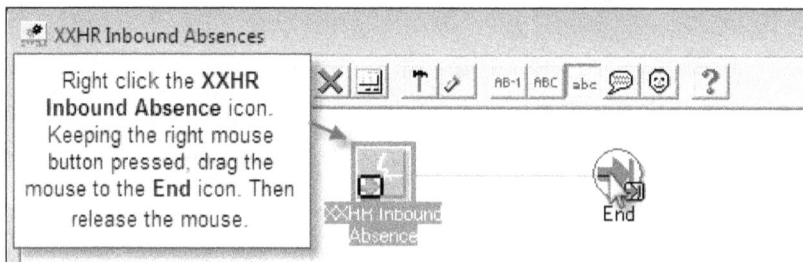

Right click the **XXHR Inbound Absence** icon. Keeping the right mouse button pressed, drag the mouse to the **End** icon. Then release the mouse.

7. A black line will show the **Start** and **End** connected as shown in the following screenshot:

8. Click on the **Save** button.

How it works...

The **End** function is a standard function that is built in to workflow and is used to represent the end of a process.

Creating attributes to store the event details

We will now create some workflow attributes to store details of event message that will trigger the workflow. We will look into business events shortly so don't worry too much about that right now as we will go through it in more detail.

How to do it...

To create workflow attributes, perform the following steps:

1. Navigate to **XXHRIABS | Attributes**.

2. Right-click the **Attributes** node and select **New Attribute** from the pop-up menu:

3. Create three new attributes and set the properties as follows:
   - EVENT_NAME
   - EVENT_KEY
   - EVENT_MESSAGE

   The following are the properties for the EVENT_NAME attribute:

Item Type	XXHR Inbound Absence Item
Internal Name	EVENT_NAME
Display Name	Event Name
Description	Event Name

Type	Text
Length	
Default Type	Constant
Default Value	`oracle.apps.xxhr.absence.inbound`

The following are the properties for the `EVENT_KEY` attribute:

Item Type	`XXHR Inbound Absence Item`
Internal Name	`EVENT_KEY`
Display Name	`Event Key`
Description	`Event Key`
Type	**Text**

The following are the properties for the `EVENT_MESSAGE` attribute:

Item Type	`XXHR Inbound Absence Item`
Internal Name	`EVENT_MESSAGE`
Display Name	`Event Message`
Description	`Event Message`
Type	**Event**

How it works...

We have created some attributes that will store the details of the event that triggered the workflow. The event message attribute will store the XML message we are going put onto the advanced queue.

Assigning the start event details

We are going to assign the event attributes in the **Event Details** tab for the `XXHR_INBOUND_ABSENCES` process. We are going to do this so that the details of the business event are captured in them at runtime.

How to do it...

To assign the event attributes, perform the following steps:

1. Navigate to **XXHRIABS | Processes | XXHR_INBOUND_ABSENCES**.
2. Open the properties of the `XXHR_INBOUND_ABSENCE` business event.
3. Navigate to the **Event Details** tab.

4. Set the following properties as shown in the following table:

Event Name	Event Name
Event Key	Event Key
Event Message	Event Message

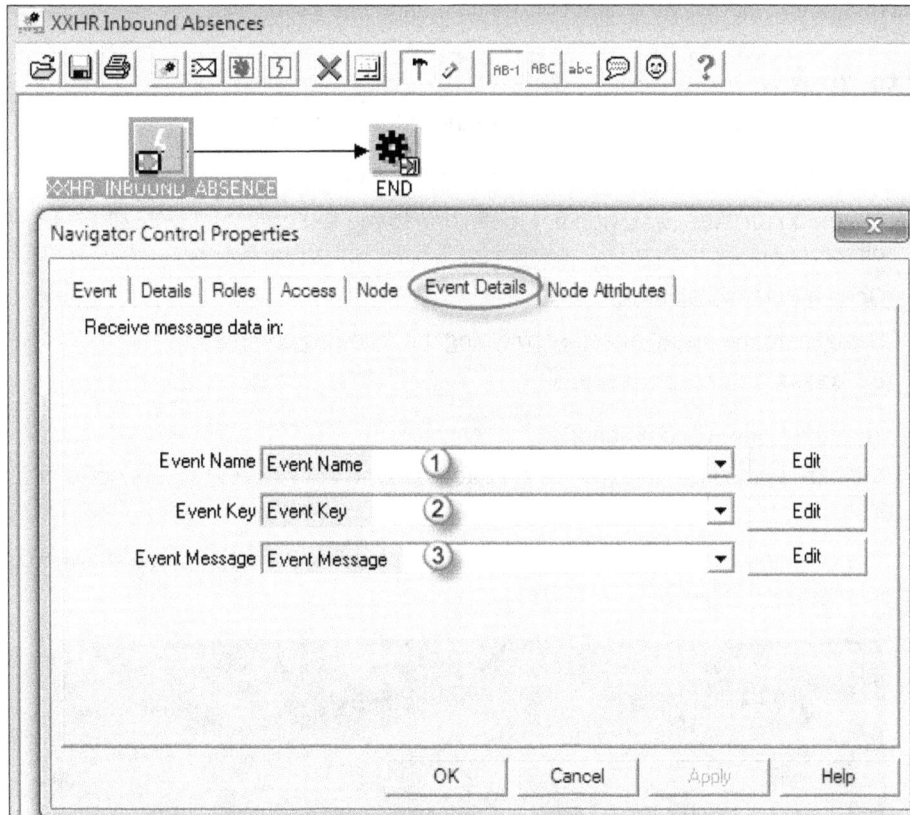

5. Click on **OK**.
6. Save the workflow.

How it works...

The event properties will be stored in these attributes and will be visible when we view the workflow during runtime. Now that we have completed the basic workflow we are going to trigger it from a business event which we will move onto later. The reason we have created a basic workflow definition first and saved to the database is because we have to select it from a list of values when we configure the business event. The list of values is generated from stored workflow definitions in the database.

Saving a workflow to the database

We will be using WinSCP to ftp the files to the server and Putty to upload the workflow to the database. To save the workflow to the database we need to ftp it to the server and upload it to the database using the command line. It is recommended that we do this rather than saving the workflow directly to the database from Workflow Builder, it should be transferred to the application tier and loaded via a script or the command line as follows.

How to do it...

To save the workflow to the database, perform the following steps:

1. Open **WinSCP** connecting to the application server.

2. Ftp the XXHRIABS.wft workflow definition to the $XXHR_TOP/install/ch5 directory.

3. Open a **Putty** session.

4. Navigate to the install directory by typing the following command:

   cd $XXHR_TOP/install/ch5

5. Type the following command:

   WFLOAD apps/<password> 0 Y FORCE $XXHR_TOP/install/ch5/XXHRIABS. wft

6. The command line will return the details of uploading the workflow as shown in the following screenshot:

```
> WFLOAD apps/apps 0 Y FORCE $XXHR_TOP/install/ch5/XXHRIABS.wft

Log filename    : L7874515.log


Report filename : O7874515.out
Oracle Workflow Definition Loader 2.6.4.0.

Access level: 0, Mode: FORCE

Uploaded 2 ITEM_TYPE record(s) to database.
Uploaded 21 LOOKUP_TYPE record(s) to database.
Uploaded 1 MESSAGE record(s) to database.
Uploaded 32 ACTIVITY record(s) to database.
Uploaded 0 ROLE record(s) to database.
```

How it works...

Now that we have created a workflow and saved it to the database it will be visible within the application when we subscribe to the business event that we will create in the next recipe. The subscription will be configured to launch the **XXHRIABS | XXHR_INBOUND_ABSENCES** workflow process. Now, each time we enqueue a message to the advanced queue, the workflow will be triggered.

Creating a business event

We are now going to create a business event that will trigger the workflow that we created in the previous recipe.

In this recipe, we will perform the following tasks:

- ▸ **Setup**—Set up the Workflow Administrator responsibility

- ▸ **Creating an agent**—The agent is a named communication point which we will configure for our advanced queue

- ▸ **Creating an agent listener**—The agent listener will monitor the advanced queue for any activity

- ▸ **Defining a business event**—The business event will be triggered each time there is a new payload added to the advanced queue

- ▸ **Subscribing to a business event**—We will finally subscribe to the business event which will launch our workflow

Setting up the workflow administrator responsibility

We need to configure which responsibility is the workflow administrator. This will allow us to view *all* of the workflows we generate. We can assign a specific responsibility as the administrator or set the value to * and all responsibilities will have administrator access. However, this is probably not advisable in a production environment.

How to do it...

To set the workflow administrator, log in as the **SYSDAMIN** user and navigate to **System Administrator | Workflow | Administrator Workflow | Administration**. On the **Administration** tab the default page will be **Workflow Configuration**. On this page we can set the **Workflow System Administrator** to the **Workflow Administrator Web (New)** responsibility and click on **Apply** as shown in the following screenshot:

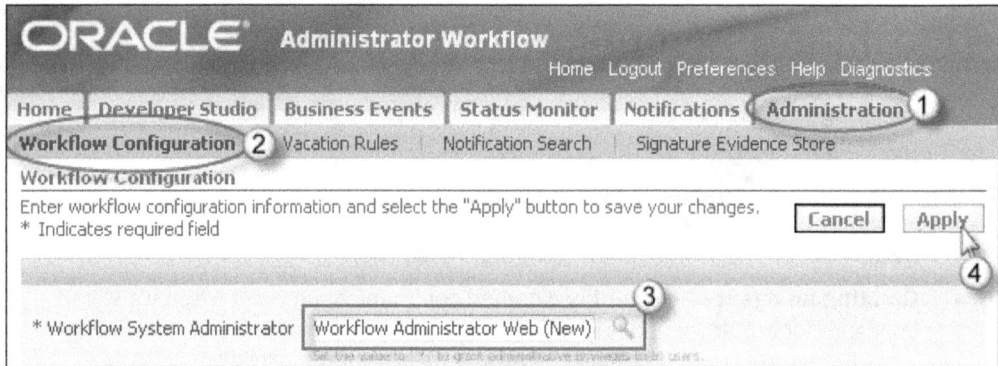

How it works...

We have set the workflow system administrator to the **Workflow Administrator Web (New)** responsibility so that we can see all of the workflow processes as they are restricted to the owner of the workflow otherwise. We could also have set the administrator to *, which allows any responsibility access to the workflows. If you do not have this responsibility assigned to your user then add it as we will be using it in the following recipes.

Creating an agent

We are now going to create an agent. This is a named point of communication between external and internal systems. Messages are sent from one agent to another.

How to do it...

To create an agent, perform the following steps:

1. Log in to Oracle with the **Workflow Administrator Web (New)** responsibility.
2. Navigate to **Business Events | Agents**.

3. Click on the **Create Agent** button as shown in the following screenshot:

4. Add the following record:

Name	XXHR_ABS_DOC_IN
Display Name	XXHR_ABS_DOC_IN
Description	Inbound document process for absence notifications
Protocol	**Sqlnet**
Address	APPLSYS.XXHR_ABS_DOC_IN@*<system name>*
System	*<system name>*
Queue Handlers	WF_EVENT_QH
Queue Name	APPLSYS.XXHR_ABS_DOC_IN
Direction	**In**
Status	**Enabled**

The *<system name>* in the **System** and **Address** fields is specific to your environment. Before you complete the **Address** field, select the **System** field using the list of values. As you can see in the following screenshot the **System** value is selected from the list of values. This can also be used to complete the value in the **Address** field.

5. Click **Apply** as shown in the following screenshot:

6. You will receive the confirmation message as shown in the following screenshot:

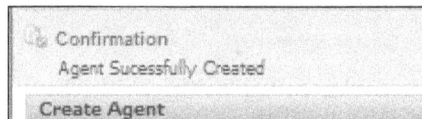

How it works...

The agent we created is to configure a named communication point for inbound messages from our advanced queue.

Creating an agent listener

We will now create an agent listener. We need to navigate to the **Workflow Manager** and create a **Workflow Agent Listener** in **Service Components**. The agent listener monitors an agent for any activity. The agent we have configured is linked to the advanced queue we created earlier. Therefore, any messages placed on the queue will trigger a business event. We will create the business event that is associated with the agent later.

How to do it...

To create an agent listener, we will have to perform the following steps:

1. Log in to Oracle with the **Workflow Administrator Web (New)** responsibility.

2. Navigate to **Workflow Manager | (Related Links) | Service Components**.

3. Click on the **Create** button as shown in the following screenshot:

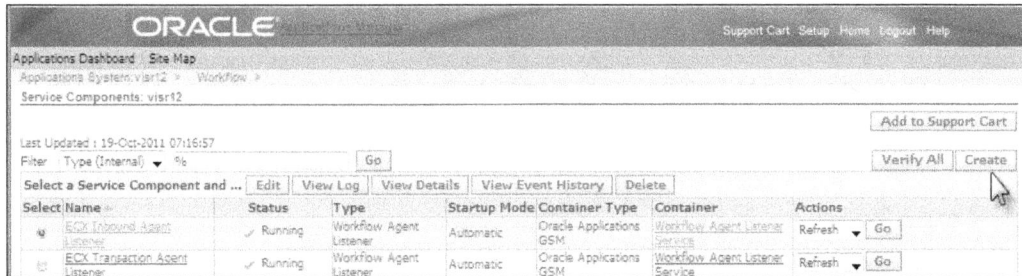

4. Select **Workflow Agent Listener** from the components list and click on **Continue**.

5. Complete **Step 1 of 4** with the data as shown in the following table and click on **Next**:

Name	XXHR Inbound Absences
Startup Mode	**Automatic**
Source Agent	
Container Type	**Oracle Applications GSM**
Inbound Agent	XXHR_ABS_DOC_IN
Outbound Agent	
Correlation ID	

6. Complete **Step 2 of 4** with the data in the following table and click on **Finish**:

Container	Workflow Agent Listener Service
Max Error Count	10
Inbound Thread Count	1
Outbound Thread Count	0
Log Level	**Error**
Processor Read Wait Timeout	0
Processor Min Loop Sleep	120
Processor Max Loop Sleep	0
Processor Error Loop Sleep	60
Processor Closed Read Timeout	Yes

7. Click on **Finish** when the **Review** screen appears as shown in the following screenshot:

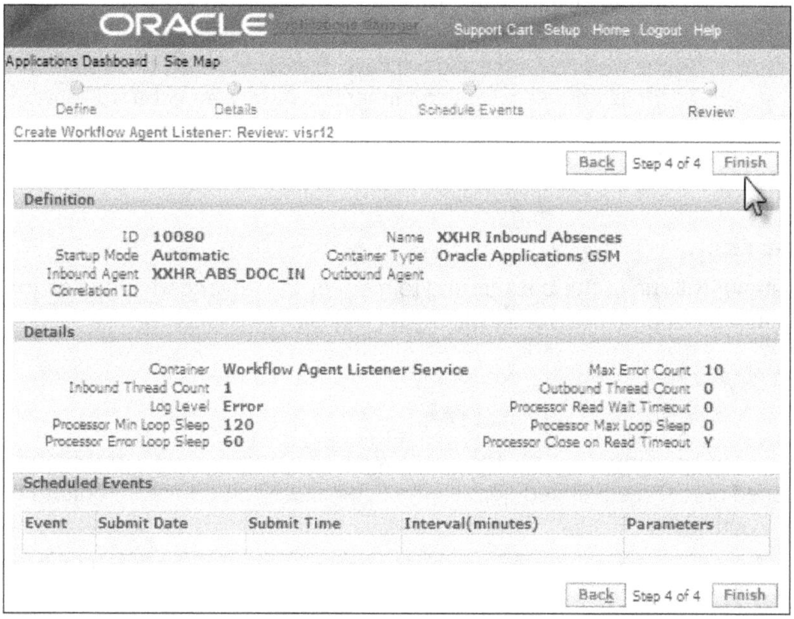

8. Check whether the service is up and running as shown in the following screenshot:

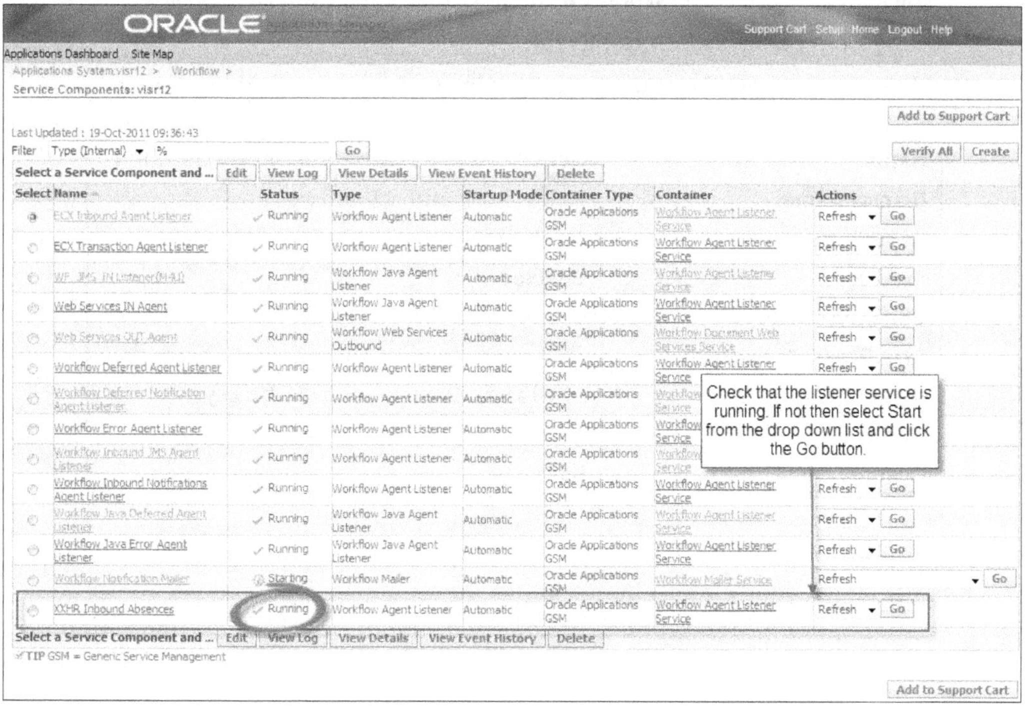

> If you are building your own workflow and you change any underlying code, for example the database package that is used by the workflow, then you will have to stop and start the workflow agent listener service. Remember this if you ever get a workflow error message saying that the underlying state of the package <XXX> has changed.

How it works...

The agent listener will run in the background to monitor the advanced queue so that any messages that are put onto the queue will trigger a business event.

Defining a business event

We will now create a business event. The event will be triggered whenever there is a message placed onto the advanced queue. The listener we just created monitors the queue for any activity.

How to do it...

To create a business event, we will perform the following steps:

1. Log in to Oracle with the **Workflow Administrator Web (New)** responsibility.
2. Navigate to **Business Events | Event**.
3. Click on the **Create Event** button and complete the event details as shown:

Name	`oracle.apps.xxhr.absence.inbound`
Display Name	`XXHR Inbound Absence`
Description	`Inbound Absence XML Payload`
Status	**Enabled**
Generate Function	
Java Generate Function	
Owner Name	`Application Object Library`
Owner Tag	`FND`
Customization Level	**User**

The Owner Name and Owner Tag fields have to be products that are licensed. We have set it to the values here as the vision instance only has these products licensed. Normally we would put the relevant module that the workflow related to.

4. Click on the **Apply** button.

How it works...

The business event we create will be triggered each time the agent listener monitors the queue and finds any new payloads on the queue.

Subscribing to a business event

We will now create a subscription to the business event. When the business event is triggered we will subscribe to the event to launch our workflow process. A business event can have multiple subscriptions that launch independent processes whenever the event is triggered. In our case whenever a message is placed on the advanced queue the business event is triggered, which will launch our workflow process.

How to do it...

To create a business event, we will perform the following steps:

1. Log in to Oracle with the **Workflow Administrator Web (New)** responsibility.

2. Navigate to **Business Events | Event**.

3. In the **Search** criteria enter `oracle%xx%` in the **Name** field and click the **Go** button.

4. Click on the **Subscription** icon.

5. In the **Subscriptions** form, click the **Create Subscription** button and enter the following details:

System	\<System Name\>
Source Type	**External**
Event Filter	`oracle.apps.xxhr.absence.inbound`
Source Agent	`XXHR_ABS_DOC_IN`@*\<System Name\>*
Phase	`20`
Status	**Enabled**
Rule Data	**Key**
Action Type	`Launch Workflow`
On Error	**Stop and Rollback**

ORACLE Administrator Workflow

Diagnostics Home Logout Preferences Help

| Home | Developer Studio | Business Events | Status Monitor | Notifications | Administration |

Events   Subscriptions   Agents   Systems

Business Events: Events >   Business Events : Events >   Subscriptions >

Cancel   Next

Update Event Subscriptions

An event subscription is a registration indicating that a particular event is significant to a particular system. An event subscription specifies the processing to perform when the triggering event occurs.
* Indicates required field

Subscriber

* System   VISR12.COM

Triggering Event

* Source Type   External ▾
* Event Filter   oracle.apps.xxhr.absence.inbound
Source Agent   XXHR_ABS_DOC_IN@VISR12.COM

Execution Condition

* Phase   20
Subscription with a phase 1- 99 are run synchronously , 100 and above are deferred.
* Status   Enabled ▾
* Rule Data   Key   ▾

Action Type

* Action Type   Launch Workflow
The Action Type controls the behaviour of the subscription
On Error   Stop and Rollback ▾

6. Click on **Next**.

7. Enter the following details:

Workflow Type	XXHRIABS
Workflow Process	XXHR_INBOUND_ABSENCE
Priority	**Normal**
Additional Options	
Owner Name	Application Object Library
Owner Tag	FND
Customization Level	**User**
Description	Inbound XML payload to create an absence

> We have selected the **Workflow Type** and **Workflow Process** from a list of values. Our workflow is listed as we saved it to the database before we configured the business event and subscription.

8. Click on **Apply** as shown in the following screenshot:

How it works...

The subscription to the business event will launch the workflow that we created each time the event is triggered. A subscription can also perform a variety of other actions such as sending an event message to another agent or to a workflow or even call custom code.

Viewing a workflow status and monitoring progress

In this recipe we are going to test the workflow that we have created so far. There are a number of test harness scripts that have been provided in the download bundle. The test harness is an SQL script that puts an XML message on to the advanced queue that we have created. The service component that monitors the queue will process the message. The workflow will be launched because we have subscribed to the business event linked to the advanced queue. We have created a workflow with only start and end objects so the workflow should complete without any errors. We will enqueue an XML payload onto the advanced queue to check that the workflow is being launched and completed. Later we will be adding a number of different objects to the workflow. We will therefore need to repeat these steps to test it.

The following are the tasks we will perform to test the workflow:

- Adding a message to an advanced queue
- Viewing a workflow in status monitor
- Viewing the workflow status monitor
- Viewing workflow attributes and event messages

Adding a message to an advanced queue

When we test the workflow we will be putting an XML message on to the advanced queue. The XML payload that we are going to use to test the workflow represents an absence record. There are SQL scripts that are provided in the download bundle that we can use to queue messages to the advanced queue. This will be explained in detail when we go through the testing tasks. The XML has the following elements:

```
<Absence>
<DateTime></DateTime>
<EmployeeNumber></EmployeeNumber>
<AbsenceType></AbsenceType>
<AbsenceReason></AbsenceReason>
<AbsenceStartDate></AbsenceStartDate>
<AbsenceEndDate></AbsenceEndDate>
<AbsenceDuration></AbsenceDuration>
</Absence>
```

Open the following two files in SQL Developer:

- ▸ CH5 Test Harness 1.sql—This script will put an XML message onto the advanced queue each time it is run. We are going to run the script and check that the message is put on the advanced queue.

- ▸ AQ Query.sql—This script contains an SQL query that will return any records in the XXHR_ABS_DOC_IN queue table.

How to do it...

We will run the scripts in SQL Developer to add a message to the advanced queue. (You can use a tool of your choice, for example if you prefer to use SQL*Plus or TOAD).

1. Open the CH5 Test Harness 1.sql script in SQL Developer.

2. Connect to your database as the **apps** user as shown in the following screenshot and run the script:

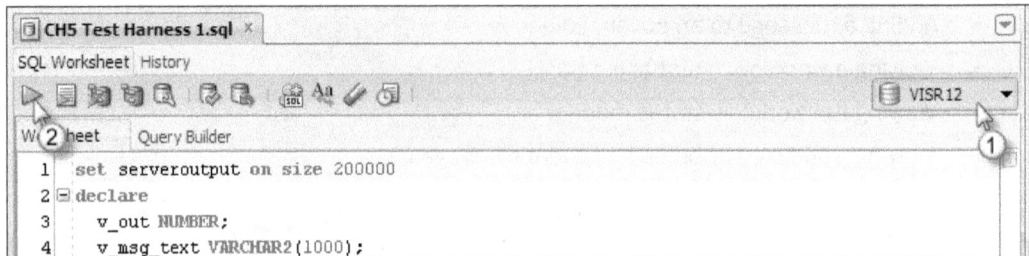

An XML message will now have been placed on the advanced queue with a temporary status of 0. This status means the message has not been processed. When the status is 2 then we will know that the message is processed and the business event will have triggered our workflow.

3. Open the AQ Query.sql in SQL Developer as the connection of the **apps** user.

4. Run the query (as shown in the following screenshot).

As you can see in the following screenshot, the payload has been added to the advanced queue but has not yet been processed. It should take no longer than a couple of minutes to process the record so re-query until the status is 2. When the status is 2 the message will trigger the business event we subscribed to, which will launch the workflow process we created.

```
1  □ SELECT     TO_CHAR (t.enq_time, 'DD-MON-YYYY HH24:MI:SS') enq_time,
2               TO_CHAR (t.deq_time, 'DD-MON-YYYY HH24:MI:SS') deq_time,
3               t.state,
4               t.delay,
5               t.priority,
6               t.user_data.event_data
7      FROM APPLSYS.XXHR_ABS_DOC_IN t
8      WHERE TO_CHAR (t.enq_time, 'DD-MON-YYYY') > sysdate - 5
9    ORDER BY t.enq_time DESC;
```

> When the state is 0 the record has not been processed. When the state is 2 then the record has been processed

Query Result ×

SQL | All Rows Fetched: 4 in 0.046 seconds

	ENQ_TIME	DEQ_TIME	STATE	DELAY	PRIORITY	USER_DATA.EVENT_DATA	
1	28-OCT-2011 09:05:32	(null)	0 (null)		0	\<Absence\>	\<DateTime\>\</DateTime\>
2	26-OCT-2011 12:35:31	26-OCT-2011 12:36:21	2 (null)		0	\<Absence\>	\<DateTime\>\</DateTime\>
3	26-OCT-2011 11:49:23	26-OCT-2011 11:50:22	2 (null)		0	\<Absence\>	\<DateTime\>\</DateTime\>
4	26-OCT-2011 11:35:58	26-OCT-2011 11:38:20	2 (null)		0	\<Absence\>	\<DateTime\>\</DateTime\>

How it works...

The XML message will be put onto our advanced queue. The agent listener will pick up the message on the queue and launch the workflow that we defined in our subscription. (The agent listener has a cycle time of 120 seconds so leave it for a while if it does not get processed immediately).

Viewing a workflow in status monitor

We are now going to view the workflow that has been triggered in the workflow status monitor within Oracle E-Business Suite.

How to do it...

To view the workflow, we will perform the following steps:

1. Log in to Oracle with the **Workflow Administrator Web (New)** responsibility.

2. Navigate to the **Status Monitor** tab.

3. In the **Monitor Search** parameters type XXHRIABS in the **Type Internal Name** field and click the **Go** button as shown in the following screenshot:

We can review the workflow by clicking on the **Select** radio button of the workflow we want to review. We can then select a number of buttons to look at details relating to the workflow. They are as follows:

- **Activity History**—The **Activity History** page shows information about the activities executed for a workflow. If a workflow is still in progress we can perform actions against the workflow such as to rewind or skip a process.

- **Status Diagram**—The **Status Diagram** page shows the process diagram for a workflow, including graphical cues about the status of the workflow and its activities. The page identifies the displayed workflow by its workflow type, internal name, and item key, as well as by its user key, if it has one.

- **Participant Responses**—The **Monitor Responses** page shows information about notifications sent by a workflow and responses from workflow participants.

- **Workflow Details**—The **Workflow Details** page shows information about a selected workflow, such as values stored in attributes and the **Event Message** that triggered the workflow.

How it works...

The status monitor allows us to see our process that has been triggered. We can view the diagram to see the message: the values are stored in attributes such as the **Event Message**. We can also see the route that the process took to complete.

Viewing the workflow status diagram

We are going to look at the status diagram which will show the path the workflow has taken.

How to do it...

To view the status diagram, we will perform the following steps:

1. Click on the radio button for the workflow that was generated (if it's not already).

2. Click on the **Status Diagram** button as shown in the following screenshot:

> The status diagram uses Java and you may get a Java Security Warning pop-up message appear. If this does appear, click on the **Run** button.

3. The status diagram will appear as shown in the following screenshot:

5. Click the browser back button to return to the search results screen.

How it works...

The process diagram shows us that our workflow has completed successfully. The process has nothing in it other than the start and end activities. Therefore, this is really just a connectivity test before we start adding activities to our workflow. We know that our workflow is now being triggered each time a new message is added to the advanced queue.

Viewing workflow attributes and event messages

We are now going to look at the workflow details. Here we can see the workflow attribute values and the **Event Message** that we passed onto the advanced queue.

How to do it...

To view the workflow attributes, we will perform the following steps:

1. Click on the radio button for the workflow that was generated (if it not already).
2. Click on the **Workflow Details** button.
3. Click on the **View Event Message** link.
4. Click on the **View Event Data** link.
5. Save the file and open it using a text editor as shown in the following screenshot:

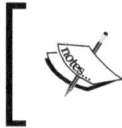

You can see from the preceding screenshot that the workflow has the three event attributes we created. The attributes have been assigned the values we passed in through the test script.

How it works...

Viewing the event message allows us to interrogate the XML message that was placed onto the queue. We can see the raw data which will help us to see the details of the message as it was given to us.

Adding a function

We are now going to go back to our workflow and create a function to call a database procedure. The procedure will store the XML in a table, validate the structure of the XML, and store the XML values in attributes in the workflow. The first thing we need to do is create the attributes in the workflow that will store the XML attributes. We will then add the function to the workflow that will parse the XML and store the attributes.

The following are the tasks required to add a function to the workflow:

- Updating an employee record for testing
- Adding attributes
- Adding a function
- Testing the workflow

Updating an employee record for testing

Before we get going we need to create a test employee record. I used an existing employee in the vision environment and updated the details.

How to do it...

We need an employee record that we are going to use throughout the testing of the workflows. We will be using the **UK HRMS Manager** responsibility. This is important as it will determine the business group you belong to.

- Add the **UK HRMS Manager** responsibility to your user and navigate to **People | Enter and Maintain**.

- When prompted with the **Find Person** screen, enter 11 in the **Number** field and click the **Find** button (the test script we use refers to employee number 11. If you choose to amend or create an employee with a different employee number then please amend the Ch5 Test Harness 2.sql script and set the variable v_emp_number in the declaration section to the employee number of the test employee you are using).

► Update the details to your own test employee record. For example, I changed the following fields:

Last	Penver
First	Andy
Title	Mr.

You will be prompted to save the record when the Last Name field is changed and you navigate out of the field. The form prompts for a save when the last name field is changed.

> When the record is saved and you are prompted with **Correction** or **Update** always choose **Correction**, otherwise a new record is created as HCM has a concept called date tracking and we don't really want to get into that right now.

Navigate to the **Office Details** tab and change the e-mail address to a test e-mail address of your own and save.

How it works...

We have now set up our test employee we are going to use. If the test employee number is different to 11 then you will need to change the CH5 Test Harness 2.sql script that we use to test the workflow. However, this is highlighted when we use the script.

Adding attributes

We need to create attributes to store data in the workflow. We can create attributes by selecting the new attribute from the menu and completing the attribute properties.

How to do it...

To add attributes to the workflow, we will perform the following steps:

1. Navigate to **XXHRIABS | Attributes**.
2. Right-click the **Attributes** node and select **New Attribute** from the pop-up menu.
3. Create the following attributes with the data in the tables (leave any other fields not specified as their default value):

   ❑ XML_DATETIME

   ❑ EMP_NUMBER

   ❑ ABS_TYPE

   ❑ ABS_REASON

- ❑ ABS_START_DATE
- ❑ ABS_END_DATE
- ❑ ABS_DURATION
- ❑ BUSINESS_GROUP_ID
- ❑ USERNAME

The properties for the XML_DATETIME attribute are as follows:

Item Type	XXHR Inbound Absence Item
Internal Name	XML_DATETIME
Display Name	XML Date Time
Description	XML Date Time
Type	**Date**
Format	**DD-MON-RRRR HH24:MI:SS**

The properties for the EMP_NUMBER attribute are as follows:

Item Type	XXHR Inbound Absence Item
Internal Name	EMP_NUMBER
Display Name	Employee Number
Description	Employee Number
Type	**Text**

The properties for the ABS_TYPE attribute are as follows:

Item Type	XXHR Inbound Absence Item
Internal Name	ABS_TYPE
Display Name	Absence Type
Description	Absence Type
Type	**Text**

The properties for the ABS_REASON attribute are as follows:

Item Type	XXHR Inbound Absence Item
Internal Name	ABS_REASON
Display Name	Absence Reason
Description	Absence Reason
Type	**Text**

The properties for the ABS_START_DATE attribute are as follows:

Item Type	XXHR Inbound Absence Item
Internal Name	ABS_START_DATE
Display Name	Absence Start Date
Description	Absence Start Date
Type	**Date**
Format	**DD-MON-RRRR**

The properties for the ABS_END_DATE attribute are as follows:

Item Type	XXHR Inbound Absence Item
Internal Name	ABS_END_DATE
Display Name	Absence End Date
Description	Absence End Date
Type	**Date**
Format	**DD-MON-RRRR**

The properties for the ABS_DURATION attribute are as follows:

Item Type	XXHR Inbound Absence Item
Internal Name	ABS_DURATION
Display Name	Absence Duration
Description	Absence Duration
Type	**Number**
Default Value	

The properties for the BUSINESS_GROUP_ID attribute are as follows:

Item Type	XXHR Inbound Absence Item
Internal Name	BUSINESS_GROUP_ID
Display Name	Business Group ID
Description	Business Group ID
Type	**Number**
Default Value	

The properties for the USERNAME attribute are as follows:

Item Type	XXHR Inbound Absence Item
Internal Name	USERNAME
Display Name	Username
Description	Username
Type	**Text**
Default Value	*<FND USERNAME>*

> Enter your *FND username* as the default value for the USERNAME attribute. This attribute will be the used as the recipient of any notifications we create later in the chapter. For testing purposes we want to send the messages to our own user. If we were implementing this for real we would set this value at runtime to be the username of the employee's manager for example.

You will end up with a list of attributes as shown in the following screenshot:

> You can toggle the hammer icon to view the objects in the navigator with their **Internal Name** or their **Display Name**.

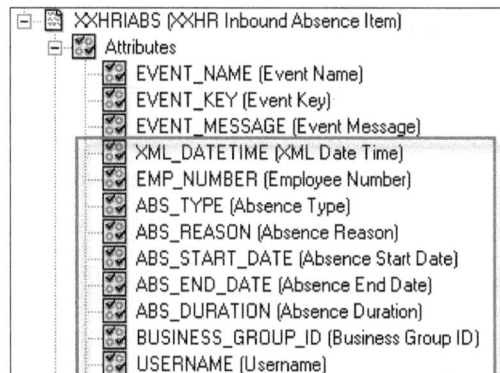

How it works...

The attributes we created here are for us to store the data that was in the XML message. We are going to create a function that will parse the XML message and store the data in the attributes. We need to store the data in the attributes so that they can be used in later activities.

Adding a function

We are now going to add a function that will call a database package to parse the XML message passed into the workflow.

How to do it...

To create a new function, we will perform the following steps:

1. Navigate to **XXHRIABS | Processes | XXHR_INBOUND_ABSENCES**.

2. Click on the **New Function** toolbar button.

3. Click anywhere in the process diagram when the cursor is a crosshair and the **Properties** window will open.

4. Complete the properties with the following values:

Item Type	XXHR Inbound Absence Item
Internal Name	PARSE_XML
Display Name	Parse XML
Description	Parse XML
Icon	FUNCTION.ICO
Function Name	XXHR_ABSENCE_IN_WF_PKG.parse_and_store_xml
Function Type	**PL/SQL**
Result Type	**<None>**
Cost	**0.00**

5. Click on the **OK** button

6. Link the function to the **START** and **END** icons as shown in the following screenshot:

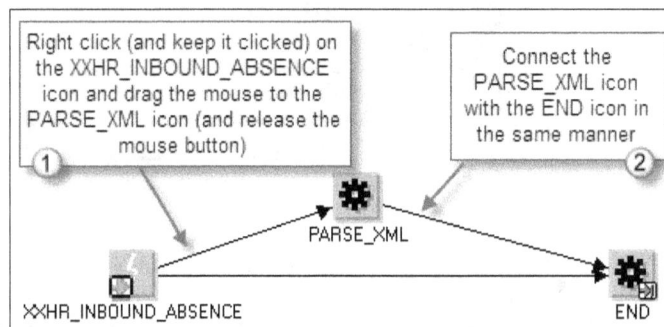

7. Delete the line linking the **START** and **END** icons as shown in the following screenshot:

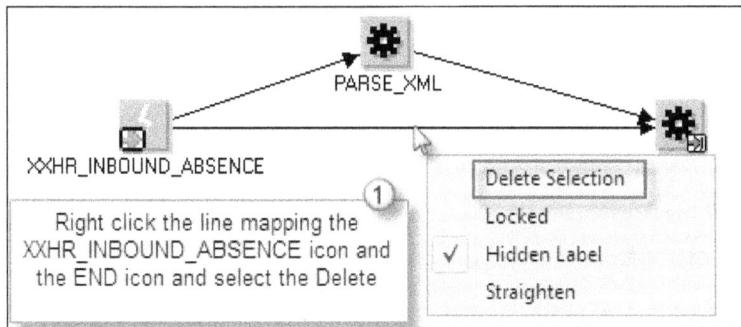

8. Now drag the **PARSE_XML** icon down in line with the other two icons as shown in the following screenshot (this is not actually necessary—it is just to tidy up the diagram):

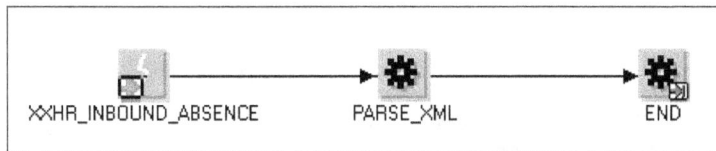

9. Save the workflow.

How it works...

The function we have just created will parse the XML from the advanced queue and check whether the XML structure is as expected. If any of the XML elements are not present then the workflow will error. The function will then parse the XML and store the values of the elements in the attributes we have just created. The code is documented so it would be a good idea to review it to ensure that you have a basic understanding of what it is doing.

There's more...

If we look at the XXHR_ABSENCE_IN_WF_PKG.parse_and_store_xml package that the function calls in more detail there are some important points to make note of. First of all notice the signature of the procedure we call:

```
PROCEDURE parse_and_store_xml ( itemtype IN VARCHAR2,
                                itemkey  IN VARCHAR2,
                                actid    IN NUMBER,
                                funcmode IN VARCHAR2,
                                resultout IN OUT NOCOPY VARCHAR2)
```

We can see that the workflow passes in a number of parameters to the procedure. Workflow definitions must always contain these parameters when calling PL/SQL procedures. Notice that there is also a parameter passed back out called `resultout`. This is interpreted by the workflow engine to determine the activity that should be executed next depending upon the logic in the workflow process. We will often use the workflow parameters to retrieve attribute values and other workflow details for the specific item, activity, or function mode.

If we look at the procedure body we make calls to the workflow specific function to get item attribute values such as:

```
WF_ENGINE.GETITEMATTRTEXT(itemtype => itemtype,
                          itemkey  => itemkey,
                          aname    => 'ABS_TYPE');
```

And workflow specific functions to set item attribute values such as:

```
WF_ENGINE.SETITEMATTRTEXT (itemtype => itemtype,
                           itemkey  => itemkey,
                           aname    => 'ERROR_MSG',
                           avalue   => v_error_msg);
```

There are also many other APIs specifically for workflow such as a call to `WF_CORE.CONTEXT`, which allows us to return context specific messages to the workflow engine that can be viewed when we monitor workflow progress.

To find out more information about the workflow APIs look through the code provided and refer to the *Oracle Workflow Developers Guide and Oracle Workflow API Reference* to gain an understanding of workflow APIs that are available.

Testing the workflow

Now we need to test the workflow. The first thing we will do is save the changes we have made to the database. We are then going to run the test harness in the download bundle called `CH5 Test Harness 2.sql`. This test harness passes an XML payload with some values stored onto the advanced queue. We are then going to view the workflow in the status monitor and check whether the element values in the test harness have been stored in the workflow attributes.

> We will summarize the testing of the workflow below. For step-by-step instructions on how to test the workflow follow the recipe we did earlier called *Viewing a workflow status and monitoring progress*. Remember to use `CH5 Test Harness 2.sql` to test the workflow.

How to do it...

To test the workflow, we will perform the following steps:

1. Ftp the workflow to the application tier and save the workflow to the database using the following command (replacing <password> with your environments **apps** password):

   ```
   WFLOAD apps/<password> 0 Y FORCE $XXHR_TOP/install/ch5/XXHRIABS.
   wft
   ```

2. Open the CH5 Test Harness 2.sql test script in SQL Developer.

3. Run the script to put an XML message onto the advanced queue.

4. Open the AQ Query.sql file and run the query to check whether a payload has been added to the advanced queue.

5. Log in to Oracle with the **Workflow Administrator Web (New)** responsibility.

6. Navigate to **Status Monitor**.

7. In the **Monitor Search** parameter screen type XXHRIABS in **Type Internal Name** field and click on **Go** button.

8. Click on the **Workflow Details** button as shown in the following screenshot:

Select Workflow and View...	Activity History	Status Diagram	Participant Responses	Workflow Details	

TIP Workflow histories are periodically purged from the system and may no longer be available for review.

Select		Status	Workflow Type	Item Key	Process Name	User Key	Owned By
◉	✓	Complete	XXHR Inbound Absence Item	1030	XXHR Inbound Absences		

9. If we scroll down to the **Workflow Attributes** region we can see that the data passed in the XML elements has been stored in the attributes we created earlier:

Workflow Attributes

Event Name	oracle.apps.xxhr.absence.inbound
Event Key	1062
Event Message	View Event Message
XML Date Time	08-FEB-2012 13:56:25
Employee Number	11
Absence Type	Sickness
Absence Reason	Cold
Absence Start Date	10-MAR-2011
Absence End Date	11-MAR-2011
Absence Duration	2
Username	APENVER

How it works...

As we make changes to the workflow we will need to repeat the process of uploading the new version to the database.

Creating a lookup

We are going to create a lookup which we will use to determine the outcome of the subprocess. There are a number of standard lookups but we can create our own when required. We are going to create a lookup type called Success/Fail which will have two values:

- Success
- Fail

To create a lookup we will perform the following tasks:

- Creating a Success/Fail lookup
- Adding an error message attribute

Creating a Success/Fail lookup

We will add a new lookup by selecting **New** from the menu when we right-click on **Lookup Types** in the navigator.

How to do it...

To create a workflow lookup, we will perform the following steps:

1. Navigate to **XXHRIABS | Lookup Types**.
2. Right-click **Lookup Types** and select **New** from the pop-up menu.

Internal Name	SUCCESS_FAIL
Display Name	Success/Fail
Description	Success/Fail

3. Click on **OK** to accept the changes.
4. Right-click the **SUCCESS_FAIL** lookup type and select **New Lookup Code** and complete the following properties:

Lookup Type	**Success/Fail**
Internal Name	SUCCESS
Display Name	Success
Description	Success

5. Click on **OK** to accept the changes.

6. Right-click the **SUCCESS_FAIL** lookup type and select **New Lookup Code** and complete the following properties:

Lookup Type	Success/Fail
Internal Name	FAIL
Display Name	Fail
Description	Fail

7. Click on **OK** to accept the changes.

You should now have created a lookup type called **Success/Fail** as shown in the following screenshot:

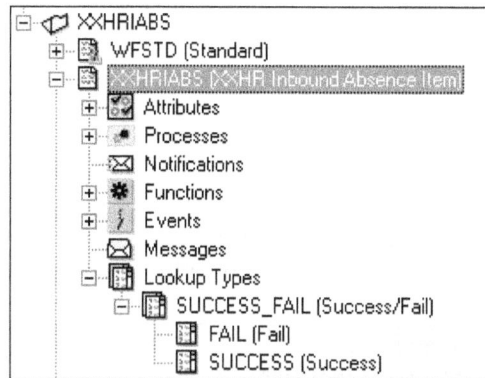

How it works...

A lookup is simply a static list of values. We will be using the lookup to define the result values of the function that we are going to create.

See also

Creating a subprocess. We will be using this lookup as the result for the subprocess when we validate the XML structure.

Adding an error message attribute

We are now going to create an additional attribute that will store any error messages we wish the user to know when the workflow runs. This will be used when we validate the XML attributes.

How to do it...

To create an error attribute, we will perform the following steps:

1. Navigate to **XXHRIABS | Attributes**.

2. Right-click the **Attributes** node and select **New Attribute** from the pop-up menu.

3. Create the following attribute (leave any other fields not specified at their default value).

    The properties for the ERROR_MSG attribute are as follows:

Item Type	XXHR Inbound Absence Item
Internal Name	ERROR_MSG
Display Name	Error Message
Description	Error Message
Type	Text

4. Save the workflow.

How it works...

The error message attribute will be used to store any messages that we can write during our activities so that it is meaningful to any users who monitor the workflow.

Creating a subprocess

We will now create a subprocess in the workflow. This will validate the attributes that have been passed in to the workflow. The subprocess will perform the following validation checks:

- That the employee exists in Oracle and is not null
- That the absence type exists in Oracle and is not null
- That the absence start date is not null
- If the absence end date is not null then it is before the absence start date

To create the subprocess we need to perform the following tasks:

- Creating a subprocess
- Adding a validate employee function
- Adding a validate absence type function
- Creating end functions
- Joining the functions
- Adding a subprocess to a parent process
- Testing the workflow

Creating a subprocess

To create a subprocess we need to navigate to processes in the navigator and select **New Process** from the menu. A subprocess is exactly the same as a normal process except the **Runnable** checkbox in the process properties is left unchecked.

How to do it...

To create a subprocess, we will perform the following steps:

1. Navigate to **XXHRIABS | Processes**.

2. Right-click **Processes** and select **New Process** from the pop-up menu.

3. Complete the properties as per the table in the following screenshot:

Internal Name	VALIDATE_XML
Display Name	Validate XML
Description	Validate XML
Icon	PROCESS.ICO
Result Type	**Success/Fail**
Runnable	☒

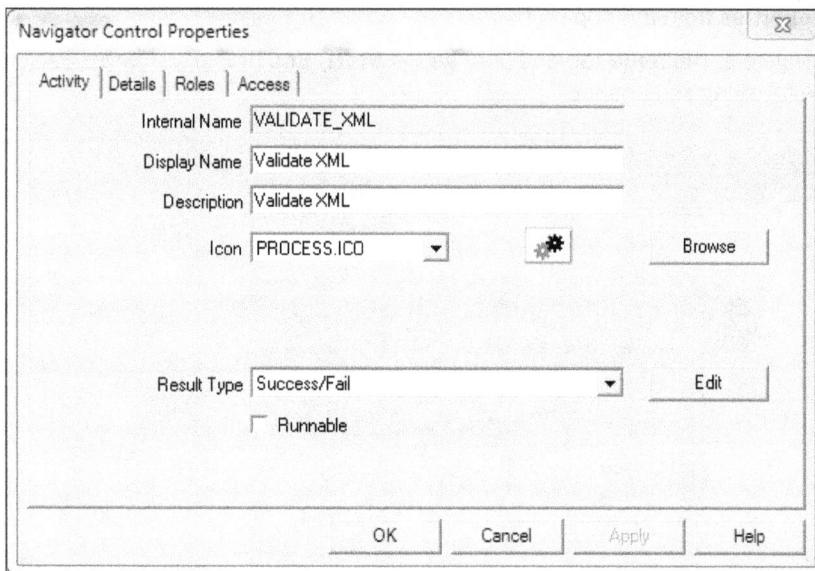

4. Double-click the **VALIDATE_XML** process to open up the **Process Diagram** window.

5. Navigate to **XXHRIABS | WFSTD | Functions | START**.

6. Drag the **START** function on to the process diagram as shown in the following screenshot:

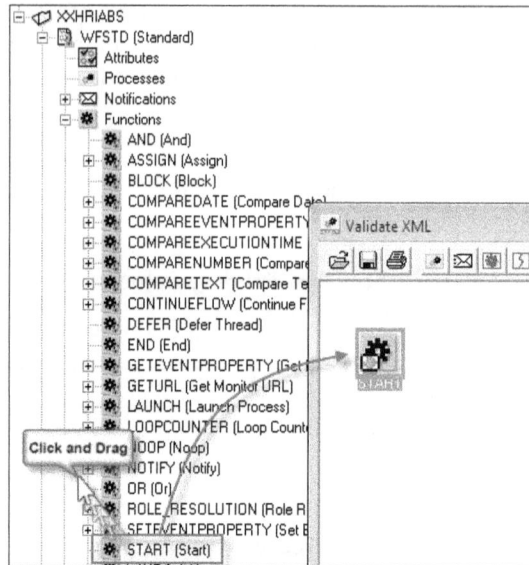

7. Right-click the **START** icon we have just created in the process diagram and select **Properties** from the pop-up menu.

8. Navigate to the **Node** tab and change the **Start/End** property to **Start** as shown in the following screenshot:

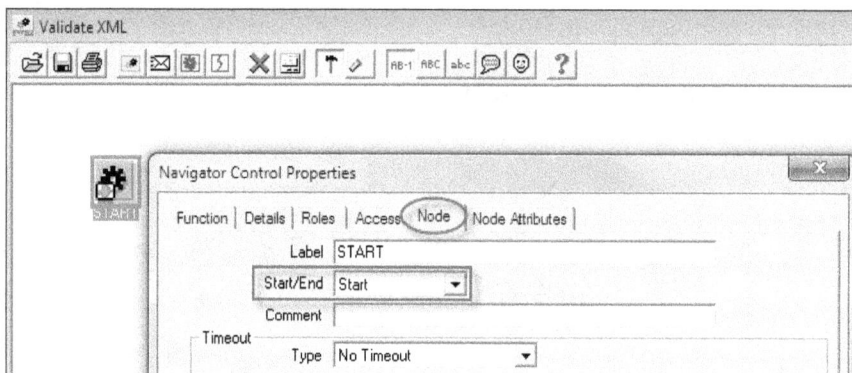

> We could have created a new standard function as we did earlier in the chapter. However it is easier to drag-and-drop standard functions onto the process diagram.

How it works...

We have created a subprocess to validate the XML message with a start activity. We will add functions to perform validation in the next recipes. A workflow can have multiple levels of subprocesses if required.

> We are using the lookup we created earlier to return a value of either success or fail.

Adding a validate employee function

We can validate the employee by adding a function to the process. It will call a database function, which we can validate if the employee number in the XML is valid.

How to do it...

To add a validate employee function, we will perform the following steps:

1. In the **Validate XML** process diagram window click the **Function Toolbar** button to create a new function.

2. Click the mouse in the process diagram when the cursor changes to a crosshair as shown in the following screenshot:

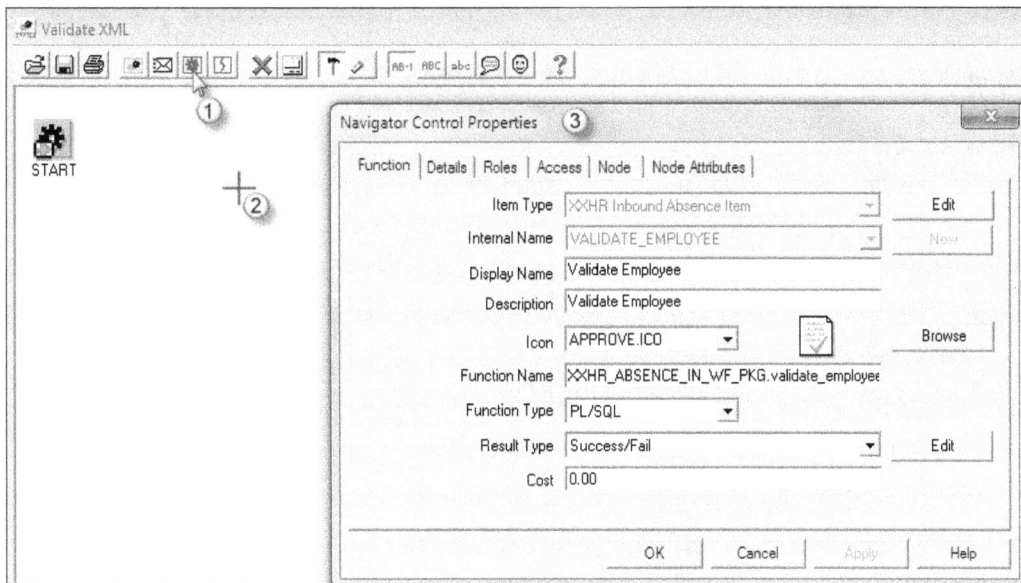

3. Complete the properties as per the following table:

Item Type	XXHR Inbound Absence Item
Internal Name	VALIDATE_EMPLOYEE
Display Name	Validate Employee
Description	Validate Employee
Icon	APPROVE.ICO
Function Name	XXHR_ABSENCE_IN_WF_PKG.validate_employee
Result Type	PL/SQL
Result Type	Success/Fail
Cost	0.00

4. Click on **OK**.

How it works...

This workflow function is used to call a package that will validate that the employee number contained in the XML message exists in Oracle.

Adding a validate absence type function

We can validate the absence type by adding a function to the process. It will call a database function where we can validate if the absence type identifier in the XML payload is valid for the business group of the **UK HRMS Manager** responsibility.

How to do it...

To add a validate absence type function, perform the following steps:

1. In the **Validate XML** process diagram window click the **Function** toolbar button to create a new function.

2. Click the mouse in the process diagram when the cursor changes to a crosshair in the same way we did earlier.

3. Complete the properties as per the following table:

Item Type	XXHR Inbound Absence Item
Internal Name	VALIDATE_ABSENCE_TYPE
Display Name	Validate Absence Type
Description	Validate Absence Type
Icon	APPROVE.ICO

Function Name	XXHR_ABSENCE_IN_WF_PKG.validate_absence_type
Result Type	**PL/SQL**
Result Type	Success/Fail
Cost	0.00

4. Click **OK**.

How it works...

This function is used to call a procedure that will validate the absence type that was passed in the XML message that exists in Oracle.

Adding a validate absence dates function

We can validate the absence dates by adding a function to the process. It will call a database function where we can validate if the dates in the XML are valid based upon the business rules we have.

How to do it...

To create a validate absence dates function, perform the following steps:

1. In the **Validate XML** process diagram window click the **Function Toolbar** button to create a new function.

2. Click the mouse in the process diagram when the cursor changes to a crosshair in the same way we did earlier.

3. Complete the properties as per the following table:

Item Type	XXHR Inbound Absence Item
Internal Name	VALIDATE_ABSENCE_DATES
Display Name	Validate Absence Dates
Description	Validate Absence Dates
Icon	APPROVE.ICO
Function Name	XXHR_ABSENCE_IN_WF_PKG.validate_absence_dates
Result Type	**PL/SQL**
Result Type	**Success/Fail**
Cost	**0.00**

4. Click **OK**.

How it works...

This function is used to call a procedure that will validate the absence dates that were passed in the XML message.

Creating end functions

Now we need to create two **END** functions. One will be for a successful outcome and the other will be where there is a validation failure in the subprocess. There needs to be two **END** functions as we defined the subprocess with a result type of **Success/Fail**. To create the two **END** functions we can drag the standard **END** function onto the diagram as follows.

How to do it...

To create the subprocess **END** functions, we will perform the following steps:

1. Navigate to **XXHRIABS | WFSTD | Functions | END**.

2. With the **Validate XML** process diagram window open drag the **END** function on to the process diagram as shown in the following screenshot.

3. Repeat and drag a second **END** function onto the process diagram as shown in the following screenshot:

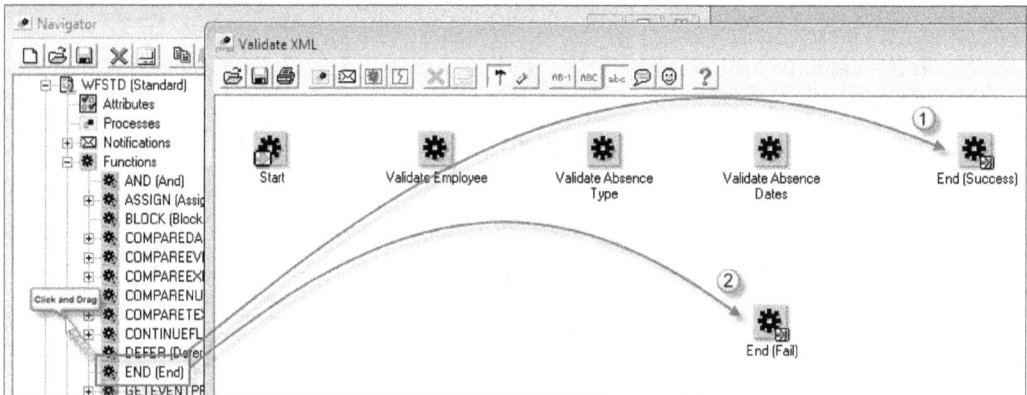

4. Right-click the first **END** icon we have just created in the process diagram and select **Properties** from the pop-up menu.

5. Navigate to the **Node** tab and set the following properties as shown in the screenshot:

Label	END-SUCCESS
Start/End	**End**
Result	**Success**

The properties should look similar to the following screenshot:

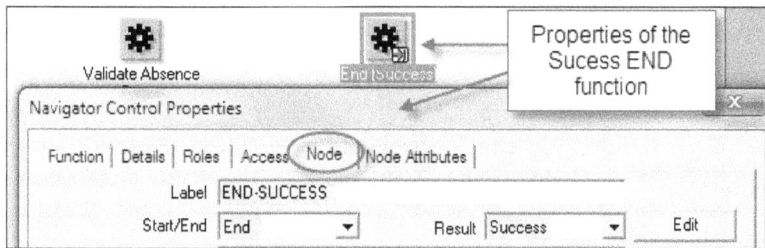

6. Right-click the second **END** icon we have just created in the process diagram and select **Properties** from the pop-up menu.

7. Navigate to the **Node** tab and set the following properties as shown in the screenshot:

Label	END-FAIL
Start/End	**End**
Result	**Fail**

How it works...

We need two **END** functions as we defined a result type to the subprocess of **Success/Fail**. This was the lookup we created earlier which had two values, **Success** and **Fail**. One **End** function will be for the **Fail** result and the other will be for the **Success** result.

Joining the functions

We can join the functions together by right-clicking the mouse button and dragging the line that appears to the function that we want to join it to. When the mouse is released on the target object, a pop-up menu appears which will allow us to select the context of the join.

How to do it...

To join the functions, we will perform the following steps:

1. Right-click on the **Start** function and drag the line to the **Validate Employee** function.

2. Right-click on the **Validate Employee** function and drag the line to the **Validate Absence Type** function, selecting **Success** from the pop-up menu.

3. Right-click on the **Validate Absence Type** function and drag the line to the **Validate Absence Dates** function, selecting **Success** from the pop-up menu.

4. Right-click on the **Validate Absence Dates** function and drag the line to the **End (Success)** function.

   We have joined the functions together to the **END (SUCCESS)** so that the completed process diagram looks similar to the following screenshot:

> The start function does not have a result type so you will not get a pop-up menu when we join it to the **Validate Employee** function. Also, you can drag the text so that it appears above the join line.

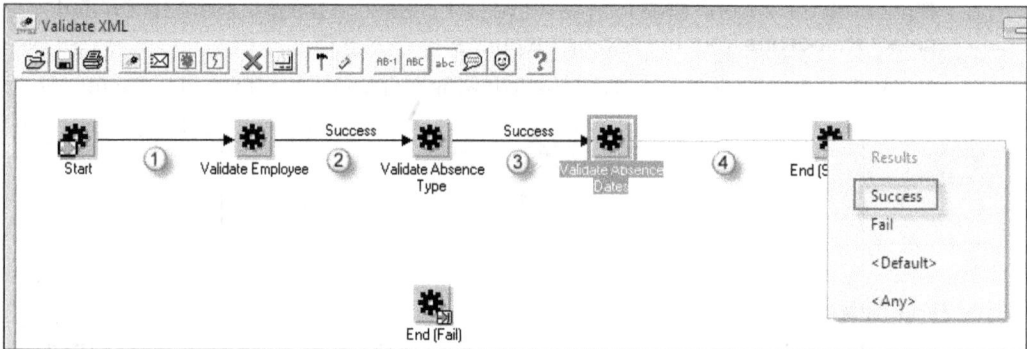

Now we will join the validate functions to the **End (Fail)** function as shown in the following screenshot. When the pop-up menu appears select **Fail** from the pop-up menu.

Right-click on the **Validate Employee** function and drag the line to the **End (Fail)** function, selecting **Fail** from the pop-up menu.

Right-click on the **Validate Absence Type** function and drag the line to the **End (Fail)** function, selecting **Fail** from the pop-up menu.

Right-click on the **Validate Absence Dates** function and drag the line to the **End (Fail)** function, selecting **Fail** from the pop-up menu.

There will be three lines mapped to the **End (Fail)** function as shown in the following screenshot:

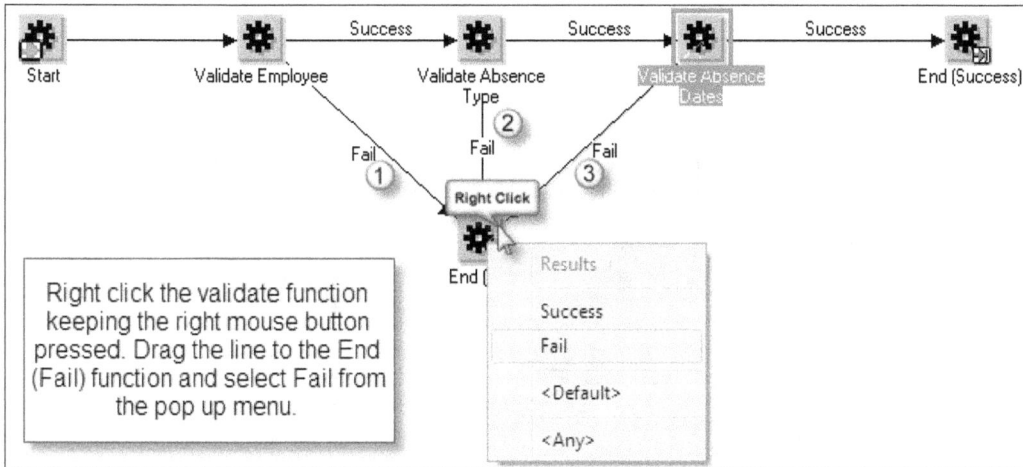

5. Now we can close the **Validate XML** window.

How it works...

We link the functions together so that if any activities fail validation they will be routed to the **END (Fail)** activity. Otherwise, each activity needs to have a successful result for the subprocess to complete with a successful outcome. Look at the code called in each of the validate procedures and you will see that the procedure has an OUT parameter called resultout. We set the resultout parameter to either 'COMPLETE:SUCCESS' or 'COMPLETE:FAIL', which is the lookup code we defined in our **Success/Fail** lookup.

Adding a subprocess to a parent process

To add the **Validate XML** sub process to the main process we can drag it from the navigator onto the **XXHR Inbound Absences** process diagram.

How to do it...

To add the subprocess to the main process, we will perform the following steps:

1. Navigate to **XXHRIABS | Processes | XXHR_INBOUND_ABSENCES**.

2. Double-click the process to open the **XXHR Inbound Absences** process diagram window.

3. Delete the line joining the **Parse XML** function and the **End** function.

4. Click-and-drag the **Validate XML** process onto the **XXHR Inbound Absences** process as shown in the following screenshot:

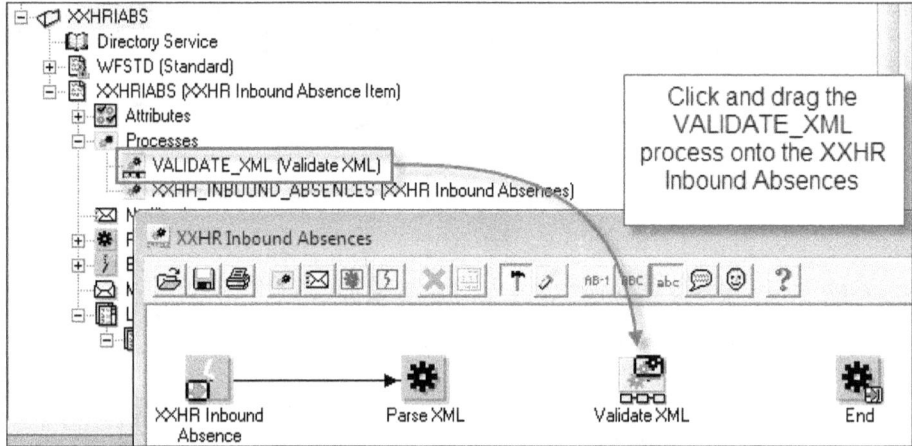

5. Join the functions from the **Validate XML** function to the **End** function.

6. Select **Success** from the pop-up menu.

7. Create a second line from the **Validate XML** function to the **End** function.

8. Select **Fail** from the pop-up menu.

9. Move the **Fail** line and create a path that is different from the **Success** path as shown in the following screenshot (we will add objects to these two paths later).

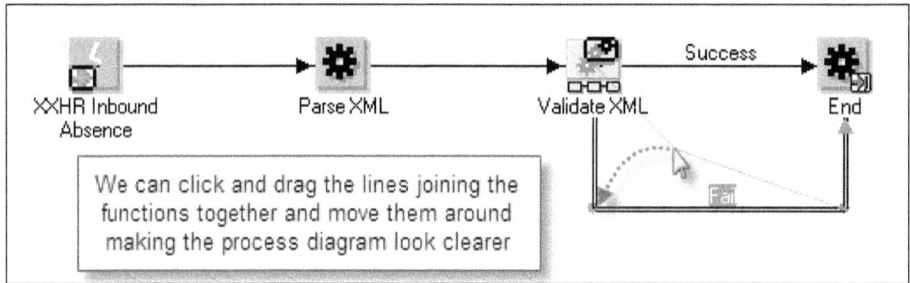

10. Save the workflow.

How it works...

We have now added the subprocess to the main process. It appears as an icon in the diagram which we can drill down into by double-clicking on it. The subprocess will have return values of either **Success** or **Fail**.

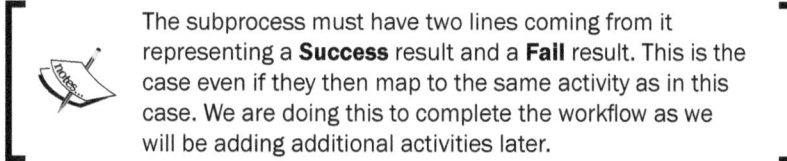

> The subprocess must have two lines coming from it representing a **Success** result and a **Fail** result. This is the case even if they then map to the same activity as in this case. We are doing this to complete the workflow as we will be adding additional activities later.

Testing the workflow

To test the workflow again we will be using the CH5 Test Harness 2.sql script. We need to upload the new version of the workflow to the database as we did previously. The steps are summarized in the following recipe.

How to do it...

To test the workflow, we will perform the following steps:

1. Ftp the XXHRIABS.wft workflow to the applications tier:

   ```
   WFLOAD apps/<password> 0 Y FORCE $XXHR_TOP/install/ch5/XXHRIABS.
   wft
   ```

2. Open the CH5 Test Harness 2.sql script in SQL Developer.

3. Run the script to put an XML message onto the advanced queue.

4. Open the AQ Query.sql script and run the query to check whether a payload has been added to the advanced queue.

5. Log in to Oracle with the **Workflow Administrator Web (New)** responsibility.

6. Navigate to **Status Monitor**.

7. In the **Monitor Search** screen type XXHRIABS in the **Type Internal Name** field and click on the **Go** button.

8. Select the workflow we have just created and click on the **Status Diagram** button.

   The completed workflow diagram will look similar to the following screenshot, where the highlighted line is the path the workflow took to complete:

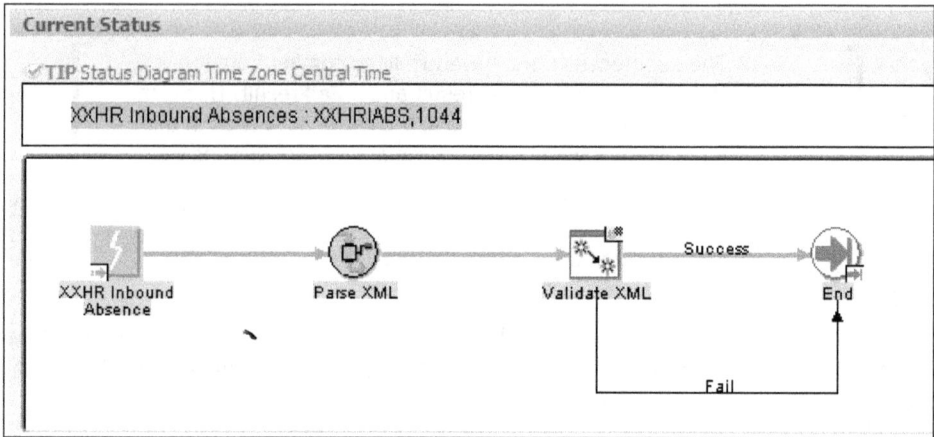

9. Double-click on the **Validate XML** process to drill down into the subprocess and it will be displayed as shown in the following screenshot:

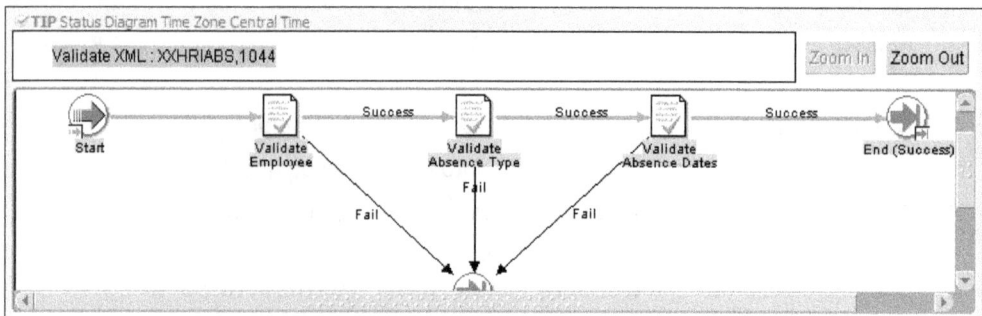

How it works...

The XML we are using to test the workflow now has some values in it. The values we used should result in a successful outcome of the workflow.

There's more...

As an additional exercise, try changing the values in the CH5 Test Harness 2.sql XML file and saving it as CH5 Test Harness xx.sql. (Do not overwrite the original script as we will be using it again later.) You can re-run the test to see if we can get the workflow to fail. Remember the conditions that will cause a fail are:

- No or invalid employee number
- No or invalid absence type
- No absence start date
- Absence end date less than the absence start date

Creating messages

When we want to send a notification we must first define a message that the notification will be based upon. We are going to create a number of messages. There will be a message to the manager of the employee to confirm the absence details. This will require a response from the manager to accept or reject the absence that was received in the XML. There will be a message to the system administrator to inform them of an error in validating the XML. Finally there will be a message to the employee to inform them that the manager has rejected the absence details. We are going to create the following three messages:

- Absence Approval
- Absence Rejection
- Invalid XML

To create messages, we will perform the following tasks:

- Creating an absence approval message
- Adding attributes to our approval message
- Creating a rejection message
- Adding attributes to our rejection message
- Creating an invalid XML message
- Adding invalid XML message attributes

Creating an absence approval message

We are now going to create an absence approval message in our workflow.

How to do it...

To create a message, we will perform the following steps:

1. Navigate to **XXHRIABS | Messages**.

2. Right-click on **Messages** and select **New Message** from the pop-up menu.

3. Complete the properties as per the following table for the **Message** tab:

Internal Name	ABS_APPROVAL
Display Name	Absence Approval
Description	Absence Approval
Priority	**Normal**

4. Complete the properties as per the following table for the **Body** tab:

Internal Name	Absence Approval for Employee Number :&EMP_NUMBER
Text Body	Please confirm the absence for the above employee.
	Absence Type: &ABS_TYPE
	Absence Start Date: &ABS_START_DATE
	Absence End Date: &ABS_END_DATE

> We can reference attributes in the e-mail by putting an & followed by the attribute name.

5. Complete the properties as per the following table for the **Result** tab:

Display Name	Approval
Description	Absence approval
Lookup Type	Approval
Default Type	Constant
Value	Approve

6. Click **OK**.

How it works...

We have defined a message for a notification that requires a response from a user to approve an absence. We have also defined tokens in the message which get replaced with values from attributes at runtime.

Adding attributes to our approval message

We must now add the message attributes that are referenced in our message.

How to do it...

To add the message attributes, we will perform the following steps:

1. Open the **Attributes** node in the navigator.

2. Click-and-drag the following attributes on to the message as shown in the following screenshot:

   ▸ EMP_NUMBER

   ▸ ABS_TYPE

   ▸ ABS_START_DATE

   ▸ ABS_END_DATE

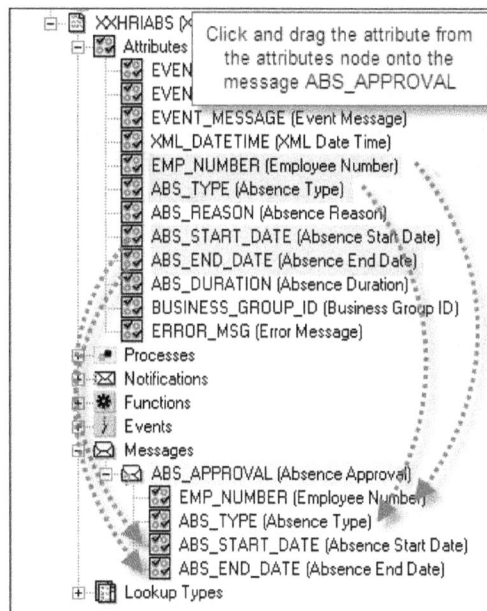

How it works...

The definition of the message has tokens in it based upon attributes in the workflow. The attributes must therefore also be in the message definition so we just need to drag them from the attributes section to the message definition.

Creating a rejection message

We are now going to create an absence rejection message.

How to do it...

To create a rejection message, perform the following steps:

1. Navigate to **XXHRIABS | Messages**.
2. Right-click **Messages** and select **New Message** from the pop-up menu.
3. Complete the properties as per the following table for the **Message** tab:

Internal Name	ABS_REJECTION
Display Name	Absence Rejection
Description	Absence Rejection
Priority	**Normal**

4. Complete the properties as per the following table for the **Body** tab:

Internal Name	Absence Rejection for Employee Number: &EMP_NUMBER
Text Body	The absence details have been rejected by your manager. Please contact your manager to confirm the absence details and resubmit the absence.

> We do not require a result for this message so we do not need to complete the **Result** tab.

5. Click on **OK**.

How it works...

We have defined a message that will be used for notifications when the approval notification returns a *Rejected* response.

Adding attributes to our rejection message

We will now add the attributes referenced in the rejection message to the message definition in the navigator.

How to do it...

To add attributes to the message, we will perform the following steps. To add attributes that are referenced in the message we must drag the attributes from the **Attributes** node in the navigator to the message.

1. Open the **Attributes** node in the navigator.
2. Click-and-drag the **EMP_NUMBER** attribute on to the **ABS_REJECTION** message:

How it works...

We have a token in the message and therefore need to drag the attribute into the message definition as we did before.

Creating an invalid XML message

We will now create a message to send when the XML validation fails. To create an absence invalid XML message we must create a new message from the navigator and complete the properties as follows.

How to do it...

To create an invalid XML message, we will perform the following steps:

1. Navigate to **XXHRIABS | Messages**.
2. Right-click **Messages** and select **New Message** from the pop-up menu.
3. Complete the properties as per the following table for the **Message** tab:

Internal Name	INVALID_XML
Display Name	Invalid XML
Description	Invalid XML
Priority	**Normal**

4. Complete the properties as per the following table for the **Body** tab:

Internal Name	Invalid XML for & EVENT_KEY
Text Body	The XML for &EVENT_NAME with an event key of &EVENT_KEY is invalid. The message that was received is &EVENT_MESSAGE

5. Click on **OK**.

How it works...

The invalid XML message is to be used by notifications sent when the subprocess returns with a result of *Fail*.

Adding invalid XML message attributes

We now need to add attributes that are referenced in the message and will therefore drag the attributes from the **Attributes** node in the navigator to the message.

How to do it...

To add the invalid XML message attributes, we will perform the following steps:

1. Open the **Attributes** node in the navigator.

2. Click-and-drag the following attribute on to the **INVALID_XML** message:

   - **EVENT_KEY**
   - **EVENT_MESSAGE**
   - **EVENT_NAME**

We should now have three messages defined as shown in the following screenshot:

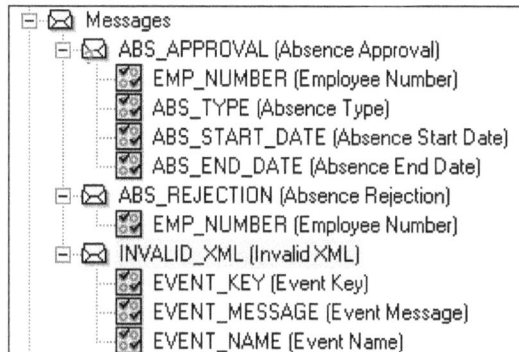

```
─ Messages
   ─ ABS_APPROVAL (Absence Approval)
        EMP_NUMBER (Employee Number)
        ABS_TYPE (Absence Type)
        ABS_START_DATE (Absence Start Date)
        ABS_END_DATE (Absence End Date)
   ─ ABS_REJECTION (Absence Rejection)
        EMP_NUMBER (Employee Number)
   ─ INVALID_XML (Invalid XML)
        EVENT_KEY (Event Key)
        EVENT_MESSAGE (Event Message)
        EVENT_NAME (Event Name)
```

3. Save the workflow.

How it works...

We are using the event attributes as tokens in this message so the event attributes are added to the message definition.

Sending notifications and processing responses

We will now use the messages we created to create some notifications in our workflow process. One notification will be sent to the manager of the employee that is absent. We will build a response into the notification. The manager will need to respond to the notification to confirm they have made contact with the employee to confirm the details of the absence. We will also create two other notifications that do not require a response. One will be a rejection notification to inform the employee that the absence that was received was rejected by their manager. The second will be a notification to the system administrator to inform them that there has been an error validating the XML message that was received.

We are now going to create three notifications that we can add into our process diagram that will be based upon the messages we created. We have to define the notifications before we add it to the process diagram. A notification placed on the diagram is an instance of a notification.

To create the notifications, we will perform the following tasks:

▶ Creating an absence approval notification

▶ Creating an absence rejection notification

▶ Creating an invalid XML notification

- ▸ Adding notifications to a process diagram
- ▸ Mapping the notifications
- ▸ Testing the workflow
- ▸ Viewing the notifications and workflow diagrams

Creating an absence approval notification

We are now going to create a notification that will be added to our workflow process to notify a user that an absence requires approval. The notification is an instance of the `Absence Approval` message we created earlier.

How to do it...

To create an absence approval notification, we must create a new message from the navigator and complete the properties as follows:

1. Navigate to **XXHRIABS | Notifications**.
2. Right-click on **Notifications** and select **New Notification** from the pop-up menu.
3. Complete the properties of the **Activity** tab as follows:

Internal Name	ABS_APPROVAL_NOT
Display Name	Absence Approval Notification
Description	Absence Approval Notification
Icon	NOTIFY.ICO
Function Name	
Function Type	**PL/SQL**
Result Type	**Approval**
Message	Absence Approval

4. Click on **OK**.

How it works...

We have now defined a notification based on the approval message we created. The notification will be added to the process diagram if we get a *Success* result from the subprocess to validate the XML.

Creating an absence rejection notification

We are now going to create a notification that is going to be added to our workflow process to notify a user that an absence approval has been rejected. The notification is an instance of the `Absence Rejection` message we created earlier.

How to do it...

To create an absence rejection notification, we must create a new message from the navigator and complete the properties as follows:

1. Navigate to **XXHRIABS | Notifications**.
2. Right-click on **Notifications** and select **New Notification** from the pop-up menu.
3. Complete the properties of the **Activity** tab as follows:

Internal Name	ABS_REJECTION_NOT
Display Name	Absence Rejection
Description	Absence Rejection
Icon	NOTIFY.ICO
Function Name	
Function Type	**PL/SQL**
Result Type	<None>
Message	**Absence Rejection**

4. Click on **OK**.

How it works...

We have now defined a notification based on the rejection message we created. The notification will be added to the process diagram if we receive a rejection response from the approval notification.

Creating invalid XML notification

We are now going to create a notification that is going to be added to our workflow process to notify a user that the XML received is invalid. The notification is an instance of the `Invalid XML` message we created earlier.

How to do it...

To create an invalid XML notification we must create a new message from the navigator and complete the properties as follows:

1. Navigate to **XXHRIABS | Notifications**.

2. Right-click on **Notifications** and select **New Notification** from the pop-up menu.

3. Complete the properties of the **Activity** tab as follows:

Internal Name	INVALID_XML_NOT
Display Name	Invalid XML Notification
Description	Invalid XML Notification
Icon	NOTIFY.ICO
Function Name	
Function Type	**PL/SQL**
Result Type	<None>
Message	Invalid XML

4. Click on **OK**.

How it works...

We have now defined a notification based on the invalid XML message we created. The notification will be added to the process diagram if we receive a result as **Fail** from the subprocess we created.

Adding notifications to the process diagram

We are now going to add the notifications we have just created to our workflow process.

How to do it...

To add the notifications, we will perform the following steps:

1. Double-click **XXHR_INBOUND_ABSENCES** to open the process diagram.

2. Navigate to **XXHRIABS | Processes**.

3. Double-click **XXHR_INBOUND_ABSENCES** to open the process diagram.

4. Delete the line linking the **Validate XML** subprocess to the **End** object. (Select the line and hit the *Delete* button). The process should now look similar to the process in the following screenshot:

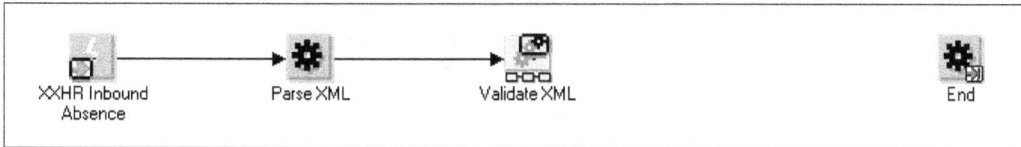

5. In the process diagram, click on the **New Notification** button.

6. When the cursor changes to a crosshair click on the process diagram to create a new notification.

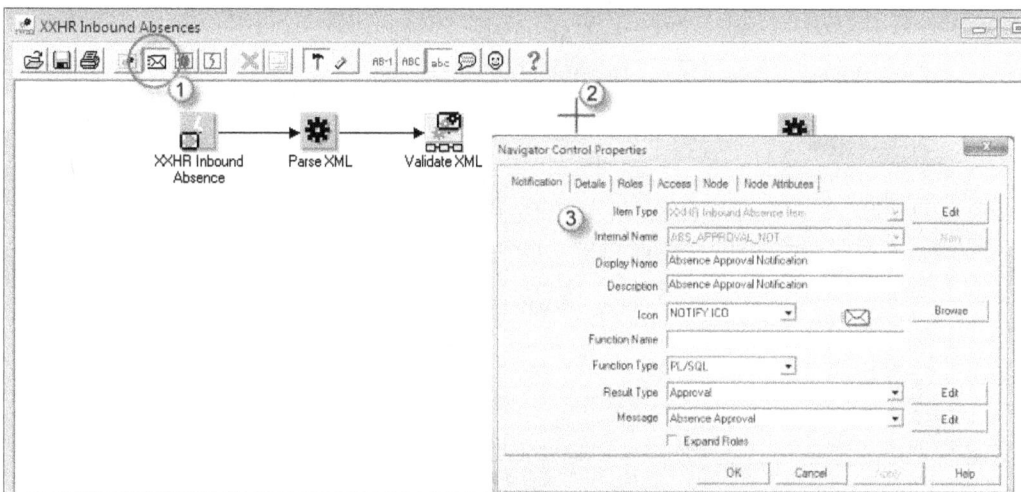

7. Complete the **Notification** tab details as in the following table to add an approval notification:

Item Type	XXHR Inbound Absence Item
Internal Name	ABS_APPROVAL_NOT
Display Name	Absence Approval Notification
Description	Absence Approval Notification
Icon	NOTIFY.ICO
Function Name	
Function Type	PL/SQL
Result Type	Approval
Message	Absence Approval

> When the **Internal Name** is selected the remaining values will automatically populate.

8. Complete the **Node** tab details as in the following table:

Label	ABS_APPROVAL_NOT
Start/End	**Normal**
Comment	
Timeout	**Relative Time**
Value	14 days 0 hours 0 minutes
Priority Type	**Default**
Performer Type	**Item Attribute**
Value	**Username**

9. Click on **OK**.

> The **Item Attribute** called **Username** should have a default value of your FND Username or SYSADMIN for testing the workflow. If we were implementing the workflow for real we would call a database package to send the message to the manager of the employee.

10. In the process diagram click on the **New Notification** button.

11. When the cursor changes to a crosshair click the mouse on the process diagram to create a new notification.

12. Complete the **Notification** tab details as in the following table to add a rejection notification:

Item Type	XXHR Inbound Absence Item
Internal Name	ABS_REJECTION_NOT
Display Name	Absence Rejection
Description	Absence Rejection
Icon	NOTIFY.ICO
Function Name	
Function Type	**PL/SQL**
Result Type	**None**
Message	Absence Rejection

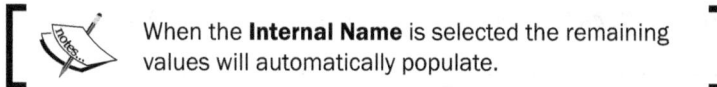

> When the **Internal Name** is selected the remaining values will automatically populate.

13. Complete the **Node** tab details as shown in the following table:

Label	ABS_REJECTION_NOT
Start/End	**Normal**
Comment	
Timeout	**No Timeout**
Priority Type	**Default**
Performer Type	**Item Attribute**
Value	**Username**

14. Click on **OK**.

15. In the process diagram click on the **New Notification** button.

16. When the cursor changes to a crosshair click on the process diagram to create a new notification.

17. Complete the **Notification** tab details as shown in the following table to add an invalid XML notification:

Item Type	XXHR Inbound Absence Item
Internal Name **	INVALID_XML_NOT
Display Name	Invalid XML Notification
Description	Invalid XML Notification
Icon	NOTIFY.ICO
Function Name	
Function Type	**PL/SQL**
Result Type	**None**
Message	Invalid XML

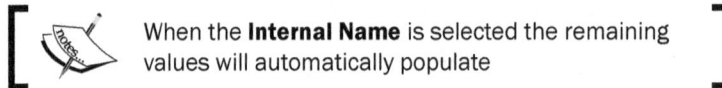

> When the **Internal Name** is selected the remaining values will automatically populate

18. Complete the **Node** tab details as shown in the following table:

Label	INVALID_XML_NOT
Start/End	**Normal**
Comment	
Timeout	**No Timeout**
Priority Type	**Default**
Performer Type	**Item Attribute**
Value	**Username**

19. Click on **OK**.

How it works...

The notification activities are now on the process diagram. When the process reaches one of these notifications the workflow engine calls an API to send the notification to the user based upon their workflow notification preferences. These preferences are set in the **Preferences** link on the login page for each user. This is set in the **Display Preferences | Notifications** region.

Mapping the notifications

To map the notifications to the diagram we must first delete any links we no longer need. As we have already done this we need to link the notifications to other objects in the diagram.

How to do it...

To map the notifications in our process diagram, we will perform the following steps:

1. Create a link between the **Validate XML** subprocess and the **Absence Approval** notification and select **Success** from the pop-up menu.

2. Create a link between the **Validate XML** subprocess and the **Invalid XML** notification and select **Fail** from the pop-up menu.

3. Create a link between the **Absence Approval** notification and the **End** function and select **Approve** from the pop-up menu.

4. Create a link between the **Absence Approval** notification and the **Absence Rejection** notification and select **Reject** from the pop-up menu.

5. Create a link between the **Absence Rejection** notification and the **End** function.

6. Create a link between the **Invalid XML** notification and the **End** function.

   The process diagram should now look similar to the diagram in the following screenshot:

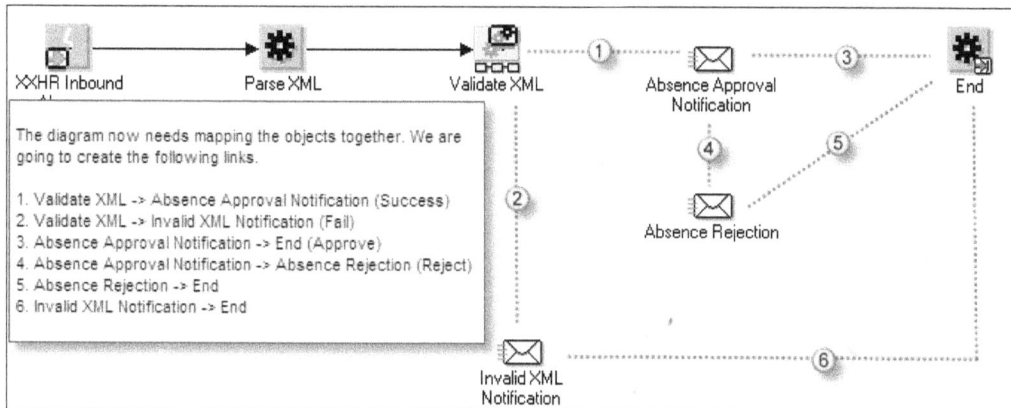

7. We will also add another link from the **Absence Approval Notification** to itself and assign it to **Timeout**. This means that if there is no response after 14 days then the message will be resent.

8. Right-click the **Absence Approval Notification** and drag the line away from the **Absence Approval Notification**. Then drag the mouse back to the **Absence Approval Notification** and release the mouse.

9. Select **<Timeout>** from the pop-up menu.

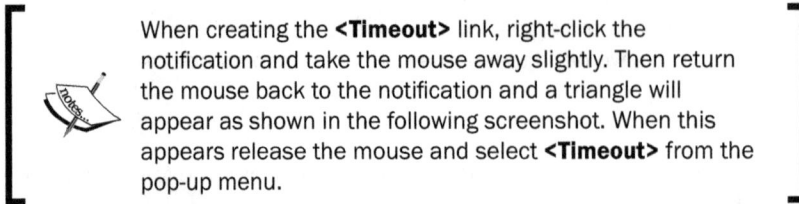

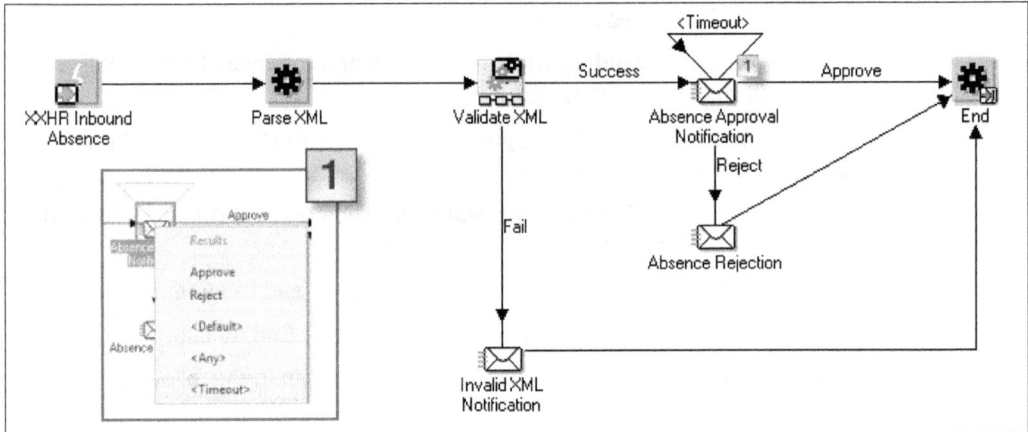

> When creating the **<Timeout>** link, right-click the notification and take the mouse away slightly. Then return the mouse back to the notification and a triangle will appear as shown in the following screenshot. When this appears release the mouse and select **<Timeout>** from the pop-up menu.

10. Save the workflow.

How it works...

We have linked the activities to complete the workflow.

Testing the workflow

We can now test the workflow again using the CH5 Test Harness 2.sql script. We need to perform the same steps as we did previously. This time though we want to test a number of scenarios:

- That the workflow completes successfully and a notification is approved
- That the workflow errors with invalid data in the XML
- That the workflow sends a second notification if the first notification is rejected

How to do it...

The steps are summarized in the following recipe:

1. Ftp the `XXHRIABS.wft` workflow to the applications tier:

   ```
   WFLOAD apps/<password> 0 Y FORCE $XXHR_TOP/install/ch5/XXHRIABS.
   wft
   ```

2. Open the `CH5 Test Harness 2.sql` in SQL Developer.

3. Run the script twice to put two XML message onto the advanced queue.

4. Open and run `CH5 Test Harness 3.sql`. (this has an invalid employee number in the XML so there is no need to amend this script.)

5. Open the `AQ Query.sql` file and run the query to check whether three payloads have been added to the advanced queue.

How it works...

We have now run the scripts to add three new XML messages onto the advanced queue so that we can test our workflow.

Viewing the notifications and workflow diagrams

We are now going to view and respond to the notifications that have been generated. If the notification mailer is running then the message will get sent to the e-mail address of the employee linked to a role in the `WF_ROLES` table. As we have not configured the notification mailer, the message will be sent internally and can be viewed in the **Notifications** tab in the workflow home page.

How to do it...

To view the notifications, perform the following steps:

1. Log in to Oracle with the **Workflow Administrator Web (New)** responsibility.

2. Navigate to **Status Monitor**.

3. In the **Monitor Search** screen type `XXHRIABS` in the **Type Internal Name** field and click on the **Go** button. We can see the three workflows we have created.

Select Workflow and View...	Activity History	Status Diagram	Participant Responses	Workflow Details		
Select		Status	Workflow Type	Item Key	Process Name	User Key	Owned By
○	✓	Complete	XXHR Inbound Absence Item	1052	XXHR Inbound Absences		
○	✓	Active	XXHR Inbound Absence Item	1051	XXHR Inbound Absences		
○	✓	Active	XXHR Inbound Absence Item	1050	XXHR Inbound Absences		

4. Navigate to the **Notifications** tab and we can see that there are now three notifications.

5. Click on the first notification and click on the **Approve** button. (It will then disappear from the list.)

6. Click on the second notification and click on the **Reject** button. (It will then disappear from the list.)

7. There will now be two notifications in the list. The **Invalid XML** and the **Absence Rejection** notifications will appear as shown in the following screenshot. Open them to view the notifications and click on the **OK** button to close the message.

8. Navigate back to the **Status Monitor** screen and query the workflows as we have done previously. Click on the **Status Monitor** button for each of the three workflows and the process diagrams will look similar to the three in the following screenshot.

9. The completed **Approved Workflow** process will look similar to the following screenshot:

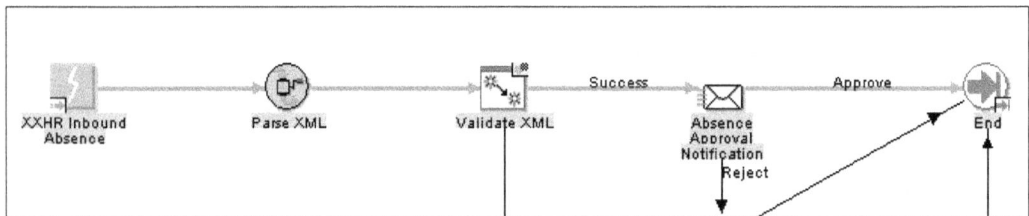

10. The completed **Rejected Workflow** process will look similar to the following screenshot:

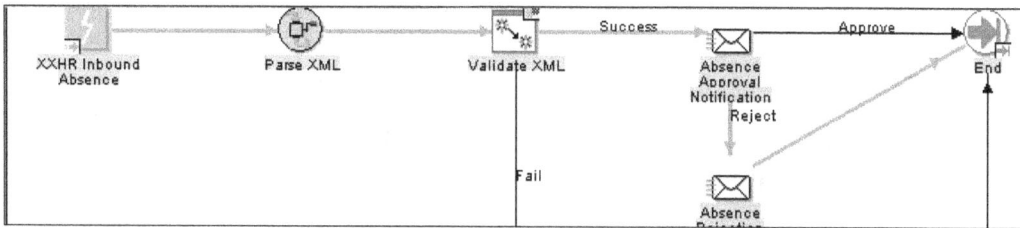

11. The completed **Invalid XML Workflow** process will look similar to the following screenshot:

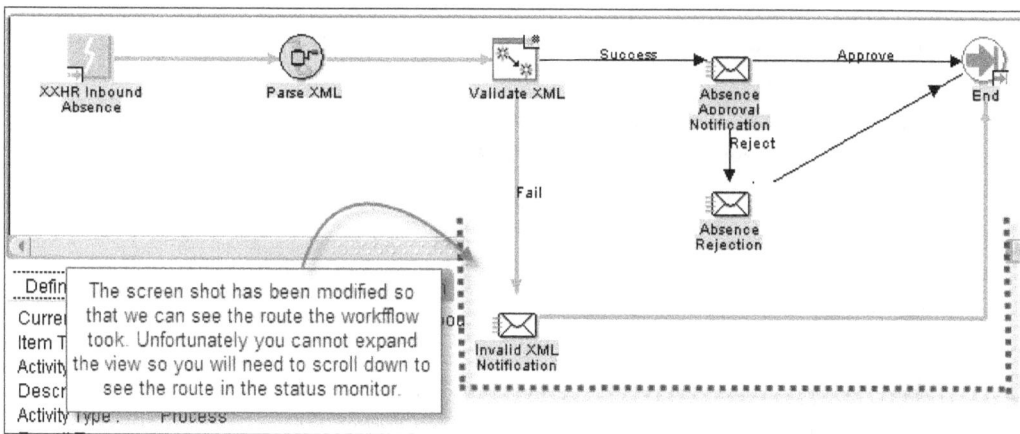

The screen shot has been modified so that we can see the route the workffow took. Unfortunately you cannot expand the view so you will need to scroll down to see the route in the status monitor.

How it works...

We have now tested the workflow checking that the three notifications have been successfully sent. We have also checked that we can respond to the approval workflow.

Calling an API

We are now going to complete the workflow by adding a call to an API if the **Absence Approval Notification** is approved.

To add this function to the diagram, perform the following tasks:

▸ Creating a function to call database package

▸ Adding a function to a process

▸ Testing the workflow

Creating a function to call the database package

We can add a new function to the workflow by selecting the **New Function** button in the **Process Diagram** toolbar. We are going to call an Oracle API to create an absence record for the employee.

How to do it...

To create a function to call an API, we will perform the following steps:

1. Open the XXHRIABS workflow in the workflow builder.

2. Navigate to **XXHRIABS | XXHR Inbound Absence Process | Processes**.

3. Double-click the **XXHR Inbound Absences** process and the **Process Diagram** window will open.

4. Click the **New Function**(⬛) icon on the toolbar in the **XXHR Inbound Absences** window.

5. Click the mouse on the process diagram when the mouse changes to a crosshair and the **Property** window will open.

6. Complete the properties with the details from the following table:

Item Type	XXHR Inbound Absence Item
Internal Name	CREATE_ABSENCE
Display Name	Create Absence
Description	Create Absence
Icon	FUNCTION.ICO
Function Name	XXHR_ABSENCE_IN_WF_PKG.create_absence
Function Type	**PL/SQL**
Result Type	**<None>**
Cost	**0.00**

7. Click on **OK**.

How it works...

We have created an activity to create the absence using the Oracle API if the workflow reaches this stage successfully.

Adding a function to a process

We are now going to add the function to the process between the **Absence Approval Notification** and the **END** function.

How to do it...

To add the function to the process, we will perform the following steps:

1. Delete the **Approve** link connecting the **Absence Approval Notification** and the **End** function. (Select the line and press *Delete*.)

2. Click-and-drag the **End** function a little to the right to make some room for the **Create Absence** function. (Any links will remain attached to the function and we will tidy it up later.)

3. Drag the **Create Absence** function in between the **Absence Approval Notification** and the **End** function.

4. Create a link from the **Absence Approval Notification** to the **Create Absence** function selecting **Approve** from the pop-up menu.

5. Create a link from the **Create Absence** function to the **End** function.

6. Tidy up the lines linking the **Absence Rejection Notification** to the **End** function and the **Invalid XML Notification** to the **End** function if desired (although this is not necessary, it just tidies up the diagram).

   The process diagram should now look similar to the diagram in the following screenshot:

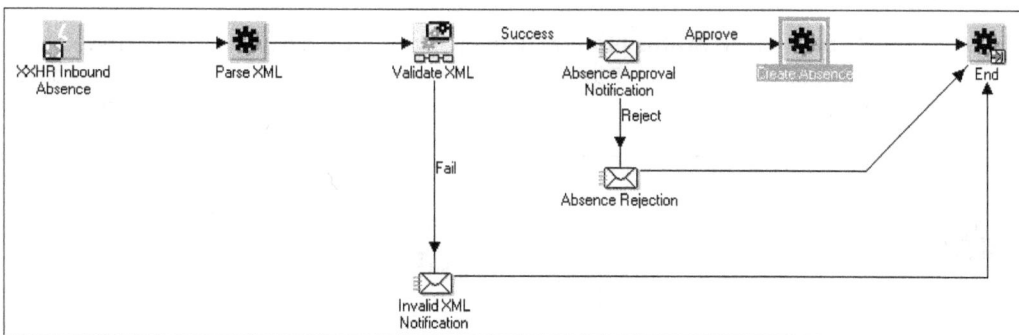

How it works...

The activity can be added to the process in the appropriate place once the absence has been approved.

Testing the workflow

We are now going to test the workflow to see if an absence has been created when a notification is approved.

How to do it...

To test the workflow, we will perform the following steps:

1. Ftp the XXHRIABS.wft workflow to the applications tier:

   WFLOAD apps/<password> 0 Y FORCE $XXHR_TOP/install/ch5/XXHRIABS. wft

2. Open the CH5 Test Harness 2.sql in SQL Developer.

3. Run the script to put an XML message onto the advanced queue.

4. Open the AQ Query.sql file and run the query to check whether a new payload has been added to the advanced queue.

5. Log in to Oracle with the **Workflow Administrator Web (New)** responsibility.

6. Navigate to **Status Monitor**.

7. In the **Monitor Search** screen type XXHRIABS in the **Type Internal Name** field and click on the **Go** button. We can see the workflow we have created.

8. Navigate to the **Notifications** tab and we can see that there is now a new **Approval** notification.

9. Click on the notification and click on the **Approve** button. (It will then disappear from the list.)

10. Navigate back to the **Status Monitor** screen and query the workflow as we have done previously. Click on the **Status Monitor** button for the workflow and the process diagram will look similar to the following screenshot for the approved workflow:

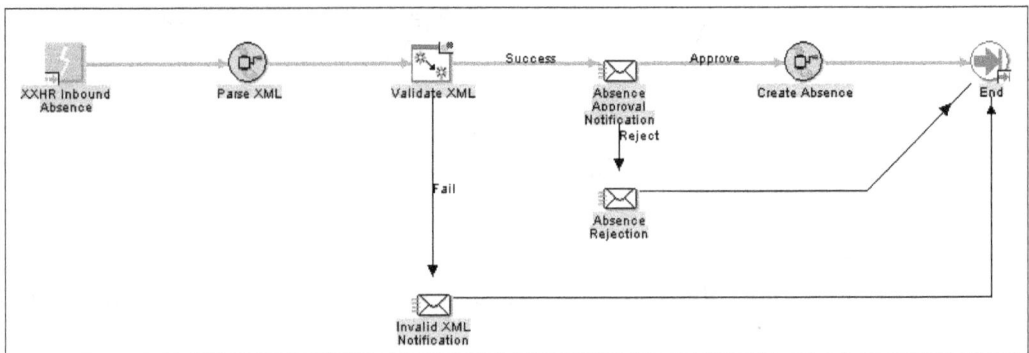

How it works...

We have passed in an XML message that will not complete the workflow successfully and should create an absence in Oracle for the employee defined in the XML message. If we now log in to Oracle as the **UK HRMS Manager** responsibility and go to the **Enter and Maintain** form. If we then query employee number 11 and click **Others | Absence** we should see the absence that has been created.

Please note if you intend to queue the same XML message more than once after we have uploaded this workflow to the database you will need to delete the absence that was created in Oracle first. To do this, log in to Oracle and query back the employee. Navigate to the **Absence** screen and delete the absence that was created. An absence cannot be created in Oracle with overlapping dates.

6
Utilities

In this chapter, we will cover the following:

- ▶ Setting the environment variables
- ▶ Starting and stopping an environment
- ▶ Creating a custom schema
- ▶ Extracting data using FNDLOAD
- ▶ Uploading using FNDLOAD
- ▶ Using a script for FNDLOAD
- ▶ Using a script for migrating objects

Introduction

In this chapter, we are going to look at some utilities that Oracle provides that will assist you as a developer to migrate code from one environment to another. We will also look at how to create a custom schema for the environment you will be working on. This would normally be done by a DBA, but we will need a custom schema for the work that we will be doing in the book. We will also look at using scripts to help with packaging scripts and running just a single script to load multiple objects.

Setting the environment variables

Throughout the book, you will see references to `$APPL_TOP` or `$XXHR_TOP`. These are like shortcuts and are set usually when we log on to the application server with the application tier OS user. On the application and database servers, the environment variables are used to navigate directly to specific directories. The variables are normally set when we log on the application server or database server. There is a file that is used to set all of the environment variables. It is a consolidated environment file called `APPS_<CONTEXT_NAME>.env`, which sets up both the Oracle E-Business Suite and Oracle technology stack environments.

In this chapter, we will show you how to perform the following:

- ▶ Setting the environment on the application server
- ▶ Setting the environment on the database server

Setting the environment on the application server

When Oracle E-Business Suite is installed, Rapid Install creates the environment file in the `APPL_TOP` directory. If the user we log in with does not execute the environment file when we log in, we will need to source the environment file and execute it manually. The environment file on the application server is in the `APPL_TOP` directory.

How to do it...

To set the environment on the application server, perform the following:

1. Open **Putty** and log on to the application server with the application's tier OS user.

2. Assuming the `APPL_TOP` directory is `/oracle/apps/r12/visr12/apps/apps_st/appl`, type the following at the command prompt:

   `./oracle/apps/r12/visr12/apps/apps_st/appl/APPS<CONTEXT_NAME>.env`

> On Windows, the equivalent consolidated environment file is called `%APPL_TOP%\envshell<CONTEXT_NAME>.cmd`. Running it creates a command window with the required environment settings for Oracle E-Business Suite.

How it works...

The environment file is normally called from the profile of a UNIX user's login. However, if it is not, then it must be set manually. This is important when running Oracle scripts as they nearly all refer to environment variables and not implicit directory structures.

Setting the environment on the database server

If we need to set the environment on the database server, we can perform the same action from the database tier owner OS user. The environment file is in the `RDBMS_ORACLE_HOME` directory.

How to do it...

To set the environment on the database server, perform the following:

1. Open **Putty** and log on to the application server with the database tier user.

2. Assuming the RDBMS_ORACLE_HOME directory is /oracle/apps/r12/visr12/ db/tech_st/11.1.0, type the following at the command prompt:

   ```
   ./oracle/apps/r12/visr12/db/tech_st/11.1.0/<CONTEXT_NAME>.env
   ```

How it works...

We must run the environment file because we use the variables to navigate to specific directories. This allows us to go directly to directories that would be commonly accessed. It is also important to set the environment as Oracle scripts refer to the variables when executing commands and not implicit directories.

Starting and stopping an environment

Normally, we would develop on an environment provided by an organization that employs a full time DBA. Their role is to manage the environment and ensure that it is up and running. Sometimes, however, we may have to manage our own environment for training purposes or if there is a small development team. Therefore, this recipe will go through the following steps:

- Starting an environment
- Stopping an environment

Starting an environment

The following steps will start an idle environment. The installation is complete and the environment is idle.

How to do it...

To start an environment, perform the following steps:

1. Open **Putty** and log on to the database server with the database OS owner.
2. Set the environment (if it is not already set).
3. Connect to SQL*Plus as sysdba with the following command:
   ```
   DB Tier> sqlplus "/as sysdba"
   ```
4. When connected to SQL*Plus, type the following command to start the database:
   ```
   SQL>startup
   ```

5. Exit SQL*Plus by typing exit.

6. When back at the UNIX prompt, start the listener by typing the following:

```
DB Tier> lsnrctl start visr12
```

> visr12 is the name of the environment I am using. You must use the name of the environment you are starting a listener for.

7. Open **Putty** and log on to the application's server with the application's OS owner.

8. Set the environment (if it is not already set).

9. Navigate to the $ADMIN_SCRIPTS_HOME directory by typing the following command at the **APPS** tier prompt:

```
APPS Tier> cd $ADMIN_SCRIPTS_HOME
```

10. Test the connection to the database by connecting to SQL*Plus as the **apps** user:

```
sqlplus apps/apps (This step is to check that application tier can
connect to Database).
```

11. Exit SQL*Plus and start the apps process by running the following script:

```
APPS Tier>./adstrtal.sh apps/apps
```

Now we can check that the environment has started by opening the home page in our browser, as shown in the following screenshot. It may take a minute or two.

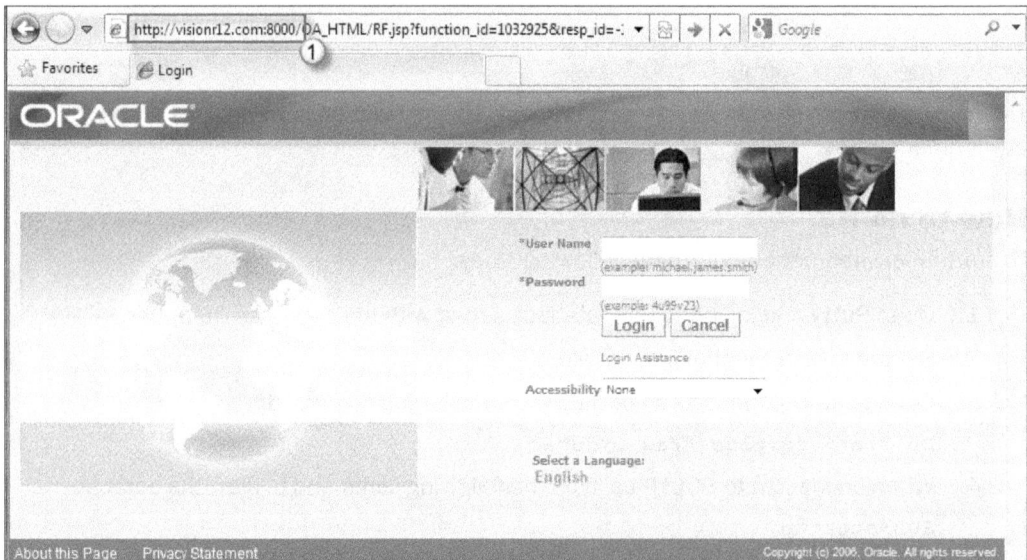

If the browser is Internet Explorer 8, then you may get the following error:

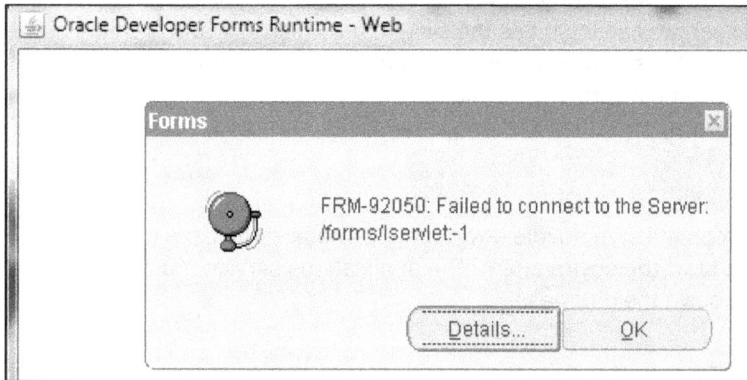

The security setting **XSS filter** needs to be disabled, as shown in the following screenshot:

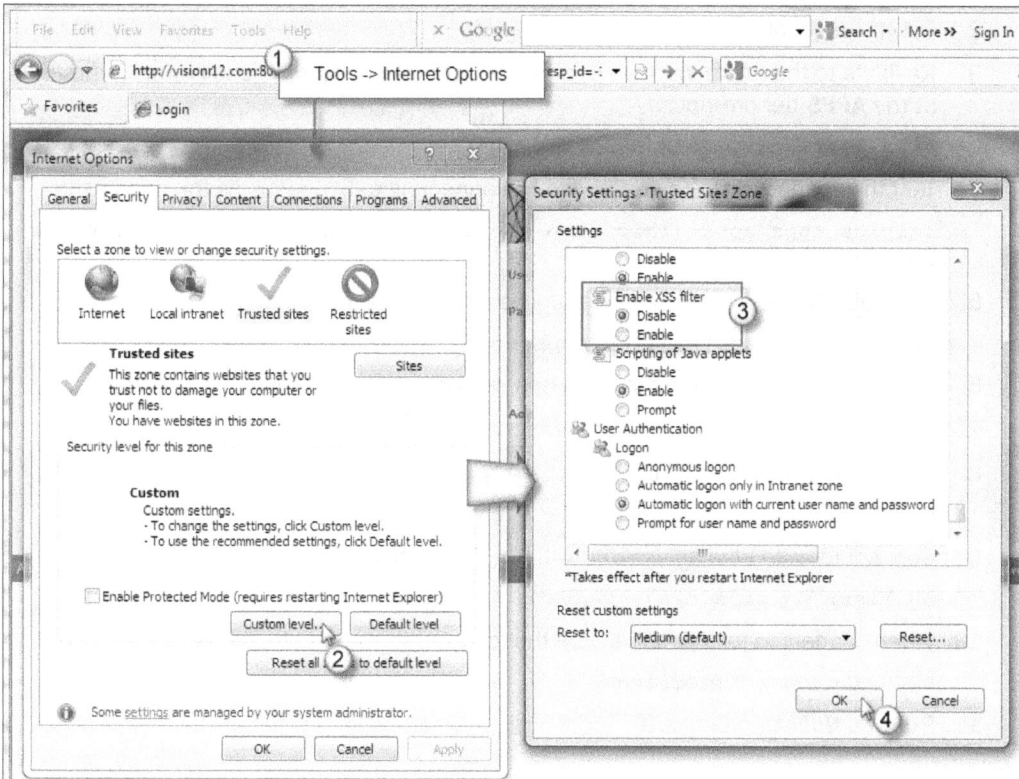

How it works...

The environment is now started and we can log on with our application's user. If we have not set up our user yet, we can log on as the system administrator and create a new user. The system administrator username is SYSADMIN and the password is SYSADMIN, by default, although this will almost certainly be changed after install.

Stopping an environment

The following steps will stop an idle environment. These steps have to be completed in the reverse order to start the environment. The applications service must always be stopped before shutting down the database.

How to do it...

To stop an environment that is running, perform the following steps:

1. Open **Putty** and log on to the application server with the applications OS owner.

2. Set the environment (if it is not already set).

3. Navigate to the $ADMIN_SCRIPTS_HOME directory by typing the following command at the **APPS** tier prompt:

    ```
    APPS Tier> cd $ADMIN_SCRIPTS_HOME
    ```

4. Test the connection to the database by connecting to SQL*Plus as the **apps** user:

    ```
    sqlplus apps/apps (This step is to check that application tier can
    connect to Database).
    ```

5. Exit SQL*Plus and start the apps process by running the following script:

    ```
    APPS Tier> ./adstpall.sh apps/apps
    ```

6. Open **Putty** and log on to the database server with the database OS owner.

7. Set the environment (if it is not already set).

8. At the **UNIX** prompt, stop the listener by typing the following:

    ```
    DB Tier> lsnrctl stop visr12
    ```

9. Connect to SQL*Plus as sysdba with the following command:

    ```
    DB Tier> sqlplus "/as sysdba"
    ```

10. When connected to SQL*Plus, type the following command to start the database:

    ```
    SQL> shutdown immediate
    ```

11. Exit *SQL*Plus* by typing exit.

How it works...

The environment has now stopped. We have performed the start-up process in reverse. Always shut down the services on the application server before shutting down the database.

Creating a custom schema

When we create custom objects, we need to put them in a custom schema. Oracle has its own schemas for each of its modules such as HR or AP. The schema is defined within Oracle EBS as an application. For each standard schema we extend, you create a custom schema. A custom schema will begin with XX so that we can identify any extension that has been applied to an environment. So, let's say we are extending HR; we will create a custom schema called XXHR.

We are going to create a schema with the following details:

SCHEMA Name	XXHR
TOP Name	XXHR_TOP
Application	XXHR Custom Application
Data Group	Standard
Request Group	XXHR Request Group
Menu	XXHR_CUSTOM_MENU
Responsibility	XXHR Custom
APPL_TOP	/oracle/apps/r12/visr12/apps/apps_st/appl
Instance Name	VISR12
Server Name	oraclevisionr12

There are several tasks that need to be completed. They are as follows:

- Making a new environment parameter
- Running **AutoConfig** (adautocfg.sh)
- Creating a CUSTOM schema directory structure
- Adding the custom schema to the environment
- Creating a new tablespace
- Creating a database user
- Registering an Oracle schema
- Registering an Oracle user

Making a new environment parameter

We are now going to create a new environment parameter for our custom application. This is the only supported way to modify parameters that **AutoConfig** maintains. Do not edit any context files manually, as they will be overwritten the next time **AutoConfig** is run.

How to do it...

To create a new environment parameter, perform the following steps:

1. Log in to Oracle with the *system administrator* responsibility.

2. Navigate to **Oracle Applications Manager | Autoconfig** and the **Applications Manager** window will open, as shown in the following screenshot.

3. Select the **Manage Custom Parameters** link, as shown in the following screenshot:

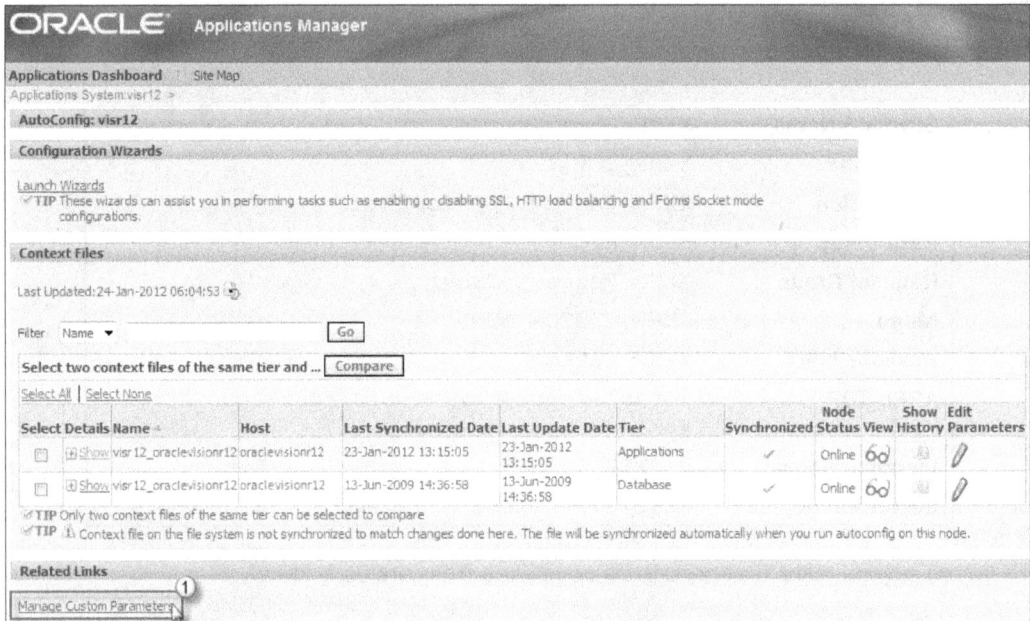

4. Select the **Add** button to add a new custom parameter to the context file, as shown in the following screenshot:

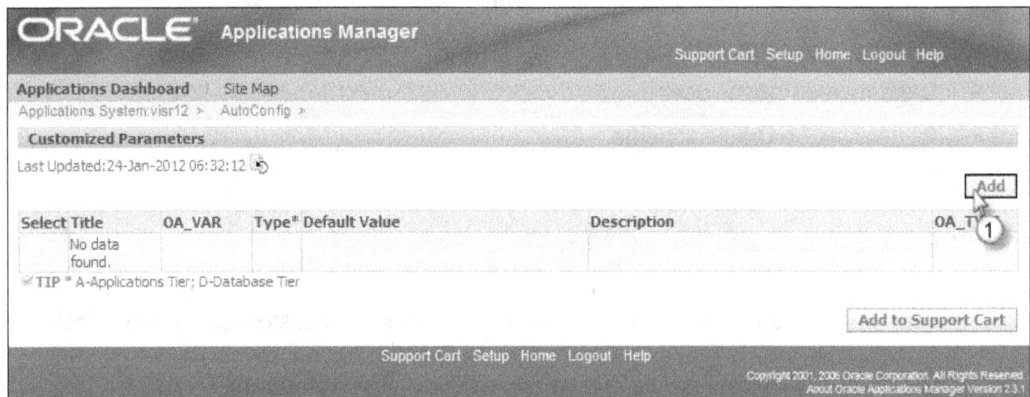

5. Select the **Applications Tier** radio button and click **Next**, as shown in the following screenshot:

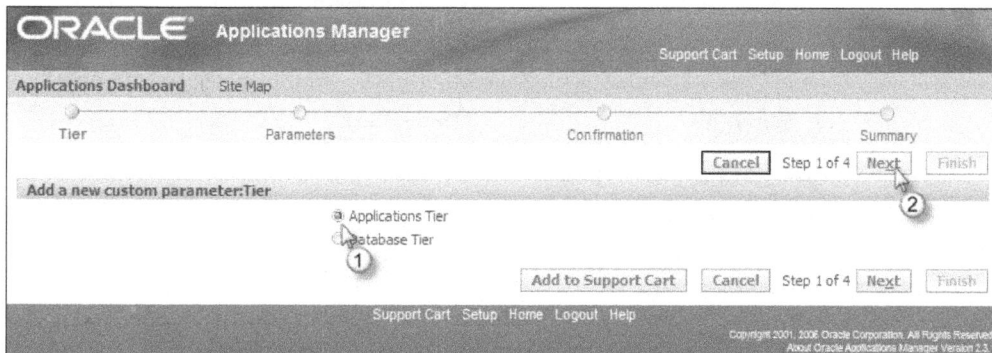

6. Enter the parameters shown in the following table and click the **Next** button:

Attribute	Value	Description
OA_VAR	c_xxhr_top	Naming convention in lowercase with no spaces and a *c_* prefix to indicate a non-standard parameter
Default Value	%s_at%/xxhr/12.0.0	Refer to the standard context-variables for the $APPL_TOP
Title	XXHR_TOP	Name of the top
Description	Custom top for HR	Description of the TOP
OA_TYPE	Select **PROD_TOP**	Define that it is a product top

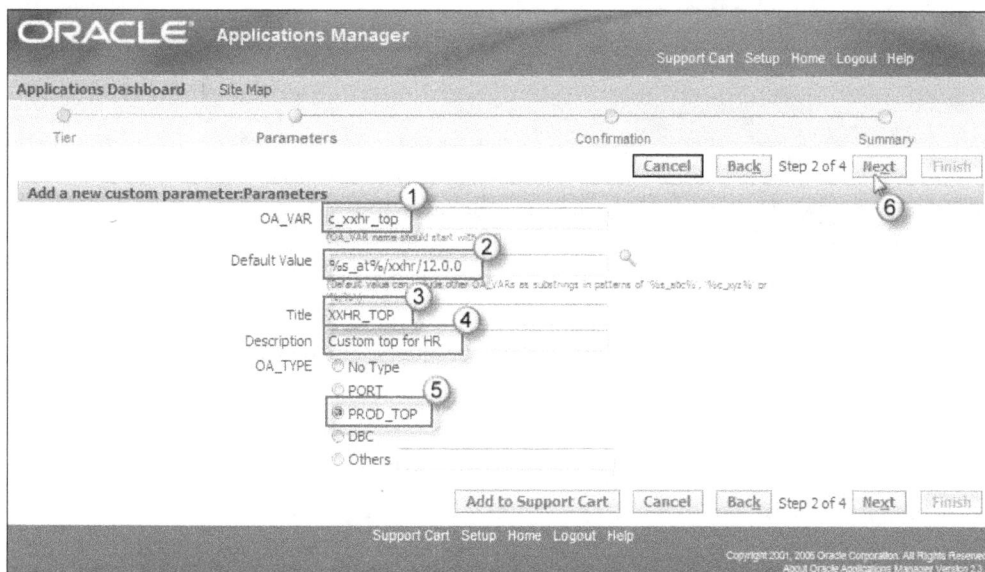

7. Click **Next**, as shown in the following screenshot, to confirm the details:

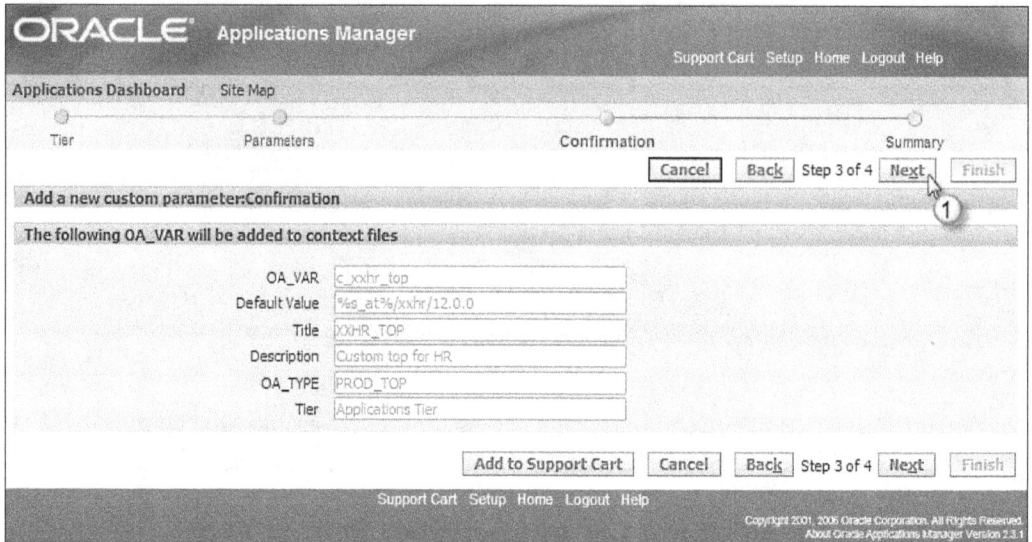

8. Click **Finish**.

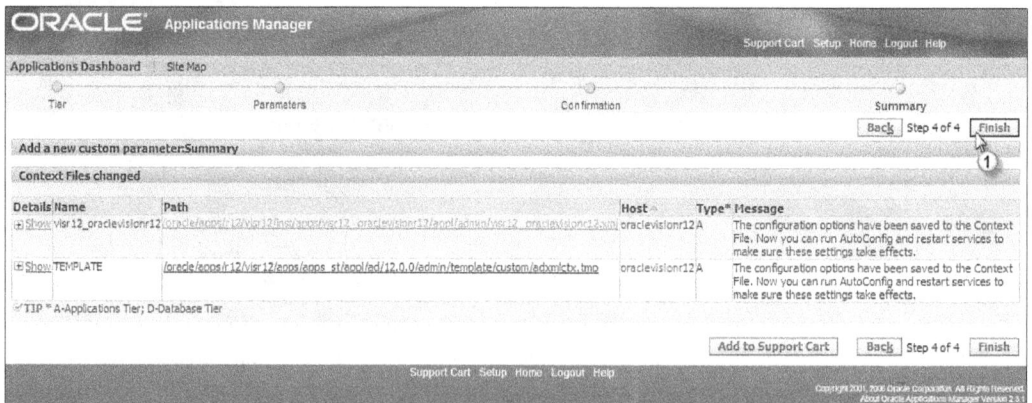

The parameter has now been created, as shown in the following screenshot:

Running AutoConfig (adautocfg.sh)

As mentioned previously, running **AutoConfig** is a utility provided by Oracle. It is run to configure the environment. It can be run both on the applications tier and the database tier, and it is run by executing a script called adautocfg.sh. We are only going to run it on the applications tier to pick up the environment parameter we have just created.

How to do it...

To run **AutoConfig**, perform the following steps:

1. Open **Putty** and connect to the application server with the OS user that owns the application tier.

2. Navigate to $INST_TOP/admin/scripts.

3. At the command prompt, type the following command to run **AutoConfig**:

   ```
   ./adautocfg.sh
   ```

4. The script will be prompt for the **apps** password, so enter it and press **RETURN**, as shown in the following screenshot:

```
[APPS_Tier@visr12]> ./adautocfg.sh  (1)
Enter the APPS user password:  (2)      Enter the apps password
                                            and RETURN
Context Value Management will no

        Updating Context file...COMPLETED

        Attempting upload of Context file and template

Configuring templates from all of the product tops...
        Configuring AD_TOP........COMPLETED
        Configuring FND_TOP.......COMPLETED
        Configuring ICX_TOP.......COMPLETED
        Configuring MSC_TOP.......COMPLETED
        Configuring IEO_TOP.......COMPLETED
        Configuring BIS_TOP.......COMPLETED
        Configuring AMS_TOP.......COMPLETED
        Configuring CCT_TOP.......COMPLETED
        Configuring WSH_TOP.......COMPLETED
        Configuring CLN_TOP.......COMPLETED
        Configuring OKE_TOP.......COMPLETED
        Configuring OKL_TOP.......COMPLETED
        Configuring OKS_TOP.......COMPLETED
        Configuring CSF_TOP.......COMPLETED
        Configuring IGS_TOP.......COMPLETED
        Configuring IBY_TOP.......COMPLETED
        Configuring JTF_TOP.......COMPLETED
        Configuring MWA_TOP.......COMPLETED
        Configuring CN_TOP........COMPLETED
        Configuring CSI_TOP.......COMPLETED
        Configuring WIP_TOP.......COMPLETED
        Configuring CSE_TOP.......COMPLETED
        Configuring EAM_TOP.......COMPLETED
        Configuring FTE_TOP.......COMPLETED
        Configuring ONT_TOP.......COMPLETED
        Configuring AR_TOP........COMPLETED
        Configuring AHL_TOP.......COMPLETED
        Configuring OZF_TOP.......COMPLETED
        Configuring IES_TOP.......COMPLETED
        Configuring CSD_TOP.......COMPLETED
        Configuring IGC_TOP.......COMPLETED

AutoConfig completed successfully.
[APPS_Tier@visr12]>
```

5. Wait for the script to complete before closing down **Putty**.

How it works...

We have now run **AutoConfig**, which will update the configuration files.

There's more...

Further information on configuring the environment can be found with the note *387859.1 Using AutoConfig to Manage System Configurations in Oracle E-Business Suite Release 12 available from the Oracle Support website.*

Creating a CUSTOM schema directory structure

Now that we have run **AutoConfig**, we need to create the directory structure for our custom application files. The directories are created on the application server under the $APPL_TOP directory. Each product then has its own directory structure under a short name or acronym. This is known as the **product top**. Oracle assumes that objects are stored in specific directories. This is why we need to be specific about the directory structure we create. We will log on to the application tier and create the directories with the applications tier user.

How to do it...

To create the Custom Top directory structure, perform the following steps:

1. Open **Putty** and log on to the application server with the applications tier user.

> We must log out of **Putty** or reset the environment after we have run AutoConfig to pick up the new environment variable for XXHR_TOP.

2. Set the environment (if it is not already set):

```
[avisr12@oraclevisionr12]$ . /oracle/apps/r12/visr12/apps/apps_st/appl/APPSvisr12_oraclevision.env
```

3. Navigate to the XXHR_TOP directory using the following command:

   `cd $XXHR_TOP`

4. Create a directory structure using the following commands:

> The directories are case sensitive and so must be created exactly as shown. You will notice that some of the directories have already been created such as log, out, and mesg.

```
mkdir $XXHR_TOP/admin
mkdir $XXHR_TOP/admin/sql
mkdir $XXHR_TOP/admin/odf
mkdir $XXHR_TOP/sql
mkdir $XXHR_TOP/bin
mkdir $XXHR_TOP/reports
mkdir $XXHR_TOP/reports/US
mkdir $XXHR_TOP/forms
mkdir $XXHR_TOP/forms/US
```

```
mkdir $XXHR_TOP/lib

mkdir $XXHR_TOP/install

mkdir $XXHR_TOP/install/ch1

mkdir $XXHR_TOP/install/ch2

mkdir $XXHR_TOP/install/ch3

mkdir $XXHR_TOP/install/ch4

mkdir $XXHR_TOP/install/ch5

mkdir $XXHR_TOP/install/ch6
```

After the directories have been created, the structure should resemble the following hierarchy:

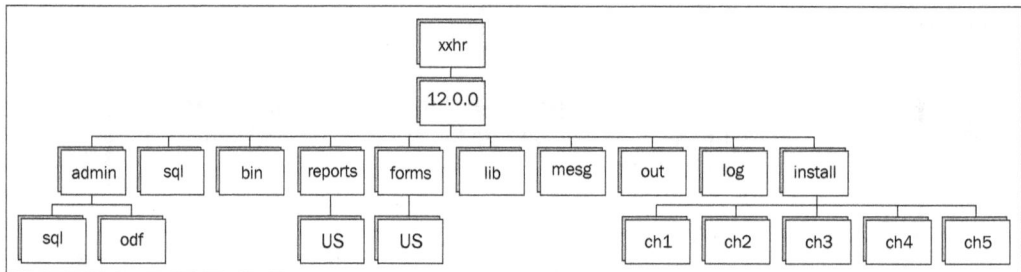

How it works...

The custom schema has been added to the context file by the configuration we performed in the previous recipe. The environment context file is an XML file that is on the application server. When we register the custom schema later, we will define the custom top called XXHR_TOP within the application. The applications context file is a repository for environment-specific details used by AutoConfig to configure the application tier. AutoConfig is a utility provided by Oracle that gets the information from the context file (and other files), automatically generates Oracle E-Business Suite configuration files, and updates relevant database profiles.

Creating a new tablespace

We now need to create a physical file to store data of our custom objects.

How to do it...

To create a tablespace, perform the following steps:

1. Log on to SQL*Plus as the **applsys** user.

2. Run the following command:

   ```
   SQL>create tablespace XXHR datafile '/oracle/apps/r12/visr12/db/
   apps_st/data/XXHR01.dbf' size 500M
   ```

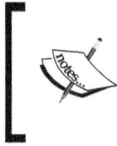

> Note that the directory in the preceding SQL statement is for the environment that is used for writing the book. The .dbf files need to be created in the DATA_TOP of the environment you are using.

3. Exit SQL*Plus.

How it works...

We have created a data file that will store all of our custom data of any database object we create in our custom schema.

Creating a database user

We also need to create a database user where we will create all of our database objects.

How to do it...

To create a database user, perform the following:

1. Log on to SQL*Plus as the **applsys** user.
2. Run the following command:

```
SQL>create user XXHR identified by XXHR
default tablespace apps_ts_tx_data
temporary tablespace temp
quota unlimited on apps_ts_tx_idx;
```

3. Exit SQL*Plus.

How it works...

We have now created a database user with the password xxhr. When we create custom objects that store any data, they will be owned by the custom user. The custom user uses the tablespace we created earlier.

Registering an Oracle schema

We must register the new XXHR schema in Oracle E-Business Suite. We need to create the application so that Oracle knows where to look on the filesystem for custom objects. We defined our environment variable in an earlier recipe that translates our application base path. We create a custom application so that we can isolate any customizations we make.

> If you already created the application in *Chapter 1, Creating Concurrent Programs*, then you will not need to do so again.

How to do it...

To register an Oracle schema, perform the following:

1. Log in to Oracle with the *system administrator* responsibility.
2. Navigate to **Application | Register** and the **Applications** window will open.
3. Enter the application details, as per the following table:

Application	XXHR Custom Application
Short Name	XXHR
Basepath	XXHR_TOP
Description	XXHR Custom Application

The screen should now look like the following screenshot:

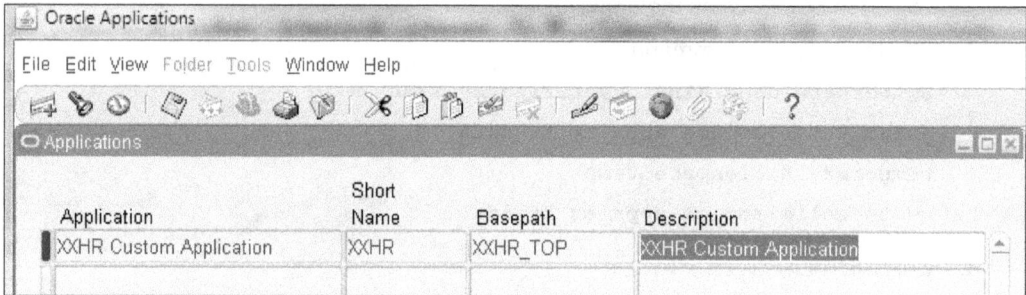

4. Save the record.

How it works...

We have now registered the custom schema in Oracle. We can see that the **Application**, **Short Name**, and the **Basepath** are defined here and this is what is used to identify where custom objects will be found.

Registering an Oracle user

We will now register the Oracle user. We have already created the database user and here we are registering that user within the **Oracle Application Library**. We only need to register an Oracle user when we create a custom application.

How to do it...

1. Log in to Oracle with the *system administrator* responsibility.

2. Navigate to **Security | ORACLE | Register**.

3. Enter the application details, as per the following table:

Database User Name	XXHR
Password	xxhr
Privilege	Enabled
Install Group	0
Description	XXHR Application User

The screen should now look like the following screenshot:

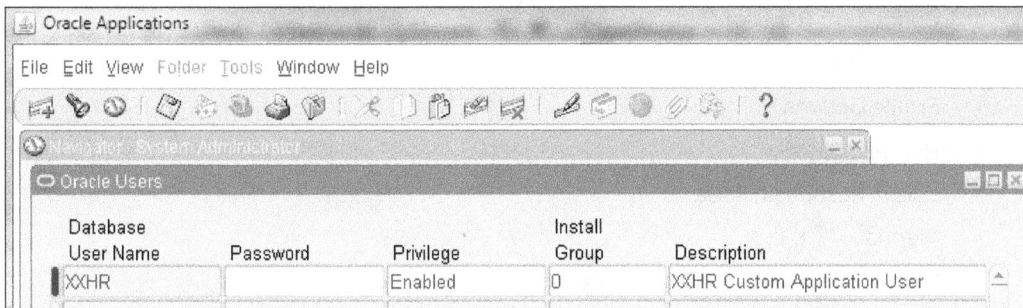

How it works...

We have now registered the database user for our custom application.

There's more...

Registering the user also enables this schema in the *gather schema statistics* concurrent program, so the schema can be analyzed by the Oracle-standard concurrent program.

Extracting data using FNDLOAD

Oracle provides a tool called **FNDLOAD**, which is also known as the **generic loader**. This tool is actually a concurrent program that performs the migration of the configuration data between instances of Oracle E-Business Suite. It is a command-line utility that is usually executed via a script. There are two stages to migrating configuration. The first step is to download the configuration from one environment and the second is to upload it to a target environment. The download process creates a file or files with an LDT extension, which is a text file. There are a number of benefits to using FNDLOAD. It means there is no manual user entry, which is prone to error. It is also much quicker to use than manual configuration. The limitation of FNDLOAD is that there are only a limited number of configuration items that can be migrated with FNDLOAD. These are the following:

- ▸ Request Groups
- ▸ Lookups
- ▸ Descriptive Flexfields
- ▸ Key Flexfield Structures
- ▸ Printer Styles
- ▸ Concurrent Programs
- ▸ Concurrent Request Sets
- ▸ Value Sets
- ▸ Profile Options
- ▸ Request Sets
- ▸ Users/Responsibilities
- ▸ Menus
- ▸ Forms, Functions, and Personalization
- ▸ Alerts
- ▸ Blobs (r12)
- ▸ NLS Languages
- ▸ Custom Messages
- ▸ Role Registration

The syntax for FNDLOAD is `FNDLOAD apps/<apps pwd> 0 Y <mode><configfile><datafile><entity> [ param ... ]`

The parameters we need to pass are as follows:

- `<apps pwd>`—This is the **apps** password.

- `<mode>`—This is either DOWNLOAD or UPLOAD. This determines if we are going to download the configuration or upload it from our datafile.

- `<config file>`—This is the configuration file that will be used to determine what it is we are uploading or downloading. It usually has a `.lct` extension. For example, there is an `LCT` file called `afcpprog.lct` that we use for migrating concurrent programs.

- `<datafile>`—The datafile is the name of the text file that is created when we download the configuration. We would normally name the file `.ldt`, but this is not mandatory. However, the extension is commonly used across implementations.

- `<entities>`—This parameter defines the entity or entities that are being downloaded. When we upload files, we upload all entities present in the datafile.

- `<param ...>`—We can add additional parameters that act as bind variables to the SQL statement that is executed. The parameter is in the format `NAME=VALUE.NAME`.

For more detailed information or any other uses of FNDLOAD, please refer to the *Oracle Applications System Administrators Guide.*

In our examples, we are going to use FNDLOAD to upload the configuration we have performed throughout the book. We are going to perform the following tasks:

- Extracting a lookup using FNDLOAD

- Extracting a descriptive Flexfield using FNDLOAD

- Extracting a concurrent program using FNDLOAD

- Extracting a concurrent request set using FNDLOAD

- Extracting a request set using FNDLOAD

- Extracting a profile option using FNDLOAD

- Extracting a form and function using FNLOAD

- Extracting a menu using FNDLOAD

- Extracting a request group using FNDLOAD

- Extracting a responsibility using FNDLOAD

- Extracting a personalization using FNDLOAD

- Extracting a message using FNDLOAD

- Downloading multiple objects

Extracting a lookup using FNDLOAD

We are going to extract a lookup we have created earlier in the book. The LCT file used for downloading lookups is `aflvmlu.lct`. We are going to run the FNDLOAD and create a file called `LU_XXHR_SOCIETY_LOV.ldt`. The text file will contain the entity definition and the data for the `XXHR_SOCIETY_LOV` lookup.

How to do it...

To download the lookup with FNDLOAD, perform the following:

1. Open **Putty** and connect to the application server with the user that owns the application tier.

2. Navigate to `$XXHR_TOP/install/ch6` by typing the following command:

   cd $XXHR_TOP/install/ch6

3. At the command prompt, type `pwd` to check the directory we are in.

4. At the command prompt, type the following command to extract the lookup:

   FNDLOAD apps/apps O Y DOWNLOAD $FND_TOP/patch/115/import/aflvmlu. lct LU_XXHR_SOCIETY_LOV.ldt FND_LOOKUP_TYPE APPLICATION_SHORT_ NAME='XXHR' LOOKUP_TYPE='XXHR_SOCIETY_LOV'

5. At the command prompt, type the following command:

   ls -al

6. Open the LOG and LDT files to check that they have been successfully created:

Just a word of warning—the `LDT` file may well have been created even though there has been a problem with the download. For example, let's say you run the following command:

```
FNDLOAD apps/apps O Y DOWNLOAD $FND_TOP/patch/115/import/
aflvmlu.lct LU_XXHR_SOCIETY_LOV1.ldt FND_LOOKUP_TYPE
APPLICATION_SHORT_NAME='XXHR' LOOKUP_TYPE='XXHR_SOCIETY_
LOV1'
```

Then we would generate a file for a lookup that does not exist. The only change is the name of the lookup, which, as mentioned, does not exist in Oracle EBS. The `LU_XXHR_SOCIETY_LOV1.ldt` file is still created. However, if you now compare the two files that have been created, the `LU_XXHR_SOCIETY_LOV.ldt` file has all of the data from the lookup and `LU_XXHR_SOCIETY_LOV1.ldt` contains nothing after the **# – End Entity Definitions –** section, as illustrated in the following screenshot:

How it works...

We have executed the command line for the FNDLOAD utility to download the `XXHR_SOCIETY_LOV` lookup we created in an earlier chapter. The FNDLOAD utility completed and generated a text file called `LU_XXHR_SOCIETY_LOV.ldt`. We can now take this text file and upload it to a different environment.

Extracting a Descriptive Flexfield using FNDLOAD

We are going to extract the Descriptive Flexfield (DFF) we created earlier in the book. The LCT file used for downloading Flexfields is `afffload.lct`. We are going to run the FNDLOAD and create a file called `DFF_XXHR_PER_SOCIETIES.ldt`. The text file will contain the entity definition and the data for the XXHR_PER_SOCIETIES DFF.

How to do it...

To download the DFF with FNDLOAD, perform the following steps:

1. Open **Putty** and connect to the application server with the user that owns the application tier.

2. Navigate to $XXHR_TOP/install/ch6 by typing the following command:

   cd $XXHR_TOP/install/ch6

3. At the command prompt, type pwd to check the directory we are in.

4. At the command prompt, type the following command to extract the DFF:

   **FNDLOAD apps/apps O Y DOWNLOAD $FND_TOP/patch/115/import/afffload.
   lct DFF_XXHR_PER_SOCIETIES.ldt DESC_FLEX APPLICATION_SHORT_
   NAME='XXHR' DESCRIPTIVE_FLEXFIELD_NAME='XXHR_PER_SOCIETIES'**

5. At the command prompt, type to check that the LDT file has been created:

   ls -al

6. Check the LOG and LDT files to check that the data has been successfully downloaded.

How it works...

We executed the command line for the FNDLOAD utility to download the XXHR_PER_SOCIETIES DFF we created in an earlier chapter. The FNDLOAD utility completed and generated a text file called DFF_XXHR_PER_SOCIETIES.ldt. We can now take this text file and upload it to a different environment.

Extracting a concurrent program using FNDLOAD

We are going to extract a concurrent program we have created earlier in the book. The LCT file used for downloading concurrent programs is `afcpprog.lct`. We are going to run the FNDLOAD and create a file called CP_XXHR_FIRST_CONC_PROG.ldt. The text file will contain the entity definition and the data for the XXHR_FIRST_CONC_PROG concurrent program.

How to do it...

To download the concurrent program with FNDLOAD, perform the following:

1. Open **Putty** and connect to the application server with the user that owns the application tier.

2. Navigate to `$XXHR_TOP/install/ch6` by typing the following command:

   cd $XXHR_TOP/install/ch6

3. At the command prompt, type `pwd` to check the directory we are in.

4. At the command prompt, type the following command to extract the concurrent program:

   **FNDLOAD apps/apps O Y DOWNLOAD $FND_TOP/patch/115/import/afcpprog.
   lct CP_XXHR_FIRST_CONC_PROG.ldt PROGRAM APPLICATION_SHORT_
   NAME="XXHR" CONCURRENT_PROGRAM_NAME="XXHR_FIRST_CONC_PROG"**

5. At the command prompt, type to check that the LDT file has been created:

   ls -al

6. Check the LOG and LDT files to check that the data has been successfully downloaded.

How it works...

We have executed the command line for the FNDLOAD utility to download the XXHR_FIRST_CONC_PROG concurrent program we created in an earlier chapter. The FNDLOAD utility completed and generated a text file called CP_XXHR_FIRST_CONC_PROG. ldt. Any associated configuration, such as the executable and value sets, are also included in the download, so we will not need to load these separately. We can now take this text file and upload it to a different environment.

Extracting a request set using FNDLOAD

We are going to extract a request set we have created earlier in the book. The LCT file used for downloading request sets is afcprset.lct. This one is slightly different in that we need to extract the request set definition and the request set links definition. We are going to run the FNDLOAD and create a file called RS_XXHR20001.ldt for the request set and RSL_XXHR20001.ldt for the request set links. The text file will contain the entity definition and the data for the XXHR20001 request set.

How to do it...

To download the request set with FNDLOAD, perform the following:

1. Open **Putty** and connect to the application server with the user that owns the application tier.

2. Navigate to `$XXHR_TOP/install/ch6` by typing the following command:

   ```
   cd $XXHR_TOP/install/ch6
   ```

3. At the command prompt, type `pwd` to check the directory we are in.

4. At the command prompt, type the following command to extract the request set:

   ```
   FNDLOAD apps/apps 0 Y DOWNLOAD $FND_TOP/patch/115/import/afcprset.
   lct RS_XXHR20001.ldt REQ_SET REQUEST_SET_NAME="FNDRSSUB3714"
   ```

> Note that the `REQUEST_SET_NAME` parameter is the **Set Code** that was automatically created by the request set wizard. Therefore, you will need to use the value that is present in the **Request Set Window**, as shown in the following screenshot:

5. At the command prompt, type the following command to extract the request set links:

   ```
   FNDLOAD apps/apps 0 Y DOWNLOAD $FND_TOP/patch/115/import/
   afcprset.lct RSL_XXHR20001.ldt REQ_SET_LINKS REQUEST_SET_
   NAME="FNDRSSUB3714"
   ```

6. At the command prompt, type to check that the `LDT` file has been created:

   ```
   ls -al
   ```

7. Check the `LOG` and `LDT` files to check that the data has been successfully downloaded.

How it works...

We have executed the command line for the FNDLOAD utility to download the XXHR20001 request set we created in an earlier chapter. The utility has completed and generated two text files called RS_XXHR20001.ldt and RSL_XXHR20001.ldt. We can now take these text files and upload them to a different environment.

Extracting a profile option using FNDLOAD

We are going to extract a profile option we created earlier in the book. The LCT file used for downloading profile options is afscprof.lct. We are going to run FNDLOAD and create a file called PROF_XXHR_WRITE_LOGFILE.ldt. The text file will contain the entity definition and the data for the XXHR Write to Concurrent Program Logfile profile option. If the profile option has a value, it will also be extracted in the extract file.

How to do it...

To download the profile option with FNDLOAD, perform the following:

1. Open **Putty** and connect to the application server with the user that owns the application tier.

2. Navigate to $XXHR_TOP/install/ch6 by typing the following command:

   cd $XXHR_TOP/install/ch6

3. At the command prompt, type pwd to check the directory we are in.

4. At the command prompt, type the following command to extract the profile option:

   FNDLOAD apps/apps O Y DOWNLOAD $FND_TOP/patch/115/import/afscprof. lct PROF_XXHR_WRITE_LOGFILE.ldt PROFILE PROFILE_NAME="XXHR_WRITE_ LOGFILE" APPLICATION_SHORT_NAME="XXHR"

5. At the command prompt, type to check that the LDT file has been created:

   ls -al

6. Check the LOG and LDT files to check that the data has been successfully downloaded.

How it works...

We executed the command line for the FNDLOAD utility to download the XXHR_WRITE_ LOGFILE profile option we created in an earlier chapter. The FNDLOAD utility completed and generated a text file called PROF_XXHR_WRITE_LOGFILE.ldt. We can now take this text file and upload it to a different environment. You may notice, if you look at the LDT text file, that the profile option values are also migrated along with the profile option definition.

Extracting a form and function using FNDLOAD

We are going to extract the form/function definitions we have created earlier in the book. The LCT file used for downloading forms and functions is afsload.lct. We are going to run the FNDLOAD and create two files called FORM_XXHRSOCC.ldt and FUNC_XXHR_EMP_SOCIETY.ldt. The text file will contain the entity definition for the **Clubs and Societies Form** and the Employee, Clubs, and Societies function.

How to do it...

To download the form and function definitions with FNDLOAD, perform the following:

1. Open **Putty** and connect to the application server with the user that owns the application tier.

2. Navigate to $XXHR_TOP/install/ch6 by typing the following command:

   ```
   cd $XXHR_TOP/install/ch6
   ```

3. At the command prompt, type pwd to check the directory we are in.

4. At the command prompt, type the following command to extract the form:

   ```
   FNDLOAD apps/apps O Y DOWNLOAD $FND_TOP/patch/115/import/afsload.
   lctFORM_XXHRSOCC.ldt FORM FORM_APP_SHORT_NAME='XXHR' FORM_
   NAME='XXHRSOCC'
   ```

5. At the command prompt, type the following command to extract the form function:

   ```
   FNDLOAD apps/apps O Y DOWNLOAD $FND_TOP/patch/115/import/afsload.
   lctFUNC_XXHR_EMP_SOCIETY.ldt FUNCTION FUNC_APP_SHORT_NAME='XXHR'
   FUNCTION_NAME='XXHR_EMP_SOCIETY'
   ```

6. At the command prompt, type to check that the LDT file has been created:

   ```
   ls -al
   ```

7. Check the LOG and LDT files to check that the data has been successfully downloaded.

How it works...

We executed the command line for the FNDLOAD utility to download the form and function definitions we created for the **Clubs and Societies** form. The FNDLOAD utility completed and generated two text files called FORM_XXHRSOCC.ldt and FUNC_XXHR_EMP_SOCIETY.ldt. We can now take this text file and upload it to a different environment.

There's more...

It is worth noting that if an object contains sub objects, then the sub objects are also included in the file extracted by the FNDLOAD. For example, if a menu has functions associated with it and the functions have forms registered with them, the menu, functions, and forms will be included in the FNDLOAD file. Therefore, it is important to remember this when downloading using FNDLOAD.

Extracting a menu using FNDLOAD

We are going to extract a menu we created earlier in the book. The LCT file used for downloading menus is afsload.lct. We are going to run the FNDLOAD and create a file called MENU_XXHR_TEST_MENU.ldt. The text file will contain the entity definition and the data for the **XXHR Administration** menu.

How to do it...

To download the menu with FNDLOAD, perform the following steps:

1. Open **Putty** and connect to the application server with the user that owns the application tier.

2. Navigate to $XXHR_TOP/install/ch6 by typing the following command:

   cd $XXHR_TOP/install/ch6

3. At the command prompt, type pwd to check the directory we are in.

4. At the command prompt, type the following command to extract the menu:

   FNDLOAD apps/apps O Y DOWNLOAD $FND_TOP/patch/115/import/afsload.
   lct MENU_XXHR_TEST_MENU.ldt MENU MENU_NAME="XXHR_TEST_MENU"

5. At the command prompt, type the following command to check that the LDT file has been created:

   ls -al

6. Check the LOG and LDT files to check that the data has been successfully downloaded.

How it works...

We executed the command line for the FNDLOAD utility to download the XXHR Administration Menu we created in an earlier chapter. The FNDLOAD utility completed and generated a text file called MENU_XXHR_MENU.ldt. We can now take this text file and upload it to a different environment.

Extracting a request group using FNDLOAD

We are going to extract a request group we created earlier in the book. The LCT file used for downloading menus is afcpreqg.lct. We are going to run the FNDLOAD and create a file called RG_XXHR_REQUEST_GROUP.ldt. The text file will contain the entity definition and the data for the XXHR Administration Menu.

How to do it...

To download the menu with FNDLOAD, perform the following:

1. Open **Putty** and connect to the application server with the user that owns the application tier.

2. Navigate to $XXHR_TOP/install/ch6 by typing the following command:

    ```
    cd $XXHR_TOP/install/ch6
    ```

3. At the command prompt, type pwd to check the directory we are in.

4. At the command prompt, type the following command to extract the request group:

    ```
    FNDLOAD apps/apps O Y DOWNLOAD $FND_TOP/patch/115/import/afcpreqg.
    lct RG_XXHR_REQUEST_GROUP.ldt REQUEST_GROUP REQUEST_GROUP_
    NAME"XXHR_REQUEST_GROUP" APPLICATION_SHORT_NAME="XXHR"
    ```

5. At the command prompt, type the following to check that the LDT file has been created:

    ```
    ls -al
    ```

6. Check the LOG and LDT files to check that the data has been successfully downloaded.

How it works...

We executed the command line for the FNDLOAD utility to download the XXHR Request Group we created in an earlier chapter. The FNDLOAD utility completed and generated a text file called RG_XXHR_REQUEST_GROUP.ldt. We can now take this text file and upload it to a different environment.

Extracting a responsibility using FNDLOAD

We are going to extract a responsibility we created earlier in the book. The LCT file used for downloading Flexfields is afscursp.lct. We are going to run the FNDLOAD and create a file called RESP_XXHR_ADMIN.ldt. The text file will contain the entity definition and the data for the **XXEBS Extending e-Business Suite** responsibility.

How to do it...

To download the responsibility with FNDLOAD, perform the following steps:

1. Open **Putty** and connect to the application server with the user that owns the application tier.

2. Navigate to $XXHR_TOP/install/ch6 by typing the following command:

   ```
   cd $XXHR_TOP/install/ch6
   ```

3. At the command prompt, type pwd to check the directory we are in.

4. At the command prompt, type the following command to extract the responsibility:

   ```
   FNDLOAD apps/apps O Y DOWNLOAD $FND_TOP/patch/115/import/afscursp.
   lct RESP_XXHR_ADMIN.ldt FND_RESPONSIBILITY RESP_KEY="XXHR_ADMIN"
   ```

5. At the command prompt, type the following to check that the LDT file has been created:

   ```
   ls -al
   ```

6. Check the LOG and LDT files to check that the data has been successfully downloaded.

How it works...

We executed the command line for the FNDLOAD utility to download the **XXEBS Extending e-Business Suite** responsibility we created in an earlier chapter. The FNDLOAD utility completed and generated a text file called RESP_XXHR_ADMIN.ldt. We can now take this text file and upload it to a different environment.

Extracting a personalization using FNDLOAD

We are going to extract the personalization we created earlier in the book. The LCT file used for downloading Flexfields is affrmcus.lct. We are going to run the FNDLOAD and create a file called PZ_PERWSHRG.ldt. The text file will contain the entity definition and the data for the **People** form personalization.

How to do it...

To download the personalization with FNDLOAD, perform the following steps:

1. Open **Putty** and connect to the application server with the user that owns the application tier.

2. Navigate to $XXHR_TOP/install/ch6 by typing the following command:

   ```
   cd $XXHR_TOP/install/ch6
   ```

3. At the command prompt, type pwd to check the directory we are in.

4. At the command prompt, type the following command to extract the personalization:

    ```
    FNDLOAD apps/apps O Y DOWNLOAD $FND_TOP/patch/115/import/affrmcus.
    lct PZ_PERWSHRG.ldt FND_FORM_CUSTOM_RULES FORM_NAME="PERWSHRG"
    ```

5. At the command prompt, type the following to check that the LDT file has been created:

    ```
    ls -al
    ```

6. Check the LOG and LDT files to check that the data has been successfully downloaded.

How it works...

We executed the command line for the FNDLOAD utility to download the personalization we created in *Chapter 3, Advanced Oracle Forms*. The FNDLOAD utility completed and generated a text file called PZ_PERWSHRG.ldt. We can now take this text file and upload it to a different environment.

Extracting a message using FNDLOAD

We are going to extract a message we created earlier in the book. The LCT file used for downloading Flexfields is afmdmsg.lct. We are going to run the FNDLOAD and create a file called MESG_XXHR_ON_HOLD_WARNING.ldt. The text file will contain the entity definition and the data for the On Hold Warning message.

How to do it...

To download the message with FNDLOAD, perform the following steps:

1. Open **Putty** and connect to the application server with the user that owns the application tier.

2. Navigate to $XXHR_TOP/install/ch6 by typing the following command:

    ```
    cd $XXHR_TOP/install/ch6
    ```

3. At the command prompt, type pwd to check the directory we are in.

4. At the command prompt, type the following command to extract the profile option:

    ```
    FNDLOAD apps/apps O Y DOWNLOAD $FND_TOP/patch/115/import/afmdmsg.
    lct MESG_XXHR_ON_HOLD_WARNING.ldt FND_NEW_MESSAGES APPLICATION_
    SHORT_NAME="XXHR" MESSAGE_NAME="XXHR_ON_HOLD_WARNING"
    ```

5. At the command prompt, type the following to check that the LDT file has been created:

    ```
    ls -al
    ```

6. Check the LOG and LDT files to check that the data has been successfully downloaded.

How it works...

We executed the command line for the FNDLOAD utility to download the XXHR_ON_HOLD_WARNING message we created in an earlier chapter. The FNDLOAD utility completed and generated a text file called MESG_XXHR_ON_HOLD_WARNING.ldt. We can now take this text file and upload it to a different environment.

Downloading multiple objects

We are going to extract all the concurrent programs we have created earlier in the book. The LCT file used for downloading concurrent programs is afcpprog.lct. We are going to run the FNDLOAD and create a file called CP_XXHR_ALL_CONC_PROG.ldt. The text file will contain the entity definition and the data for the concurrent programs starting with XX.

How to do it...

To download the concurrent programs beginning with XX, perform the following steps:

1. Open **Putty** and connect to the application server with the user that owns the application tier.

2. Navigate to $XXHR_TOP/install/ch6 by typing the following command:

   ```
   cd $XXHR_TOP/install/ch6
   ```

3. At the command prompt, type pwd to check the directory we are in.

4. At the command prompt, type the following command to extract the concurrent program:

   ```
   FNDLOAD apps/apps O Y DOWNLOAD $FND_TOP/patch/115/import/
   afcpprog.lct CP_XXHR_ALL_CONC_PROG.ldt PROGRAM APPLICATION_SHORT_
   NAME="XXHR" CONCURRENT_PROGRAM_NAME="XXHR%"
   ```

5. At the command prompt, type the following to check that the LDT file has been created:

   ```
   ls -al
   ```

6. Check the LOG and LDT files to check that the data has been successfully downloaded.

How it works...

We have executed the command line for the FNDLOAD utility to download all the concurrent programs, beginning with XXHR. The changes we made to the command line were the name of the LDT file to CP_XXHR_ALL_CONC_PROG.ldt and we also put a wildcard into the CONCURRENT_PROGRAM_NAME parameter. It became "*XXHR%*".

Uploading using FNDLOAD

We are now going to upload the LDT files that we have created. The idea is to upload the FNDLOAD files to a separate environment, as this is what we would do if we did it for real. We will perform the following *fnd* upload tasks:

1. Uploading a lookup using FNDLOAD
2. Uploading a Descriptive Flexfield using FNDLOAD
3. Uploading a concurrent program using FNDLOAD
4. Uploading a request set using FNDLOAD
5. Uploading a profile option using FNDLOAD
6. Uploading a form and function using FNDLOAD
7. Uploading a menu using FNDLOAD
8. Uploading a request group using FNDLOAD
9. Uploading a responsibility using FNDLOAD
10. Uploading a personalization using FNDLOAD
11. Uploading a message using FNDLOAD
12. Modifying the LDT file

Uploading a lookup using FNDLOAD

We are going to upload a lookup we have created in the earlier recipes. The LCT file used for uploading lookups is `aflvmlu.lct`. We are going to run FNDLOAD and upload the file we created called `LU_XXHR_SOCIETY_LOV.ldt`. The text file contains the entity definition and the data for the `XXHR_SOCIETY_LOV` lookup.

How to do it...

To upload the lookup with FNDLOAD, perform the following steps:

1. Open **Putty** and connect to the application server with the user that owns the application tier.
2. Navigate to `$XXHR_TOP/install/ch6` by typing the following command:

   ```
   cd $XXHR_TOP/install/ch6
   ```

3. At the command prompt, type `pwd` to check the directory we are in.
4. At the command prompt, type the following command to upload the lookup:

   ```
   FNDLOAD apps/apps O Y UPLOAD $FND_TOP/patch/115/import/aflvmlu.lct
   LU_XXHR_SOCIETY_LOV.ldt
   ```

5. At the command prompt, type the following:

   ```
   ls -al
   ```

6. Open the LOG and LDT files to check whether they have been successfully created.

How it works...

We have executed the command line for the FNDLOAD utility to upload the XXHR_SOCIETY_LOV lookup into a new environment.

Uploading a Descriptive Flexfield using FNDLOAD

We are going to upload the Descriptive Flexfield (DFF) we created in the earlier recipes. The LCT file used for uploading Flexfields is affload.lct. We are going to run FNDLOAD and upload the file we created called DFF_XXHR_PER_SOCIETIES.ldt. The text file contains the entity definition and the data for the XXHR_PER_SOCIETIES DFF.

How to do it...

To upload the DFF with FNDLOAD, perform the following steps:

1. Open **Putty** and connect to the application server with the user that owns the application tier.

2. Navigate to $XXHR_TOP/install/ch6 by typing the following command:

   cd $XXHR_TOP/install/ch6

3. At the command prompt, type pwd to check the directory we are in.

4. At the command prompt, type the following command to upload the DFF:

   FNDLOAD apps/apps O Y DOWNLOAD $FND_TOP/patch/115/import/affload. lct DFF_XXHR_PER_SOCIETIES.ldt

5. At the command prompt, type the following to check that the LDT file has been created:

   ```
   ls -al
   ```

6. Check the LOG and LDT files to check that the data has been successfully downloaded.

How it works...

We executed the command line for the FNDLOAD utility to upload the XXHR_PER_SOCIETIES DFF into a new environment.

Uploading a concurrent program using FNDLOAD

We are going to upload a concurrent program we have created in earlier recipes. The
LCT file used for uploading concurrent programs is afcpprog.lct. We are going to run
FNDLOAD and upload the file we created called CP_XXHR_FIRST_CONC_PROG.ldt. The
text file contains the entity definition and the data for the XXHR_FIRST_CONC_PROG
concurrent program.

How to do it...

To upload the concurrent program with FNDLOAD, perform the following steps:

1. Open **Putty** and connect to the application server with the user that owns the
   application tier.

2. Navigate to $XXHR_TOP/install/ch6 by typing the following command:

   cd $XXHR_TOP/install/ch6

3. At the command prompt, type pwd to check the directory we are in.

4. At the command prompt, type the following command to upload the
   concurrent program:

   **FNDLOAD apps/apps O Y DOWNLOAD $FND_TOP/patch/115/import/afcpprog.
   lct CP_XXHR_FIRST_CONC_PROG.ldt**

5. At the command prompt, type the following to check that the LDT file has
   been created:

   ls -al

6. Check the LOG and LDT files to check that the data has been successfully downloaded.

How it works...

We have executed the command line for the FNDLOAD utility to upload the XXHR_FIRST_
CONC_PROG concurrent program into a new environment. The FNDLOAD utility completed and
generated a text file called CP_XXHR_FIRST_CONC_PROG.ldt. Any associated configuration,
such as the executable and value sets, are also included in the download, so we will not need to
load these separately. We can now take this text file and upload it to a different environment.

Uploading a request set using FNDLOAD

We are going to upload a request set we have created in the earlier recipes. The LCT file used
for uploading request sets is afcprset.lct. This one is slightly different in that we need
to upload the request set definition and the request set links definition. We are going to run
FNDLOAD and upload the two files we created called RS_XXHR20001.ldt for the request set
and RSL_XXHR20001.ldt for the request set links.

How to do it...

To upload the request set with FNDLOAD, perform the following:

1. Open **Putty** and connect to the application server with the user that owns the application tier.

2. Navigate to $XXHR_TOP/install/ch6 by typing the following command:

   ```
   cd $XXHR_TOP/install/ch6
   ```

3. At the command prompt, type pwd to check the directory we are in.

4. At the command prompt, type the following command to upload the request set:

   ```
   FNDLOAD apps/apps 0 Y DOWNLOAD $FND_TOP/patch/115/import/afcprset.
   lct RS_XXHR20001.ldt
   ```

5. At the command prompt, type the following command to upload the request set links:

   ```
   FNDLOAD apps/apps 0 Y DOWNLOAD $FND_TOP/patch/115/import/afcprset.
   lct RSL_XXHR20001.ldt
   ```

6. At the command prompt, type the following to check that the LDT file has been created:

   ```
   ls -al
   ```

7. Check the LOG and LDT files to check that the data has been successfully downloaded.

How it works...

We have executed the command line for the FNDLOAD utility to upload the XXHR20001 request set into a new environment.

Uploading a profile option using FNDLOAD

We are going to upload a profile option that we created in the earlier recipes. The LCT file used for uploading profile options is afscprof.lct. We are going to run FNDLOAD and upload the file we created called PROF_XXHR_WRITE_LOGFILE.ldt. The text file contains the entity definition and the data for the XXHR Write to Concurrent Program Logfile profile option.

How to do it...

To upload the profile option with FNDLOAD, perform the following steps:

1. Open **Putty** and connect to the application server with the user that owns the application tier.

2. Navigate to $XXHR_TOP/install/ch6 by typing the following command:

   ```
   cd $XXHR_TOP/install/ch6
   ```

3. At the command prompt, type `pwd` to check the directory we are in.

4. At the command prompt, type the following command to upload the profile option:

   FNDLOAD apps/apps O Y DOWNLOAD $FND_TOP/patch/115/import/afscprof. lct PROF_XXHR_WRITE_LOGFILE.ldt

5. At the command prompt, type the following to check that the LDT file has been created:

   ls -al

6. Check the LOG and LDT files to check that the data has been successfully downloaded.

How it works...

We executed the command line for the FNDLOAD utility to upload the XXHR_WRITE_LOGFILE profile option into a new environment.

Uploading a form and function using FNDLOAD

We are going to upload the form \ function definitions we created in earlier recipes. The LCT file used for uploading forms and functions is `afsload.lct`. We are going to run the FNDLOAD to upload the two files we created, called FORM_XXHRSOCC.ldt and FUNC_XXHR_EMP_SOCIETY.ldt.

How to do it...

To upload the form and function definitions with FNDLOAD, perform the following steps:

1. Open **Putty** and connect to the application server with the user that owns the application tier.

2. Navigate to $XXHR_TOP/install/ch6 by typing the following command:

   cd $XXHR_TOP/install/ch6

3. At the command prompt, type `pwd` to check the directory we are in.

4. At the command prompt, type the following command to upload the form:

   FNDLOAD apps/apps O Y DOWNLOAD $FND_TOP/patch/115/import/afsload. lct FORM_XXHRSOCC.ldt

5. At the command prompt, type the following command to upload the form function:

   FNDLOAD apps/apps O Y DOWNLOAD $FND_TOP/patch/115/import/afsload. lct FUNC_XXHR_EMP_SOCIETY.ldt

6. At the command prompt, type the following to check that the LDT file has been created:

   ls -al

7. Check the LOG and LDT files to check that the data has been successfully downloaded.

How it works...

We executed the command line for the FNDLOAD utility to upload the form and function definitions that we created for the **Clubs and Societies** form.

Uploading a menu using FNDLOAD

We are going to upload a menu we have created in the earlier recipes. The LCT file used for uploading menus is afsload.lct. We are going to run FNDLOAD and upload the file we created called MENU_XXHR_TEST_MENU.ldt. The text file contains the entity definition and the data for the XXHR Administration menu.

How to do it...

To upload the menu with FNDLOAD, perform the following steps:

1. Open **Putty** and connect to the application server with the user that owns the application tier.

2. Navigate to $XXHR_TOP/install/ch6 by typing the following command:

   cd $XXHR_TOP/install/ch6

3. At the command prompt, type pwd to check the directory we are in.

4. At the command prompt, type the following command to upload the menu:

   FNDLOAD apps/apps O Y DOWNLOAD $FND_TOP/patch/115/import/afsload.lct MENU_XXHR_TEST_MENU.ldt

5. At the command prompt, type the following to check that the LDT file has been created:

   ls -al

6. Check the LOG and LDT files to see whether the data has been successfully downloaded.

How it works...

We executed the command line for the FNDLOAD utility to upload the XXHR Administration Menu into a new environment.

Uploading a request group using FNDLOAD

We are going to upload a request group we created in the earlier recipes. The LCT file used for uploading menus is afcpreqg.lct. We are going to run FNDLOAD and upload the file we created called RG_XXHR_REQUEST_GROUP.ldt. The text file contains the entity definition and the data for the XXHR Administration menu.

How to do it...

To upload the menu with FNDLOAD, perform the following steps:

1. Open **Putty** and connect to the application server with the user that owns the application tier.

2. Navigate to $XXHR_TOP/install/ch6 by typing the following command:

   cd $XXHR_TOP/install/ch6

3. At the command prompt, type pwd to check the directory we are in.

4. At the command prompt, type the following command to upload the request group:

   FNDLOAD apps/apps O Y DOWNLOAD $FND_TOP/patch/115/import/afcpreqg.lct RG_XXHR_REQUEST_GROUP.ldt

5. At the command prompt, type to check that the LDT file has been created:

   ls -al

6. Check the LOG and LDT files to check that the data has been successfully downloaded.

How it works...

We executed the command line for the FNDLOAD utility to upload the XXHR Request Group into a new environment.

Uploading a responsibility using FNDLOAD

We are going to upload a responsibility we have created in the earlier recipes. The LCT file used for uploading Flexfields is afscursp.lct. We are going to run FNDLOAD and upload the file we created called RESP_XXHR_ADMIN.ldt. The text file contains the entity definition and the data for the **XXEBS Extending e-Business Suite** responsibility.

How to do it...

To upload the responsibility with FNDLOAD, perform the following steps:

1. Open **Putty** and connect to the application server with the user that owns the application tier.

2. Navigate to $XXHR_TOP/install/ch6 by typing the following command:

   cd $XXHR_TOP/install/ch6

3. At the command prompt, type pwd to check the directory we are in.

4. At the command prompt, type the following command to upload the responsibility:

   FNDLOAD apps/apps O Y DOWNLOAD $FND_TOP/patch/115/import/afscursp.lct RESP_XXHR_ADMIN.ldt

5. At the command prompt, type to check that the LDT file has been created:

   `ls -al`

6. Check the LOG and LDT files to check that the data has been successfully downloaded.

How it works...

We executed the command line for the FNDLOAD utility to upload the **XXEBS Extending e-Business Suite** responsibility into a new environment.

Uploading a personalization using FNDLOAD

We are going to upload the personalization we created in the earlier recipes. The LCT file used for uploading Flexfields is affrmcus.lct. We are going to run FNDLOAD and upload the file we created called PZ_PERWSHRG.ldt. The text file contains the entity definition and the data for the **People** form personalization.

How to do it...

To upload the personalization with FNDLOAD, perform the following steps:

1. Open **Putty** and connect to the application server with the user that owns the application tier.

2. Navigate to $XXHR_TOP/install/ch6 by typing the following command:

   cd $XXHR_TOP/install/ch6

3. At the command prompt, type pwd to check the directory we are in.

4. At the command prompt, type the following command to upload the personalization:

   FNDLOAD apps/apps O Y DOWNLOAD $FND_TOP/patch/115/import/affrmcus.lct PZ_PERWSHRG.ldt

5. At the command prompt, type the following to check that the LDT file has been created:

   `ls -al`

6. Check the LOG and LDT files to check that the data has been successfully downloaded.

How it works...

We executed the command line for the FNDLOAD utility to upload the personalization we created in *Chapter 3, Advanced Oracle Forms*.

Uploading a message using FNDLOAD

We are going to upload a message we have created in the earlier recipes. The LCT file used for uploading Flexfields is `afmdmsg.lct`. We are going to run FNDLOAD and upload the file we created called `MESG_XXHR_ON_HOLD_WARNING.ldt`. The text file contains the entity definition and the data for the `On Hold Warning` message.

How to do it...

To upload the message with FNDLOAD, perform the following steps:

1. Open **Putty** and connect to the application server with the user that owns the application tier.

2. Navigate to `$XXHR_TOP/install/ch6` by typing the following command:

   ```
   cd $XXHR_TOP/install/ch6
   ```

3. At the command prompt, type `pwd` to check the directory we are in.

4. At the command prompt, type the following command to upload the profile option:

   ```
   FNDLOAD apps/apps O Y DOWNLOAD $FND_TOP/patch/115/import/afmdmsg.
   lct MESG_XXHR_ON_HOLD_WARNING.ldt
   ```

5. At the command prompt, type the following to check that the LDT file has been created:

   ```
   ls -al
   ```

6. Check the LOG and LDT files to check that the data has been successfully downloaded.

How it works...

We executed the command line for the FNDLOAD utility to upload the XXHR_ON_HOLD_WARNING message into a new environment.

Modifying the LDT file

We can edit the LDT text files once they are created. However, do so with care as it may invalidate the LDT. An example would be that we have created some configuration in the application. The user that is extracted from the development environment is stored in the LDT file that was extracted. In this example, we are going to change the user to a common setup user that exits in our target environment.

How to do it...

To edit an LDT file, perform the following steps:

1. Open the CP_XXHR_ALL_CONC_PROG.ldt file from the download bundle.

2. Search and replace APENVER in the text file, as shown in the following screenshot:

3. Save the file, giving it a new name.

How it works...

We have modified the owner of the objects in the LDT file. Ensure that the user exists in the target environment before performing an upload.

Using a script for FNDLOAD

In the download bundle for *Chapter 6, Utilities*, you will also find two scripts. One of the scripts will download the FNDLOAD definitions. The second uploads the LDT definitions. When downloading multiple objects in a script, the order in which they are downloaded makes no difference. However, pay special attention when using a script to upload LDT definitions and pay attention to dependencies. Some of the definitions will extract dependent items and store them in the one LDT file. Open the scripts to take a look. These can be reused by adding and removing FNDLOAD statements.

How to do it...

To use the script, perform the following steps:

1. Open **Putty** and connect to the application server with the user that owns the application tier.

2. Navigate to $XXHR_TOP/install/ch6 by typing the following command:

   ```
   cd $XXHR_TOP/install/ch6
   ```

3. At the **UNIX** prompt, type the following command to execute the script:

   ```
   APPS Tier> fndload_download.sh <apps_pwd>
   ```

4. Check each LDT file to ensure that they have been generated with data.

How it works...

We have used a script to download some of the LDT files from the development environment. The advantage of using a script is that it saves a lot of time and reduces manual errors as there is only one executable to run.

Using a script for migrating objects

You may have noticed that there is a script for most of the chapters to install the database objects. In this final recipe, we will look at the script and how you can modify it to install any database object.

How to do it...

The following screenshot shows the header of the script. It provides details of the script, what it does, and how to run it. It also contains revision details:

```
  4842_06_01.sh

   1    #! /bin/ksh -p
   2    # Commented out for debugging and error trapping
   3    #set -x
   4    #****************************************************
   5    #
   6    # (c) 2011 NU-TEKK Ltd All Rights Reserved
   7    #
   8    #******************************************************************************
   9    # MODULE NAME:          4842_06_01.sh
  10    # ORIGINAL AUTHOR:      Andy Penver
  11    # DATE:                 15-SEP-2011
  12    # DESCRIPTION:
  13    #
  14    # Installation Script for Chapter 6 to be installed within APPS database schema
  15    #
  16    # PARAMETERS:
  17    #
  18    # NAME               TYPE          DESCRIPTION
  19    # --------------     ------        -------------------------------------------
  20    # ID_PSWD            CHAR          Schema username and password (e.g. apps/apps123)
  21    # INSTALL_FROM       CHAR          Installation Directory
  22    #
  23    # CHANGE HISTORY:
  24    #
  25    # VERSION  DATE             AUTHOR              DESCRIPTION
  26    # -------- ------------     -----------------   ----------------------------
  27    # 1.0      15-SEP-2011      Andy Penver         Initial Version
  28    #******************************************************************************
  29    #
  30    #+----------------------------------------------------------+
  31    #+ Parameters obtained from concurrent request              +
  32    #+----------------------------------------------------------+
  33    #
```

> This section is just comments. It contains details about who wrote the script and how to run it.

The following code shows the parameters that are passed into the script. We pass in the **apps** username and password in the format `apps/<appswd>` (this could be another user if running the script from another schema; however, it is preferable to grant permissions to the **apps** user, so that the script can be run from the **apps** user while providing the schema notation before the object is owned by another schema, for example, `XXHR.TABLE_NAME`).

> This is one parameter without spaces. The second parameter is where the script will look for the installation files. If no parameter is passed, then the script will search in the directory the script was run from. The third parameter is used to name the `LOG` file that is produced while running the script. The script will err if there is no reference parameter defined.

The next section defines the name of the `LOG` file and checks that a username and password have been passed into the script.

```
34      echo "Started Script"
35      l_apps_user_pswd=${1}   (1)    1. The 1st parameter we pass in is the apps user and password
36                                     e.g. apps/apps
37      l_install_from=${2}     (2)    2. This is where the script will look for the files to run. If no
38                                     parameter is passed then the script will look in the directory the
39      CUST_TOP=$XXHR_TOP             script is run from.
40
41      l_reference="4842_06_01"  (3)  3. The reference is used as a reference when naming a log file
42                                     produced by the script.
43      if [ -z "${l_reference}" ] ; then   (4)  4. An error is raised if there is no reference
44          echo                                 defined.
45          echo "Extension reference is not set"
46          echo                           5. Checks that a username and password
47          exit                           have been supplied when executing the
48      fi                                 script.
49
50      l_log_file=XXHR_${l_reference}.log
51                                                                                        (5)
52      rm -f ${l_log_file} 1>/dev/null 2>/dev/null
53
54      if [ -z "${l_apps_user_pswd}" ] ; then
55          echo
56          echo "Must supply username and password for APPS e.g. apps/apps123"
57          echo
58          exit
59      fi
```

The following part of the script checks if the script has access to the FNDLOAD utility:

```
60
61   #
62      #+-----------------------------------------------------------+
63      #+ Check that we have access to FNDLOAD                      +
64      #+-----------------------------------------------------------+
65      #
66      whence FNDLOAD 1>/dev/null 2>/dev/null
67      status=$?
68      if [ ${status} -ne 0 ] ; then
69          echo "ERROR :- Unable to access FNDLOAD.  Please add the FNDLOAD to PATH"
70          exit
71      fi
```

Each of the variables in the next part of the script is where we define the files that we want the script to run. Each file is separated by a space and each line has a backslash. There are multiple variables for the different types of files that we have. The name of the variable explains the type of file that should be assigned to it. For example, the **l_control_file_list** contains the LDT files for the FNDLOAD files, as shown in the following screenshot:

```
72
73   l_control_file_list="$FND_TOP/patch/115/import/aflvmlu.lct LU_XXHR_SOCIETY_LOV.ldt \
74                        $FND_TOP/patch/115/import/afffload.lct DFF_XXHR_PER_SOCIETIES.ldt \
75                        $FND_TOP/patch/115/import/afcpprog.lct CP_XXHR_FIRST_CONC_PROG.ldt \
76                        $FND_TOP/patch/115/import/afcprset.lct RS_XXHR20001.ldt \
77                        $FND_TOP/patch/115/import/afcprset.lct RSL_XXHR20001.ldt \
78                        $FND_TOP/patch/115/import/afscprof.lct PROF_XXHR_WRITE_LOGFILE.ldt \
79                        $FND_TOP/patch/115/import/afsload.lct FORM_XXHRSOCC.ldt \
80                        $FND_TOP/patch/115/import/afsload.lct FUNC_XXHR_EMP_SOCIETY.ldt \
81                        $FND_TOP/patch/115/import/afsload.lct MENU_XXHR_TEST_MENU.ldt \
82                        $FND_TOP/patch/115/import/afcpreqg.lct RG_XXHR_REQUEST_GROUP.ldt \
83                        $FND_TOP/patch/115/import/afscursp.lct RESP_XXHR_ADMIN.ldt \
84                        $FND_TOP/patch/115/import/affrmcus.lct PZ_PERWSHRG.ldt \
85                        $FND_TOP/patch/115/import/afmdmsg.lct MESG_XXHR_ON_HOLD_WARNING.ldt "
86
87   l_profile_list=""
88                                                        This is where we put all of our FNDLOAD (Upload) list.
89   l_value_set_list=""                                  The script will execute each entry and load the ldt files.
90
91   l_conc_progs_list=""
92
93   l_seed_list=""
```

We have other examples of different types of files being assigned to variables in the list. We can use the script to load SQL scripts, triggers, packages, and workflows, as shown in the following screenshot:

```
94
95   l_db_object_list="XXHR_PER_SOCIETIES.sql \
96                     XXHR_PER_SOCIETIES_SYN.sql \
97                     XXHR_PER_SOCIETIES_V.sql \                    ①
98                     XXHR_PER_SOCIETIES_SEQ.sql \                  List our SQL
99                     XXHR_PER_SOCIETIES_SEQ_SYN.sql \              scripts here
100                    XXHR_PERSON_DETAILS_V.sql \                   to create our
101                    XXHR_PERMGR_DETAILS_V.sql \                   database
102                    XXHR_PER_MEDIA_SUBS.sql \                     objects.
103                    XXHR_PER_MEDIA_SUBS_SYN.sql \
104                    XXHR_PER_MEDIA_SUBS_V.sql \
105                    XXHR_PER_MEDIA_SUBS_SEQ.sql \
106                    XXHR_PER_MEDIA_SUBS_SEQ_SYN.sql \
107                    XXHR_XML_WF_IN.sql \
108                    XXHR_XML_WF_IN_SYN.sql \
109                    XXHR_EVENT_ENQUEUE_S.sql"
110
111  l_trigger_list=""
112
113  l_db_pkg_list="XXHR_PER_SOCIETIES_PVT.pks \        ②  List our DB
114                 XXHR_PER_SOCIETIES_PVT.pkb \            package scripts
115                 XXHR_GEN_VALID_PKG.pks \               here to create our
116                 XXHR_GEN_VALID_PKG.pkb \               database
117                 XXHR_ABSENCE_IN_WF_PKG.pks \           packages.
118                 XXHR_ABSENCE_IN_WF_PKG.pkb"
119
120  l_wf_list="XXHRIABS.wft"  ③  List our workflows here to load workflows
```

You will see that there are other variables for installing other objects. These can be left blank if we do not have any. We do not need to edit the rest of the script. We just need to add the objects that we want to load. Remember to list the objects in the correct order. For example, if we have a script for a DB package specification and body, then ensure that the script for the specification is listed before the script for the body. Always check any dependencies between objects.

How it works...

We have created a number of objects that we are going to use in the coming recipes. The table XXHR_PER_SOCIETIES will store details relating to clubs or societies that the employee belongs to. We have created a synonym to the **apps** user as all of our objects need to be accessed by the **apps** user. The table will store the raw data and so we have also created a view which has the meanings and descriptions visible to the user as well. We will use the views when we create the form and we will go into that a little bit later. The sequence we have created will generate a unique number each time a new record is created. Finally, the package we have created stores all of the procedures and functions related to database activity within the form, such as inserting, updating, or deleting records.

Index

host script 16
hyperlink
    configuring, on spreadtable 272

I

immediate program 16
installing
    database objects 78-80, 327, 328
    Oracle Developer Suite 104-108
invalid XML message
    creating 387, 388
invalid XML message attributes
    adding 388, 389
invalid XML notification
    creating 391, 392
item addition
    block, creating for 199-202
item names
    finding 245
item properties
    setting 203
    setting, for detail block 142, 143
    setting, for master block 121-123
items
    adding, to block 265, 266
    creating, in query block 175, 176
    adding, to pop-up menu 228
    positioning, on tabbed canvas 205, 206
    sizing, on tabbed canvas 205, 206
item type
    creating 330, 331

J

Java stored procedures 16
Java Virtual Machine (JVM) 3
JDeveloper 97
JTF_GRID_EVENT trigger 273
JTF_GRID library
    attaching 266, 267
JTF_GRID object group
    about 273
    adding 264

K

key flexfields (KFF) 232

L

layout
    modifying, for form 160, 161
LDT file
    modifying 446, 447
left-hand toolbar 101
library
    about 100
    attaching, to CUSTOM library 252, 253
    attaching 266, 267
    compiling, on application server 254, 255
list item
    creating 167, 168
list of values *See* LOV
log file
    about 16
    procedure, writing for 57, 58
    viewing 60
    writing 58, 59
logic
    coding, for message display 192, 193
lookup
    creating 137, 138, 217, 218, 368
    error message attribute, creating 369, 370
    extracting, FNDLOAD used 426, 427
    Success/Fail lookup, creating 368, 369
    uploading, FNDLOAD used 438, 439
LOV
    about 100
    creating, LOV wizard used 218-220
    creating, for society name field 163-166
    new record group, assigning to 320, 321
    record group, altering 316
LOV wizard
    used, for creating LOV 218-220

M

machine 3
master and detail blocks
    relationships, creating between 204
    relationship, creating 143, 144
master block
    block properties, setting 120, 121
    canvas properties, setting 123, 124
    creating 116

[PACKT] PUBLISHING   enterprise
professional expertise distilled

Thank you for buying
Oracle E-Business Suite R12 Core Development and Extension Cookbook

About Packt Publishing

Packt, pronounced 'packed', published its first book "*Mastering phpMyAdmin for Effective MySQL Management*" in April 2004 and subsequently continued to specialize in publishing highly focused books on specific technologies and solutions.

Our books and publications share the experiences of your fellow IT professionals in adapting and customizing today's systems, applications, and frameworks. Our solution-based books give you the knowledge and power to customize the software and technologies you're using to get the job done. Packt books are more specific and less general than the IT books you have seen in the past. Our unique business model allows us to bring you more focused information, giving you more of what you need to know, and less of what you don't.

Packt is a modern, yet unique publishing company, which focuses on producing quality, cutting-edge books for communities of developers, administrators, and newbies alike. For more information, please visit our website: www.PacktPub.com.

About Packt Enterprise

In 2010, Packt launched two new brands, Packt Enterprise and Packt Open Source, in order to continue its focus on specialization. This book is part of the Packt Enterprise brand, home to books published on enterprise software – software created by major vendors, including (but not limited to) IBM, Microsoft and Oracle, often for use in other corporations. Its titles will offer information relevant to a range of users of this software, including administrators, developers, architects, and end users.

Writing for Packt

We welcome all inquiries from people who are interested in authoring. Book proposals should be sent to author@packtpub.com. If your book idea is still at an early stage and you would like to discuss it first before writing a formal book proposal, contact us; one of our commissioning editors will get in touch with you.

We're not just looking for published authors; if you have strong technical skills but no writing experience, our experienced editors can help you develop a writing career, or simply get some additional reward for your expertise.

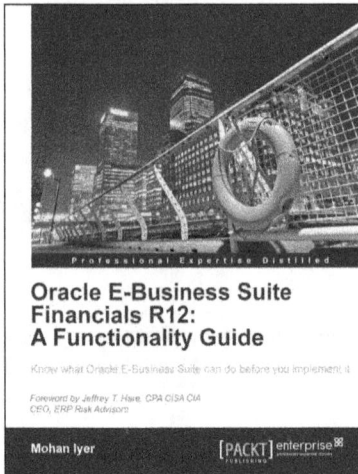

Oracle E-Business Suite Financials R12: A Functionality Guide

ISBN: 978-1-84968-062-2   Paperback: 336 pages

Know what Oracle E-Business Suite can do before you implement it

1. Take a deep dive into the key elements of Oracle EBS financial transaction processing

2. Understand the functionality and critical configuration steps

3. Master Oracle EBS product highlights and their effective usage

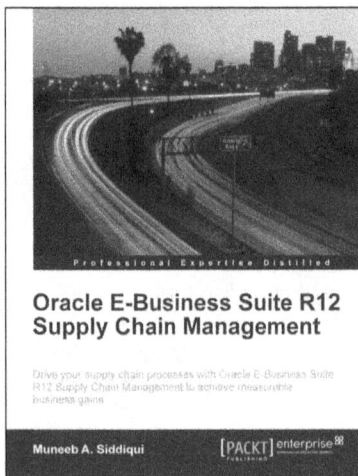

Oracle E-Business Suite Financials R12: A Functionality Guide

Know what Oracle E-Business Suite can do before you implement it

Foreword by Jeffrey T. Hare, CPA CISA CIA
CEO, ERP Risk Advisors

Mohan Iyer   [PACKT] enterprise ⊠

Oracle E-Business Suite R12 Supply Chain Management

ISBN: 978-1-84968-064-6   Paperback: 292 pages

Drive your supply chain processes with Oracle E-Business Suite R12 Supply Chain Managment to achieve measurable business gains

1. Put supply chain management principles to practice with Oracle EBS SCM

2. Develop insight into the process and business flow of supply chain management

3. Set up all of the Oracle EBS SCM modules to automate your supply chain processes

4. Case study to learn how Oracle EBS implementation takes place

Oracle E-Business Suite R12 Supply Chain Management

Drive your supply chain processes with Oracle E-Business Suite R12 Supply Chain Management to achieve measurable business gains

Muneeb A. Siddiqui   [PACKT] enterprise ⊠

Please check **www.PacktPub.com** for information on our titles

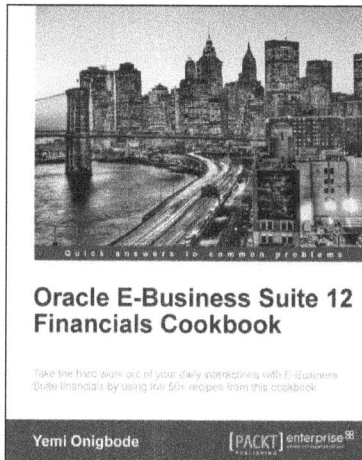

Oracle E-Business Suite 12 Financials Cookbook

ISBN: 978-1-84968-310-4   Paperback: 384 pages

Take the hard work out of your daily interactions with E-Business Suite financials by using the 50+ recipes from this cookbook

1. Delivers practical solutions that can be easily applied in functional EBS environments

2. A step-by-step tour through the EBS R12 Financials core modules in this book and eBook

3. Demonstrates the functional integration points between the EBS R12 Financial modules

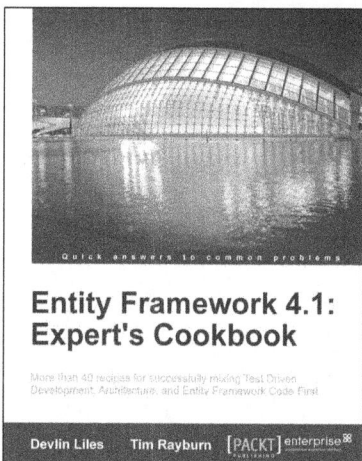

Entity Framework 4.1: Expert's Cookbook

ISBN: 978-1-84968-446-0   Paperback: 352 pages

More than 40 recipes for successfully mixing Test Driven Development, Architecture, and Entity Framework Code First

1. Hands-on solutions with reusable code examples

2. Strategies for enterprise ready usage

3. Examples based on real world experience

4. Detailed and advanced examples of query management

5. Step-by-step recipes that will guide you to success

Please check **www.PacktPub.com** for information on our titles